Latin American Social Movements

Latin American Social Movements

Globalization, Democratization, and Transnational Networks

EDITED BY HANK JOHNSTON AND PAUL ALMEIDA

ROWMAN & LITTLEFIELD PUBLISHERS, INC.
Lanham • Boulder • New York • Toronto • Oxford

ROWMAN & LITTLEFIELD PUBLISHERS, INC.

Published in the United States of America
by Rowman & Littlefield Publishers, Inc.
A wholly owned subsidiary of The Rowman & Littlefield Publishing Group, Inc.
4501 Forbes Boulevard, Suite 200, Lanham, Maryland 20706
www.rowmanlittlefield.com

P.O. Box 317, Oxford OX2 9RU, UK

British Library Cataloguing in Publication Information Available

Library of Congress Cataloging-in-Publication Data

ISBN-13: 978-0-7425-5331-6 (cloth : alk. paper)
ISBN-10: 0-7425-5331-0 (cloth : alk. paper)
ISBN-13: 978-0-7425-5332-3 (pbk. : alk. paper)
ISBN-10: 0-7425-5332-3 (pbk. : alk. paper)

Printed in the United States of America

♾™ The paper used in this publication meets the minimum requirements of American National Standard for Information Sciences—Permanence of Paper for Printed Library Materials, ANSI/NISO Z39.48-1992.

CONTENTS

Part I

Popular Protest in the Neoliberal Era

Chapter 1

NEOLIBERAL GLOBALIZATION AND POPULAR MOVEMENTS IN LATIN AMERICA

Paul Almeida and Hank Johnston

Throughout Latin America, social and political protests seem to be occurring with greater frequency and intensity, and under the banner of new demands, claims, and repertoires of contention. Globalization processes, especially the effects of neoliberal economic policies, serve as the catalysts of many of these protests. These macro-processes are often perceived as threats in the immediate political and social environments of affected groups (Tilly 1978; Goldstone and Tilly 2001). The *negative* conditions typically associated with "austerity" measures and neoliberal policies are numerous, but a short list must include the following: rising costs of living, cuts in social services, informalization and fragmentation of national economies, ponderous foreign debt, hyperurbanization and, for many workers, low wages, harsh working conditions, and insecure employment in newly privatized enterprises and export processing zones. Under such conditions, aggrieved collectivities begin to act in concert in order to avoid being made worse off by the unwanted economic changes (Walton and Shefner 1994; Veltmeyer and Petras 2000) or in reaction to violation of their perceived social citizenship rights (Eckstein and Wickham-Crowley 2003).

However, the existence of economic grievances and social claims by themselves do not explain the unprecedented wave of Latin American popular protest in the last decade. A full understanding must consider other processes at work, some of which occur in tandem with economic globalization, such as the growth of transnational non-governmental organizations, transnational advocacy networks, and global communications and information exchange. Another key process is democratization: the opening of Latin American polities, more competitive elections, and the slow and sometimes fitful creation of new channels for grievance articulation and the waning of old ones.

This book deepens our understanding of popular mobilizations in several different Latin American countries by looking at the intersection of these three themes: neoliberal economic globalization and how it affects the articulation of claims, democratization and the opening of political opportunities for challenging groups, and the networks of advocacy and support organized on a transnational scale.

SOCIAL MOVEMENTS AND THE GLOBAL POLITICAL ECONOMY

While social movement researchers have given considerable attention to globalization processes, the tendency has been to focus on only one of these three themes: namely, the rise of transnational actors and their effects on national arenas of contention (Tarrow 2005a, 2005b; Rothman and Oliver 1999; Lewis 2000). The number of international nongovernmental organizations (INGOs), transnational social movements (TSMOs), and linkages between transnational activists expanded rapidly in the 1990s, establishing new and significant players on a global scale. Sikkink and Smith observed a 300 percent increase in the number of these organizations between 1973 and 1993 (Sikkink and Smith 2002: 31). These groups and organizations worked at an international level to establish human rights, democracy, women's rights, and environmental protection regimes and exerted pressure on national politics to conform to emerging global norms in exchange for a place in the interstate system (Smith 1997; Keck and Sikkink 1998a, Smith and Johnston 2002). For example, human rights accords and their monitoring by TSMOs such as Amnesty International can confer a modicum of legitimacy to newly industrializing states in the global South to assuage first-world consumers and transnational subcontractors. These global players, their operations, and their resources are mostly located in the global North and it is fair to say that their influence is mostly exerted at the policy level rather than in popular mobilizations.

A related tendency of social movement research has been to focus on the antineoliberal globalization movement (or global justice movement), which also primarily has developed in the global North (J. Smith 2001b). These studies look at the transnational organization and participation in protest events (Bédoyan, Van Aelst, and Walgrave 2004) and campaigns (Tarrow 2005a) directed at the main agencies of neoliberal policies, such as the IMF, World Bank, G-8 meetings, and WTO rounds (Almeida and Lichbach 2003; Fisher et al. 2005). Also relevant here is the growth of radical-democracy elements of the global justice movement such as the various social forums in different countries (della Porta 2005). While this research is important, the result has been, first, that theories of protest mobilization tend to deemphasize those precise locales where the negative impacts of globalization are most directly felt; and second, that theories of protest mobilization in general tend to de-emphasize how national polities outside the global North are structured by the system of global dependency.

The other side of the coin is that scholarship on global economic dependency has paid little attention to popular mobilizations in the developing world. Dependency theory (Frank 1978, 1980; Amin 1976) and world-system theory (Wallerstein 1974; Chase Dunn 1992; Chase-Dunn and Hall 1993) focus on the unequal and exploitative nature of global economic relationships and their effects on national economies and societies. However, it is fair to say that, with respect to collective action, the dependency perspective did not move far beyond the basic equation that surplus extraction by the West plus anti-imperialist ideology plus revolutionary organizations equal popular insurgencies (see Wickham-Crowley 2001). World-system theory itself says little about collective action: it links labor unrest and labor peace to hegemonic cycles; and some scholars have proposed the general pattern that social and political movements are associated with hegemonic descent. It also proposes a relationship between world-system position and political contention by associating the prosperity of core status with a growing middle class that finds political expression in democratic institutions. At the same time, national elites find political legitimacy in electoral processes and stronger guarantees of civic and human rights, with the result that civil unrest is quelled. Conversely, state repression and lack of basic freedoms are associated with underdeveloped peripheral states, where insurgencies, coups d'état, and revolutionary movements tend to be more common (Goodwin 2001).

Since the 1970s empirical trends in Latin America (and elsewhere) have complicated the broad categories of dependency and world-system theories and have given rise to numerous popular mobilizations that fall outside their theoretical schemata. First, several Latin American states came to occupy a middle level in the global division of labor—becoming *newly industrializing states*, or NICs (Mexico, Brazil, Argentina, Chile)—or in world-system lexicon, semiperiphery. It was precisely in these countries that some of the major mobilizations against neoliberal reforms occurred, but also—it is fair to say—that the semiperiphery is probably the most understudied and undertheorized economic region in world system theory, and there is limited research about the unique shape of popular mobilization there (but see Jenkins and Schock 1992; Boswell and Chase-Dunn 2000).

For decades, the economies of Mexico, Argentina, Brazil, and Chile were characterized by import substitution industrialization (ISI) as a developmental strategy, which privileged urban workers and created large urban-rural disparities. By the 1980s, protectionist ISI policies were rejected in favor of free-trade, export-oriented industrialization (EOI), with significant effects on traditional political and class alignments. Old clientelist foundations of state legitimacy and social control eroded and were replaced by networks of more autonomous citizens and civic organizations that emerged and grew as political democratization occurred throughout Latin America. As industrialization and democratization moved forward (Chile being the anomalous case), dependency and world-system theories offered little theoretical guidance to understand the social and political movements that developed at the same time. Prior to 1970, economic injustice had always been linked with restriction of political freedoms, and the macroscopic theorizing of both dependency and world system approaches left little room for the unique historical and social environment of Latin America, such as clientelism, national political cultures, and the social configurations of ISI development. Similarly, because the field of social and political movements developed almost entirely out of the analysis of Western political contexts, there was equally little space for Latin American structural and cultural uniqueness (Davis 1999). The result was that the eruptions of austerity protests in these countries and elsewhere were both unexpected and undertheorized.

A second complicating trend in Latin America was the rapid growth of debt in the late 1970s as countries borrowed to underwrite domestic spending and finance state enterprises for ISI development. By the early 1980s, a global recession, floating interest rates and falling commodity prices—frequently combined with bad planning and corruption—made it impossible for most countries to meet payment schedules, leading to debt crisis in Latin America (see Roddick 1988; Pastor 1989; Walton and Seddon 1994 for detailed discussions). Since around 1980, global financial institutions (such as the IMF and World Bank) and trade organizations have exerted increasing pressure to abandon ISI policies and open national economies to global market forces (Green 2003).

6 Paul Almeida and Hank Johnston

Indebted Latin American states were structurally dependent on these financial institutions to ensure future capital flows into their respective national territories and economies (i.e., new loans, foreign investment, and favorable credit ratings). The externally imposed structural adjustments included cutting back domestic national budgets/expenditures—especially in the public sector workforces and wages, subsidies to basic food and transportation, as well as in the education, public health, and retirement/pension sectors. In addition, governments were instructed to devalue their local currencies and sell off productive state assets such as government-run industries and infrastructure (e.g., mines, natural resource deposits, ports, telecommunications, power and water distribution, healthcare services, etc.) and use the privatization receipts to make debt repayments or at least to pay the interest on previous loans.

State managers in Latin America were also strongly encouraged by the IFIs to find other sources to generate revenue such as increasing the sales tax (or value-added tax) on most consumer items (Babb 2005). This particular neoliberal policy is widely viewed by the popular sectors as a regressive taxing measure in a region where over 45 percent of the population lives at or under the poverty line (Figueroa Ibarra 2002; Robinson 2004). Another neoliberal economic development strategy, found largely in the Caribbean basin countries (Mexico, Central America, and the Caribbean), is to establish free trade zones for light export manufacturing (Robinson 2003). In this case, the neoliberal state itself actively constructed new social actors for potential contention by concentrating large numbers of young women in similar social and economic production relations (see the Bandy and Bickham-Mendez chapter in this volume). The ultimate objective of the above programs and policies centers on making the Latin American economies more outward-oriented, focusing on the export sector and developing specific niche products to compete effectively in international markets. In accord with this extraverted economic approach, governments are given incentives to liberalize their national economic laws and engage in bilateral and multilateral free trade accords.

DEBT, INTERVENTION, AND AUSTERITY PROTESTS

With some important exceptions, the major mobilization campaigns witnessed in Latin America over the past decade have focused on economic issues directly or indirectly connected to the foreign debt crisis, structural adjustment policies, and global economic integration. The *Argentinazo* of December 2001 (looting and mass demonstrations including pot banging—*cacerolazos*—against state-mandated bank freezes and other unfavorable policies), the indigenous uprising in Ecuador in January 2000 against an impending dollarization of the economy (Walsh 2001), the ongoing water and gas wars in Bolivia in 2000, 2003, and 2005 (privatization of utilities and natural resources), and the free trade protests in Central America and Ecuador between 2002 and 2006 are easily traceable to economic liberalization policies. It is interesting to note that these are all mass-based movements bringing tens of thousands of people into the streets (and at times highways) in order to prevent, slow down, or renegotiate the unwanted economic changes. In order to explain the variation in how these macroeconomic threats lead to different levels of contention, however, we need an understanding of how larger global pressures intersect with local political conditions—or what Javier Auyero (2001) calls "glocal" political struggles.

These collective actions have variously been labeled anti-austerity protests, food riots, or anti-IMF protests. The earliest protests against austerity measures began in the mid-1970s. They were not limited to Latin America, but no other region of the world experienced as many cost-of-living-related protests, and some of largest erupted there.

There were a total of 146 protest events globally between 1976 and late 1992 occurring in almost one-half of the debtor countries worldwide and especially frequent and intense in Peru, Bolivia, Chile, Argentina, and Venezuela. The vast majority occurred in cities (see Walton 1989; Walton and Seddon 1994; Walton and Shefner 1994). Early research observed a peak between 1983 and 1985, when the international debt crisis and IMF intervention also peaked. After an apparent lull during the early 1990s, it is impressive that this trend seems to have either reemerged or intensified into the late 1990s and early 2000s (Almeida 2002).

It is significant that, prior to the IMF austerity programs, there was a marked absence of popular uprisings in Latin American countries where economic hardships and belt-tightening were common (Walton and Seddon 1994: 44). Key elements in the first wave of protests seem to have been hyperurbanization and intrusion of international agencies in national politics and national economic planning. According to Walton and Ragin (1990), other plausible causes such as size of debt, rapid inflation, export dependency, and level of industrialization did not significantly predict protest events. They observe that austerity protests were highly correlated with a lack of prior uprisings, the absence of face-value deprivation as measured by indexes of economic development and inflation, and IMF intervention. These findings suggest the diffusion of a globally informed way of interpreting price hikes, social service cuts, or unemployment that specifies the IMF, other international agencies, and transnational corporations as key antagonists. Also, they suggest that this interpretive frame links outside intervention with the delegitimization of local and national political elites. Many of the riots had an element whereby participants attacked government buildings and vilified local politicians (see Auyero's chapter in this volume). Dense urban networks provided the structural and practical context for rapid mobilization of people into the streets when price increases were announced. The level of spontaneity varied according to the particular outburst, but it was common, and still is, that some organizational involvement helped mobilize the vast numbers of participants—labor unions, civic associations, neighborhood associations, and nascent or emergent social movement organizations.

Social histories of food riots occurring in the eighteenth century point to a moral economy of rights and obligations associated with traditional social structure that articulated the townsfolk's sense of injustice. This moral economy held immediate antagonists—local millers and merchants—to blame for the "abandonment of consumer protections in free-market reforms that served the centralization of capital and state power" (Walton and Seddon 1994: 52). We mention this because contemporary austerity programs also interrupt established social relations and daily routines (see Auyero's and Wolford's chapters). The key difference is that the IMF and World Bank are distant forces, not the local merchants and tradesmen encountered every day. Since the 1980s, an anti-globalization master frame has become a powerful lens through which to view local grievances. It incorporates the local moral economy of aggrieved populations within a larger and sophisticated schema of understandings about the global economy. The rise of TSMOs and INGOs has been one factor in the master frame's diffusion. Another factor is an expanding web of transnational activist linkages (Keck and Sikkink, 1998a; Caniglia 2001; and Olesen's chapter). Finally, local activists, opposition politicians, and labor leaders have further elaborated the frame by identifying the ties of IMF, World Bank, and transnational corporate managers with national elites, thereby providing close-range targets for collective action.

While there is a great deal to be learned by aggregating austerity riots and analyzing them in terms of broad measures of economic and political trends, (see chapter 2 by

Shefner, Pasdirtz, and Blad), there also is much to be gained from a more fine-grained approach to Latin American social movements (see Wolford's chapter for elaboration of this argument). To this end, Eckstein and Wickham-Crowley (2003) have identified several areas in terms of moral economy of rights that are threatened by neoliberal globalization (see also Eckstein 2001a, 2001b for related inventories). Drawing on their discussion of how basic "subsistence rights" are challenged by neoliberal adjustments (Eckstein and Wickham-Crowley 2003: 11), several patterns within the category of austerity protests and austerity-inspired social movements can be identified. Of course, all are related to neoliberal policy adjustments in one way or another, but it is noteworthy that closer inspections reveal that—in varying degrees—not all of these protests are spontaneous outbursts in reaction to suddenly imposed deprivation, but rather are given form and motion, at least in early stages, by preexisting organizations and civil society groups. What we present is a short list of major categories of social movements that are most directly related to neoliberal policies—it is not intended to be exhaustive (see Eckstein and Wickham-Crowley 2003 for elaborations).[1]

Protests against Cuts in Urban Services. The category of urban services includes public transportation (in which fare hikes can cause real hardships for the poor), provision of electricity, water, and sanitation, cost of fuel, public heath, food subsidies, housing, and even the security of banking services (which are especially relevant for the urban middle and working classes). It is fair to say that this category can claim the largest and most violent outbursts of protest, such as the *caracazo* in Venezuela (see Lopez-Maya and Lander's chapter) and the numerous outbursts in Argentina, including the *Argentinazo* in 2001 (see Auyero's chapter in this volume). While superficially appearing to be spontaneous riots, and certainly there is often a spontaneous quality to their development, many of these protests have labor, leftist political parties, and neighborhood civic groups playing mobilizing roles as well (see Almeida's chapter 4). For example in 2000, during the protests in Cochabamba, Bolivia, against the privatization of municipal water services, civil society groups made a decisive contribution in sustaining mobilization (Albro 2005).

Also significant under this category are movements for adequate housing. Squatter invasions in the semiurban periphery had been a widespread form of mobilization in Latin America that were tolerated by regimes fostering ISI development based on an urban labor force (see Holzner's chapter 5). Although many squatters' movements tapered off in the 1990s, urban housing movements remained, especially in Mexico City (building on organizations created after the 1985 earthquakes there) and in Brazil, where the Roofless Peoples Movement mobilized in several cities (Eckstein and Wickham-Crowley 2003: 20). A sister Movimiento Sin Techo movement has also mobilized thousands in Paraguay, and by 2001 claimed urban land and building occupations sufficient to house 2,000 families.

Strikes and Labor Struggles. Unions continue to be a significant presence in Latin American society, but the recent trend is that popular mobilization is less and less union-inspired. Corporatist unions enjoyed a privileged place under ISI development policies and were often the transmission belts of regime-supported social mobilization. When regime change occurred, union organizations remained as forces to be reckoned with and frequently provided preexisting networks for protest mobilization. While the strength and scope of operation for unions varied during the neoliberal period, waning under military governments, waxing initially after democratic transition, they have consistently resisted neoliberal policies on two fronts: the privatization of national enterprises and the suspension of labor rights in EPZ manufacturing. In the case of privatization, it is typical that the guarantees of minimum wage, employment, health and safety, hours, and pension are either threatened or suspended in the transfer. In the case of EPZ—or *maquila*— manufacturing, it is common that in addition to tax breaks and guarantees of infrastructural development, states grant concessions, either explicit or tacit, against union organizing so that wages remain low (Armbruster-Sandoval 2005). As Bandy and Mendez's chapter in this volume demonstrates, the combined effects of transnational solidarity networks and local shopfloor organization can successfully counter the anti-union efforts of the *maquila* sector.

Gender-based movements. While the subordination of Latin American women by traditional cultural patterns of patriarchy and male privilege is well known, significant political and economic changes have broken women's quiescence in many sectors and, where women's activism has been historically evident, given rise to new patterns of mobilization. Earlier, during the 1960s and 1970s, Latin American women participated in the revolutionary insurgencies that were common throughout the region (Shayne 2004). Later, during the first wave of structural adjustments, urban women were often at the forefront of protests against curtailment of services and rural women were active in development claims (Nash and Safa 1986). Also, women's activism was significant in protesting against the brutal repression of military regimes and demanding transition to democracy. In Chile, Noonan (1995) notes how the military coup created new spaces for women's mobilization based on traditional conceptions of motherhood, but which soon expanded to include demands for democratic return. Women were instrumental in protests against the dictatorship and also against the regime's neoliberal shock therapy for the Chilean economy. In Argentina, the Madres movement became emblematic of women's concerns for basic human freedoms of life and liberty as they demanded accountability for their children who disappeared under military repression. Borland's chapter in this volume chronicles how today's Madres movement has expanded its scope after the democratic transition to include economic justice claims. Finally, the extension of *maquila* production in EPZs has raised new issues for women. *Maquila* production overwhelmingly draws upon women as a cheap and flexible labor source and it is common that unions are prohibited or co-opted by corporatist (and male-dominated) national unions (Tiano 1994). This is translated into low wages, lack of job security and dangerous and exploitative working conditions (Sklair 1989, 1995; Bailey, Parisotto, and Renshaw 1993). Bandy and Bickman Mendez's chapter focuses on how labor demands in the *maquila* industry are overwhelmingly women's issues, and how they draw upon transnational labor and feminist networks to press their claims.

Rural movements. This category refers to mostly rural claims such as demands for land and/or land seizures, price supports, water rights and development, agricultural loans, crop subsidies, and communal land access. As peasant-based guerrilla movements decrease (with the exception of Colombia), new rural movements have appeared to voice claims against neoliberal restructuring in agriculture and development policies, often taking the form of protests against displacement from land by large development projects, especially dams, and restriction of access to means of livelihood—such as rural landless workers movement, the rubber tappers movement in Brazil, and the *cocalero* movement in Bolivia. Because indigenous populations are mostly rural, these economic claims are often overlaid with ethnic-identity and cultural-diversity claims that have become part of a master indigenous-rights frame. Although indigenous movements are not new in Latin America—for example, Bolivia's Katarista movement in the 1960s had strong cultural and identity elements—the number, strength, and tactics of indigenous movements since the 1980s are noteworthy (Yashar 2005). Especially significant is the pressure various indigenous movements have been able to exert on central governments via their adeptness at developing transnational solidarity networks and drawing upon resources of TSMOs.

Land ownership throughout Latin America tends to be highly concentrated, which has spurred class-based insurgencies, land seizures, and revolutions for decades, but agricultural restructuring policies under neoliberalism impart even greater advantages to large landowners and further squeeze small peasant farmers. The mostly mestizo-based Movement of Rural Landless Workers (*Movimento Dos Trabalhadores Rurais Sem Terra,* or simply MST) is arguably the largest social movement in contemporary Latin America (Wright and Wolford 2003). Beginning in 1984, 250,000 land occupations have been initiated by MST. Brazil's agricultural restructuring caused thousands of families to be cast off the land they had worked, and thousands more rural workers were left idle by agroindustrial concentration and mechanization. The MST movement arose with the simple repertoire of seizing idle land from large landholders and expanded to demand social welfare rights such as health care, education, and services. The MST movement was also able to draw some transnational support, especially via international linkages with Christian churches and charitable organizations (Mainwaring 1986). Wolford's chapter in this volume traces the individual decisions that swelled the ranks of the MST during the late 1980s and 1990s. Since 2000, an MST movement has expanded in rural Bolivia after the Agrarian Reform Institute ceased legally recognizing new land settlements in the late 1990s.

In Brazil, the rubber tappers' movement was able to develop strong transnational linkages by merging its claims with environmental and indigenous rights issues—patterns exhibited by other rural movements. By the mid-1970s, the livelihood of rubber tappers was pressured by land encroachment from the development of the Amazon region, especially loss of forest due to ranching and agriculture encouraged by Brazilian development projects. The movement itself began as a class-based movement but shifted its focus to reflect environmental issues. Conservationists in Washington, D.C., concerned about rainforest loss were among the first to raise awareness of the rubber tappers' plight. Later, activists of the Sierra Club, Environmental Defense Fund, National Wildlife Federation, and Charles Steward Mott Foundation began to work with the movement to pressure the World Bank for sustainable development programs (see Keck and Sikkink 1998a: 133-144). A similar pattern was evident in Brazil's anti-dam movement, which began in 1979 to press claims by peasants displaced by large projects in the Uruguai river basin but which later cultivated ties with environmental INGOs to leverage influence at the national and local levels (Rothman and Oliver 1999).[2]

Indigenous movements combine claims for political and cultural rights with a cosmopolitan awareness of how their grievances are linked with neoliberal globalization. At the end of 2005 in Bolivia, such a synthesis propelled Evo Morales to the presidency backed with the largest electoral majority in the country's recent history. Indigenous groups also incorporate strategies that develop links with TSMOs and cultivate global solidarity with related movements and with "conscience constituents" in the global North (McCarthy and Zald 1977). The movements that follow this general pattern are many and include *La Confederación de Nacionalidades Indígenas del Ecuador* (CONAIE), the Zapatista rebellion in Mexico, indigenous organizations in Ecuador's and Bolivia's Amazon region, the San Blas Kuna rights mobilizations in Panama, the Movimiento Indígena Pachacutik in Ecuador, Yanomami mobilizations in the Amazon region of Brazil, indigenous protests in Bolivia among *altiplano* Aymara and Quechua groups and pan-Mayan communities in Guatemala (see Stewart's chapter in this volume).

Ecuador's "national indigenous uprising" (*el levantamiento nacional indígena*)—as it came to be called—is representative of this form of contention. In June 1990, tens of thousands of highland Indians in Ecuador staged a spectacular national protest. Growing out of a nationally coordinated indigenous umbrella coalition called CONAIE, the movement was characterized by broadening its demands beyond a purely agrarian focus to include economic, territorial, political, cultural, and linguistic rights. CONAIE was formed in 1986 by several indigenous organizations from the high sierra and the equatorial regions. At this time, large agroindustrial producers prospered from Ecuador's free trade policies, but smaller—typically indigenous—farmers could not compete because of higher interest rates and rising costs of basic necessities. The movement was distinguished from peasant-based interest groups of the past by a deemphasis of class-based land claims and the promotion of cultural and territorial rights and a framing of Ecuador's indigenous populations as ethnic groups in a multiethnic society (Zamosc 2004). The frame of multiethnic diversity and conservation of traditional lands resonated with many NGOs in the global North to provide resources for pushing the movement's claims.

The macroeconomic conditions of Ecuador strongly paralleled those in Mexico, with the additional factor that Mexican growers faced impending competition from the U.S. under conditions of NAFTA. On January 1, 1994, the day that NAFTA went into effect, about 3,000 armed Mayan Indians from the state of Chiapas seized the capital, San Cristóbal de Casas, and several other surrounding municipalities, inaugurating the Zapatista uprising. The rebels' grievances stressed ethnic-regional inequalities in addition to political claims against Mexico's ruling party—especially regarding regional favoritism. Like CONAIE, there was a global awareness in framing of the demands. Zapatista spokesman, Subcomandante Marcos describes the global context: "Billions of tons of natural resources go through Mexican ports . . . [to] the United States, Canada, Holland, Germany, Japan . . . [but] poor people can not cut down trees [because foreign timber companies own the rights.]" (quoted in McMichael 2000: 271). Also like Ecuador, support from human rights INGOs played an active role. Several observers have stressed the importance of global linkages in the Zapatista rebellion: anti-NAFTA NGOs in Canada, Mexico, and the U.S. disseminated information about the rebellion (Schulz 1998: 594-597; also see Olesen's chapter in this volume). These ties seem to have been instrumental in mobilizing international protests against the Mexican army's counteroffensive. Solidarity demonstrations occurred in Canada, the U.S., Great Britain, France, Germany, and Spain. Likewise, Maney (2001b) stresses the role of global resources via transnational SMOs in the successful movement for land rights among Panama's San Blas Kuna Indians. He also partly attributes the less successful pursuit of land rights by Brazil's Yanomani to their weaker transnational ties.

DEMOCRATIZING POLITIES

No overview of Latin American protest would be complete without reference to the veritable wave of democratization that swept the region between 1979 and 1990. Military governments and/or personal dictatorships were replaced by elected civilian regimes in Argentina, Bolivia, Brazil, Chile, Ecuador, El Salvador, Guatemala, Haiti, Honduras, Nicaragua, Panama, Paraguay, Peru, and Uruguay. Some of these political transitions were elite-led, but several were equally driven by popular movements from below (Foweraker and Landman 1997). In Chile, for example, shantytown dwellers, students, progressive clergy, human rights organizations, and labor unions played key roles in placing pressure on the General Augusto Pinochet regime to liberalize

Argentine & Brazil Milt govts

12   *Paul Almeida and Hank Johnston*

(Schneider 1995). Similar types of coalitions applied weight on the Argentine and Bra-zilian military governments to initiate system-wide democratization in the early 1980s. In Central America, especially in the cases of El Salvador, Guatemala, and Nicaragua, armed insurgents and civil society allies forced out (or negotiated out) decades-old brutal dictatorships and military governments (Paige 1997; Jonas 2000; Wood 2000; Robinson 2003; Booth, Walker, and Wade 2006).

democratiza & debt crisis grows

Recognizing that there were a variety of forms of popular mobilizing in pre-democratic transition Latin America, we focus here on the new terrain of relatively more open polities in the 1990s and 2000s, and the likelihood of social movement emergence and associated forms of popular mobilization. But not only did political movements for democratic rights represent a significant category of protest, the democratization of Latin American states was a structural influence that had important effects on the wave of economic protests discussed above. Figure 1.1 demonstrates that democratization and debt crisis have grown together over the past two decades in Latin America and suggests that this sets the stage for popular struggles in the 1990s and early 2000s covered in the proceeding chapters. The figure brings the political and the

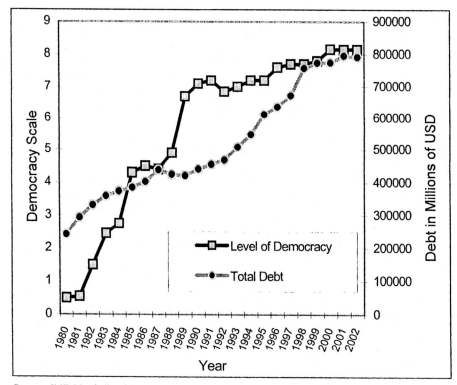

Sources: IMF; Marshall and Jaggars (2002). The countries included in these data are: Argentina, Bolivia, Brazil, Chile, Colombia, Costa Rica, Dominican Republic, Ecuador, El Salvador, Guatemala, Honduras, Jamaica, Mexico, Nicaragua, Panama, Paraguay, Peru, Trinidad Tobago, Uruguay, and Venezuela.

Figure 1.1 Democracy and Foreign Debt in Latin America, 1980-2002

economic together, which we believe are critical in understanding the current wave of contention in the region. The democracy index is constructed from Marshall and Jag-gar's (2002) Polity Index. A score of 10 corresponds to full democratization and a score of -10 equals complete authoritarianism. The index was compiled by averaging the annual scores of twenty Latin American and Caribbean countries between 1980 and 2002. The figure shows that the region had a very low democratization average in the early 1980s. By the late 1990s and early 2000s, the region was high in the democracy index, with an average of around 8. Latin America's foreign debt has also clearly sustained an upward trend since the regional economic meltdown in the early 1980s.

In the early days of Latin America's democratic transitions, commentators observed a *decrease* in overall popular movement organizing (Oxhorn 1996; Chalmers, Martin, and Piester 1997).[3] The demands and grievances centering on issues relating to repressive authoritarian rule were no longer as salient as regimes moved on to convoke competitive multiparty elections at the local and national levels (Linz and Stepan 1996; Eckstein 2001b; Salazar Villava 2002). The emerging institutional politics would be dominated by traditional and newly established political parties inside the polity (Canel 1992). The social movement sector in each of the emerging new (or renewed) democracies had to recalibrate its organizational and mobilizing strategies in the context of this more open political environment. Oppositional movements and civil society groups needed to adapt to the new rules of the political game (Foweraker 1995). Everyday forms of resistance such as "oppositional speech acts" (Johnston 2005), clandestine organizational structures (Johnston and Figa 1988), and absolute resistance to regimes gave way to new forms of more open organizing and alliances with ideologically similar political parties (Hellman 1992).

At the same time that surviving social movements and oppositional collectivities from the pre-transition era were readjusting their organizational forms and stratagems, increasing democratization made it possible for the growth and spread of several types of civic groups and associations. Such civil society organizations included a variety of nongovernmental organizations (NGOs) such as environmental, public health, indigenous rights, women's rights, gay rights, and cultural groups—to name just a few (Alvarez, Dagnino, and Escobar 1998). A democratizing regime allows for more of such groups to exist and possibly obtain legal status. Many of the newly emerging NGOs maintain transnational ties to international entities through loose affiliation, financing, or serving as the local chapters of development organizations (Keck and Sikkink 1998b; Korzeniewicz and Smith 2000). From this universe of NGOs (which vary enormously in mission and political ideology), an organizational infrastructure is created that in part may be appropriated during mobilizing campaigns against unwanted neoliberal policy changes, reforms, and "modernization" programs.

Potentially even more important for the Americas, though, is the increasing density of *regional* cross-border ties (Korzeniewicz and Smith 2004). Several inter-American organizations and bodies now hold annual gatherings such as the São Paulo Forum (Robinson 1992), the various World Social Forums (*Foro Social Mundial*) hosted in Brazil, Argentina, Uruguay, Paraguay, Ecuador, and Venezuela, and the *Foro Mesoamericano* in Central America. These regional encounters provide a critical social space whereby local NGOs, social movement organizations (SMOs), political parties, and like-minded individuals exchange information, develop long-term contacts, and reaffirm social solidarity around a pan-Latin American identity with a strong flavor of anti-neoliberalism. Thomas Olesen's contribution to this volume shows parallel dynamics during the convocation of the pro-Zapatista intercontinental *encuentros*.

We would also predict that the more "classical social actors" (Calderón 1995: 20) in the labor and educational sectors (i.e., unions, students, and teachers) would be freer to organize once they adapted to the liberalizing political environment (Cordero Ulate 2004). Finally, neighborhood groups, informal sector workers (especially market and street vendors, but also newly mobilized collectivities such as sex workers), and peasant associations and cooperatives should also have an easier time organizing with a *relatively* more publicly accountable political regime. In brief, state practices of regime liberalization and democratization provide system-wide "structural" changes in political opportunity (Meyer and Minkoff 2004) favorable to multiple subaltern and excluded social groups to launch mobilizing campaigns (Goldstone 2004). System-wide political opportunities or changes in the larger political environment associated with Latin American democratization and favorable for popular mobilization include a relaxation in state repression (McAdam 1996a), competitive elections and relatively more access to state institutions (Tarrow 1998; Almeida 2003). Indeed, as Tilly states, democratization is intimately tied to the spread of social movements:

> democratization in itself promotes formation and proliferation of social movements. It does so because each of its elements—regularity, breadth, equality, consultation, and protection—contributes to social movement activity. It also does so because it encourages the establishment of other institutions (e.g., political parties and labor unions) whose presence in turn usually facilitates social movement claim making. (2004: 137-138)

Moreover, the most potent SMOs and political organizations in the region, in terms of the numbers of people mobilized in collective action, tend to have been founded in the transition period or the post-authoritarian era of their respective countries. This pattern seems to be represented by a wide array of cases such as the Confederation of Indigenous Nationalities of Ecuador (CONAIE), the *Central de los Trabajadores Argentinos* (CTA), the *Movimento dos Trabalhadores Rurais Sem Terra* (MST) in Brazil, the *Bloque Popular* in Honduras, and the *Confederación Sindical Única de Trabajadores Campesinos de Bolivia* (CSUTCB) along with a variety of newer SMOs in Bolivia (e.g., coca-grower federations, municipal associations in El Alto and Cochabamba, etc.). As a general proposition, movements founded in a democratizing political environment would likely mobilize more rapidly and extensively because their prevailing organizational structures and practices would be geared toward a liberalizing regime and imprinted at the time of the movement's birth (Stinchcombe 1965). On the other hand, SMOs left over from the pre-democratic period would have to expend precious time and resources overcoming sunk costs by shedding outdated modes of struggle while simultaneously learning new tactics and behaviors consistent with a competitive electoral system.[4] Nonetheless, enduring traditions and repertoires of resistance from past movements may be transmitted over time and space to contemporary movements such as the roadblocks currently used by the unemployed workers' movement in Argentina (*los piqueteros*) that were first used in southern Santa Fe province by rural groups in the early twentieth century (Giarracca and Bidaseca 2001) or displaced unionized miners in Bolivia transferring their organizing skills to the newly-settled tropical cocoa-growing provinces in Cochabamba as a major asset in the *cocalero* movement (Vargas and Córdova 2004).

At the same time, there exists substantial variation within and between countries in the level of popular mobilization that cannot be accounted for by system-wide openings in political opportunity associated with regime democratization. Scholars must therefore explain how changes in "issue specific" political opportunities (Meyer and Minkoff 2004) affect the likelihood for mobilization for particular social sectors and groups. These would include such positive policy shifts as the establishment of new state agencies that potentially favor particular groups such as an institute of agrarian reform or the implementation of new laws protecting and/or recognizing indigenous people's rights, languages, and autonomy as in the cases of Ecuador in the 1980s and Bolivia in the 1990s (Vargas and Córdova 2004). In the latter case, such positive state actions legitimate pre-existing collective identities (i.e., ethnic identity) that may empower specific culturally defined groups to engage in future rounds of collective action in terms of increasing the probability of gaining new benefits or advantages (Amenta and Caren 2004).

Of course, we have delineated a rosy picture of post-authoritarian Latin America. If this were the case, much of the popular mobilization witnessed would largely focus on gaining even more advantages, collective goods, and extending democracy even further. The democratic regimes that have emerged in the region are still plagued by widespread official corruption, institutional racism, legitimacy problems, and severe economic constraints (Oxhorn and Ducatenzeiler 1998; Diamond 1999; Figueroa Ibarra 2002).[5] In short, even after the democratic transitions, there remains a major gap between democratic procedures in principle and upholding the rule of law in practice (Foweraker and Landman 1997). Indeed, the chapters by Auyero on Argentina and Holzner on Mexico in this volume demonstrate both the triggering and constraining roles of local state corruption in collective action dynamics.

It appears that the new wave of anti-austerity protests throughout the region is driven at the macro-level by several years of democratization (which peaks in the late 1990s and early 2000s) and the increasing economic threats associated with neoliberal globalization (Korzeniewicz and Smith 2000). Democratization seems to have a "lag effect" on mass contention in the region. The "cooling off" period of diminished social movement activity observed in the early years of the democratic transition in the Americas is giving way to intensified protest campaigns against unwanted economic changes. Just as structural adjustment policies reconfigured the relationship between citizens and the state in terms of social and economic distribution (Portes and Hoffman 2003), the social movement sector in each country of the region has "readjusted" to the prevailing political-economic environment from authoritarian-developmentalism to neoliberal democracy. This process was time dependent as new organizational structures, alliances and collective identities developed to effectively respond to the emerging political formation of today's neoliberal democracies.

Each of the chapters in this volume presents social movement cases that operate in this larger macro-context. The individual studies demonstrate the national and sectoral variations of these struggles, from women fighting for basic rights in garment factories and squatters for land rights, to unemployed and state workers struggling for employment and owed back wages. Even the paradigmatic movement against authoritarianism and human rights abuses in the region—*Los Madres de Plaza de Mayo* in Argentina—has integrated into its claim-making repertoire issues related to the social consequences of free market economic policies. The Plaza de Mayo itself served as ground zero for the pitched battles between unarmed protesters and police on December 20, 2001—at the height of the *Argentinazo* (see Borland's chapter 8).

THE STUDIES

We have selected most of the chapters in this volume according to the main themes of (1) popular protest against neoliberal policies, (2) occurring in the context of democratization, (3) and drawing on the support of transnational advocacy networks and TSMOs. Several other chapters have been selected because they shed light on (4) how neoliberalism and democracy affect gender issues related to social movement participation and (5) how they shape the moral economy of protest. These patterns of protest occurrence comprise the book's five thematic sections.

The early chapters in this volume examine large-scale collective actions by civil society against economic liberalization policies. In chapter 2, Shefner, Blad, and Pasdirtz take a comparative perspective by analyzing anti-austerity protest trends in Mexico and Argentina using a data set that updates and extends Walton and Seddon's decade-old protest-event data. A key finding is that, using economic modeling techniques similar to the IMF's but with social and political factors highlighted, neoliberal economic policies have a negative effect on the standard of living in those countries, which in turn, affect the occurrence of protest.

The next two chapters present examples of the scope, focus, and tactics of two important anti-neoliberal protests. López Maya and Lander (in chapter 3) present an impressive compilation of protest event data from Venezuela—spanning from the 1950s, through the *Caracazo* uprising of 1989 against IMF-sponsored price hikes, to the contentious Chávez years of the early 2000s. Almeida then presents a detailed study (chapter 4) of how negative policy impacts on public health care led to major mobilizations in El Salvador. He demonstrates how public sector employees that organize civil society groups and align with strong oppositional political parties sustained one of the largest campaigns in Latin America to prevent privatization—the outsourcing of El Salvador's state-run hospitals and medical services.

We then present two studies that explore the effects of democratization on protest mobilization—both focusing on Mexico but with implications that extend to other states as well. In Holzner's important study of a squatter settlement community mobilization on the outskirts of Oaxaca city, Mexico (chapter 5), the strong ties of patron-client relations are shown to have endured well into the neoliberal democratizing era inhibiting autonomous collective action for particular actors, while weak ties with newer political parties open up possibilities for independent mobilization. Holzner provides a sobering warning against studies that tend to overestimate the autonomy of civil society once a democratic transition commences. In strong corporatist states such as Argentina, Mexico, and Brazil, patron-client cliques may well carry over into the democratic period in some of the most impoverished social sectors such as urban squatter communities. Wada presents an innovative technique in chapter 6 for examining the changing demands or claims by oppositional groups over four decades—spanning from the developmentalist-authoritarian era to the current period of neoliberal democracy. He shows that claim making in Mexico has increasingly become politicized in the neoliberal era as challengers mix economic and social claims with demands for political rights.

The studies by Borland (chapter 7) and Bandy and Bickham-Mendez (chapter 8) combine the three forces of neoliberal trends, democratization, and transnational influences in terms of women's mobilization. Borland shows how the movement that captured the imaginations of human rights activists and feminists across Latin America and the globe, Argentina's Las Madres de Plaza de Mayo, matured both organizationally and ideologically to embrace anti-neoliberal platforms while maintaining original demands of an accounting for *los desaparecidos* of Argentina's dirty war and punishment of its perpetrators. Bandy and Bickham-Mendez's chapter focuses on how export processing zones open up new forms of mobilization led by female activists and women's advocacy groups. At the same time, they show how these movements must navigate the delicate (and understudied) within-movement contradictions of patriarchic organizations and traditional authority structures in developing strategies of coalition formation and tactical choices. Such struggles for democratic practices within non-state organizations (including SMOs) are an often-neglected arena by analysts of social movement politics in Latin America (Alvarez, Dagnino, and Escobar 1998).

The next two chapters offer in-depth case studies of particular groups and countries in their popular struggles during the neoliberal transformation of the region over the past two decades. Auyero (in chapter 9) employs an ethnographic account of two major social conflicts in the mid-1990s that were the immediate precursors to the development of Argentina's nation-wide unemployed workers' movement (*los piqueteros*)—the largest such movement in the Americas. He gathered the rich interview and archival data in the critical years immediately *preceding* Argentina's social eruptions at the end of 2001. Drawing from the work of E.P. Thompson and James Scott, Auyero calls for a "moral politics" understanding of popular collective action. The chapter offers an innovative way of tackling a daunting task for students of collective action— bringing macro economic changes (structural adjustment and public sector privatization) to the micro level of the interpretations of the specific communities impacted by these major shifts—municipalities outside the often-studied capital megacities. Auyero teaches us that reactions to negative economic changes associated with structural adjustment policies are clearly not simply knee-jerk reactions or the work of outside agitators and alienated political elites (as commercial media accounts often suggest), but rather connected to local beliefs about proper economic and political arrangements between regional powerholders and the popular sectors, and the potentially explosive consequences when those tacitly understood arrangements are violated. For example, in Auyero's case of Santiago del Estero, the pattern of looting and vandalism clearly shows that the grievances were directed at local state institutions and state managers— those blamed for the official corruption and responsible for wage arrears of civil servants.

Wolford's contribution to this volume (chapter 10) compares two distinct regions of landless worker's movement (MST) mobilization in Brazil. She contends that MST members' spatial construction of their communities, especially prevailing norms of property rights associated with specific rural economic arrangements, plays a decisive role in the timing of poor farmers' decision to join the high-risk landless movement. Similar to Auyero's work on the moral economy of protest, she complements the important macro explanations of the MST's rise based on grievances, political opportunities, and institutional resources by demonstrating the *multiple* pathways of membership based on regional and social class variations in productive relations and their associated meanings attached to land usage.

We close with three contributions that demonstrate the role of transnational advocacy networks and the difficulties of building and sustaining them. Olesen (chapter 11) analyzes the strategies of transnational framing that brings together a global solidarity network for the Zapatista struggle in Chiapas, Mexico. Stewart (chapter 12) examines the role of transnational resources in how indigenous activists make claims against the Guatemalan government for atrocities in the 1980s. Both of these studies demonstrate how becoming part of a transnational solidarity network is a dynamic and transformational process. Movements work to create a convergence of their interests with members of a transnational network. In contrast to Keck and Sikkink's boomerang hypothesis—that transnational strategies result from closed national and local opportunities— these two chapters show that a local to transnational shift requires new elaborations of the movements' discourse, ideologies, tactics, and goals.

The final chapter focusing on transnational linkages uses case studies of labor organizing in two Mexican maquiladoras. It traces how workers successfully resisted

low wages and poor working conditions through international network building and information sharing. Key to the success in both cases was the role that nonstate actors played in domestic and international politics, operating outside of national borders to simultaneously target the local, national, and international level. This chapter by Victoria Carty draws on social movement and international relations literature to conceptualize the transnationalization of grassroots efforts to pressure multinational corporations and host governments to respect labor laws, trade agreements, and national and self-mandated corporate codes of conduct.

In summary, the following contributions offer an important sampling of the various types of social movement struggles that are carried out in Latin America under the relatively new contexts of political and economic liberalization and with the possible salience of TSMOs and transnational advocacy networks. These movements range from export-processing zone workers and austerity-based protest movements, to unemployed workers, rural movements, indigenous movements, and human rights-based movements. The lessons learned from these cases will be insightful to activists, students and scholars as Latin America appears to remain on its current trajectory of deepening neoliberal democratization and heightened levels of popular mobilization.

NOTES

1. We do not include exclusively environmental campaigns nor the several armed insurrections and civil wars that occurred throughout Latin America. We do not discuss student protests, which sometimes arise from increases in tuition, cuts in the number of classes, faculty layoffs, or reductions of university resources—in other words, educational issues. Student protest often occurs in solidarity with workers and leftist organizations. Also, protests that focus on economic issues strictly defined, such as tax increases or currency devaluations are not covered. In the next section on democratic openings, we discuss political protests, as such.

2. In 1987 the movement's SMO, Comissão Regional de Antingidos por Barragens (Regional Committee of those Displaced by Dams) won an agreement with the state power utility that provided for fair reimbursement in cash or resettlement of those affected, but it was the leverage of the transnational organizations plus openings in Brazilian democracy that were critical for the success.

3. Eckstein (2001b) notes, however, that labor strikes increased in the late 1980s and early 1990s in Latin America and then tapered off with increasing levels of democratization and neoliberal reforms.

4. Of course we acknowledge that there were several democratic and semi-democratic regimes in existence before the 1980s in Latin America such as Costa Rica, Colombia, and Venezuela. We focus our analysis here on general regional trends.

5. In terms of regime legitimacy, we have witnessed the fall of several democratically elected governments in the early 2000s, including Haiti (2004); Argentina (2001); Ecuador (2000 and 2005); Bolivia (2003 and 2005); and briefly Venezuela (2002), while Nicaragua seemed to be teetering on the brink of executive removal for most of 2005.

Chapter 2

AUSTERITY PROTESTS AND IMMISERATING GROWTH IN MEXICO AND ARGENTINA

Jon Shefner, George Pasdirtz, and Cory Blad

This chapter compares austerity protests in Mexico and Argentina throughout the decade of the 1990s. International Monetary Fund (IMF) austerity policies imposed on Mexican and Argentine governments resulted in these states eliminating or decreasing national social and economic protections. Subsequently, these nations' reduced social investment spending created situations of widespread socioeconomic hardship that, when integrated with existing political opportunities, often resulted in protest actions. Mexico and Argentina are important cases to demonstrate the impact of austerity policy, given the size and strength of their economies, the relatively large number of protests each nation suffered, and the important political outcomes found in each nation. Mexico by the beginning of the millennium had democratized a political system long founded on exclusion and Argentina entered a period of great political instability in large part due to the ongoing imposition of austerity policies.

COMPARING MEXICO AND ARGENTINA

For decades, Mexico's economy flourished under a program of import-substitution industrialization governed by a one-party state that governed with a creative blend of clientelist and corporatist strategies. Using the state apparatus to employ many citizens in government-owned enterprises but providing only limited political access, the PRI (Partido Revolucionario Institucional) held largely unshakeable power by providing some measure of material provision. With a growing economy, the state was able to maintain power by selectively making openings to opposition parties, distributing the

19

fruits of growth through clientelist relationships, all the while consistently committing electoral fraud, punctuated by moments of fierce repression.

Cracks in the system emerged in the late 1970s, as economic slowdown and increasing debt limited the state's ability to address growing social needs. Temporarily buoyed by the discovery of oil reserves, the Mexican miracle of economic growth officially ended in 1982 when the government's inability to pay its public debt shocked global policymakers. From 1982 to 1994, Mexican economic policy was defined by austerity, both to repay debt and to reposition the nation within the global economy. The costs were substantial—Mexican citizens suffered extensive unemployment, wage declines, increased poverty, and decreased social spending as the government imposed austerity measures that reversed much of the previous thirty years of social advances.

As neoliberal policy increasingly defined economic policy, the government's patronage base declined, diminishing its capacity to employ state workers and reward them and other clients with health care, housing and education, and urban infrastructure. As the potential rewards to supporters declined, electoral competition increased. So, too, did social movement activity, as urban movements pushed for infrastructure, rural groups for land security, indigenous groups for autonomy, and all calling for democratization.

The Salinas administration (1988-1994) was forced to respond to unprecedented social movement and electoral opposition. Salinas' apparent fraudulent victory was ushered in amid massive street demonstrations throughout the nation. Despite maintaining policies that continued to impoverish millions of Mexicans, Salinas's public relations efforts were partially successful, as he directed spending to ameliorate the worst of the economic harm in areas vulnerable to opposition campaigning. The success of the NAFTA negotiations led Salinas to pursue membership in the G-8.[1] Yet, the success proved illusory with the 1994 confluence of the Zapatista rebellion, political assassinations, and finally the peso devaluation. The peso devaluation, timed to follow the election of another PRI president, would provide great impetus for social movements in Mexico.

On March 17, 1995, thousands of farmers—campesinos and larger landholders alike—joined middle-class debtors in responding to the call by El Barzón. El Barzón had begun in the state of Jalisco as an organization articulating the needs of indebted farmers, and grew to become an important voice of Mexicans impoverished by the nation's neoliberal policies. The protestors gathered in Mexico City's main plaza as well as outside the U.S. embassy. Their action followed on the heels of protests by "fashionable housewives armed with cellular telephones and Gucci bags," and wearing "designer sunglasses" who demonstrated at the Presidential Palace in that same city. Accompanied by their maids, the women spoke out against the soaring interest of credit cards that had reached 60 percent, car loans of 50 percent, and home mortgages over 40 percent.

In general, Mexicans saw the emergency austerity measures announced between December 1994 and March 1995 favoring investors and banks at the expense of middle-class, working-class, and poor citizens. Between January and March, a series of measures were announced, including a 35 percent rise in gas prices, a 20 percent increase in electricity prices, a significant rise in value added taxes, elimination of four government ministries, and caps on wage increases, as well as the steep rise in interest rates. Early protests included a march in the Federal District of thousands of workers, focusing especially on rising food, gas, electricity, and telephone prices. Almost 900 bank branches were closed during the March protests as the result of a "debtor's strike" called by El Barzón while the crisis continued to deepen. Twenty thousand students protested in Guererro, and thousands of businesses participated in a work stoppage in Oaxaca (Williams 1996; 2001).

Participants in the bailout included the governments of the United States and Canada, the International Monetary Fund (IMF), and private international banks; the size of the funds devoted to Mexico's needs reached US$50 billion. The austerity announcements continued, as Stanley Fischer, managing director of the IMF "welcomed the substantive measures adopted by the Mexican authorities to strengthen their economic program." Thousands of farmers, laborers, shopkeepers, businessmen, lawyers, and accountants continued their protests, marching on government buildings as interest rates continued to rise, with mortgage and credit cards approaching 150 percent. Manufacturers such as Volkswagen laid off 10 percent of their work force, while "Labor Secretary Santiago Onate admitted that as many as 500,000 people may lose their jobs in the next six to seven months."[2]

Argentina's post-WWII economic and political system displays much more instability than Mexico's. The Peronist corporate tradition privileged the military and urban working class as its most important partners. Military intervention often responded to the Argentine leader's perceived inability to keep the active working and middle classes under control. In the early years of the first Peron regime (1946-1955), the populist policies resulted in a sharp rise in standards of living, and economic growth, as the government attempted to limit foreign influence in the economy. Such gains were quickly undercut by economic recession, and the Peronists' policy responses included tightening credit and reductions in government spending, all with the intent to get the Argentinean economy under control to facilitate a quick return to social progress. Despite a populist government, the active role of the military from the 1950s through the 1970s proved that access to politics was often illusory.

Elections demonstrating Peronist partisans' strength were consistently overturned by either military governments or by civilian governments at the behest of the military. The coup of 1966 showed the government becoming more decisively anti-civilian in its governing stance than its earlier interventions. At the same time the military ushered in a period of increasing repression. For economic policy, the military relied on its technocratic decisionmakers who increased an external search for investment and economic direction. Contact with the IMF began with one of the few non-military governments of the 1960s, which had relied on the IMF for aid, accepting conditions of cutting subsidies and public spending while limiting wages and devaluing the currency in exchange for IMF credit. Later, during her brief presidency, Isabel Perón in 1976 also imposed austerity in exchange for IMF aid.

Increasing repression defined succeeding military governments, until the emergence of a revolutionary left using violent tactics supplied a rationale for the dirty war of the 1970s. Thousands died and disappeared while the military governments' economic policymakers privileged the private sector and sought to reduce the public sector, following neoliberal precepts of limiting wages and interest and privatizing state-owned enterprises.

The Falklands debacle and surging inflation weakened the military's nationalist and technocratic claim to efficiency. By 1983, the military gladly gave control of an Argentinean economy careening out of control to newly elected president Raúl Alfonsín. Exploding debt forced the president to seek new loans from the IMF, which were accompanied by new austerity conditions. Alfonsín's neoliberal measures did little to control the economy, as inflation roared out of control. Alfonsín took the unprecedented step of leaving office early, when Carlos Menem took over as president. In the early 1990s, Menem pursued orthodox neoliberal policies to get the economy under control: further privatizations of state-owned industry, slashing taxes, facilitating foreign trade and investment, and pegging Argentina's peso to the U.S. dollar. Other government strategies such as strike breaking and wage freezes demonstrated that the new Peronism had left its populist legacy behind. Inflation plummeted, and a vestige of stability returned. Yet, the medium-term costs of neoliberal polices were soon to be felt.

The 1992 privatization of the state-owned oil company, YPF, yielded mass unemployment in towns of Cutral-Co and Plaza Huincul. By 1996 the local conditions had deteriorated to the point of crowds responding with roadblocks and clashes with police. Protestors were joined at the barricades by teachers and other residents, especially after a passerby was shot and killed by police (see Auyero's chapter in this volume). In 1997 teacher's unions held a nationwide strike in mid-April and protest spread as sympathetic rioters soon attacked public buildings in Buenos Aires and Mendoza.

As protest continued into May 1997, the organized character of the movement became increasingly apparent. In the provinces of Santa Fe and Tucuman, as well as in the city of Buenos Aires, the contention was led increasingly by unions, such as in the town of San Lorenzo, Santa Fe, where 40 percent of the workforce was unemployed. Neighborhood uprisings continued and cuts to university budgets led to hunger strikes and street demonstrations by teachers and students in Buenos Aires and elsewhere. By the end of May, violent protests occurred throughout Argentina, including road blockages and takeovers of bridges and government buildings.

The sell-off of state industries and layoffs of state employees continued into the spring, as did high unemployment. Lower-middle and middle-class families that had been insulated from previous periods of reform now felt the hardships of austerity, and joined vendors, union members, and law students in the streets. As the Mendoza provincial government decided to privatize the local utility, the power worker's union protested, hurling stones at the government building where the legislation was being debated. Police responded with rubber bullets and tear gas, as they had in several other protests throughout the nation.

With the summer of 1997, some of the protest quieted, but not the anger. A visit by David Copperfield led to the popular joke enjoyed by Buenos Aires residents that the magician "begged President Menem to teach him how to make an entire middle class disappear." Government workers' bitterness remained especially deep, reflecting federal employment cuts from 1 million workers in 1991 to 300,000 in 1997. Mid-August protests showed the respite was temporary as a successful general strike led by government employees and unions, bus drivers and teachers paralyzed the country. The strategies of blockades reemerged in over 20 provinces, as the nation roiled under the impact of seemingly ceaseless austerity and responding protest.[3]

The previous descriptions introduce two extended periods of political ferment engendered by austerity policies. The imposition of such policies, usually at the urging of the IMF, resulted in protests around the globe during the 1980s (Auvinen 1996; Walton 1989; Walton and Ragin 1990; Walton and Seddon 1994). Despite the fact that the antiglobalization protests in cities of the Global North have achieved a higher profile among journalists and activists, the wave of protests in the Global South has continued throughout the 1990s to the current day. These protests have had important implications for the political life of powerful nations in the developing world well beyond the more publicized events of Seattle, Quebec, Prague, and elsewhere.

This chapter examines such protest events and their political outcomes in two nations in Latin America, Mexico and Argentina. We focus on these two nations for several reasons. First, Latin America is the locale of the greatest number of austerity protests that we have been able to document. Second, Argentina and Mexico are two of Latin America's giants, measured in size and importance of their economies. The size of these nations and the fact that their political systems have been rocked by austerity policies confirm the importance of this wave of protest.

Theoretically, this chapter argues that some of the contributions of political opportunity theory may be expanded if we look at how hardships themselves influence the political and cultural landscape of nations experiencing international pressure. We argue that IMF policies and other external political economic pressures work in the following way: Austerity expectations and other external pressures decrease national social investment. IMF pressures both directly and indirectly increase hardships. Increased hardships lead directly to protest. Hardships will also indirectly lead to protest in the presence of high levels of political access. Alternatively, high levels of political participation could limit levels of protest in two ways: (1) under certain circumstances, by providing channels of participation which supersede protest as a way to express political demands; or (2) by forcing national governments to resist the extent of their agreements with the IMF, thereby limiting IMF pressure.

FROM DEBT TO CONDITIONALITY

The debt crisis of the 1980s, and the subsequent design of austerity policies, has been traced to the mid-1960s European recession. Lasting into the 1970s, the recession was accompanied by increasing oil prices and consequently greater OPEC funds in western banks. Banks holding a large amount of capital began to lend more heavily to Global South and socialist nations. Many developing nations were already suffering balance of payment deficits due to steadily rising import prices, while others were enjoying substantial aggregate growth. Many nations borrowed at unprecedented levels in order to pursue greater production capacity or to address social welfare needs. Capital became increasingly internationalized (Block 1977) not only because of increasing OPEC profits strengthening the Eurodollar market, but "also based on flows from within the industrialized countries, attracted by the lack of regulation" (Wood 1986: 79).

The effects of recession in the late 1970s and early 1980s became felt simultaneously with declining prices in exports. Few indebted nations could pay their debts. In response, the IMF required nations to change domestic economic policy as conditions of debt renegotiation (Stiglitz 2002; Larner 2000).[4] The conditions suggested by the IMF and imposed by national governments have consistently taken the form of "shock treatments" intended to elicit economic stabilization.[5] Common features of these policies include currency devaluation and reduction of public-devoted expenditures such as social welfare spending and consumer subsidies. These policies follow free-market ideology by reducing state control of domestic industry, often by privatizing state-owned enterprises. Stabilization policies also facilitate foreign investment by cutting wages, increasing focus on export production, and dismantling protectionist industrial policies (Stiglitz 2002; Walton 1989; Harris and Seid 2000).

The policies have had savage effects on almost all sectors of the Global South. Globalization has meant increasing penetration of imported food in these nations, that, when coupled with currency devaluations, makes food buying more expensive. Wage freezes amid inflation further reduce buying power. Reductions and/or privatization of public spending means that the quality and quantity of education, health care, housing, and other social services have declined. Often basic foodstuffs and transportation are subsidized; the removal of those subsidies cuts an already thin margin of survival. Increased interest rates have meant increased debt among the middle class while employment drops when small business owners find it harder to obtain capital. Finally, increasing the access of foreign business using capital-intensive production methods, coupled with cutting protection for local industry, has meant the dissolution of local business relying on labor-intensive production. Again, employment drops, local production falters, and populations fall into poverty.

Despite popular protest and opposition by national governments, IMF activities and influence have expanded. This expansion has increased the numbers of agreements between the IMF and member nations. Prior to 1986, there was a 22 percent probability of any developing nation being part of an IMF program; from 1986 to 1997 the probability increased to 51 percent (Evrensel 2002). Indeed, many member countries "have been under the IMF's care almost continuously" (Evrensel 2002: 578). Further, neoliberal precepts have become the policies prescribed for all economic ills suffered by nations of the Global South and ex-members of the Soviet bloc. The policies once designed to address debt are now implemented by nations undergoing other reforms as a way to induce economic growth by "opening" markets. Conditionality has now been imposed on many nations addressing needs above and beyond debt payment.

Research on the "lost decade" of the 1980s demonstrated that IMF intervention in national economies had severely negative consequences for the Global South (Onimode 1989; Bello et al. 1982; George 1988; Pastor 1987a, 1987b; Korner et al. 1986; Wood 1986; MacEwan 1990; Bradshaw 1987). The implementation of these policies, and the accompanying subsequent economic and social devastation, has continued to the current day. Although the Global South no longer suffers from the zero to negative growth of the early 1980s, average annual growth rates of the 1990s (measured by GDP) have declined from the 1980s level of 4.4 percent among World Bank-designated low-income nations to 2.4 percent. Average annual growth rates among World Bank-designated middle income countries have varied little, ranging from 3.2 percent to 3.5 percent across the same decades. Total external debt increased from a 1990 level of $1.4 trillion to a 1998 level of $2.5 trillion in low- and middle-income nations (World Bank 2001). Debt and subsequent national vulnerability to policy dictates of international financial agencies continues to define the economic policies of nations in the developing world even more now than it did twenty years ago (Harris and Seid 2000; Nef and Robles 2000; González de la Rocha 2000).

EXPLAINING IMF PROTEST

Since 1990, research on protest in developing nations has proliferated. Some of this work examines other forms of protest (Jenkins and Schock 1992; Auvinen 1996); much of it follows on Walton and Ragin's (1990) groundbreaking work, both reinforcing and challenging their findings that the extent of austerity protest is positively and significantly related to IMF intervention, debt service ratio, inflation, and urbanization. For example, Maney (2001a) suggests that the evidence addressing world systems-derived hypotheses linking economic marginalization and political protest is conflicting. Auvinen (1996), on the other hand, acknowledges the connection between economic hardships and political protest, but questions the role of the IMF in the occasion of protest. Indeed, Auvinen concludes that being subjected to IMF conditionality may stabilize national politics if these programs improve economic performance. Evrensel (2002) finds exactly the opposite: not only do IMF-suggested measures fail to achieve their avowed intentions, they leave nations increasingly economically destabilized and politically vulnerable.[6]

Other researchers address the relative influence of external and internal characteristics. Moaddel, for example, finds that neither modernization nor world systems theory offers sufficient explanation for political conflict. Instead, according to Moaddel, "domestic characteristics" within nations explain such protest (1994: 294). Auyero (2001, 2004) agrees in part: although he recognizes that the global economy influences protest, he suggests we learn more by examining individual events to discover how global pressure is mediated by local politics. Jenkins and Schock (1992) also examine contrasting explanations generated by political process and global economy theories to explain domestic political conflict, and advocate for a synthesis of the different theoretical explanations.

The role of the state complicates the issue. On the one hand, the state functions as the intermediary between the IMF and local citizens. Austerity policies are designed internationally, but are applied nationally through domestic policy adjustments. This creates a methodological problem in determining the true extent that national institutions promote hardships and conditions of poverty, especially given the secrecy surrounding such negotiations. On the other hand, the state maintains a sufficient level of authority to administer or mediate such policy reforms. Indeed, at times governments work to counter the pervasive problems that accompany such externally imposed shocks. Yet, if states resist the externally "suggested" reforms, they often suffer substantial consequences such as the loss of loan monies needed for national development or even the maintenance of national economic systems (Manley 1987).

The protests that we have documented provide evidence that support della Porta's and Kriesi's (1999) observation that despite globalization, the state remains the main actor in conflicts with its constituency. Even if the roots of a conflict or problem are global, the reach of most protestors is national. Della Porta argues that states are targeted even in cases where conflict has international roots because of the difficulties of holding non-state entities accountable. Yet, lack of accountability, as we have seen in earlier accounts of these protests, does not mean lack of attribution (Walton and Shefner 1994). Protestors may strategically target the state while understanding full well that the state has been forced to acquiesce to an international regime.

Jenkins and Klandermans tell us that "the state shapes the conflict and alliance systems that shape social movement emergence and development" (1995: 4). Given this recognition, it is not unreasonable to think that if the state is the organ of national political policy, a similar logic applies internationally. International political policy similarly structures national political policy through state action (Bello 2001). But states also provide targets and opportunities for movements, as Jenkins (1995) suggests. States in the neoliberal context provide the very reason for movement emergence and action. They do so by acquiescing to IMF neoliberal dictates, removing protections that provided a shelter from hardships while imposing new and sharp hardships on traditionally and newly vulnerable populations alike.

In Latin America, hardships imposed by neoliberal adjustments push movements to work in ways that they were not previously able to within clientelist or corporatist states. As external neoliberal pressures rise, the state loses preexisting means of legitimization, such as provision of material goods and services, and must rely increasingly on coercion. Still, because of the difficulty for national movements to address international entities, the target remains national even with clear attribution to the international power center.

Austerity protests continue to be an important form of global political contention. Yet, protest does not neatly follow the imposition of austerity in each nation. What explains the surge of protests in Mexico and Argentina?

We examine austerity protests by analyzing the interaction of a complex set of indices. We created two different indices that operationalize different kinds of external pressure. One, following Walton and Ragin (1990) is an IMF pressure index. The second measures the level of international aid. We know IMF pressure has important influences on budget allocations in indebted nations, decreasing expenditures in national social investments. We suggest that increased IMF pressure will result in two kinds of hardships, one directly affecting households, and another mediated through states.[7] International aid may have contradictory effects on hardships. Various forms of economic aid, such as food aid or agricultural assistance, may ameliorate some of the damage felt by households experiencing neoliberal pressures. Alternatively, further "free market" conditions may accompany international aid, making such aid a further indication of external pressure to impose neoliberal policy.

The direct harm to households is operationalized by an index measuring prices and inflation levels. The second index demonstrates a whole series of state-mediated economic hardships, including health and education expenditures. These state social investments are consistently targeted by IMF conditionality measures. As one critic observed, "studies at the World Bank show that such strife is systematically related to adverse economic factors . . . that can be produced by excessive austerity" (Stiglitz 2002: 78). However, we believe that different hardships or different hardship intensities may have diverging implications for austerity protests. González de la Rocha (2000) suggests that immiseration in much of the developing world has reached a level such that household survival is threatened. In fact, extreme levels of immiseration may curtail ability for protest. Thus, those nations that most deeply experience dangers to survival may not protest given the energy devoted to survival. Less dramatic levels of hardship may instead yield the most severe protest.

We measure how neoliberal a nation's policies are based on the *Wall Street Journal*'s indicators of "economic freedom," which we have renamed *extent of neoliberalism*. Our argument is that the more neoliberal the government policies, the more that hardships will result in severe protest. We also construct an index of government access by joining indicators of political and civil rights with other measures of government openness. Here our argument is that in the presence of high government access, protest severity will be tempered due to the presence of institutional channels of claim making (Tilly 1978). A contrasting approach draws upon the work of Piven and Cloward, who see protest and institutional political activity as more complementary and less separable (1979, 1993). This gives an alternative hypothesis that the greater the political access, the more a population will respond with protest in the face of external pressure and hardships. To explain further, we root our argument in the political opportunity framework.

A key theme in this chapter is that an analysis of hardships, *as such,* has been sorely lacking in recent social movement theory and that the kind of hardships associated with austerity protest can be profitably thought of as giving rise to their own unique political opportunities through the agency of the populations most affected. Marks and McAdam comment that "movements emerge and develop in response to shifts in the broader political environment that render their opponents (both in and out of government) more or less vulnerable to challenge" (1999: 98). We suggest that both the activities of international agencies and the hardships they impose may be understood as shifts in that broader environment. We do not want to stretch the concept of political opportunity too thin, as Kriesi and others have warned (Kriesi 2004; see also Goodwin and Jasper 2004), yet the framework of political opportunity should be flexible enough to address one of the reasons that movements emerge, namely, the existence of shared hardships.

Certain hardships provide political opportunities for protest when they are widespread, allowing for mobilization of a large cross section of a public. Additionally, hardships may further provide opportunities when they weaken state legitimacy based in welfare provision or other state-centered domination such as clientelism or corporatism. The basis of such systems, found in both Mexico and Argentina, are founded on a contract of reciprocal obligation, either explicitly articulated or implicitly structured (Roniger 1990). Attacking the capacity to discharge a series of welfare obligations disrupts the moral economy of survival (Thompson 1971), and makes the state unable to fulfill its side of the social compact.

Hardships may further structure political opportunities if they are sufficiently intense that the state is significantly weakened. If the regulatory capacity of the state, its ability to maintain domestic order, or its sovereignty within international conflicts are weakened, hardships will emerge that provide opportunities to mobilizing groups. State legitimacy may also be damaged with a clear shift in allegiances to defined constituencies. When allegiance of the state is increasingly transferred to elites, transnational or otherwise, client or corporate actor constituents may react drastically to the subsequent withdrawal of material provision. In short, people can make their own opportunities (Kurzman 1996) drawing on shared hardships when that affects their relationships with states. In so doing, they exert agency given structural opportunities provided by shared hardships.

DATA AND SAMPLE

This chapter is part of a larger project in which we searched fifty-eight national and international English-language newspapers in the *Lexis-Nexis General News* database to collect events for the current data set. In order to maintain some broad comparative possibilities, we maintained the sixty-nation sample originally created by Walton and Ragin (1990). We followed their general criteria for defining an austerity protest: "(a) mass actions that (b) specifically addressed austerity policies . . . , and (c) stemmed from actions by governments that were strongly urged by international institutions (typically the IMF)" (Walton and Ragin 1990: 882). We reviewed over 25,000 articles and documented 828 events as austerity protests for the period of 1990-1999.[8]

Each protest event was coded for the number of cities involved, duration, level of violence, form, and participation. We refined Walton and Ragin's coding scheme by making two important changes. First, the violence scale was expanded, and second, the scale for "Social Composition of Participants" was changed to a "Social Power Scale for Participants." This new coding places protest participants in a basic hierarchy of social power and adds the categories of small and large alliances/coalitions. This set of measures provides our index of protest severity.

Despite the large number of events identified for this ten-year period, we argue it is a very conservative measure of the actual number of protests within each nation and across the database. First, most events are not covered in national newspapers, let alone those published in English. Second, the inclusion criteria were followed very closely and many possible events were not included due to lack of direct support.[9] Third, we could have expanded the search terms and periodical list to include more events, but time constraints forced a compromise with coverage. Finally, evidence collected from many articles describe uncodeable events or list numbers of related protests which show that our numbers are much lower than the actual events. One example comes from a March 22, 1995, article on Mexico from the *Independent* (London): "One day recently, there were 100 separate anti-government protest marches in this capital of more than 20 million people." Without supporting materials for each individual protest, however, we were unable to code these events. That is, each coded event supplied information about place, participants, form of protest, and precipitating policy imposed by national governments at the urging of international agencies. In the absence of these documented details, the events were not included in the data set.

Additionally, cross-national data on each of the sixty countries was collected from a variety of sources including World Bank and United Nations databases, IMF reports, the Polity IV dataset, Freedom House, and independent reporting agencies. Access to international comparative data has vastly increased over the past decade, and therefore allowed for substantial choice when selecting indicators to represent economic, political, and social realities.

ANALYSIS

Any attempt to describe IMF policy impacts forces us to confront a number of difficult issues. IMF staff use econometric models in an attempt to understand how their policymaking might affect a given country. Protest and ongoing immiseration demonstrate that these models are wrong, as we will see. The IMF is "too wedded to their traditional models of how to fix troubled economies" (Blustein 2001: 18). The IMF policy manipulations had a number of unintended consequences, including generating protest responses from affected populations. If the IMF models were wrong, why were they wrong? What are the right models and how might they be constructed?

Our work suggests two critiques of IMF policy, one conceptual and the other methodological. Conceptually, we believe that neoliberals commit great errors when they fail to account for wide political, cultural, and social histories of the societies for which they design policy. In effect, they commit the errors that Polanyi points out are common to those who believe too much in the magic of the market: ignoring that economies are embedded in wider societies and that the prioritizing of the market will have savage effects on citizens (Polanyi 1944).

The implication of Polanyi's critique is that we cannot understand the operations of economies in isolation from a whole set of systemic dynamics. Kalman (1980) agrees with this position, and has argued that econometric models are wrong precisely because they ignore the dynamics of the social systems they seek to explain. A country cannot simply be described as a neoclassical market economy existing in a societal equilibrium which is interrupted only occasionally by "exogenous variables" representing important cultural and political events and institutions. Complex social and political dynamics must be accounted for; in our case these include external and internal political pressures, levels of political access, and variations in protest, among others. Far from being exogenous, such dynamics are intrinsic to these social systems as manifestations of both historical social structure and contemporary social problems.

Methodologically, IMF policy has been driven by econometric modeling vulnerable to Kalman's critique. Societies are complex entities, with multiple historical, social, cultural, political, and economic phenomena occurring at any time. Some of these are measurable, others are less so. Much quantitative work seeks to hold many of these issues constant, and yields explanations that minimize historical interactions. Economic growth theories, for example, suggest that the simple investment of capital will induce growth, ignoring the social, political, and cultural ramifications of the new investment. Yet, errors are endemic to modeling that ignores the interaction of such events. For example, we know that both external and internal investment is fostering massive growth in China. We do not know, however, the extent of the political, social, and cultural changes that such investment will bring. Neither do we know how subsequent impacts on labor markets, urbanization, and the environment will play out in China—and econometric models that try to hold analysis constant over time, space, culture, and politics will not shed much light on these changes.

Our method instead *highlights* those historical interactions over time. Our regressions have been run through time-series techniques that bring social change over time into account. In this way, we are confident of making causal statements regarding the impact of neoliberal IMF policy on hardships in the nations subjected to such policy, like Mexico and Argentina, as well as the impact of such policy on protest.

These simulation techniques also are able to provide another benefit over common econometric techniques. In effect, we are able to conduct historical experiments, or examine counterfactual possibilities. That is, our simulations allow us to ask questions like: What would have happened in the absence of IMF pressure? Simulations provide a way to extract variables (such as IMF pressure and foreign aid) over time, while tracing a myriad of other social and political phenomena. Our simulations predict levels of growth and inequality in the absence of IMF pressure. That is, we answer the question: What would Mexico's and Argentina's economies have looked like without the imposition of IMF "pro-growth" austerity policies? The difference between our counterfactual simulation techniques and the econometric modeling of the IMF is that we address interactions within a system, while holding one variable constant, while they look at the effects of one variable while holding the system constant. As we will see, the results of these models demonstrate the ongoing impoverishment of Argentina and Mexico. They demonstrate not only that IMF policy results in increased immiseration and protest, but it has exacerbated long-term patterns of unequal economic growth and poverty. The result of immiserating growth in both real and counterfactual history demonstrates the great error of neoliberal thought: that nations can grow out of poverty. We will say more about this shortly.

We use systems theory as the starting point to capture complex system dynamics (Kalman 1980). Systems theory is essentially the search for the simplest dynamic model that can link a real complex system to an abstract theoretical representation. It is superior to other techniques because it addresses a number of problems that obstruct cross-national quantitative studies, such as missing data and measurement errors. Additionally, systems theory allows a time series analysis, and addresses issues of complexity and hierarchy. That is, societies present a complex unit of analysis that cannot be observed directly but only through measurable inputs and outputs, and are embedded in both regional systems and in the world system that requires a multilevel analysis to disentangle hierarchical effects.

Systemic modeling requires the use of indices rather than the manipulation of single variables. Index construction also mirrors our position that economic, social, and political life is too complex to be addressed by examining the effects of single variables. We have constructed certain indices following Walton and Ragin's (1990) work, aggregating variables which help give a full picture of protest severity (by joining variables of protest frequency, severity as defined by injuries and deaths, duration, actors involved, and spread), as well as of IMF pressure (by joining variables defining numbers of IMF negotiations and restructurings over the 1990s, as well as ratio of borrowed money to IMF reserves).

In addition, we designed indices that measure elements of our model. To construct a comprehensive index of social investment, for example, we aggregated measures of public spending in education, central government debt, and health, and budget deficits among other variables. To construct an index of hardships, we aggregated measures of populations without access to safe water or sanitation, human poverty measures, population below poverty level, and unemployment. To construct an index of political conditions, we aggregated measures of openness of political institutions, political rights, and civil rights. Present also in this index is a variable of neoliberalism, which measures the level of openness the national economy is to the "free market."

Construction of these indices helps us create a model that allows the testing of relative importance of varying systemic characteristics. From an initial set of eleven indexes, we used general-system techniques to reduce them to five variables measuring protest, economic conditions (to include export commodity concentration, inequality, GNP, etc.), social conditions (to include measures of demographic pressure, short-term and long-term hardship), and external political conditions (IMF pressure and international aid), the latter being taken as the exogenous policy variables.[10] We can now state our hypotheses for testing[11]:

> H1:   As external political pressure increases, protest will increase, to a point.
> H1.1: External political pressure that directly worsens social conditions will result indirectly in protest.
> H1.2: For countries experiencing immiserizing growth, if external political pressure increases economic growth then the deterioration in social conditions resulting from economic growth will result in protest.
> H2:   As internal social conditions deteriorate, protest will increase, to a point, regardless of increased economic growth.
> H3:   As internal political conditions improve, protest will decrease.

Figure 2.1 demonstrates the different trends of protest in Mexico and Argentina. In Mexico, protest numbers (totaling 103 over the course of the decade) peaked during the 1995 peso crisis, when Mexico was under so much duress. After 1995, protest in Mexico slowly tapered off until the late 1990s when an upward surge began again. In Argentina, where we documented a total of 75 protests over the decade, there was more of a cycle of increase and decrease over the decade. Although the peaks did not reach the extent of Mexico's, the consistent pattern set the stage for the explosion of 2001 and later.

Table 2.1 presents the estimated regression coefficients for the model showing year-to-year changes. For Mexico, the external political index, Xpolitical[1], has the largest impact on protest while economic conditions, Economic[1], also display a positive impact. That is, declining international aid and increasing economic growth stimulated protest, as did increasing IMF pressure. This confirms our hypothesis linking external pressure and protest.

The model estimated for Argentina was specified somewhat differently than the model estimated for Mexico because we found different patterns of protest—more linear in Mexico, and more cyclical in Argentina (see figure 2.1). To account for the different pattern of protest dynamics in Argentina, we added a nonlinear term, Protest[1]^2. The largest negative impact, -0.93, is from deteriorating social conditions. The next largest impact, -0.41, is from deteriorating economic conditions.[12] That is, declining economic performance and deteriorating social conditions stimulated protest in Argentina, again as we have hypothesized.

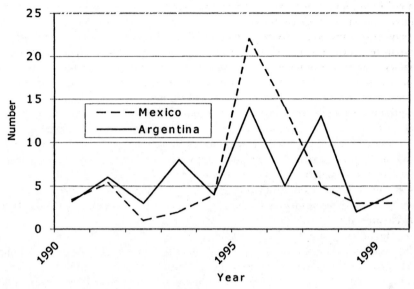

Figure 2.1. Protest in Mexico and Argentina

	Protest Index[t]	Economic Index[t]	Political Index[t]	Social Index[t]
Protest Index[t-1]	-0.35	-0.09	0.48	-0.08
Economic Index[t-1]	-0.41	0.43	-0.75	-0.76
Political Index[t-1]	0.01	0.05	0.27	-0.18
Social Index[t-1]	-0.93	-0.02	-0.36	-0.11
Xpolitical Index[1,t-1]	0.01	0.08	-0.63	0.07
Xpolitical Index[2,t-1]	0.27	0.18	0.37	-0.43
Protest Index[t-1]^2	-0.24	0.03	-0.24	0.10
Constant	0.26	0.16	0.00	-0.11

Table 2.1. Estimated Policy Impacts and Short-Run Growth Dynamics for Argentina.[13]

	Protest Index[t]	Economic Index[t]	Political Index[t]	Social Index[t]
Protest Index[t-1]	-0.06	0.02	0.16	0.03
Economic Index[t-1]	0.23	0.27	0.21	-0.29
Political Index[t-1]	-0.33	0.15	0.32	-0.21
Social Index[t-1]	-0.26	-0.28	-0.21	0.31
Xpolitical Index[1,t-1]	0.71	-0.02	-0.38	0.07
Xpolitical Index[2,t-1]	0.76	0.28	0.00	-0.25
Constant	-0.04	0.18	0.17	-0.21

Table 2.2. Estimated Policy Impacts and Short-Run Growth Dynamics for Mexico.[14]

The coefficent -0.35 in Protest[1] demonstrates that protest itself in one time period limits protest in a later time, unless the previous action was met by governmental policy addressing social needs. Dissenters are thus more likely to protest against austerity policies if their previous actions have borne some fruit. External political pressure, Xpolitical[2], also demonstrates a positive impact on protest—IMF and other international pressure does lead to protest, as our journalistic evidence shows. The non-linear protest component, Protest[1]^2 = (-0.24) tells us that protest can reach a limit, which will limit protest in future time periods. For both countries, improving social conditions would have decreased protest. Historically, of course, social conditions were deteriorating.

Economic conditions in the short term affected our two cases differently. In Mexico, increasing economic conditions stimulated protest. The neoliberals were right: their policies created growth. Yet, the growth was immiserating—distributed in ways that led to protest. In Argentina, economic growth depressed protest directly, but indirectly led to deteriorating social conditions—what we call hardships—and in this way led to protest.

Figures 2.2 and 2.3 display the criterion simulation for the endogenous variables. In this figure, we demonstrate how well our model has predicted historical change in Mexico and Argentina. A criterion simulation sets the initial conditions of all endogenous variables to their historical values and then solves the model numerically for all the remaining time points. The performance of the criterion simulation for Argentina is somewhat poorer than in Mexico, with protest providing the worst prediction. However, each model does track the basic historical data.

For Mexico, negative social conditions, Social[1] (demographic pressure, long-term and short-term hardship), increased while economic growth increased, reaching a plateau toward the end of the decade, again demonstrating our thesis of immiserating growth (Miyagiwa 1993). Toward the end of the decade, internal political conditions, Political[1], stopped growing, that is, the growth of neoliberalism and political access halted, amid a decline in national social investment.

For Argentina, social conditions, Social[1], deteriorated, as in Mexico. However, economic growth reached a plateau earlier in the decade than in Mexico. Neoliberalism was increasing, that is, the economy became more open to the free market while national social investment decreased. Political access remained constant, reflecting the earlier accomplishment of democratization in Argentina than in Mexico.

Tables 2.3 and 2.4 show coefficients for long-run system dynamics. Notice the long-run negative relationship between economic growth and social conditions (-1.14 and -1.22) in Mexico, again demonstrating the pattern of immiserating growth (Miyagiwa 1993). The long-run negative impact of economic growth on social conditions in Argentina (-0.01 and -0.96) again demonstrates a pattern of immiserating growth, but is less pronounced than in Mexico. Internal political dynamics are different in Argentina than in Mexico, as we discuss below. Therefore, in the long run, improved political conditions decreased protest in Mexico but increased protest in Argentina.

Comparing the coefficients in tables 2.1 and 2.2 show the differences in the short- and long-run determinants of protest. In both countries, deteriorating social conditions lead to protest in both the short run and in the long run. In Mexico, economic growth also increases protest both in the short run and in the long run. In Argentina, in the short run, political access was constant over time, and so has little effect. National social investment peaked and then declined, and neoliberalism increased over time. This scenario set Argentina up for the explosions of 2001. In nations, declining economic and social conditions and increasing economic growth led to protest. It should also be noted that protest in Argentina was more volatile and cyclical.

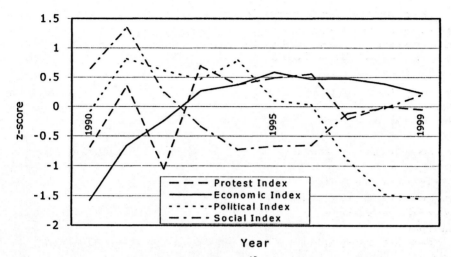

Figure 2.2. Criterion Simulation for Argentina[15]

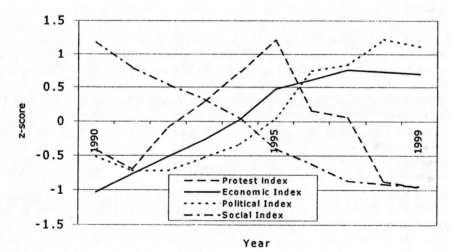

Figure 2.3. Criterion Simulation for Mexico[16]

	Protest Index	Economic Index	Political Index	Social Index
Protest Index	0.86	-0.06	0.69	-0.13
Economic Index	0.14	1.65	-1.13	-0.96
Political Index	0.22	0.12	1.55	-0.35
Social Index	-0.80	-0.01	-1.06	1.14

Table 2.3. Long-Run Growth Dynamics for Argentina[17]

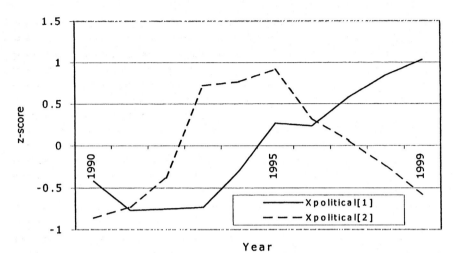

Figure 2.4. External Political Pressure Index for Argentina.[18]

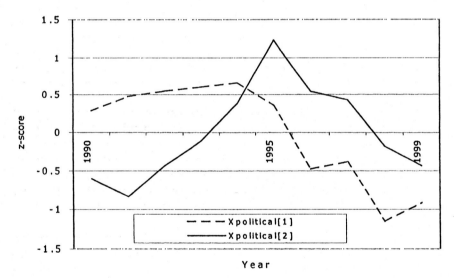

Figure 2.5. External Political Pressure Index for Mexico

	Protest Index	*Economic Index*	*Political Index*	*Social Index*
Protest Index	0.91	0.13	0.29	-0.11
Economic Index	0.40	2.10	1.15	-1.22
Political Index	-0.21	0.77	1.97	-0.94
Social Index	-0.44	-1.14	-1.18	2.27

Table 2.4. Long-Run Growth Dynamics for Mexico[19]

How much of the observed history is due to internal dynamics and how much is due to external intervention? Figures 2.4 and 2.5 display the patterns of external pressure for Mexico and Argentina. For Mexico, the first component XPolitical[1,M] measures declining international aid which, over time, was substituted with increasing IMF pressure. The second component, XPolitical[2,M], measures cycles in international aid and IMF pressure. The peak in 1994 shows the peak of international aid and the low point of IMF pressure. For Argentina, XPolitical[1,A] measures growth in international aid associated with declining IMF pressure. The second component, XPolitical[2,A], illustrates the mid-decade peak in both international aid and IMF pressure. For both countries, then, there were trends in substitution between international aid and IMF pressure, albeit in different directions, and there were mid-decade peaks in the application of external political pressure.

Returning to Figure 2.1, the peak in international aid and substitution for IMF pressure tracks the pattern of protest very clearly. In Argentina, the pattern is less clear. Since we know from tables 2.1 and 2.2 that protest has strong interactions with other social forces, how do we disentangle the effects of external political pressure? Essentially, the question for our counterfactual simulation technique is: "How would the course of history have been different with a different pattern of external political pressure?"

Figures 2.6 and 2.7 display the counterfactual simulations for Mexico and Argentina. Typically, a counterfactual simulation alters the time path of a given exogenous variable to see what effect a different policy program might have had. As we have said, a counterfactual simulation is essentially an historical experiment run on the model rather than the real social system. For the present counterfactual simulation, we eliminate the effect of external political pressure—that is, IMF pressure and international aid—on Mexico and Argentina.

Notice that social conditions would still have declined while economic growth would have increased without IMF intervention and international aid. The level of economic growth is almost the same as actually achieved. By the end of the decade, Mexico would have almost reached an equilibrium level of economic growth matched by relatively poor social conditions compared to the beginning of the decade. In Mexico then, IMF policy did little that would not have occurred without it, with the exception of generating hardships and protest. The policy suggested by the IMF by which Mexico was to grow out of its poverty clearly did not work.

By removing the effects of external political pressure, Argentina would have converged to equilibrium much more quickly than in Mexico. Economic growth would have stabilized at about the same level, maybe even somewhat higher, than was actually observed at the end of the decade. That is, the growth policies designed by the IMF retarded growth in Argentina. In Argentina also, the effect of IMF policy was most notable in its influence on generating hardship and subsequent protest. Our simulation demonstrates that both Argentina and Mexico have been caught in a long-term history of economic growth that has actually impoverished most of its citizens. The neoliberal policies to which the IMF subjected these nations actually exacerbated this immiserating growth, and generated a great deal of social protest over the 1990s.

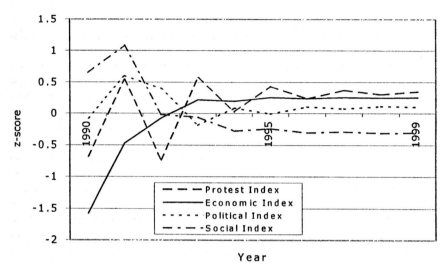

Figure 2.6. Counterfactual Simulation for Argentina

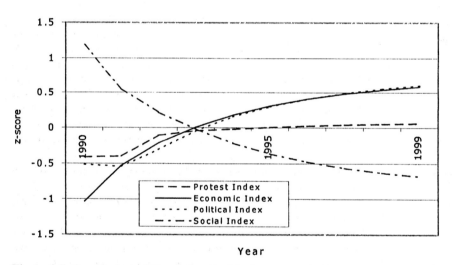

Figure 2.7. Counterfactual Simulation for Mexico

DISCUSSION AND CONCLUSION

Some clear conclusions can be drawn from our results. First, external political pressure accounted for the complex paths of social conflict in both Mexico and Argentina during the decade of the 1990s. Second, deteriorating social conditions, a direct result of IMF pressure, drove protest. Third, both Mexico and Argentina display a pattern of immiseration demonstrated by increased economic growth accompanying deteriorating social conditions. Unlike the theoretical perspectives that focus on the effects of policy measures, such as tariffs, in creating immiserating growth (Miyagiwa 1993), our results indicate that immiseration is a fundamental part of the societal dynamic in these countries. Although foreign aid and IMF stabilization policies might have been based on defensible reasoning, stop-and-go policies designed to stimulate economic growth are clearly not the answer. The policies of the IMF, consistently couched in the trickle-down rationale that growth alleviates poverty, is fundamentally incorrect.

Both nations demonstrate a cycle of policy and protest. As external pressure increases so, too, do hardships resulting from austerity. Protest answers the hardships, and governments respond in turn with some temporary upsurge in investment in programs that address social needs. After a peak in social investment spending, such spending decreases, again in response to IMF pressure. Social conditions again deteriorate, and protest once again answers the imposed hardships.

Mexico showed some interesting patterns. Throughout the decade, the democratization movement (Shefner 2006) succeeded in opening political access, simultaneous with increased pressure imposed by the IMF.[20] As in Argentina, protest increased as a result of increased IMF pressure and deterioration of social conditions, which we have called hardships. During the 1995 peso devaluation and banking crisis, both IMF pressure and protest peaked. Subsequently, IMF pressure decreased, while other forms of international pressure increased. Protest decreased as political access increased, with no indication that social conditions were improving. This suggests that hardships, in a context of increasingly open political access, are less likely to spur protest, confirming Tilly's (1978) position that open politics limits protest activity.

Although the model estimated for Argentina demonstrates much similarity to the Mexican case, the protest dynamic is very different. Unlike Mexico, protest in Argentina increased over the decade. Political access appeared to have less of an impact in Argentina than in Mexico. Although our model estimation shows some decrease in political access, the importance here is limited, as the equivalent of Mexico's democratization (although carried through in very different way) occurred some 15 years earlier in Argentina. We can conclude that opening political access, while an important issue in Mexico, was much less so in Argentina. This indicates further that the importance of political access as it interacts with protest is larger at moments of transition than during periods of stability. That is, greater opening of "normal" political channels affects protest in a system previously characterized by limited political rights. Ongoing political access is less important to protest in a system with a longer history of such access.

External political pressure also followed a different route in Argentina. IMF pressure declined after significant increases in both countries. Yet, our other index of pressure, international aid, declined in Argentina while it increased in Mexico. This indicates that the international community, newly perceiving Argentina as a success, continued to enter with increasing trade without following up with international aid. Where international aid has been influential, however, is in maintaining a nation's neoliberal policies. This suggests that we should think of international aid neither as fulfilling some kind of independent foreign aid goal, nor as ameliorating the damage of neoliberalism. Instead, we must conceive of aid as fully a part of the neoliberal toolbox, as conditions on international aid delivery bolster austerity policies. Finally, neoliberalism of the national economy increased in both nations, confirming the impact of the external pressure on internal policymaking.

One of our clearest results for both Mexico and Argentina both critiques the foundation of IMF policy while confirming basic world-system theory contributions (Wallerstein 1974, 1980, 1989). We refer to the clear pattern of social immiseration despite aggregate economic growth. The main assumption of neoliberal theorizing on poverty is that poverty alleviation cannot occur without aggregate economic growth. Managing a national economy in such a way that the role of the state is minimized forces the economy to grow, according to neoliberals (Dillon and Oliveros 1987; Khan and Knight 1985; Heller 1988). The clear message of neoliberal policy is that the rising tide of economic growth will indeed float all boats.

Our work demonstrates that neoliberalism's growth model is wrong. Aggregate economic growth does not address poverty. In fact, the clear pattern of immiserating growth that we have documented suggests exactly the opposite: that as national economies of peripheral nations grow, their citizens become more impoverished. Clearly that result does not apply to all citizens, as elites in these nations have been well-placed to benefit from the spoils of privatization and changing trade relations. But, the expanding fortunes of elites notwithstanding, our analysis brings neoliberal policy-making deeply into question. Econometric predictions of aggregate growth are wrong when they fail to take into account national and international histories of inequality and polarization. If economic measures could be applied in the absence of political power and privilege, not to mention historical inequalities, perhaps the neoliberal's policies might work. As we know, it is impossible to divorce economics from political power.

Our evidence confirms basic world system tenets that economic growth of peripheral nations will do little if anything to address poverty and inequality in those nations. Our counterfactual simulations are especially instructive in demonstrating that peripheral world system position generates poverty even in the absence of international pressure. Growth in Mexico and Argentina led to deteriorating social conditions. Layering IMF austerity policy on top of long-term inequalities made a bad situation worse in the medium range. The fact that the political instability we have documented over the decade of the 1990s can clearly be linked to international pressure firmly challenges the IMF recipe of stimulating growth as the medicine to address poverty, while confirming what many others have already demonstrated—that growth without redistribution maintains internal and international inequality.

Another clear result shared by both Mexico and Argentina is the important role of declining social conditions, which we call hardships, in explaining austerity protest. Our findings clearly demonstrate that externally imposed policy provoked a decline in social conditions in a way that subsequently led to wide-ranging protest. The relationship is not linear. Deprivations in social conditions often lead more toward household survival efforts than political action. Declining social conditions coupled with immiserating economic growth offer opportunities for mobilization by providing targets and mobilizing people experiencing identifiable and shared hardships. The role of internal political change (neoliberalism and political access) is less clear due to differences in historical timing between Mexico and Argentina. The historical differences, however, still lead us to link increased neoliberalism to austerity protest, and to suggest that increased political access will mediate protest contingent on specific histories of closure or openness of political systems.

These consistent results suggest that new attention be paid to the theoretical role of hardships and mobilization. We believe political opportunity theories offer the best vehicle with which to pursue this question. Kriesi (2004: 80) warns against interpreting movement emergence as a mechanistic process derived from political opportunities, insisting that such elements

> define only a set of necessary conditions for the emergence of contention—its "opportunity set." The transformation of a potentially explosive situation into the unfolding of the events within the interaction context is historically contingent, and therefore, quite unpredictable.

We do not suggest a mechanistic process, but instead argue that examining hardships and their impact on mobilization, strategies, and cultures of contention will widen our understanding of how protestors express agency in response to oppressive structures. Hardships themselves, if deep, shared, and clearly attributable to state actors, may provide opportunities for mobilization. Indeed, we believe that recent explorations into the role of emotion in social movement activity should reinforce our claim (Goodwin, Jasper and Polletta 2001). If people indeed engage in social movement activity in part because they are angry, passionate, altruistic, or motivated by some other emotional response, it makes sense to understand the hardships in which some of these responses are rooted.

Certainly we cannot think of austerity protests in Mexico and Argentina—and other nations in Latin America and the Global South—as caused by a recipe of adding external pressure to internal hardships, stir and wait for protest to ferment. Austerity protestors responded to various political (and subsequently material) changes in a system that had provided a moral economy of survival in some class contexts, and of progress in others. Yet, we have demonstrated that the shifting external political variable of external neoliberal pressure does have predictable outcomes for protest.

Neoliberal globalizers have proven to be quite flexible. The capacity to enter and leave emerging markets and to set conditions for policymaking of less powerful state actors are characteristic of current relations between international financial institutions, global capital, and national states. The austerity protests we have documented challenge such efforts in individual nations. Although the hardships to which they respond are indeed global, these are not currently transnational movements, which may limit their global influence. It is likely that both movements and state resistance to the global economy will have to become transnational for states to gain greater sovereignty over economic policymaking and more fully respond to their citizens' needs.

Our research provides new avenues for the study of states, social movements, and international agencies in the neoliberal global economy. Kentor (2001: 440) suggests that "higher levels of inequality are likely to generate political instability, resulting in policies that favor redistribution of income." This political instability is responsible for recent electoral change throughout Latin America, which has brought governments from the left and center-left into power. We suspect the histories of austerity policies and protest have influenced elections and other governmental changes in Argentina, Bolivia, Brazil, Chile, Ecuador, Uruguay, and Venezuela. This is the subject of our future work. For now, given the extent and duration of protest, joined with national political history, we can suggest such protest against neoliberal measures translated into significant political change in the short and medium-term in Mexico and Argentina. Whether such changes will have subsequent economic impact alleviating the misery of protestors, or whether the new political systems will attempt to legitimate the assault on citizens is yet to be revealed. Another possibility is that the electoral wave of center-leftist governments in Latin America will provide a coalesced challenge to neoliberal globalization. The possibility of that challenge, and the contribution to it from protestors on the streets provides both new research questions and new hopes.

NOTES

1. The G-8, or Group of Eight, meets to determine global, political, and economic policies and is composed of representatives of the top global economic powers. The Group is made up of seven full members (Canada, France, Germany, Italy, Japan, the United Kingdom, and the United States) and Russia, which has participated in the annual meetings since 1994.

2. This description is compiled from newspaper articles published by the *Washington Post* (3/11/95, 3/15/95); the *Independent* (3/18/95, 3/22/95); *Latin American Weekly Report* (3/30/95); the *Guardian* (1/13/95, 1/14/95); and the *Los Angeles Times* (3/17/95). The quotes at the beginning of the description come from the *Washington Post* (1/13/95), and the final quote comes from the *Los Angeles Times* (3/12/95).

3. This description draws on articles from the *Latin American Weekly Report* (5/20/97; 5/27/97; 6/3/97), the *Financial Times* (4/15/97), the *Miami Herald* 4/15/97), the *Houston Chronicle* (8/15/97), and the *New York Times* (5/22/97). The David Copperfield quote is from the *Washington Post* (6/22/97).

4. These new policies were not merely imposed from without, but often welcomed by a new group of national economic policymakers convinced of the propriety of neoliberal thought (Larner 2000, Babb 2001, Centeno 1997, Stiglitz 2002).

5. Over the past three decades, IMF policies have been variably named shock treatments, stabilization policies, structural adjustment, and austerity policies.

6. Ragin and Bradshaw (1992) and Bradshaw and Huang (1991) also share the perspective that IMF policy further damages national economies and immiserates poor populations.

7. IMF austerity policies require alterations in state spending and policy priorities. The IMF has no authority over national populations, but in exchange for IMF funds, states must conform to neoliberal political economic requirements. Thus, the state mediates external austerity policies through reductions in domestic social welfare spending such as education, health care, and trade protections.

8. At least one qualifying event was found for 45 of the 60 countries.

9. We should note that our searches revealed another 200 protests that did not fit our criteria. Instead, these protests responded to other international pressures; we called these "neoliberal protests'"or "globalization" protests, and we will address them in future work.

10. In our index of national politics, neoliberalism and national social investment are always inversely related. As measures of how open a government is to the "free market" increases, national social investment decreases.

11. More extensive discussion of research methods may be found on our project website at axle.do it.wisc.edu/~gwp/global/

12. The coefficients are the solution to the super matrix

$$\begin{vmatrix} \mathbf{A} \\ \mathbf{B} \end{vmatrix} \text{ in } \mathbf{F}_t = \mathbf{F}_{t-1}\mathbf{A} + \mathbf{X}\mathbf{B}$$

where the columns of $\mathbf{F}$ each contain one index computed from the measurement model $\mathbf{Y} = \mathbf{FS}$. The input matrix $\mathbf{X}$ contains exogenous policy variables (external political pressure) and nonlinear terms (Protest Index$[t-1]^2$). Nonlinear terms capture limits to growth from the generalized logistic equation

$$q_t = rq_{t-1}\left(1 - \frac{q_{t-1}}{M}\right) = rq_{t-1} - \frac{r}{M}q_{t-1}^2 = \beta_1 q_{t-1} + \beta_2 q_{t-1}^2$$

where M is a maximum value or limit to growth. The nonlinear term was added to the Argentina model to capture the saw-tooth pattern as protest reached limits observable in figure 2. The system and measurement equations form a Dynamic Mode State Space model (Aoki 1990) that is equivalent to an autoregressive moving average model with a one period lag, AR[1]. Each index is standardized such that $\mu = 0$ and $\sigma = 1$. Therefore, the coefficients are standardized so that comparisons of strength effects can be made within and across models. A test statistic to determine the statistical significance of the model can be developed by taking the largest characteristic root, λ_1, of $\mathbf{E}^{-1}\mathbf{H}$ from the determinental equation

$$|\mathbf{H} - \lambda\mathbf{E}| = 0$$

where $\mathbf{E} = \mathbf{FF} - (\mathbf{ZC})\mathbf{ZC}$ is the error matrix and $\mathbf{H} = (\mathbf{ZC})\mathbf{ZC}$ is the hypothesis matrix and

$$C = \begin{bmatrix} A \\ B \end{bmatrix} \text{ and } Z = \begin{bmatrix} F & X \end{bmatrix}.$$

The empirical distribution function (EDF) of λ_1 is computed using a computer intensive technique, the bootstrap (Efron 1987). The bootstrap EDF of λ_1 for Argentina shows that

$$P[2.2e^6 < \lambda_1 = 1.32e^7 < 5.9e^7] = 0.98.$$

Since λ_1 does not bracket zero, the model had a significant effect on explaining the time path of the state variables.

13. The bootstrap EDF of λ_1 for Mexico shows

$$P[1.3e^6 < \lambda_1 = 1.1e^7 < 7.5e^7] = 0.98.$$

Since λ_1 does not bracket zero, the model had a significant effect on explaining the time path of the protest state variables (see explanatory text in table 2.1).

14. A negative change in social conditions has a positive impact on protest in this interpretation.

15. Theil's index of inequality (Theil 1958: 40)

$$U = \frac{\sqrt{(p - a)' W(p - a)}}{\sqrt{p'Wp} + \sqrt{a'Wa}}$$

is used to compare predicted and actual outcomes, p and a respectively, with $W = 1/n\mathbf{I}$. U varies across $[0,1]$ with values close to zero indicating good prediction. The average total Theil (1958: 40) statistic is 0.23. Values closer to zero are considered better and 0.30 is considered the upper limit of acceptability.

16. The average total Theil (1958: 40) statistic is 0.23. Values closer to zero are considered better and 0.30 is considered the upper limit of acceptability (see explanatory text in figure 2.2).

17. Long-term impacts can be calculated for the endogenous variables by solving the system equation (see table 2.1) for the long-run equilibrium values, $F^\top = XB(1 - A)^{-1}$. The solution matrix $(1 - A)^{-1}$ captures the system's long-run dynamics and is displayed in table 2.3.

18. See the explanation in note 17.

19. See explanation in note 17.

20. Judith Hellman minimizes the importance of austerity protest in Mexico, relegating it to action that was "sporadic, generally uncoordinated with groups beyond the local setting" (1997, 4). Her explanation is that control of labor by PRI unions limited mobilization in response to austerity. Other scholars, however, point to a rapid rise and increase in both mobilization and action on the part of affected Mexican groups (Carr 1986; Ramirez 1989; Williams 1996). The research of these scholars refutes the contention that protest mobilization and action was limited. Shefner also consistently links austerity policies to the Mexican democratization movement. In this view, anger at ongoing austerity was channeled into efforts to democratize Mexico. This suggests that the impact of austerity in generating protest was much greater than Hellman argues (Shefner 2006, 2004, 2001).

Chapter 3

POPULAR PROTEST IN VENEZUELA: NOVELTIES AND CONTINUITIES

Margarita López Maya and Luis Lander

Since the mid-1980s, Venezuela has been perceived both at home and abroad as a society in constant mobilization. Following the *El Amparo* massacre in 1988 and the so-called *Caracazo* in 1989, the number of protests registered has generally been high, although naturally some years have been more turbulent than others. By way of contrast, in the early 1980s Venezuela was generally considered one of the countries in Latin America least prone to popular mobilizations. It was argued that its firm democratic institutions, together with substantial oil revenue, had facilitated the consolidation of efficient mechanisms for mediation and representation, thus avoiding internecine social conflict. The Venezuelans were "different" from the rest of Latin America precisely because they had apparently succeeded in overcoming the sociopolitical turbulence endemic to the region. In academic circles this attitude was reflected in the literature that postulated the "exceptionalism" of Venezuela within the Latin American context. The sharp contrast between these two perceptions obliges us to re-examine the question of "street politics" in Venezuela since 1958.

This chapter examines popular protest both before and after the 1980s in order to demonstrate that, despite changes, the protests of the past were not substantially different from the more recent ones, neither in their frequency, nor in their motives and other aspects. Using the empirical information available in the Database El Bravo Pueblo (BDEBP) and in the Annual Reports published by the Programa Venezolano de Educación y Acción en Derechos Humanos (Venezuelan Program for Education and Action on Human Rights—Provea), we conclude that the characteristics of popular protest in recent decades are less of a novelty than has been assumed, while the peace and harmony associated with the 1970s are more an illusion than a reality. In this earlier period, there were also moments of acute social tension and important street mobilizations; the difference is that they did not seriously undermine the legitimacy of the political system, of its principal actors or of the state structure whose foundations had been established in 1958.

RECENT PROTESTS: VISIBILITY AND CHARACTERISTICS

In response to the macroeconomic adjustment program announced by Carlos Andrés Pérez's recently installed government (1989-1993), a massive social uprising shook Caracas and the other principal Venezuelan cities between February 27 and March 3, 1989. The *Caracazo*, as it came to be known, was a popular protest that stands out in recent Venezuelan history due to its duration, geographical coverage, intensity, and violence.[1] The disturbances revealed the extent to which the legitimacy of the political system had already been undermined. They also contributed to a political crisis soon to be reflected in the frustrated military coups in 1992 and the destitution of President Pérez in 1993. This uprising had been preceded in October 1988 by another violent incident (less well-known outside Venezuela) that also contributed to a questioning of the legitimacy of the Venezuelan state: the *El Amparo* massacre. Venezuelan police and military forces had assassinated a group of local villagers on a fishing trip near the Colombian border, presenting the incident as an encounter with a Colombian guerrilla group. The unanticipated survival of two of the villagers and the subsequent mobilization of the local community brought the truth to light and provoked widespread indignation. These two episodes represented a turning point for the dimensions of popular protest in Venezuela and oblige us to examine a phenomenon that had always existed but that has previously received little attention: *street politics*. By this, we refer to the interaction in a public space—the street—between social and political actors (including the multitude) and different representatives of the authorities. Those who opt for street politics are, above all, from weaker social sectors distant from the centers of power (Eckstein 1989: 28).

As a result of the *Caracazo*, Provea (a nongovernmental organization for the defense of human rights) was founded and began to publish annual reports on the human rights situation in the country, including a detailed monitoring of the right to demonstrate peacefully on the streets. Thanks to this initiative, we now count on a reasonably reliable source of information on popular demonstrations during the last decade and a half: how many there were, the actors involved, their motives, and the response of the authorities.

More recently, additional information has been made available as the result of an independent academic initiative in the Central University of Venezuela: the creation of a database on popular demonstrations *El Bravo Pueblo* (BDEBP) designed to eventually cover the entire twentieth century. While Provea draws on a variety of national and regional newspapers to feed its database, BDEBP has a more restricted coverage: it registers the information available in just one of the national dailies (*El Nacional*) since its appearance in 1944; and registers that available in other dailies for earlier years. Nevertheless, the information in BDEBP is more detailed than that of Provea and, as noted, it covers a far longer period. We count on sufficient information between the two sources to examine the demonstrations in recent years and compare them with those that took place before the *Caracazo*.

Despite their well-known limitations, newspaper sources have been increasingly accepted as a useful contribution to research on social conflicts (Tarrow 1989: 357-

365; Franzosi 1996: 377). However, we need to bear in mind the characteristics of this kind of source, together with the differences between the two databases we are using. As already mentioned, both databases rely on information offered by the newspapers and therefore to some extent reflect their limitations as a source. The daily press tends to register what is considered "newsworthy," and will thus give preference to conflictive or violent events rather than those with more routine characteristics. Editorial policy also affects coverage and may change over time, modifying the frequency and the way in which protests are reported. On the other hand, our two databases are designed differently. Provea registers protest incidents while for BDEBP the reference is to the news items that appeared in *El Nacional*. Furthermore, Provea's annual reports cover from October to September of the following year. As a result, the numbers offered by the two sources are not strictly comparable. Nevertheless, since we are not aiming at precise quantification, the information available is sufficient to give us a reliable general picture of the modifications in, and the characteristics of, popular protest in Venezuela, before and after the *Caracazo*.

THE INFORMATION FROM THE DATABASES

According to Provea, during the fourteen years from October 1989 to September 2003, there were a total of 12,889 demonstration protests in the country, an average of 2.52 per day, including weekends and holidays (see table 3.1). The totals do not include strikes and work stoppages, as they are not considered a form of mobilization. During these years, there are two periods of particularly intense activity: between 1991 and 1994; and between 1999 and 2003.

      During the first of these periods, there was an acute political crisis reflected most dramatically in the aborted military coups in February and November 1992. From then on, the Pérez government rapidly lost political support until May 1993, when the National Congress dismissed the president after the Supreme Court had decided there were sufficient merits for accusing him of the misappropriation of public funds. He was replaced by an interim government headed by historian Ramón J. Velásquez, until Rafael Caldera assumed the presidency as a result of the December 1993 elections. During these years we find that the daily average number of protests rises to 2.75. The second peak, between 1999 and 2003, coincides with the years of the Chávez government. In this case, a new political elite was trying to implement an alternative project for the country, generating massive demonstrations, both in favor of and against it. In these years, the daily average rises to 3.50. This would appear to indicate a degree of mobilization appreciably higher than before, although it must be taken into account that for 2001-2002, Provea for the first time includes work stoppages as a form of mobilization, thus increasing the average.

      On the other hand, for the years it covers, BDEBP registers a total of 3,416 news items on protests, an average of 0.55 per day. This database also indicates years of activity peaks. The first is 1983. In February, on what has become known as "Black Friday," the Luis Herrera government devalued the national currency, and introduced exchange controls, in the process revealing the dimensions of the economic crisis and contributing to the victory of the opposition candidate, Jaime Lusinchi, in the presidential elections in December. As in the case of Provea, DBEBP also reflects the peak provoked by the *Caracazo* and the increase in mobilizations during the early years of the Chávez administration.

Year	Total Protests Provea	Total News Items BDEBP
Oct. 1983 to Sept. 1984	---	283
Oct. 1984 to Sept. 1985	---	157
Oct. 1985 to Sept. 1986	---	191
Oct. 1986 to Sept. 1987	---	124
Oct. 1987 to Sept. 1988	---	121
Oct. 1988 to Sept. 1989	---	225
Oct. 1989 to Sept. 1990	675	156
Oct. 1990 to Sept. 1991	546	220
Oct. 1991 to Sept. 1992	873	159
Oct. 1992 to Sept. 1993	1047	185
Oct. 1993 to Sept. 1994	1099	190
Oct. 1994 to Sept. 1995	581	176
Oct. 1995 to Sept. 1996	628	245
Oct. 1996 to Sept. 1997	632	197
Oct. 1997 to Sept. 1998	422	186
Oct. 1998 to Sept. 1999	855	272
Oct. 1999 to Sept. 2000	1,414	329
Oct. 2000 to Sept. 2001	1,312	---
Oct. 2001 to Sept. 2002	1,262	---
Oct. 2002 to Sept. 2003	1,543	---
Total	12,889	3,416
Average per period	921	201

Source: Provea, *Situación de los derechos humanos* (Annual Reports) and Database *El Bravo Pueblo.*

Table 3.1. Protests and Protest News Items (1983-2002)

BDEBP ON CHARACTERISTICS AND MOTIVES

In the BDEBP, the protests reviewed are classified in terms of three categories: conventional, confrontational, and violent. Conventional actions are those day-to-day protests that although frequently legal, do not provoke fear or anxiety among participants, observers, and the authorities. Confrontational actions are those that provoke fear and anxiety, although without involving physical aggression or damage to property. Examples of the latter are roadblocks, non-authorized combative demonstrations, or marches and hunger strikes. Finally, violent protests are those that provoke damage or destruction of public or private property and/or affect the physical integrity of persons, whether participants or not. The greater incidence and visibility of confrontational and violent protests – particularly confrontational ones – indicate that the society is undergoing a period of turbulence and/or socio-political transformation (Tarrow 1989). In the following table (3.2), we register the distribution of the protests in the BDEBP, according to this classification.

Year	Total News Items BDEBP	Conventional		Confrontational		Violent	
		N	%	N	%	N	%
Oct. 1983 to Sept. 1984	283	164	57.9	98	34.6	21	7.4
Oct. 1984 to Sept. 1985	157	105	66.9	40	25.5	12	7.6
Oct. 1985 to Sept. 1986	191	154	80.6	33	17.3	4	2.1
Oct. 1986 to Sept. 1987	124	72	58.1	14	11.3	38	30.6
Oct. 1987 to Sept. 1988	121	81	66.9	22	18.2	18	14.9
Oct. 1988 to Sept. 1989	225	86	38.2	63	28.0	76	33.8
Oct. 1989 to Sept. 1990	156	51	33.7	74	47.4	31	19.9
Oct. 1990 to Sept. 1991	220	111	50.5	53	24.1	56	25.5
Oct. 1991 to Sept. 1992	159	16	10.6	71	44.7	72	45.3
Oct. 1992 to Sept. 1993	185	45	24.3	70	37.8	70	37.8
Oct. 1993 to Sept. 1994	190	54	28.4	70	36.8	66	34.7
Oct. 1994 to Sept. 1995	176	61	34.7	50	28.4	65	36.9
Oct. 1995 to Sept. 1996	245	45	18.4	104	42.4	96	39.2
Oct. 1996 to Sept. 1997	197	84	42.6	67	34.0	46	23.4
Oct. 1997 to Sept. 1998	186	79	42.5	70	37.6	37	19.9
Oct. 1998 to Sept. 1999	272	42	15.4	172	63.2	58	21.3
Oct. 1999 to Sept. 2000	329	153	46.5	125	38.0	51	15.5
TOTAL	3.416	1.403	---	1.196	---	817	---
Average per period	201	83	41.3	70	34.8	48	23.9

Source: Database *El Bravo Pueblo*

Table 3.2. Nature of the Protests (1983-2000)

The first striking fact is that the items reporting violent protests, less than 10 percent of the total in the earliest years of the series, consistently register double digit percentages after 1986. Violence peaks in 1991-1992 and 1992-1993 as a result of the political crisis during the second Pérez government, and again in 1995-1996. This second period corresponds to the implementation of the economic adjustment program known as the *Agenda Venezuela* (Venezuelan Agenda). From then on, the tendency is for the percentage of violent protests to decline.

The definition of "violent protests" adopted by BDEBP naturally includes those subject to state repression. Provea, as an organization dedicated to the defense of human rights, offers a detailed, year-by-year report on the mobilizations that were repressed by the state.[2] According to the Provea information, during Pérez's second presidential period (1989-1993), violent state repression of protest was commonplace. One of every three protests was repressed with an elevated cost in human lives. In addition to the atrocious repression during the *Caracazo*, 26 deaths were registered as a result of pacific demonstrations in the days following the abortive February 1992 coup (Provea 1991-1992).

Modifications in the patterns of the official response to pacific demonstrations were evident during the second Caldera administration (1994-1998) when levels of repression were lower. At the same time, the emergence of new political actors in the

regional and local governments also led to changes of attitude toward pacific manifestations. The criminalization of protest, which dated back to the 1960s when it
formed part of the response to the armed struggle, now became less common as a
result of new efforts to submit cases of repression to a body of rules (López Maya
2003b). Toward the mid-term of Caldera's period, the proportion of demonstrations
repressed had fallen to 1 of every 6. Deaths in public demonstrations were also fewer
and in 1996 not a single one was registered. There was also less evidence of the use
of arms in demonstrations (Provea 1994-1998).

With the Chávez government, there has been a greater recognition of the right to
protest and this has been institutionalized. In 1998-1999, one of every 25 protests
was repressed, in 2000-2001 one of every 28, and in 2002-2003, one of every 36
(Provea 1998-2003). The use of arms in public demonstrations continued to fall and,
in fact, was prohibited in the 1999 Constitution. During the first five years of the
current government, there were a total of five deaths registered in public demonstrations (Provea 1998-2003)[3]. This tendency evidently contributed to a reduction in the
incidence of violence, although the most recent Provea Report registers another increase in violence in 2002-2003 related not so much to state repression, as to the
acute political confrontation associated with the April coup and its aftermath (Provea
2002-2003).

Protests classified as "confrontational" in BDEBP are an increasing proportion of
the total number in the years after 1988-1989. In the previous period, the proportion
had been an average of 21.4 percent. From 1988-1989 to 2000, the proportion rises
to an average of 38.5 percent. During the second half of the 1990s, at the same time
as violent protests became less frequent, those defined as "confrontational" accounted for 43 percent. Finally, it can be observed that the incidence of conventional
protests is in almost inverse relation to that of violent protests. At the outset of the
series, conventional protests account for far more than half the total, but their proportion falls during the years of political turbulence in the early 1990s, recovering once
again in the second half of the decade.

The BDEBP also classifies the protests on the basis of their motives, using more
than 90 different categories. For our present purposes, however, we have classified
the motives into two broad groups: the first includes those related to material living
standards, and the second covers civic and political concerns (table 3.3). The following table registers the totals, together with the percentage that they represent. A final
column registers the cases in which the motives are not altogether clear. The lack of
coincidence between these totals and those registered in table 3.2 is due to the fact
that a protest may have various motives and may therefore be registered in both of
our two broad groups.

As can be observed in table 3.3, an overwhelming majority of the protests are
motivated by socio-economic concerns. However, it can be appreciated that, in a few
isolated years, those that reflect civic and political concerns account for more than a
third of the total, as in 1986-1987, 1991-1992 and 1998-1999. Although a detailed
analysis of this phenomenon goes beyond the objectives of this chapter, it is clear
that the dates coincide with moments in which there are particularly high levels of
political agitation. Between 1986 and 1988 there were important mobilizations in
favor of political reforms, particularly those related to the process of decentralization. These demonstrations helped to foment the climate necessary to back the reforms recommended by the Comisión Presidencial para la Reforma del Estado
(Presidential Commission for the Reform of the State—Copre) and which led to the
legislation favoring decentralization (Gómez Calcaño and López Maya 1990). The

years 1991-1992 witnessed the first abortive military coup and 1998-1999, the first year of the Chávez government, was subject to massive mobilizations in favor of the Constituent Assembly.

Year	Total Motives	Socio-economic		Civic and Political		Others	
		Total	%	Total	%	Total	%
Oct. 1983 to Sept. 1984	296	253	85.5	37	12.5	6	2.0
Oct. 1984 to Sept. 1985	174	151	86.8	18	4.8	5	2.9
Oct. 1985 to Sept. 1986	215	198	92.1	16	7.4	1	0.5
Oct. 1986 to Sept. 1987	135	71	52.6	62	46.0	2	1.5
Oct. 1987 to Sept. 1988	125	86	68.8	39	31.2	0	0.0
Oct. 1988 to Sept. 1989	312	223	71.5	82	26.3	7	2.2
Oct. 1989 to Sept. 1990	176	149	84.7	23	13.1	4	2.3
Oct. 1990 to Sept. 1991	54	42	77.8	9	16.7	3	5.6
Oct. 1991 to Sept. 1992	223	127	57.0	91	40.8	5	2.2
Oct. 1992 to Sept. 1993	221	159	71.9	60	27.1	2	0.9
Oct. 1993 to Sept. 1994	226	175	77.4	41	18.1	10	4.4
Oct. 1994 to Sept. 1995	204	142	69.6	49	24.0	13	6.4
Oct. 1995 to Sept. 1996	293	241	82.3	38	13.0	14	4.8
Oct. 1996 to Sept. 1997	218	178	81.7	32	14.7	8	3.7
Oct. 1997 to Sept. 1998	199	149	74.9	40	20.1	10	5.0
Oct. 1998 to Sept. 1999	304	195	64.1	106	34.9	3	1.0

Source: Database *El Bravo Pueblo*
Table 3.3. Motives of the Protests (1983-1999)

Year	Socioeconomic				Civic and Political			
	Total	A %	B %	C %	Total	A %	B %	C %
Oct. 1983 to Sept. 1984	253	7.5	25.3	67.2	37	56.8	21.6	21.6
Oct. 1984 to Sept. 1985	151	12.6	30.5	57.0	18	33.3	16.7	50.0
Oct. 1985 to Sept. 1986	198	11.1	20.7	68.2	16	56.3	12.5	37.5
Oct. 1986 to Sept. 1987	71	1.4	42.3	56.3	62	85.5	6.5	8.1
Oct. 1987 to Sept. 1988	86	29.1	27.9	43.0	39	64.1	23.1	12.8
Oct. 1988 to Sept. 1989	223	32.7	34.5	32.7	82	70.6	18.3	8.5
Oct. 1989 to Sept. 1990	149	10.7	44.3	45.0	23	30.4	21.7	47.8
Oct. 1990 to Sept. 1991	42	26.2	54.8	19.0	9	44.4	11.1	44.4
Oct. 1991 to Sept. 1992	127	18.9	48.8	32.3	91	57.1	7.7	35.2
Oct. 1992 to Sept. 1993	159	26.4	26.4	47.2	60	45.0	16.7	38.3
Oct. 1993 to Sept. 1994	175	2.,7	48.6	25.7	41	80.5	14.6	4.9
Oct. 1994 to Sept. 1995	142	7.8	50.0	42.3	49	57.1	22.4	20.4
Oct. 1995 to Sept. 1996	241	26.6	34.0	39.4	38	65.8	10.5	23.7
Oct. 1996 to Sept. 1997	178	21.9	36.0	42.1	32	59.4	31.3	9.4
Oct. 1997 to Sept. 1998	149	20.1	24.2	55.7	40	50.0	27.5	22.5
Oct. 1998 to Sept. 1999	195	18.5	33.3	48.2	106	47.2	14.2	38.7

Source: Database *El Bravo Pueblo*
Table 3.4. Motives of Protests by Subgroups (1983-1999)

In order to examine these motives in greater detail, we have divided each of the two broad groups into three subgroups (table 3.4). The first subgroup (A) of the socio-economic group includes motives related to productive activity, like the demand for access to land, subsidies, credits, taxes, etc. The second (B) covers those concerns related to public services, health, education, water, transportation, etc. The third (C), groups together the motives related to income: wages, collective contracts, pensions, work, etc. The motives of a civic and political nature are divided between a first subgroup (A) that covers human rights, repression, killings, mistreatment, etc. Subgroup B includes motives related to civil rights, justice, freedom of expression, laws, regulations, etc. And, finally, the third subgroup (C) is composed of explicitly political concerns, election fraud, democratization, autonomy, corruption, etc. Table 3.4 registers the respective percentages corresponding to each of these subgroups.

Within the socioeconomic group, the predominant motives are those that fall within subgroups B and C, that is to say, those concerned with income and public services. Combined, they consistently account for more than 70 percent of the total. During the 16 annual periods examined, the main concern in 11 of them is income. Within the broad range of civic and political motives, in 13 of the 16 years the predominant theme is human rights and in 11 of them, these account for more than half of the respective totals.

In sum, these recent years have been characterized by elevated levels of protest that, according to Provea, amount to an average of more than two demonstrations per day, including holidays and weekends, and even (until the 2001-2002 Report) without taking into account work stoppages, one of the most important forms of protest in Venezuela. After the mid-1980s, the percentage of protests registered in BDEBP as violent is generally in the two-digit range, although there is a tendency for it to decline during the late 1990s, largely as a result of a change in the attitude of the state toward the right to demonstrate. The forms of protest characterized as confrontational were less than a quarter of the total prior to the *Caracazo*, but it subsequently rose to a yearly average of about a third of the total for the 1990s, and reached 43 percent for the second half of that decade. This tendency suggests a society in which power relationships are undergoing a transformation. As we have seen, the most important motives for protesting throughout these years are the cost of living and public services, but toward the end of the 1990s protests over civic and political issues begin to increase in numbers. Of the latter, the majority are related to human rights and the defense of the citizens' personal dignity and physical integrity.

PROTEST SINCE 1958 IN COMPARATIVE PERSPECTIVE

We will now examine the extent to which the characteristics of protest of recent years can be considered a novelty; to do so we need to examine more closely the evidence available on protest in the decades immediately following 1958. First we will present what could be regarded as the conventional wisdom on protest activity before the *Caracazo*.

Juan Carlos Rey, a renowned Venezuelan political scientist, considers the apparent passivity of the masses one of the basic conditions for explaining the successful functioning of the Venezuelan political system during the decades that precede the period we have been discussing. With the overthrow of the Pérez Jiménez dictatorship in January 1958, there followed a series of democratic governments that were to be considered a model for the rest of Latin America. Shortly after the *Caracazo*,

Rey argued that Venezuelan democracy rested on the consolidation of a limited number of large and highly disciplined political party organizations that fomented political stability by establishing between themselves a relationship that avoided zero-sum situations. The politicians who promoted the pact on which Venezuela's democracy was based had feared that, if popular demands were not channeled by the political parties, the system would be uncontrollable and could even collapse. Avoiding a zero-sum situation was made possible as a result of the resources available to the state from oil revenue. Thus, according to Rey, the stability of Venezuela's democracy depended on the demobilization and lack of participation of the masses. From what we have already discussed, it is apparent that at least in recent years, the restraints on mobilization and participation have been seriously undermined.

In another influential analysis of the Venezuelan political system, Moisés Naím and Ramón Piñango comment that "the first decades of the democratic experience reveal a surprising absence of permanent open conflicts" (1984: 553). They argued that open conflict appeared not to be an essential element in the prevailing social dynamics and that processes provoking serious traumas in other countries, in Venezuela had occurred free of major turbulence. As examples, they pointed to the way in which the armed conflict of the 1960s had given way to a successful pacification in the 1970s, and the prevalence of harmonious labor relations.

On the other hand, Steve Ellner (1995) has argued that, while it is true that such analyses have a certain basis, exaggerating these arguments has led to the adoption of misleading and even erroneous conclusions. As far as mobilizations are concerned—what we have termed "street politics"—such affirmations appear to suggest that they were infrequent before the mid-1980s and scarcely relevant for an understanding of the dynamics of the society. It has also been argued that the protests during the initial stages of the post-1958 democratic experience were more ideologically motivated and less concerned with everyday conditions of life, and that they were less intense and conflictive than in the more recent period we have examined (Escobar 1997, personal interview). To what extent is all this in fact true?

As of yet, BDEBP has not completed its coverage of popular protest for the entire post-1958 period, so we have opted for examining the information available for two years in each of the succeeding decades in order to establish comparisons. We are interested in the frequency of the protests, their characteristics and their motives. As the information available is not exhaustive, we have opted against the adoption of sophisticated criteria for the choice of the years to be examined. We have simply taken, for each decade, an election year together with a second, non-election year. We opted for 1958 and 1959 because, apart from the general criteria, they cover the initial experiences of the recently installed political system. And for the 1990s, we have used 1998 (an election year) and 1999, the first year of the Chávez government. As we have already insisted, what we are looking for is not statistical precision but rather an estimate of the frequency and characteristics of the protests.

Contrary to the conventional wisdom, even among those of us who have studied recent popular mobilizations, the data do not reveal appreciable differences in the frequency of protests registered between the earlier decades and the more recent years examined in detail in the first part of this chapter. If we take the period prior to the 1980s (keeping in mind that the quantification cannot be considered precise), we have an annual average of 356 protests registered, appreciably more than what is registered in table 3.1. Perhaps most striking is the information available for the 1970s: in 1973 there are 843 protests, in 1977, 744 and in 1978, 561. Surprisingly, this suggests that even those researchers such as Richard Hillman who have recognized the permanent presence of mobilizations and protests in Venezuela's contemporary history, have wrongly assumed that, unlike the 1960s and the 1980s, the decade of the 1970s was a period of relative calm, with the conflicts cushioned by the resources of the oil boom (1994: 4).

Table 3.5 presents the information on protests for the two chosen years for each decade, organized according to the BDEBP criteria. As can be observed, the idea that the protests and mobilizations were less violent in earlier decades is a simple illusion. While it is true that in the initial two years of the democratic period violent protests represented less than 10 percent of the total, they were more frequent in the 1960s and 1970s. In addition, 1963 was a particularly violent year in that it was an electoral year when those political forces committed to the armed struggle called for a policy of abstention. The confrontation between the Betancourt government and the rebels was intense and violent and this situation undoubtedly accounts for the numbers registered. For the years covered, the numbers registered for confrontational conflicts are erratic. Understandably, by limiting our coverage to two years per decade, we can hardly expect to register any tendencies. However, there are two years, 1959 and 1970, when confrontational protests are more than a third of the respective totals. Only on the basis of long-term and uninterrupted annual series could we identify prolonged periods of turbulence like that of the late 1990s, but the possibility cannot be discarded. Finally, the more conventional protests are a majority in 6 of the 10 years we have chosen and, just as we have seen in table 3.2, they tend to be less visible in years that register elevated levels of political turbulence.

In the following tables, we have registered the motives of the protests. The first one (table 3.6), as in the case of table 3.3, separates the motives into the same two broad categories we have used previously (socioeconomic and civic-political) in order to indicate their relative percentages.

In table 3.6, as in table 3.3, it can be appreciated that protests motivated by socioeconomic concerns are the majority (except for 1963). However, the prevalence of this motivation is not as marked in the period prior to the 1983 Black Friday as in the following years. Whereas during the first six years registered in the table (1958-1973), the average percentage of protests motivated by socioeconomic considerations is 55.7 percent of the total, during the last four years registered it reaches 75 percent (a difference of almost 20 points). This contrast appears to apply to the entire period from 1983 to 1999, as the uninterrupted series registers an annual average of 74.3 percent. As in the previous table, 1963 stands out as an untypical year in which, as we have already noted for periods of political tension, the relative weight of protests motivated by civic and political considerations increases substantially.

Table 3.7 looks more closely at the motives at play, dividing each of the broad categories into three subgroups. As in table 3.4, we can appreciate here the importance of socioeconomic motives, specifically those registered in categories B and C, which refer to living standards and public services. The two categories account for more than 80 percent of the total. Once again, those related to living standards are the more important. Among the protests motivated by civic or political considerations, subgroup C covering those which are strictly political (democracy, corruption, elections, politics, autonomy, etc.) are the most numerous in 3 of the first 6 years. This marks a difference with the post-1980s period when concern over human rights is the most prevalent motive.

Year	Total	Conventional		Confrontational		Violent	
		Total	%	Total	%	Total	%
1958	358	230	64.3	95	26.5	33	9.2
1959	221	133	60.2	79	35.8	9	4.1
1961	211	132	62.6	55	26.1	24	11.4
1963	153	55	36.0	25	16.3	73	47.7
1970	353	22	6.2	268	75.9	63	17.9
1973	843	431	51.1	271	32.2	141	16.7
1983	163	148	90.8	8	4.9	7	4.3
1989	236	80	33.9	87	36.9	69	2.2
1998	168	77	45.8	68	40.5	23	1.7
1999	354	43	12.2	239	67.5	72	20.3

Source: Database *El Bravo Pueblo*

Table 3.5. Nature of the Protests (Various Years)

Year	Total Motives	Socioeconomic		Civic and Political		Others	
		Total	%	Total	%	Total	%
1958	385	193	50.1	178	46.2	14	3.6
1959	234	128	54.7	86	36.8	20	8.5
1961	207	134	64.7	64	30.9	9	4.3
1963	154	37	24.0	99	64.3	18	11.7
1970	403	292	72.5	104	25.8	7	1.7
1973	851	580	68.2	167	19.6	104	12.2
1983	163	134	82.2	27	16.6	2	1.2
1989	325	250	76.9	70	21.5	5	1.5
1998	182	142	78.0	33	18.1	7	3.8
1999	392	246	62.8	143	36.5	3	0.8

Source: Database El Bravo Pueblo

Table 3.6. Motives for the Protests (Various Years)

Year	Socioeconomic				Civic and Political			
	Total	A %	B %	C %	Total	A %	B %	C %
1958	193	10.4	24.4	65.3	178	30.0	7.3	60.7
1959	128	6.3	21.1	72.7	86	50.0	18.6	31.4
1961	134	16.4	30.6	53.0	64	29.7	14.1	56.3
1963	37	2.7	16.2	81.0	99	12.1	2.0	85.9
1970	292	4.8	49.7	45.5	104	27.9	45.2	26.9
1973	580	8.6	35.5	55.9	167	49.7	19.8	30.5
1983	134	16.4	26.1	57.5	27	81.5	7.4	11.1
1989	250	29.2	36.0	34.8	70	75.7	7.1	17.1
1998	142	25.4	27.5	47.2	33	60.6	27.3	12.1
1999	246	16.7	38.6	44.7	143	41.3	10.5	48.3

Source: Database *El Bravo Pueblo*

Table 3.7. Motives for the Protests by Subgroup (Various Years)

CONCLUSIONS

Popular protest, which has become such an important everyday ingredient of social experience in Venezuela since the 1980s, is much less of a novelty than many believed. The frequency of protests in earlier decades is similar, if not greater, than those registered during the most recent decade and a half. At the same time, despite minor differences in emphasis, the motives for protesting are the same.

Nevertheless, it is important to underline the differences that we have detected. From 1958 until the early 1970s, there is a greater numerical equilibrium between those protests stimulated by socioeconomic considerations and those motivated by civic and political considerations. From then on, the former are much more numerous than the latter. Furthermore, in the early years of the democratic experience, of those protests stimulated by civic and political considerations, those strictly political in nature (subgroup C) are the most common. This evidently reflects the climate of political turbulence during the first decade of the democratic period until the 1970s; the hegemony exercised by those who had signed the 1958 pact had been firmly established. In Provea's most recent reports, there are signs that suggest that we have once again entered into a similarly turbulent phase: during the last four years, the number of politically motivated protests has clearly been increasing, in both absolute and relative terms; and many of those protests that are presented as prompted by socioeconomic considerations are also politically motivated (Provea 2001-2002: 500). Indeed, we are witnessing once again a struggle for hegemony that has yet to be resolved.

The resolution of the struggle for hegemony in favor of those who signed the political pacts at the outset of the democratic period strengthened the legitimacy of the system and of its principal actors. These circumstances, together with the oil boom during the same decade, explains, at least partially, the generalized sensation of social peace and harmony, as reflected in the literature that presented Venezuelan society as though it were devoid of open conflicts. These depictions lend themselves to interpretations referring to the "exceptionalism" of the Venezuelan society. The evidence offered by the BDEBP indicates that in the early 1980s protests largely assumed conventional forms, with single-digit percentages for violent protests.[4] From a longer historical perspective, however, this was not a normal situation, but rather a brief "truce." Historical circumstances of social and cultural exclusion that had not been resolved, together with the deteriorating living conditions of the general populace once the oil boom had passed, renewed the pressures for a new cycle of conflicts and political struggle. Nevertheless, there are indications of changes in the political demands typical of the more recent protests. Since the *El Amparo* massacre and, even more so, after the *Caracazo*, there has been an evident advance in public consciousness and repudiation of violations of human rights.

Protest is, and has always been, a dimension of experience in Venezuelan society, and it is thus seriously misleading to highlight a supposedly passive behavior on the part of the popular sectors during prolonged periods. What does change, however, is the role of protest in the dynamics of the society. In periods of struggle over hegemony, *street politics* contributes directly to a questioning of the established power structure and this is reflected in changes in its characteristics and motives. In those situations, it becomes more confrontational and violent and the strictly political considerations come to the fore. By way of contrast, during periods in which hegemonic control is not in question, when the system counts on a greater legitimacy and stability, protests motivated by socioeconomic considerations are by far the most common. At the same time, the room for maneuver on the part of those to whom the demands are directed is far greater. In contrast with the situation in the 1960s when protest was criminalized and energetically repressed, thus contributing to spiraling violence, since the mid-1980s and above all during the Chávez government, this criminalization has diminished together with the violence. As a result, the hegemonic struggle is now fought out primarily on the basis of confrontational collective action.

Between the early 1970s and the mid-1980s, the Venezuelan state counted on extraordinary levels of oil revenue in order to maintain protest at bay. Its capacity for overcoming conflicts contributed to a disarticulation of the attempts of independent popular sectors to organize themselves. Frequently, protest was a mere prelude to negotiations between trade union bureaucrats and the political parties or state institutions. Despite high levels of protest, this pattern could not open real prospects of creating solid social movements or organizations. However, with the sustained economic deterioration and the undermining of the legitimacy of the political system, especially during the late 1980s, the situation was transformed. Protest once again returns to the center of the stage in the political struggle and the socioeconomic demands could no longer be countered by relying on the clientelistic and corporative mechanisms of the past. The conditions have been created for transcending protest and establishing an autonomous dynamic for popular movements and social organizations.

More recently, new elements that have not been discussed in this study have complicated this already complex situation. Since the last months of 2001, new actors have appeared in street politics. In the current struggle for hegemony in Venezuela, sectors of the upper and middle classes have also taken to the streets. This new ingredient has made protest even more visible than before because these new sectors count on important economic resources and, above all, are backed by the private mass media that share and promote the aims of the mobilizations. These sectors also face the challenge of improving and consolidating their relationship with the Venezuelan state and democracy.

In the course of this chapter, we have attempted to shed some light on the complexity of the relationship between state and society in Venezuela, as expressed by street politics. By examining the different modalities, characteristics, and motives of the protests within a historical perspective, we have been able to identify continuities and changes in the interaction between popular actors and those closer to the seats of power. We have seen how, in certain periods, the patterns of protest reflect the relative legitimacy of the political system and its actors. The application of this same methodology on a wider scale in Latin America could provide comparative insights capable of enriching the analysis of this relationship, particularly now that street politics has been assuming novel, creative forms throughout the entire continent.

ACKNOWLEDGMENTS

This chapter originally appeared in *Latin America Perspectives* 32 (2) (March 2005). The original article was translated by Dick Parker. The article is reprinted here with permission of Sage.

NOTES

1. For information and analysis of the *Caracazo*, see *Cuadernos del Cendes* (1989), *Politeia* (1989), Coronil and Skurski (1991) and López Maya (2003a)

2. López Maya (2003b) analyzes the relationship between repression and the increasing violence of the demonstrations.

3. The deaths occasioned by state repression during the April 11, 2002, coup and during the following two days are not included in the totals of the Provea report: in the case of events occurring on April 11 because to date there is no reliable account of what happened; and in the case of April 12 and 13 because the responsibility lies with the de facto Carmona regime. In the 2002-2003 report, four deaths are registered, although three of them are the result of repression of a violent demonstration.

4. In addition to 1983, which is registered in table 3.5 with 5.1 percent for violent protests, BDEBP indicates 7.3 percent for 1981 and 5 percent for 1982.

Chapter 4

SOCIAL MOVEMENT UNIONISM, SOCIAL MOVEMENT PARTYISM, AND POLICY OUTCOMES: HEALTH CARE PRIVATIZATION IN EL SALVADOR

Paul Almeida

Between 1999 and 2003, Salvadoran health care unions and their civil society support groups launched two massive campaigns in order to prevent the partial privatization of the public medical system. The mobilizations were the largest in post-civil war and newly democratized El Salvador. The labor strikes by the public health care sector unions alone were the longest in the history of the country—not an easy feat in a nation with a long tradition of mass organizing. Besides the impressive level of popular mobilization, however, is the outcome of the struggle. On two separate occasions, the movement forced the government to concede and formally agree to halt the outsourcing of public hospital units and services. In neoliberal Latin America, preventing an unwanted economic policy via mass mobilization is more the exception than the rule. Certainly, neoliberal policy implementation frequently sparks mass mobilization in Latin America (Walton and Shefner 1994; López Maya 1999; Eckstein 2001b; Almeida 2002; Auyero 2002). I concentrate here on the dimensions associated with a movement actually turning back such efforts—a less common phenomenon but key to understanding the prospects for deeper structural reforms in the region. The conditions associated with these movement-favorable policy outcomes constitute the subject of this chapter.

Public sector privatization has served as the cornerstone of neoliberal policies throughout Latin America over the past two decades (Edwards 1995). As part of a larger policy reform package, ranging from currency devaluations, lowering of import tariffs, subsidy reductions on basic consumer goods, transportation and public spending in general, privatization of public industries, infrastructure, and services has provided a rapid and short-term means to generate badly needed revenue. Public sector privatization emerged especially strong in the 1990s and early 2000s in Latin America. Privatization is intimately connected to a country's indebtedness. International lending institutions condition loans on a nation's ability to sell off public assets to make payments on past foreign borrowing. Government privatization programs have been carried through in all countries on the continent, usually with meager public opposition. Nonetheless, at times privatization has triggered some of the most intense and dramatic waves of popular unrest observed in the last ten years in the region.

In Bolivia, Peru, Costa Rica, and Paraguay privatization of public resources, services, and utilities has generated massive civil society resistance. Both the privatization of natural gas deposits and potable water distribution served as the roots of multiple episodes of popular unrest in Bolivia between 2000 and 2005, leading to the fall of two presidents, several states of siege, the death of at least 70 demonstrators, 500 additional people injured, and a constitutional crisis (Lewis 2004). The attempted privatization of electricity distribution in Arequipa, Peru, in mid-2002, sparked large-scale protests leaving several dozens of Peruvian citizens injured, and two dead, and causing over $100 million in property damage. In March and April 2000, the attempted privatization of telecommunications and electricity in Costa Rica (*Ley de transformación del ICE*) led to mass street marches and roadblocks. Witnessing the largest public demonstrations in recent history, the ruling PUSC and social-democratic opposition (PLN) parties backpedaled from their plans to open up state-run electricity and telecommunications to international markets. In Paraguay between 2002 and 2005, workers, students, public employees, and *campesinos* sustained a major campaign to prevent the privatization of telecommunications, water, and the railroads under legislative Laws 1615 and 1932 (*La Nación* July 1, 2005). Early in the protest campaign, in July 2002, two demonstrators were killed by security forces and President González Macchi declared a state of siege to end rioting and property damage (*BBC News* July 16, 2002). Given the recent historical import of these major national crises in the Americas, we need a greater understanding of the conditions associated with the actual implementation of privatization and other neoliberal measures versus the circumstances when civil society successfully blocks or rolls back such policies.

SOCIAL MOVEMENT THEORY AND POLICY OUTCOMES

A relatively less developed part of social movements research, as opposed to movement emergence or individual recruitment, is in the area of the consequences or impacts of social movements (Stearns and Almeida 2004; Jenkins and Form 2005). Though there has been considerable empirical and theoretical work on social movement outcomes in recent years to overcome this deficit (Giugni, McAdam, and Tilly 1999; Amenta, Caren, and Olasky 2005), the majority of these studies focus on policy outcomes of *new benefits and advantages* for aggrieved groups. Given that much of the mobilization in contemporary Latin America tends to be defensive and driven by neoliberal economic programs, scholars need to give more attention to the ability of social movements to prevent the implementation of *unwanted* economic and social policies (i.e., collective bads) as well as protect popularly favored ones from austerity cuts. This is the milieu in which policy battles are being waged in the Americas in the twenty-first century. The present chapter concentrates on conditions drawn from the political sociology and social movement literature to explain successful mobilization in Latin America against these unpopular economic policies.

The present chapter employs political mediation theory that centers on the political context in which social movements struggle and seek to have an impact on political and economic elites (Amenta, Caren, and Olasky 2005). Political mediation theory predicts that, "it takes a combination of favorable political contexts, mobilization, and assertive actions to bring about far-reaching state outcomes" (ibid.: 515). We apply these analytical insights on movements struggling to influence unwanted neoliberal policies in Latin America. Our framework centers on three conditions that seem most critical for political challengers attempting to prevent the loss of economic and social benefits; these conditions include 1) favorable public opinion; 2) social movement unionism; and 3) social movement partyism. These three key dimensions reflect the combination of an encouraging political context, mobilization, and forceful action that will be discussed in relation to the economic liberalization policies that have transformed the role of the state in Latin American society over the past twenty-five years.

PUBLIC OPINION AND DEMOCRATIZATION

In democratizing and democratic states, public opinion matters to policymakers. Nonetheless, in the early years of a democratizing regime public attitudes may only slowly penetrate into the calculations of policymakers. In the beginning phases of a democratic transition, with all the corresponding political uncertainties (e.g., which political parties and constituencies will triumph?, will the transition be completed?, etc.), it is not evident to state actors what the consequences may be for varying responses to issues that garner widespread public attention. In addition, authoritarian legacies left over from the pre-democratic era likely weaken the influence of public opinion in fledgling democracies. An authoritarian political culture as well as the survival of political parties and state bureaucrats with direct links to nondemocratic rule all act as forces inhibiting the permeation of popular sentiments about key national themes into the halls of elite political decision making. Over time, though, we would expect policymakers to become increasingly receptive to public opinion as the state continues on a consistent path of democratization (i.e., successive competitive national elections, peaceful transitions of executive power, relative political stability, etc.) (Booth 1995). This is the political context for several Latin American states between the mid-1980s and early 2000s.

Once a democratic transition occurs and when over 50 percent of the public rejects a particular policy, it places reelection in serious question for ruling political parties and minority parties that support the policy (Burstein 1979). Unfavorable public attitudes also threaten job security of appointed ministry officials and their staffs (e.g., the oscillating fortunes of ministers of the economy and finance in several Latin American states). Of course, the saliency of the policy to the general public would also be important (Burstein and Linton 2002) or what social movement scholars refer to as the "centrality" of a policy to a society's larger belief system (Snow and Benford 1988: 205). Across-the-board new sales taxes or increasing the retirement age to receive pension payments are likely to be meaningful policies in the everyday lives of large numbers of the citizenry. These kinds of neoliberal proposals, if implemented, may eventuate in negative consequences in future elections for the parties and officials serving as the main proponents and boosters of the policy.

However, governments, legislators, and executives debate and pass all kinds of legislation and policies in the interlude between national elections. A negative neoliberal measure may be balanced out by other policies that have popular support such as "get tough on crime" laws or cultural issues where there is a large societal consensus. In addition, lesser-developed countries often implement neoliberal policies because they are in a dependency relationship with international financial institutions to make debt-servicing payments and secure future lines of credit (Walton and Seddon 1994). This may push especially dependent governments and state managers to carry out unfavorable economic policies despite a public against such changes. Additionally, neoliberal governance has become institutionalized in world society as the appropriate way for domestic political elites to manage national economies (Fourcade-Gourinchas and Babb 2002; Henisz, Zelner, and Guillén 2005) in order to appear legitimate with international financiers and trading partners. It is for these reasons that public opinion alone, even in democratic states, might not be a sufficient condition to prevent the implementation of an unpopular economic policy. Indeed, the rather abrupt historical transition in twenty-five years from a state-led development program to a neoliberal strategy in most countries in Latin America provides evidence that state managers more often than not adopt these economic development policies even when there is mild to strong opposition within public opinion. A well-organized social movement campaign combined with public opinion against a free market policy raises the costs significantly for national policymakers to implement an impending unfavorable economic plan.

SOCIAL MOVEMENT UNIONISM

Beyond public opinion, the emergence of a social movement would boost civil society's leverage against privatization or other unwanted economic policies. Public opinion as portrayed in representative national surveys and polls offers a snapshot in time of individual feelings about a particular policy. A social movement is a *collective* struggle that demands varying levels of time, resources and commitment from its volunteer members (Snow, Soule, and Kriesi 2004). Thus, a social movement is clearly a higher level of organized discontent than public opinion sentiment. At the same time, a social movement thrives in an environment where public opinion is in alignment with its own goals (i.e., both wanting to stop an impending policy).[1] Democratic governments are much less likely to ignore or repress a social movement that enjoys public opinion support for its objectives. Social movements also give embodiment to public opinion attitudes as an organized expression of civil society's dissension with a state's neoliberal policy-making trajectory.

The character of the social movement also matters. A movement organized in a single sector with few allies has a much more difficult time bringing about favorable policy outcomes (Almeida and Stearns 1998). In the case of neoliberal policy implementation, the social movement campaign usually begins with the sectors most affected or threatened by the policy change. For example, in the case of telecommunications privatization, if a movement materializes, it would likely begin with workers in the government-run institution—the state telephone workers union. The catalyst to mobilization would involve fears of union decertification, mass layoffs, and other uncertainties related to the privatization process. Theories of social movement unionism inform us that labor campaigns that focus on two features—community mobilization and non-institutional tactics—are more successful than campaigns that lack these properties (Seidman 1994; Schock 2005). We apply the insights from the social movement unionism literature to the impact of anti-neoliberal policy protests in Latin America.

Wider community mobilization. When a unionized workforce serves as the primary affected constituency of a neoliberal policy, theories of social movement unionism suggest that the labor union must attempt to organize or cooperate with other sectors in order to sustain the struggle. Focusing only on the narrow concerns of the workers in the sector to be privatized (though certainly not a "narrow" issue to the workers in question), such as job loss and indemnification matters, will not likely harness the support of outside groups such as other labor unions and community groups. When the labor unions targeted by a neoliberal measure effectively reach out to other social sectors to mobilize in a sustained campaign against unwanted policy shifts, they give *social* expression to public opinion that is already against the policy. Public opinion ceases to act solely as an abstract construct of unconnected individuals and begins to amass as an organized force that represents a broad cross-section of civil society. Favorable public opinion to a movement's goals also makes a multi-sectoral or social movement unionism campaign easier to assemble (Van Dyke 2003)—strengthening the overall "mobilization potential" of the populace (Klandermans 1997: 16). Challengers invest much less time in socially constructing the neoliberal policy as a social problem in need of redress (e.g., through popular education campaigns) if public opinion already stands against it (Snow and Benford 1988). A societal "demand" exists for political change (Klandermans 2004). Instead, activists direct scarce resources into coordinating strategies leading to much more rapid and widespread mobilization than if public opinion had to be swayed or built from scratch. Thus, prevailing public opinion provides a kind of "coat rack" in which several sectors can "hook on" to the oppositional coalition.

In Costa Rica in 2000, such a widespread community-labor alliance emerged to prevent the privatization of the state telecommunications and electrical power system (ICE). The number of organized state workers in the ICE was no more than 15,000. The ICE workers aligned with the university community, NGOs, environmentalists, community groups, and port workers in early 2000 to launch a successful campaign to prevent the privatization process. With the added support of these actors external to the labor organization, the scale of popular mobilization in March and early April of 2000 reached unprecedented levels with street marches of tens of thousands of demonstrators and protest actions reported in all seven of Costa Rica's provinces. A similar amalgamation of public employees and NGOs—along with indigenous organizations, successfully coalesced in Ecuador in November 1995 to prevent the privatization of several state enterprises and the social security system (Zamosc 2004).

If labor unions, facing a looming unfavorable neoliberal policy shift such as privatization, fail to coordinate a larger campaign beyond the union's organizational boundaries they will likely face an uphill battle and be deemed a privileged labor aristocracy enjoying socioeconomic benefits that the majority of the nonpublic sector workforce lacks (e.g., retirement system, health care coverage, recreational facilities, vacation, seniority privileges, etc.). For example, Sandoval (2001: 184-185) reported that in a 1995 opinion poll of São Paulo, Brazil, residents that, "84.3% felt that employees of state enterprises were privileged workers."

Non-institutional tactics. Another facet of social movement unionism besides a multisectoral coalition (i.e., labor unions, community groups, students, nongovernmental organizations acting in concert) resides in the use of non-institutional tactics. A defining characteristic of social movements involves the employment of strategies for political influence that clearly appear outside the conventions of institutionalized politics such as mass disruption, street marches, boycotts, and expressive actions (Snow, Soule, and Kriesi 2004; Trevizo 2006). Along with community support, these non-institutional tactics constitute the "social movement" in social movement unionism. Legislators and executives may fail to listen to civil society demands against neoliberal reforms because of international financial institution pressure and/or because elections remain too far off to be worried about the political repercussions. In such cases of government intransigence, a labor-community coalition will likely engage in disruptive protest campaigns to try and force state managers to negotiate or retract the policy. Non-institutional tactics provide a negative inducement that can create greater levels of uncertainty for policymakers (Piven and Cloward 1979; McAdam 1982 [1999]; Almeida and Stearns 1998), providing political and economic elites an incentive to negotiate or offer some concessions to the anti-neoliberal coalition in exchange for a cessation in disorderly movement actions.

In June of 2004, Guatemalans launched a successful disruptive protest campaign against an impending increase in the national sales tax. The campaign involved a general strike, mass street marches, and roadblocks placed strategically throughout the country impeding traffic on major roads and highways. A day into the national strike, the government of Oscar Berger temporarily rescinded the tax hike and set up a special commission to analyze the necessity of such an austerity measure. Developing a wide multi-sectoral coalition that employs institutionally disruptive tactics certainly does not ensure a mobilization drive will succeed against socially harmful economic liberalization measures. Having an ally inside the polity aids an anti-neoliberal social movement campaign further in terms of pressuring for change *within the government* and reaching a legally binding resolution to the conflict. A strong oppositional political party likely serves as the most important ally inside the polity.

SOCIAL MOVEMENT PARTYISM

The social movement literature counts a substantial number of studies that emphasize the role of external actors facilitating collective action for disempowered groups as well as increasing the likelihood of movement-generated gains (Jenkins and Perrow 1977; Almeida and Stearns 1998). Outside groups play such an important role in social movement politics that Tarrow (1998: 79-80) places "influential allies" as one of the five defining features of the structure of political opportunity that shapes the external environment in which challengers struggle.[2] In a survey of studies using the political process theory of social movements, McAdam (1996a: 27) consigns "the presence or absence of elite allies" as one of four key elements on his "highly consensual list of dimensions of political opportunity." Out of the universe of these potential external and influential allies (e.g., institutional and political elites, cultural producers, scientists, celebrities, etc.), movement-sympathetic groups *inside the government* or state actors seem to be especially important in terms of attaining policy success (Trevizo 2006). Social movement scholars have referred to this relationship as state-movement "interpenetration" (Wolfson 2001) or the "state-movement intersection" (Banaszak 2005).

In a recent article focusing on movement-state alliances shaping favorable policy impacts for national environmental movements, Stearns and Almeida (2004) found that the more ties an anti-pollution movement establishes with state actors—local governments, courts, political parties, and state agencies—the more likely it is to achieve movement-desired outcomes (e.g., stricter environmental standards, compensation payments for pollution victims, etc.). We focus here on the relationship between the anti-neoliberal labor-community coalition and one particularly important state actor, an oppositional political party. The best scenario in terms of influencing policy outcomes would be for the labor-community alliance to link with the dominant political party in the legislature and/or the executive branch since such a party has the political capital to implement policy change (Stearns and Almeida 2004). Nonetheless, such a situation is highly unlikely in the sense that it is the dominant political party that is most often committed to the neoliberal agenda for both economic and ideological reasons (Babb 2001). Moreover, it is likely that the dominant party generated part of the crisis in the first place by bringing the free market reforms into formal political debate.

It is more probable that the labor-community coalition will form a relationship with an oppositional political party with whom it has an ideological affinity (Maguire 1995; Stearns and Almeida 2004). In the arena of Latin American neoliberalism, such a relationship is most likely to form with a left-of-center or nationalist political party. While the most important contribution an oppositional political party can make to a social movement unionism campaign centers on acting as an ally inside the legislature (Burstein, Einwohner, and Hollander 1995: 289) and impeding the neoliberal policy reform, there exist other roles a political party can play to sustain opposition.

Besides acting as an advocate inside the polity, an oppositional political party may aid a social movement campaign by sending official representatives to protest events, encouraging rank-and-file party supporters to participate in social movement activities, and allow local governments under its control to support the social movement campaign, including city workers. Just as a traditional labor union can turn to more social movement forms of collective action by organizing other social sectors and engaging in non-institutional tactics, so too can a political party. Such was the case in Nicaragua in April and May of 2005 over the issue of rising public transportation rates (climbing between 15 and 30 percent) linked to the sudden increase in global petroleum prices (Carrillo and Enríquez 2005). Bus driver cooperatives, university students, and community groups, aligned with the largest oppositional political party in the country—the Frente Sandinista para la Liberación Nacional (FSLN)—to pressure the national government to lower bus fares. After a month of intense street protests, FSLN mayors (benefiting from recent electoral gains) and legislative deputies successfully achieved a three-month government subsidy to prevent a bus fare price hike.

The involvement of electoral parties in contentious movement-type activities will not come as a surprise to scholars of collective action since many political parties began their careers as social movements (Keck 1992; Aminzade 1995; Goldstone 2004).[3] This conversion process of movement to political party slowly unfolded over several decades in many advanced capitalist democracies. In Latin America's democratic transition, however, many political parties just recently completed the move from social movement to an electoral political party within a single generation (e.g., the Workers' Party in Brazil, the Partido de la Revolución Democrática in Mexico, FREPASO and Polo Obrero in Argentina, Movement toward Socialism in Bolivia, the Alianza Nueva Nación in Guatemala, FSLN in Nicaragua, Frente Amplio in Uruguay, FMLN in El Salvador, Pachakutik in Ecuador, etc.). The trend continues in the late 1990s and early 2000s in the region and appears especially evident with indigenous movements forming electoral political parties (Van Cott 2005).

This recent social movement history means that many of the leaders and members of oppositional political parties have organizational experience in various social movement organizations (SMOs), while active rank-and-file party affiliates retain overlapping memberships in SMOs, nongovernmental organizations (NGOs), and their respective electoral party. For instance, Seidman (1994) found that in the early years of Brazil's Partido dos Trabalhadores (PT) in the mid-1980s, the Party's membership was largely composed of unionists affiliated with the militant labor federation Central Única dos Trabalhadores (CUT). In a more recent example, in 1996, social movement organizations in Ecuador associated with the Confederación de Nacionalidades Indígenas del Ecuador (CONAIE), Confederacón Única de Afiliados del Seguro Social Campesino (CONFEUNASSC), and the Coordinadora de Movimientos Sociales founded the indigenous-based political party—el Movimiento de Unidad Plurinacional Pachakutik Nuevo País (MUPP-NP), which has grown to be one of the strongest opposition political parties in the country (Collins 2004; Zamosc 2004). In sum, in several Latin American countries the boundaries appear blurred between social movements outside the polity and political parties inside (see also Goldstone [2004] for cases beyond Latin America). The larger the oppositional political party (in terms of absolute size and political representation in local and national government) that aligns with the social movement unionism campaign, the more influence it commands in mobilizing people and pressing for policy change inside the state. We place all of these movement-contributing roles of an electoral political party (inside and outside of the polity) under the rubric of "social movement partyism."

To summarize, unfavorable public opinion alone is unlikely to stop neoliberal policy reform and such reforms are rarely put to a popular referendum. Labor unions in sectors most threatened by economic liberalization will be more successful if they can move to a social movement unionism organizing strategy—that is, mobilizing other sectors beyond their own organizational boundaries. Such widespread mobilization is difficult to generate, but if achieved, will help pressure for policy change. Finally, a strong oppositional political party that practices social movement partyism in concert with social movement unionism may provide the kinds of coalitions and accumulation of social forces necessary to compel the government to rescind its unfavorable policies. I examine this framework below with the case of public health-care privatization in El Salvador and then discuss the implications of the findings for other similar struggles in the region.

PUBLIC HEALTH CARE PRIVATIZATION IN EL SALVADOR

With the conclusion of El Salvador's civil war at the beginning of 1992, the country began to deepen its level of global economic integration and move onto a stricter path of neoliberal policymaking.[4] The pro-neoliberal political party—the National Republican Alliance (ARENA)—came to executive power in 1989. Through the mid-1990s, ARENA controlled a majority of El Salvador's 262 local governments, legislative seats, and ministerial cabinets. The dominant neoliberal party, along with its think tanks and pressure from international financial institutions, embarked on a state "modernization" program throughout the decade of the 1990s. The economic program began in earnest in 1989 through the early 1990s with the re-privatization of the banking system, agro-export sector, and the closure of the basic grains regulatory institute. During the tenure of ARENA president Calderón Sol (1994-1999), neoliberal policymaking picked up pace with a formal "state modernization" program passed by the legislature in 1995. The modernization legislation called for the retirement of 15,000 state employees, raising the value-added tax by three percent, and the privatization of sugar refineries, telecommunications, electricity distribution, and the government-run pension program.

These neoliberal policy packages passed through the legislature with mixed public opinion and mild to moderate opposition by the affected public employees. State workers protested massive layoffs in 1995 and early 1996 with sporadic strikes, street marches, and hunger strikes. The state telephone workers led the largest demonstrations against privatization of the telecommunications system between 1995 and 1997. Their campaigns rarely brought in larger sectors of civil society and in the end lost out to privatization, which reduced the telecommunications work force by two-thirds. All these protest campaigns in the mid-1990s rarely produced a street march of over 10,000 people.[5] It was not until the government attempted to privatize part of the public health care system that widespread and sustained anti-neoliberal mobilization materialized.

PUBLIC OPINION AND HEALTH CARE PRIVATIZATION

While public opinion has been mixed on various privatization programs implemented by the Salvadoran government in the mid-1990s, the public has consistently opposed privatization of El Salvador's two main public health care systems.[6] Nationally representative public opinion polls taken by the most prestigious survey institutes in the country between 1997 and 2003 show that between 55 and 87 percent of the public opposed health care privatization (see Table 1.0).[7] Though the national government undertook small steps toward privatization in the mid-1990s in both public health care systems with the subcontracting of some health and maintenance services to private firms, in 1999 the government moved forward with a pilot program to begin privatizing two of the Salvadoran Social Security Institute (ISSS) hospitals located in greater San Salvador. Health care unions responded in mid-to-late 1999 by launching sporadic work stoppages demanding both an end to the privatization process and respect for a collective bargaining agreement signed by the previous administration of Calderón Sol in 1998. Buttressed by the strong public sentiment against health system privatization, the health care unions in the ISSS began a formal strike campaign in November 1999.

SOCIAL MOVEMENT UNIONISM IN PUBLIC HEALTH CARE

The campaigns to prevent health care privatization in El Salvador consist of two distinct waves. The first campaign was launched between November 1999 and March 2000. The second wave spanned from September 2002 until June 2003. Both waves included the ISSS health care unions reaching out to other sectors besides their own, making them true social movement unionism campaigns as defined above. In the fall of 1999, the government made public its plans to partially privatize the ISSS Amatepec and Roma hospitals. The ISSS health care workers' union—Sindicato de Trabajadores del Instituto de Seguro Social (STISSS)—launched a strike wave demanding the cessation of privatization and respect for its previously signed collective contract. In November 1999, the doctor's union of the ISSS (SIMETRISSS) strategically allied with STISSS, demanding an end to private concessions in the ISSS hospital system.

The central government and the ISSS officials refused to negotiate with the striking health care unions and fired 221 workers affiliated with STISSS. Fortunately for the health care unions, in the year prior to the strike a renewed effort commenced to unify public sector unions in a formal coalition. The Movimiento de Organizaciones Laborales Integradas (MOLI) formed in 1998 to prevent further job cuts and privatization in the public sector as a whole. MOLI brought twelve public sector unions and associations under a single coordinating umbrella representing 50,000 state workers. Several of the MOLI unions supported the health care workers' strike and demands by making public statements, threatening solidarity strikes, holding short work stoppages, and participating in street actions.

	In Agreement	*In Disagreement*	*Other*	*N*
Would you be in agreement or disagreement if the ISSS were privatized? (November 1997)	23.4%	55.5%	21.1%	1202
Would you be in agreement or disagreement if the ISSS were privatized? (December 1999)	16.5%	74.3%	9.2%	1326
Are you in agreement with the privatization of health care? (January 2003)[a]	12.65%	87.35%	0.0%	2040

Sources: Centro de Opinión Pública and Instituto Universitario de Opinión Pública
Note: [a] This poll was administered in greater San Salvador. The other polls are nationally representative.

Table 4.1. Public Opinion and Health Care Privatization

As the strike dragged on into December and January, STISSS and SIMETRISSS also brought out other social sectors such as university students and NGOs to support them in their street marches. Early in the strike campaign, in late November 1999, SIMETRISSS called a special meeting with civil society groups including representatives of NGOs, agricultural cooperatives, and university students, to convince them that health care privatization was a national issue. Their coalition building seems to have paid off. On December 8, 1999, a mass march for "Public Health" took place in which an estimated 20,000 people participated, including health care workers, students, labor unions, and community groups.

Over time the marches increased in size with more social groups present in February and early March of 2000. In early February 2000, peasants traveled from Chalatenango, San Vicente, and Usulután departments to hold simultaneous marches to the ISSS administrative offices in San Salvador demanding an end to public health care privatization. Peasant participation provides a clear illustration of the level of social movement unionism achieved, in that poor rural groups do not pay into the Social Security health system nor are they covered by it. Peasant organizations felt a sense of solidarity with the health care unionists and a threat to the public health system as a whole in which they are beneficiaries. Around this same time (February 2000), an ad hoc coalition of civil society groups formed to support the striking health care workers called the "Coordinadora de Organizaciones Sociales en contra de la Privatización" (COSCP). Street marches and public rallies were also held in at least a dozen towns outside of San Salvador, including Usulután, San Miguel, Santa Tecla, Santa Ana, Sonsonate, Aguilares, Apopa, San Vicente, and Zacatecoluca. On March 6, riot police used water cannons, tear gas, and rubber bullets to disperse doctors and their supporters holding a sit-in on a street in the public hospital sector of San Salvador. The tear gas diffused into the nearby hospitals and affected several patients. In response, STISSS and SIMETRISSS along with their civil society supporters in the COCSP convoked a mass march on March 8 to the presidential palace. The demonstration drew an estimated 50,000 participants (by SIMETRISSS accounts). Finally on Saturday, March 11, the government negotiated with the unions and agreed to halt the privatization process—a day before national parliamentary and municipal elections.

Part of the accords reached in March 2000 between the health care unions and the state included the formation of a special commission composed of unions, health care administrators and recipients, NGOs, and the government. The goal of the multi-party

Source: Imágenes Libres

Figure 4.1. The *Marcha Blanca,* Avenida Cuscatlán, San Salvador, October 23, 2002.

commission was to generate a health care reform program with the consent of the most relevant sectors in provisioning and receiving public health care. In the summer of 2002, the proposal of the workgroup was ignored by the central government. At this same time, at an annual meeting of large private enterprise associations, the business groups introduced their own plan to be presented to the legislative assembly, which included a partial privatization of the ISSS public health system. These unfavorable gestures led to a new strike wave in the fall of 2002.

Both STISSS and SIMETRISSS began employing work stoppages in the ISSS hospitals in September 2002. The health care unions had been already meeting with NGO groups and communities throughout El Salvador in the summer of 2002, leading teach-ins and seminars about health care privatization. By October 2002, a broad, pre-existing coalition of NGOs called the *Foro de la Sociedad Civil*, threw in its support for the striking health care workers. The Foro represented over fifty NGOs and community associations. By the end of October, members of the Foro de la Sociedad Civil joined with other groups of students and labor organizations to form the *Alianza ciudadana contra la privatización* (ACCP). In addition to peasant, student, and labor groups, the ACCP represented women's rights associations and ecology/consumer defense-focused groups. These civil society organizations engaged in street protests, vigils, and roadblocks on behalf of the striking doctors throughout the campaign. The roadblocks, marches, and sit-ins created a climate of mass disruption from October 2002 until May 2003 in San Salvador and the major towns and highways of the republic. Observers at the time acknowledged the health care workers' adroitness at constructing mobilization appeals consistent with public misgivings about health privatization, especially concerning the rising costs and increasing exclusion of the poorest sectors from access to medical services (González and Alvarenga 2002).

In addition to this extensive civil society camaraderie, the ISSS unions had the backing of workers and doctors in the general public health care system (the MSPAS). Health care workers in the MSPAS system engaged in both short-term work stoppages and longer strikes in solidarity with the ISSS workers between October 2002 and May 2003 (as they also carried out in the 1999-2000 strike). The efficacy of the second anti-health care privatization campaign—which was much larger and more intensive than in 1999-2000—was manifested in the seven *marchas blancas* (white marches) convoked in late 2002 and early 2003 (see figure 4.1). Beginning on October 16, 2002, the ISSS unions and their civil society allies organized mass street demonstrations in El Salvador whereby they deployed their symbolic capital (Giarracca and Bidaseca 2001) by dressing in white apparel and applying white body paint to display solidarity with the public health care profession (Umaña 2003). The immense white marches signified that "we are all health care workers." One common white t-shirt worn and distributed by STISSS unionists during the strike and marches read on the backside, "Unidos defendamos la salud de todo el pueblo."

The largest white marches attracted up to 200,000 participants from all social backgrounds, making them clearly the largest mobilizations in the post-civil war era (Schuld 2003). STISSS and SIMETRISSS membership combined totaled less than 7,000 unionists. Thus, the multitudinous *marchas blancas* displayed a heightened level of social movement unionism. Whereas the largest marches in the protest wave of the late 1970s preceding the civil war were often funeral processions for fallen activists and victims of state-sponsored violence, the white marches called for an end to privatization and the "merchandizing" of public health—marking a clear historical shift in popular claims-making from the era of authoritarian developmentalism to neoliberal democracy.

THE FMLN AND SOCIAL MOVEMENT PARTYISM

Both protest campaigns enjoyed the support of the largest opposition political party, the Farabundo Martí Front for National Liberation (FMLN), which was legalized as an official party after the negotiated end to the civil war in 1992. The former insurgents effectively transformed from a guerrilla army to a legal electoral party. The FMLN was relatively weak in the early to the mid-1990s as it adjusted to conventional and institutional politics. In the 1994 parliamentary elections (the party's first electoral competition), the FMLN won 21 out of 81 parliamentary seats. However, in a bitter factional split, seven legislative deputies abandoned the party in 1995, reducing the FMLN representation in the legislative assembly to 14 seats. The seven defecting legislative deputies subsequently colluded with the ruling ARENA party to pass a regressive sales tax hike in 1995—a common measure in neoliberal policy packages. In the 1994 local elections, the FMLN only won 13 of 262 municipal government councils (Montgomery 1997). Nonetheless, in each successive local, legislative, and presidential election between 1994 and 2004 the opposition party gained more votes.

The 1997 legislative elections were a turning point for the FMLN. The party took control of the capital, San Salvador, and over four dozen other municipalities, while winning many seats in the unicameral national legislature. From this foothold, the FMLN continued to make gains in the 2000 and 2003 legislative and municipal elections. Thus, in the formative years of neoliberal reform in the early 1990s, social movements had few allies inside the polity to give them a hearing to prevent unpopular economic policies. By the late 1990s, however, this all began to change. The big breakthrough for the electoral opposition arrived with the 1997 elections.

In the 1997 legislative and local elections, the FMLN won 27 of 81 parliamentary seats, which clearly distinguished itself as the second largest political force in the country after the neoliberal ARENA party (Montgomery 1997). The FMLN also took control of 51 municipal governments, including 6 of the 14 provincial capitals (including San Salvador itself)—none of which the party had won in 1994. Though by the time it came to exercise its newly acquired oppositional power it was too late to prevent privatizations that ARENA already pushed down the legislative pipeline (such as the state telecommunications company ANTEL), the FMLN would be a leading voice to prevent public health care privatization between 1999 and 2003.

The FMLN's behavior in supporting the health care unions can be characterized as "social movement partyism." Not only did this oppositional political party act as a friend inside parliament voting against legislation allowing for private contracts in the public health care system, but also in supporting social movement mobilization efforts (Harnecker 2003). The FMLN along with other oppositional political parties supported a bill early in the 2002-2003 strike that constitutionally prevented the government from privatizing the public health sector. The anti-privatization legislation passed on two separate occasions in October and November of 2002, but was overturned when the ruling ARENA party aligned with a smaller center-right party to pass counter legislation in December of 2002 (Schuld 2003). Hence, parliamentary struggle alone was not sufficient to put the brakes on the privatization process.

The legislative representatives of the FMLN often participated in street marches. The legislative deputies of the FMLN marched in unison as a distinct column in the *marchas blancas* of 2002 and 2003, carrying their own banner stating solidarity with the health care workers. The oppositional party had also began a tradition in June 2002 of holding a weekly public gathering in downtown San Salvador on Friday evenings called the *Tribuna Abierta*. During the 2002-2003 health care strike, elected FMLN officials openly encouraged the audience at the *tribunas abiertas* to participate in the *marchas blancas* and contribute to the anti-privatization campaign.

Party members and high-ranking FMLN politicians also participated in the more risky and disruptive protest tactics such as roadblocks, which at times were dispersed with tear gas, rubber bullets, and mass arrests. In October of 2002, FMLN mayors and legislative representatives showed up at highway sit-ins in diverse locations around the country including in the western department of Ahuachapán and in the southeastern region at the Puente de Oro to protest health care privatization and economic liberalization. City employees of FMLN-controlled municipalities of greater metropolitan San Salvador also served as a key support group in major protests.[8] Finally, FMLN representatives acted as advocates within the justice system by publicly demanding the release of protesters arrested during the health care strike campaigns (Meza 2003). Voters rewarded the FMLN handsomely. Both protest campaigns peaked during the election season for legislative and municipal elections. In both elections (2000 and 2003), the FMLN made significant electoral gains and held on to their 1997 victories at the local and parliamentary levels—a payoff from movement-party interdependence.

Both rounds of anti-health care privatization mobilization resulted in the government negotiating a formal agreement (in March 2000 and June 2003) to halt the privatization process while in exchange the health care unions and their civil society support groups ceased work stoppages and disruptive and creative street actions. Thus, if we measure social movement outcomes by the stated goals of the main protagonists (Burstein, Einwohner, and Hollander 1995), these campaigns proved to be relatively successful. The level of mobilization was national, with health care union-community coalitions reproduced on a local scale in dozens of municipalities. Arguably, the El Salvador anti-health care privatization campaigns represent some of the largest and longest sustained struggles against a *particular* neoliberal policy in Latin America (with the possible exception of the Bolivian mobilizations against natural gas privatization and export). Even more important, however, is that the Salvadoran anti-health care privatization protests succeeded in halting the privatization process via social movement actions—a relatively rare occurrence in neoliberal Latin America.

In sum, the best that social movements can do in neoliberal Latin America may be to slow down the *rate* of economic change (Polanyi 1944: 37). One movement-generated victory against privatization or other neoliberal measures does not ensure that pressures for economic liberalization will not remerge. In El Salvador in the early 1990s, public opinion was mixed about various government measures and schemes to privatize key public services and industries. Social movements that tried to mobilize against the reforms in the early to mid-1990s were usually only organized within their own sector and experienced a challenging time sustaining their protests—such as the state telecommunications workers' unions. At this same moment, oppositional political parties with ideological leanings against neoliberal reforms were relatively weak and controlled few legislative seats or municipal governments. Thus, the early to mid-1990s in El Salvador were neither favorable to social movement unionism nor to social movement partyism (not to mention a society exhausted by over eleven years of civil war in the midst of reconstruction).

When the government moved to privatize *relatively* affordable and accessible services such as public sector health care, the ISSS health care unions tapped into public opinion misgivings and brought in other social sectors to support the struggle—including other public sector unions, teachers, students, women's rights groups, NGOs, and agricultural cooperative associations. In the late 1990s, when the health care privatization process commenced, the opposition political party with a strong anti-neoliberal ideology climbed to a much more potent political position within the Salvadoran polity, controlling a third of legislative seats and the municipal governments where a majority of the population resided. These favorable conditions (public opinion, social movement unionism, and social movement partyism) converged to create a multi-layered barrier against health care privatization on two separate occasions. The Salvadoran protest campaigns eventuated in one of the largest and most intensive mobilizations witnessed in the hemisphere against privatization.

LESSONS FOR LATIN AMERICA

The Salvadoran social movement campaigns against health care privatization may be instructive for similar types of policy struggles in contemporary Latin America. Regional public opinion seems to be turning against privatization. In Bolivia, the popular upheavals in the early 2000s went even a step further than most anti-neoliberal struggles in the Americas by calling for the nationalization of natural gas reserves partially privatized at bargain rates back in 1996. Bolivians also drew on public opinion (in which over 80 percent supported nationalization of natural gas deposits), widespread multisectoral and multicultural organizing (e.g., indigenous groups, students, teachers, neighborhood-based associations), and oppositional political parties that practiced social movement partyism (i.e., the MAS and the Movimiento Indígena Pachakuti) (Lewis 2004). Similar types of coalitions have materialized in Paraguay and Costa Rica to prevent government privatization programs.

Additionally, we should consider negative cases whereby mass mobilization failed to achieve desired policy outcomes against neoliberal measures (the more common outcome). For example, in Guatemala in March of 2005, the legislature ratified the Central American Free Trade Agreement (CAFTA)—a neoliberal measure to open markets and reduce trade barriers between Central America, the United States, and the Dominican Republic. Mass protests occurred before, during, and after the parliament voted in favor of the treaty. The anti-CAFTA campaign was multisectoral with the participation of key labor federations, NGOs, Mayan peasant groups, students, and human rights associations. The movement employed roadblocks and street marches through the first three weeks of March. The security forces killed at least one demonstrator at a roadblock of teachers and peasants in Colotenango, Huehuetenango. Private enterprise estimated economic losses of 85 million quetzales from the protests, which shut down the central business district of Guatemala City for several days (Canahui 2005). Despite the mass uprisings, the government held to its position regarding CAFTA. What factors may help explain this negative movement outcome?

First, national public opinion polls taken back in December 2004 showed that nearly 70 percent of the Guatemalan public was unaware of CAFTA, making it less than a salient public issue. For those who were aware of the trade agreement, more thought it would benefit the country than harm it. Second, inside the parliament the voting was dramatically skewed in favor of CAFTA. Out of 158 legislators, 126 voted in favor of signing the free trade agreement, twelve deputies from the center-left opposition voted against it, and the remaining twenty were absent (Paredes Díaz 2005). Hence, two of the key conditions outlined previously—public opinion and social movement partyism—were relatively weak, providing a very *unfavorable* context for mass disruption to influence public policy. Though the cross-sectoral representation of the protest participants in the Guatemalan anti-CAFTA campaign was impressive as well as the intensity of the contention for a short period, the movement fizzled out by late March—during the traditional Easter holiday season in Central America.

It should also be noted, though, that one major variable in this study—social movement partyism—contains other political costs and benefits beyond the immediate protest campaign. Movement-political party links may best serve the needs of social movements in ad hoc relationships. Over time, a movement could be co-opted by a political party and have its original goals displaced or ignored (i.e., removal of austerity policies) such as was the case with the labor movement and political parties in the late 1980s and early 1990s in Argentina, Mexico, and Venezuela (Murillo 2001). After the labor movement in these respective countries assisted in securing electoral victories for erstwhile pro-labor parties, the parties, once in power, managed the state in a neoliberal fashion through the early 1990s (ibid.). In Ecuador in 2003, an anti-neoliberal coalition in alliance with the indigenous-based political party Pachakutik (MUPP-NP), played a critical role in Lucio Gutiérrez' presidential victory. However, in less than 8 months, president Gutiérrez made a rapid U-turn and attempted to implement several neoliberal policies connected to an IMF standby loan, breaking his pact with the social movements and oppositional political party (MUPP-NP) that delivered him to executive power (Zamosc 2004; Almeida 2005).

On the other hand, an oppositional political party may be able to convert social movement and legislative success into more electoral power, which has the potential to win the executive branch and a legislative majority. Such a government may be able to partially hold back the tide of neoliberal reforms, or at least the most harmful ones to social welfare, but this seems to remain an open question in contemporary Argentina, Bolivia, Brazil, Chile, Uruguay, and Venezuela. These two conflicting scenarios indicate that more research needs to be carried out on both the long-term risks and potential payoffs of social movement partyism.

To summarize, tax hikes, cuts in the national retirement system, and the privatization of public utilities and services are the kinds of policies that are likely to mobilize significant subsets of the population. Such forms of neoliberal policymaking provide a structural potential for multisectoral organizing beyond a single group or labor union. The existence of a strong oppositional political party acting as an advocate for the movement inside and outside the polity further strengthens the potency of the coalition(s) struggling against the unwanted economic policy (at least in the short term). Future research should examine more precisely and across more cases the likelihood of such a combination of social and political forces converging, the conditions under which they do, and the outcomes they achieve in terms of neoliberal policy implementation/non-implementation.

ACKNOWLEDGMENTS

The author appreciates the comments provided by Hank Johnston on a draft of this chapter. The author benefited from research support by the Texas A&M Office of the Vice President for Research and the College of Liberal Arts. An earlier version of this work was presented at the Melvin G. Glasscock Center for Humanities Research Faculty Colloquium Series on February 15, 2005, at Texas A&M University.

NOTES

1. Social movements may influence public opinion negatively or positively. My focus here is how social movements and public opinion have an additive and cumulative influence on policy outcomes.

2. We also should mention that part of the social movement literature finds a demobilizing function of external groups when they align with the indigenous base of an insurgent group because of cooptation and goal displacement (McAdam 1982).

3. Of course, this is only one path to the establishment of a formal electoral party. An alternative path

could be from a schism among contending political elites that leads to the formation of a new party.

4. Since the late 1970s El Salvador was embroiled in violent political conflict. The civil war officially ran from the January 1981 guerrilla offensive to the signing of a United Nations brokered Peace Accords in January 1992. An estimated 80,000 Salvadorans lost their lives in the long and drawn-out conflict.

5. Other significant protest actions in this time period included campaigns by ex-paramilitaries for government indemnification payments, struggles over land redistribution connected to the Peace Accords, and intermittent battles between street vendors and local police in San Salvador.

6. El Salvador maintains two separate public health care systems. One is for the general population and is referred to as the Ministry of Public Health and Social Assistance (MSPAS). The MSPAS covers about 80 percent of the population. The other system is the Salvadoran Social Security Institute (ISSS) and it provides health care services for between 15 and 20 percent of the population (or roughly about 1 million people). The ISSS is catered to the formal workforce where employees and employers pay into the system. The clientele are workers in the state sector and in large private firms and under the protection of collective contracts. Retirees and family members of the formal workforce that have made payments into the ISSS also have access to its health care services.

7. It should be noted that even though public opinion polls consistently registered majorities against public health care privatization, public opinion was more mixed on the tactics used by the health care unions and their supporters during strike campaigns.

8. Political parties allied on both sides of the conflict to the point that in the 2004 presidential elections, ARENA chose as its vice presidential candidate, Ana Vilma de Escobar, the former director of the ISSS during the 1999-2000 conflict and in favor of partial privatization. The FMLN picked the leader of the Colegio Médico as its vice presidential candidate—a leading organizer of the doctors' labor union and opponent to ISSS privatization initiatives.

Part II

Democratization and the New Contentious Politics

Chapter 5

CLIENTELISM AND DEMOCRACY IN MEXICO: THE ROLE OF STRONG AND WEAK NETWORKS

Claudio A. Holzner

This chapter analyzes the stubborn resilience of clientelist organizations and practices in Mexico despite a strengthening civil society and growing electoral competition at all levels. Under the electoral hegemony of the PRI (Party of the Institutionalized Revolution)—Mexico's ruling party from 1929 until it lost the 2000 presidential elections—the bulk of political activity by lower-class groups in Mexico was channeled through corporatist and clientelist organizations linked to the state and the PRI. As a result, political activity by the rural and urban poor was severely circumscribed, consisting primarily of ritualistic and regime-supportive activities (Cornelius 1974, 1975; Eckstein 1977).

This was all supposed to change with the advent of democracy and the deepening of neoliberal reforms. Together these twin transformations have weakened the ability of the state and of political parties to dole out patronage, making traditional mechanisms of clientelistic control much less effective. Recent research across Latin America has in fact documented the rise of new forms of political organizing among the urban poor that emphasize political autonomy and democratic participation (Dietz 1998; Levine 2006; Levine and Romero 2002; Oxhorn 1995; Stokes 1995). The period since the 1980s has also seen a dramatic revitalization of civil society in Mexico, characterized by increased organizational pluralism and a growing willingness of organizations to actively resist political clientelism. In Mexico the trend is most evident in cities such as Mexico City and Guadalajara where grass roots organizations have fought for greater organizational autonomy and have had notable success in "scaling up" their movements by linking with other organizations in broader coalitions (Alonso

1986, 1988; Bennett 1992; Fox 1992; Ramírez Sáiz 1986; Shefner 1999, 2001).

Though these trends are undeniable, the fact is that clientelism has not gone away in Mexico and may even be strengthening in many areas (Fox 1994; Hellman 1994; Holzner 2002). The staying power of clientelism despite greater organizational pluralism, increased political competition, and drying up of state patronage is puzzling and largely unanticipated by recent scholarly work on Mexico's process of democratization. This chapter attempts to shed light on this puzzle through a close examination of the development of rival organizations in a single squatter settlement in the city of Oaxaca, located in southeastern Mexico. In a pattern repeated across Mexico, an electoral victory by an opposition party in the municipal elections—in this case the right-of-center PAN (National Action Party)—created the opportunity and incentives for a group of squatters to desert the PRI, establish an independent neighborhood association, and work to resist clientelist relations with political parties and the local government. However, a large minority of residents remained loyal to the PRI, rejected the new administration's land titling program, and continued to push their claims through traditional clientelist channels even while members of a rival group were receiving land titles from the city government. The emergence of an autonomous organization seeking independence from the PRI fits the broader patterns described by recent studies; but why a large minority clung to their PRI ties even after patronage stopped flowing and other residents were receiving land titles from the city government remains unexplained. This chapter undertakes the task of solving this puzzle.

I conducted the research for this chapter between October 1998 and November 1999 in the Solidaridad settlement (not its real name) and surrounding squatter settlements located on the outskirts of Oaxaca. Though I did not live in the neighborhood, I was a regular visitor there during the entire period, participating in weekly *tequios,*[1] and attending community assemblies as well as meetings of the two main neighborhood associations. I carried out in-depth interviews with current and past neighborhood leaders, and I was able to build enough trust to gain access to members of both rival networks. In all, I interviewed more than forty-five residents, community and city leaders, including the former mayor and several members of the sitting administration. I witnessed numerous protests and rallies staged by supporters of both the PRI and the PAN, and had access to documents dealing with the city's land titling program.

To be sure, the push and pull of clientelism are not limited to one neighborhood or to Mexico alone; it is a common experience among the urban and rural poor across Mexico and Latin America. A focus on a single case helps focus our attention on the processes through which clientelist organizations endure in democratic settings despite significant organizational pluralism. I will argue that the answer lies in part in strong ties. Granovetter's (1973) distinction between strong and weak networks is helpful in revealing the power of strong ties in maintaining loyalty to clientelistic organizations even when other options appear and the benefits of membership decline. Unlike weak ties that link disparate groups together and promote the flow of information, strong face-to-face networks give leaders enormous power to monitor the behavior of members and to isolate them by controlling and filtering information flows. Without access to unbiased information, people who belong to strong networks are less likely to find out about new opportunities; and even if they do, they may not view them as real, credible, or trustworthy. The prevalence of strong ties among clientelist organizations and the information constraints they create helps account for the staying power of clientelism in democratic settings.

THE PUZZLE: CLIENTELISM AMID DEMOCRACY

At the height of the power of the PRI, independent organizations in civil society were few in number, faced a chronic shortage of resources, and struggled against repression and cooptation. Because Mexican civil society existed at the margins of the political system, scholars and analysts alike considered it to be politically inconsequential and incapable of effecting social and political change. But after decades of tight control by the PRI regime over grassroots and interest organizations such as labor unions and peasant federations, organizations in civil society became more diverse and assertive in the 1980s. Many students of Mexican politics have pointed to the 1985 earthquake and 1988 presidential campaign of Cuauhtémoc Cardenas as watershed moments in the maturation of Mexican civil society. Hundreds of grassroots associations, human rights organizations, neighborhood associations, feminist groups, environmental organizations, church groups, and independent poor people's organizations sprung up at this time. They asserted their autonomy from corporatist PRI controls and breathed life into democratic movements from below (Alonso, Azis, and Tamayo 1992; Bennett 1992; Foweraker and Craig 1990; Levy, Bruhn, and Zebadúa 2001; Ramírez Sáiz 1992).

The expansion of organizational pluralism in Mexico has continued into the 1990s. At the top end, new political parties and interest groups emerged representing more diverse interests, often challenging and sometimes replacing traditional corporatist organizations. At the grass-roots level, thousands of less formal organizations have sprung up to fill the vacuum of service provision left by the shrinking Mexican state. The late 1980s and early 1990s saw a proliferation of social movements and networks of organizations that aggressively maintained their autonomy from the state and remained outside the control of the PRI. This was especially true in rapidly growing urban areas such as Mexico City where the PRI was slow to adapt to the huge expansion of squatter settlements and lost control over territorial organizations. Though much scholarly attention has been paid to the CONAMUP movement in Mexico City, these developments were not unique to the nation's capital. Other powerful regional movements and independent organizations emerged in places like Durango (Haber 1994), Juchitán (Rubin 1997), Guadalajara (Shefner 1999, 2001), and Guerrero (Bartra 1996; Bennett 1992) that were key players in forging a democratic challenge from below to the PRI, undermining its electoral hegemony. Squatter's groups such as those I encountered in Solidaridad were part of this trend.

For optimists, the end of clientelism was near. Analysts of Mexico's political economy and of popular movements shared an insistence that the state's mechanisms of clientelistic political control were rendered ineffective due to a combination of economic crises, declining legitimacy, neoliberal reforms that reduced the size of the state, and democratic reforms that increased political competition at all levels. At the same time, the emergence of an autonomous and plural civil society in Mexico's urban centers (and in some of its rural areas) helped break the state's monopoly over organizational life and decreased poor people's dependence on a single source of essential goods and services. This was especially true when grassroots organizations were able to form broader coalitions with other groups and define their goals as national, collective, and embedded within a set of wide political rights (Shefner 2001).

Upon closer examination the picture is less rosy. Voting results indicate that the PRI continues to exert significant control over the political behavior of Mexico's poor, especially outside of Mexico City and Guadalajara. An increase in competition among political parties has give citizens more choice than ever when it comes to electing candidates for public office.[2] And yet, the majority of the poor continue to vote for the PRI.[3] Hellman in particular has pointed to the limited impact that popular movements have had on the democratization process in Mexico, in part because new movements tend to follow the logic of clientelism that has always guided the political strategies and tactics of political parties (Hellman 1994). Shefner's close reading of local politics in Guadalajara also shows that popular and even middle-class groups remain vulnerable to clientelistic control (Shefner 2001). The staying power of clientelist politics despite increasing alternatives and declining benefits of membership requires an explanation if we are to have a fuller understanding of the limits of democratic representation in Mexico.

Most theoretical writing on pluralism and organizational involvement is uniformly optimistic about the capacity of grassroots organizations to stimulate political action and enhance the voice of the poor, and so it sheds little light on our puzzle. Political scientists in particular are generally optimistic about the role of nonpolitical associations and civil society in promoting an active, democratically inclined citizenry.[4] According to these theories, membership in voluntary organizations produces positive externalities for members in several ways: it provides individuals with opportunities to acquire politically relevant skills (Verba, Schlozman, and Brady 1995); it provides opportunities for members to experiment with debate, deliberation, and compromise, providing them with an informal education and socialization into democratic practice (Pateman 1970); it builds trust and social capital (Putnam 1993); and it instills democratic attitudes and culture that combat clientelistic tendencies (Lipset 1981; Tocqueville 1961).

Social movement scholars also emphasize the importance of grassroots organizations and strong networks for collective action—although there are notable exceptions.[5] Their theories have highlighted the work that strong networks do in recruiting members, developing a collective consciousness, and mobilizing members for contentious collective action. For example, studies of the American civil rights movement by Doug McAdam, Charles Payne, and others stand out as examples of research documenting the critical role played by both formal and informal grass-roots organizations in the emergence and evolution of the American civil rights movement (McAdam 1982; Payne 1995). The strong networks within black churches and community organizations built trust and solidarity among members that allowed them to undertake difficult and dangerous tasks. They provided sites where collective identities were strengthened and where new repertoires of action—sit-ins, peaceful marches, and boycotts—were developed and deployed, energizing the movement and giving it a force it did not previously possess (see also Tarrow 1998). Research in Chile, Argentina, and Brazil has also documented the democratizing impact of movements from below, especially in stimulating what Garretón has called the "invisible transition" (Eckstein 1989; Garretón 1989; Mainwaring and Viola 1984; Oxhorn 1995; Schneider 1995).

Much of the recent scholarship of Mexico's democratic transition has been influenced by these theories largely developed on the basis of experiences in the United States and in South American countries. However, these lessons do not transfer easily to the Mexican case, where the state had an almost monopolistic control over organizational life and the transition to democracy has been gradual and largely controlled by the PRI. The strength of these approaches lies in their ability to explain much about the dynamism of Mexican civil society, but they cannot explain the rest of the picture: why the poor continue to cling to clientelist organizations.

Another strand of scholarship tackles this question more directly, attributing the political loyalty and quiescence of the poor to various forms of political irrationality, false consciousness, or hegemonic subordination (Booth and Seligson 1978).[6] Susan Stokes, for example, found a bifurcated pattern of political behavior among residents of a shantytown in Lima. While many residents overcame a history of quiescence by joining social movements that worked for deep political and social change, many remained loyal to clientelist neighborhood associations and expressed a strong preference for petitions, conciliatory tactics, and clientelistic relations with organizational leaders and the state. She explains this bifurcated nature of political activism and organizational behavior in terms of the power that hegemonic ideas have over rational behavior. That is, while protests, marches, and similar regime-challenging political acts were rational in that they were designed to achieve actors' real self-interest, clientelist practices, she argued, were cognitively and substantively irrational but were nonetheless common because of the influence that hegemonic ideologies exerted over the goals, norms, and beliefs of some actors (Stokes 1995: 117-132). These hegemonic controls needed to be broken before Lima's poor could even think of leaving clientelist relations.

This is an appealing argument for the case of Mexico since the PRI has often been described as a hegemonic party exerting ideological control over citizens, especially the poor. But this position also falls short. On the one hand, the hegemonic influence of the PRI and the state was at best incomplete and at worst nonexistent (Rubin 1997). If citizens choose to remain loyal to the PRI despite policies that appear to be contrary to their long-term interests, we should not assume that they are irrational, but look at the ways in which their choices are constrained. Most of the people with whom I spoke are shrewd political players, acting strategically to maximize their personal and community gains within the constraints of their socioeconomic and structural position. By identifying the constraints to choice that individuals face, we can understand why they make the decisions that they do and better specify the conditions under which their political behavior will change, namely when constraints are removed and new opportunities for action become available.

Granovetter's insights about the relative strength of strong and weak ties hint at two sources of opportunities and constraints: (1) the ability of organizational leaders to monitor behavior and (2) control the flow of information reaching members (Granovetter 1973). According to Granovetter, organizations based on strong ties or networks are characterized by densely knit clusters of social interaction, with many points of contact among individuals within the network but few outside of it. Sometimes, because of geographic isolation or other structural features, grassroots organizations favor strong networks out of necessity; quite often, however, leaders encourage strong ties as a way to develop loyalty to the organizations, promote group consciousness, and increase their power by isolating members. Organizations that emphasize weak ties, on the other hand, seek out links with other organizations and allow—even encourage—members to establish links across groups and strong networks. Membership in such groups may be less cohesive and more heterogeneous, making collective action more difficult to organize. But once groups mobilize, weak ties facilitate the diffusion of information and the spread of movements (Tarrow 1998).

As we will see, strong ties do not necessarily make for strong movements from below. This is because the same characteristics of dense social networks that motivate and strengthen political participation can be used by leaders to stifle or control the participation of rank and file members. We know that clientelist organizations can exert powerful control over their members because patrons have a variety of tools at their disposal with which to control their clients. These include ideological tools, the manipulation of affective ties, support from government officials, and outright repression. Most agree, however, that the root of a patron's power is the near monopolistic control over essential resources, which gives patrons the ability to coerce, cajole, and otherwise shape client's political behavior (Roniger 1990; Scott 1972). These features are all important, but the resilience of clientelism in Mexico despite eroding regime legitimacy, declining state resources, and increasing competition among potential patrons suggests that other factors are also at work. In fact, because clientelist organizations in Mexico are usually based on strong networks, patrons have two additional tools with which to manipulate the political behavior of Mexico's poor: the ability to monitor and sanction their behavior, and to filter the information to which they have access.

The following passage by Rosenstone and Hansen illustrates how the capacity of strong social networks based on strong ties of family, friendship, and community to control the dissemination of information, monitor behavior, and sanction noncompliance gives leaders within such networks enormous power to enable and constrain the political behavior of their constituents.

> Members of social networks can identify readily those who comply with social expectations and those who don't, that is, those who vote and write and attend and otherwise participate in politics and those who do not. In turn, because members of social networks can distinguish participants from pikers, they can also selectively reward the one and sanction the other. Finally, because they can reward and sanction discerningly, they can also create and enforce expectations that many will act in concert. (Rosenstone and Hansen 1993)

Though they wrote about democratic forms of political mobilization in the United States, their words might as well have been written to describe clientelistic political mobilization during the heyday of the PRI.

Filtering information is an especially powerful method of controlling behavior because it does not require coercion, it skews member's perceptions about what the available opportunities outside the organization are, all the while maintaining the legitimacy of the organization because people feel like they are making the best possible decision given known constraints. On the other hand, the particular strength of weak ties for changing participatory practices among the poor in Mexico lies in their potential for counteracting the deleterious effects of restricted information flows and expanding choice. If poor people in Mexico can gain access to information about political opportunities, alternative sources of resources, or new political repertoires, political behavior—even clientelistic behavior that has been patterned and reinforced for decades—can change very quickly.

A TALE OF TWO NETWORKS

Local politics in Mexico provides a particularly good setting in which to explore these issues. Oaxaca is among the poorest states in Mexico and patron-client relationships are still very strong, making local politics among the most restrictive and least democratic in all of Mexico. Nonetheless, political and electoral reforms begun in the early 1980s have given local governments greater fiscal autonomy and administrative responsibility, have made some local political systems more competitive and democratic, and overall have begun to transform municipalities into increasingly important arenas of political participation. In addition, Oaxaca has a history of organizational activism linked to progressive elements of the Catholic Church, and has more recently been targeted by participatory government and NGO-sponsored development projects. As a result of these conflicting pressures, democratic local governments and practices have spread unevenly across the state—much as they have across the rest of Mexico—creating a complex mix of pluralist enclaves coexisting with authoritarian strongholds and semi-democratic subnational regimes.

The rest of this chapter tells the story of two rival groups in Solidaridad—a squatter settlement on the outskirts of the city of Oaxaca, the state's capital—and the effect that these groups have had on the political activity of their members. The first group is affiliated with the PRI and controlled the neighborhood association, or *comité vecinal* between 1990 and 1996. The second organization emerged in 1996 and gained control of the *comité vecinal* after the pro-business PAN won the local mayoral elections and encouraged members to break with the PRI and establish an autonomous neighborhood association.

Solidaridad is one of approximately a dozen squatter settlements located in the hills above the colonial city of Oaxaca, on the north side of the Pan-American Highway leading out toward Mexico City. Before 1990, the hills were completely barren and unused, too steep and too dry for agriculture and too far from the center of town to be attractive as a residential site. But Oaxaca was growing very quickly as a result of immigration from rural villages and from the surrounding states of Veracruz and Puebla (INEGI 1996). Between 1960 and 1995 the city's population more than tripled to 245,000 residents, thousands of whom now live in squatters' neighborhoods that sprawl in all directions from the center of town.[7] By the 1980s, the need for affordable housing far outpaced the supply but the city government had few resources to carry out the road building and other infrastructure projects needed to make the steep hillsides amenable to human inhabitants. Political entrepreneurs and popular groups began organizing and carrying out land invasions on both public and private lands surrounding the historical center of the city. The number of squatter settlements mushroomed after 1990, tacitly encouraged by local administrations that realized that land invasions were a stopgap measure to prevent wider and more disruptive public unrest (Francisco Segura 1999).

The common image of Latin American land invasions is that they are popular movements in which landless individuals organize and actively participate in risky and challenging acts of defiance against local governments. Individuals who participate develop strong collective identities and become socialized into norms that value solidarity and exalt the value of participatory politics. But the movement that gave birth to Solidaridad and the neighboring *colonias* was not particularly participatory, nor dangerous, and did not have the effect of generating collective identities.[8] According to the founding residents of Solidaridad who participated in the initial land invasion, the movement was planned and executed in 1990 by a small group of organizers from the community of San Jacinto Amilpas, an *ejido* community with indigenous roots that claimed to have ancestral rights to the land. In exchange for a symbolic quota of $50 to $100 pesos, individuals who could demonstrate that they did not have a house of their own were given rights to a 10x20 meter plot of land, assigned to them more or less at random. Sergio described his participation in the land occupation:

> You can't really say that they sold me the land because I was invited by other people to come to San Jacinto Amilpas to request a piece of land,

because they were providing land for people who did not have their own place to live. At the time I was renting and when I went to the city hall in San Jacinto, they asked me for $50 pesos, more as a contribution than a payment. Then they told me to come here (to the *colonia*) on a specific day and time for the distribution of plots. When I got here there were hundreds of people! [The organizers] began measuring out plots of land and distributing them up high, at the top of the hill. They had a notebook with the names of people and they would measure out two, three, four lots and assign them to the next people on the list. When it was my turn I got this lot of land. It is only 9x20 meters because they had to cut part of it away to widen the road. . . . It was only later that we started to organize ourselves to solicit titles for our land and get services from the city.[9]

Many of the founding residents paid their quota only a day or two before the invasion was scheduled. Even so, only a few of the plots of land in Solidaridad were immediately occupied and many people sold off their lot immediately for profit. For others the living conditions were too difficult to bear so they gave up their rights to the land after a couple of years. At least one-third of the current residents did not participate in the original land invasion, having bought their plot of land after much of the most difficult work of opening up roads and walkways and securing some basic services had been accomplished.[10] This more or less random process of settlement created a heterogeneous community, where residents did not know each other before arriving and where collective identity formation, based on shared problems, proximity to each other, and cooperative activities was incomplete.

In the first few months following the land invasions the early settlers drew on the *tequio*, an indigenous tradition of community work and service, to organize and coordinate community improvement projects. At the same time, party activists began the process of creating formal neighborhood organizations (*comites vecinales)* by recruiting local leaders and holding neighborhood assemblies in which the leaders of the *colonias* were selected. These organizations have a similar structure across neighborhoods. The governing board consists of a president, treasurer, and secretary, in addition to several officers responsible for specific tasks or issues.[11] All officers are typically elected in general assemblies for three-year terms, although in some neighborhoods ambitious local leaders hang on to power for much longer.

The basic function of neighborhood associations is to mediate links with the local, state, and national government, petition for and coordinate public works projects, and pressure the authorities for land titles. In this sense, they act as pressure groups and the legitimacy of leaders is measured in terms of the benefits they can secure for residents. During the early years most leaders—including the leaders of Solidaridad's first neighborhood association—cultivated clientelistic ties with the PRI, which controlled local, state, and national-level government resources.[12] Though there were efforts by PRD militants to organize squatters into autonomous organizations, their efforts were largely ineffective. As a result, between 1990 and 1997 most squatters' organizations in the area functioned as de facto PRI-based committees and members' political participation became increasingly ceremonial as leaders monopolized the links and contacts with city leaders.

Neighborhood committees also serve two other important functions: coordinating *tequios* and enforcing local property rights. The president of the organization is responsible for coordinating and enforcing residents' participation in the *tequios,* the importance of which extends beyond improving living conditions in the community. In Solidaridad and other illegal settlements in Oaxaca where property rights are not covered by legal institutions, individuals hold a right over a plot of land only as long as other residents of the neighborhood recognize that claim. Contributing one's labor to the improvement of the community through *tequios* is the primary way that residents stake a socially recognized claim on their plot. As long as a social consensus exists among neighbors as to who possesses which plot, they work together to defend and enforce local property rights against rival claimants, whether they are other squatters, the state, or the original owners. If, on the other hand, a settler and his family fail to participate in *tequios* over a period of time, they lose community recognition of their claim to the plot and risk being evicted forcibly from their plot. Quite often, disputes over who "owns" a particular plot of land or over property limits are resolved in a general assembly where the community as a whole arrives at an enforceable consensus as to who possesses rights to the land. Thus, by organizing *tequios* and keeping track of residents' participation in community events, neighborhood associations have the power to enforce local property rights and settle disputes among neighbors. Given the lack of a presence of the central state, neighborhood organizations function as ad hoc local governments, taxing residents (through *tequios*), enforcing property rights, and coordinating projects to provide public goods for residents.

This discretionary power lends itself easily to abuse by ambitious and corrupt leaders who, with the support of PRI and government officials, take advantage of residents' tenuous property rights to shake them down for cash contributions and to control their political activity. The original *comité vecinal* was run much like other clientelistic, PRI base organizations. The leader was a PRIista who used his personal connections to supply goods for the community and encouraged a dense network of contacts and activities among members, including weekly *tequios*. While the leaders of the *comité vecinal* visited government offices and met with party officials on an individual basis, they made no effort to form alliances with other neighborhood groups in the area and discouraged residents from interacting with other local organizations, even if they were also affiliated with the PRI. Consequently, all links and all information coming from outside organizations and the government were mediated and filtered through a small number of leaders.

Early on settlers mobilized frequent marches to city hall and to government agencies to demand water, electricity, trash pickup, and land titles. However, in a process repeated across squatter settlements in Oaxaca, Mexico City, and other major metropolitan centers,[13] once the president of Solidaridad's neighborhood association became affiliated with the PRI, the political participation of settlers became increasingly constrained and lost its vitality. More often than not, the president made decisions without consulting residents. Protests, petitions and other pressure tactics waned, giving way to direct negotiations between neighborhood leaders and government officials. Where once rank-and-file members took active roles in the organization, their political activity became ritualized, centering on clientelistic voting and participation in civic and political rallies instead of on the local concerns that previously motivated their participation. By 1995, political participation in Solidaridad was minimal and largely symbolic, focusing on self-help modes in which residents worked together to provide the public goods that the state could not or would not provide. Contentious, autonomous political action was discouraged and rare. The social movement—to the extent that it ever existed—was exhausted and ineffective.

This situation changed dramatically in 1995 when the PRI lost the local elections and the PAN took the reins of city hall for the first time in Oaxaca's history. In 1996, the recently elected PAN municipal administration encouraged squatter neighborhoods to adopt a new organizational structure called a COMVIVE[14] in order to break patterns of clientelism that existed in most popular neighborhoods. COMVIVEs were designed to be organizations run democratically without party affiliation and with safeguards to prevent political parties from co-opting local leaders and from dominating the political activities of residents. Given this opportunity, residents of Solidaridad ousted their leaders who had run the PRI-affiliated neighborhood organization for six years and voted in an open assembly to establish a COMVIVE in their neighborhood. According to city officials with whom I spoke, the experiment had mixed results in other squatter settlements but was a huge success in Solidaridad, particularly because the newly elected leaders cut off all ties with the PRI and strongly encouraged direct resident involvement in all the important neighborhood decisions.

However, not everyone wanted to sever ties to the PRI, believing that linkages to the ruling party were still the best way to secure access to government resources. This caused a split in the neighborhood. Approximately one-third of the residents withdrew their support from the COMVIVE within a year of its formation and remained loosely linked to local PRI networks. Most of these were long-time residents who had been founders of the *colonia* and members of the original PRI-led *comité vecinal*. They mistrusted the new leadership and withheld their support because they were afraid to lose out on PRI patronage. Though they did not establish a formal organization to challenge the COMVIVE, they formed a distinct clique that maintained close ties to the PRI and pursued land titles and solutions to other pressing needs independent of the COMVIVE. This was the situation when I arrived in Solidaridad in 1998: the neighborhood was split into two cliques with virtually no communication between them. Rumormongering, mistrust, and false accusations dominated relations between the two camps. [15]

The difference in the political activity of the members of these two cliques—the COMVIVE and the PRI-based network—was glaring. Members of the PRI network abstained almost completely from community affairs. Instead, their political participation was limited to voting for the PRI and to dealing with local PRI leaders on an individual basis about individual problems, emphasizing their continued loyalty to the ruling party. They isolated themselves from the COMVIVE by not attending any neighborhood assemblies and refusing to participate in the weekly *tequio*. They also avoided participation in any projects sponsored by the city government or the COMVIVE, including the city's plan to legalize land titles, preferring instead to solicit resources and services from local PRI organizations.

While the PRI clique continued to show traits of strong ties and clientelist practices, the COMVIVE leadership encouraged openness and actively sought links and information from other neighborhood organizations, all three political parties, and with the state and local governments. Members were encouraged to initiate and carry out such contacts on their own, meaning that links to actors outside the organization were decentralized. Members of the COMVIVE participated in weekly work groups, attended and spoke at regular community assemblies, and volunteered for political actions to pressure the city and state governments for services. They voted regularly and tended to vote for either the PAN or the PRD, rejecting efforts by the PRI to recruit them with promises of patronage.

What accounts for the differences in the political strategies pursued by residents of Solidaridad? Mainstream explanations of differences in political participation are based almost exclusively on individual preferences or in the individual resource constraints they face. However, from a sociological standpoint, the members of the PRI and of the

COMVIVE group are essentially identical. All have similar migratory experiences, similar educational and income levels, and similar personal resources they can bring to bear on political activity. If anything, the members of the PRI group were among the most involved during the first six years of the neighborhood association, and so were among the most predisposed to participate in politics, and had the greatest opportunity to acquire politically relevant skills.[16] And in my interviews, members of both groups mentioned the same set of basic needs they wanted the local and state governments to address: water service and land titles. Individual preferences and individual attributes do not explain the divergence in political strategies I observed.

The answer lies instead in the difference between strong and weak networks. Studies of clientelism often emphasize the sanctioning power of patrons whose control over essential resources allows them to reward supporters and punish defectors of the clientelist bargain. The power of sanctions is no doubt important, but dwindling access to state resources makes these mechanisms of political control ineffective. In such a context of declining benefits and increasing political competition, monitoring compliance, and controlling information flows becomes critical to the survival of clientelist organizations. The following sections show how neighborhood associations used these two strategies effectively to maintain the loyalty of their members even though they were unable to distribute any goods or services to them.

MONITORING

PRI leaders of grassroots organizations go to great lengths to monitor and enforce the political behavior and loyalty of members, especially since their power and prestige within the party depend directly on their ability to mobilize their membership for key political events. In March 1999 I attended a rally in Oaxaca's main square organized by the PRI's Movimiento Territorial (Territorial Movement), a loose federation of neighborhood associations linked to the PRI. José Murat, the governor of the state of Oaxaca was scheduled to speak, so it was important for leaders of squatter organizations to demonstrate to the local PRI leadership that they were capable of mobilizing large number of residents for political events. Each neighborhood committee prominently displayed a sign with the group's name so that the governor and his entourage could see it. As the rally got underway, the moderator called out the name of each neighborhood group over the loudspeaker, and when each group was called the members of that group enthusiastically waved a small banner with the word "*Presente*," signaling to the leadership that they were present in great numbers. The PRI was in effect taking roll, and no doubt someone was writing down which groups had mobilized the largest number of followers.[17]

Leaders of Oaxaca's squatter organizations use different strategies to ensure participation in key events such as the Movimiento Territorial rally, but all of them tap into dense interrelationships to monitor member behavior. The ability of local leaders in Oaxaca to monitor participation in *tequios*, and hence over property rights in squatter communities, is one of the main ways that PRI neighborhood organizations constrain squatters' political activity. For example, Salomon, the president of Solidaridad's first neighborhood association, exempted residents who attended PRI rallies from the requirement to work the *tequio* for that week. Whether or not residents actually supported the PRI, their precarious land-tenure situation was reason enough to acquiesce to his demands to support the PRI at key rallies because his capacity to monitor participation in *tequios* made his threats and promises credible.

Strong networks like Salomon's play an even more important role in monitoring less observable behavior, such as how clients vote. The basic clientelistic contract in which political leaders exchange material resources for votes would quickly break down if patrons did not have the ability to observe how clients actually vote. Were this not the case, the poor would in principle be free to accept goods and services and then vote for whomever they pleased. The relative secrecy of the ballot is therefore important for the power balance between patrons and clients. The greater the secrecy of the ballot, or more accurately, the greater the *perception* that the vote is secret, the greater the political freedom of citizens and the more the balance of power shifts in favor of the poor.

In the past, especially in rural communities where there were no independent election observers present at any polling booth, it was almost impossible to guarantee the secrecy of the ballot.[18] During the 1990s the government implemented a series of electoral reforms aimed at protecting the secrecy of the vote. These measures included new voter identification cards with pictures, requiring all polling booths to have electoral observers from opposition parties present, and allowing citizen groups, such as *Alianza Cívica* to staff polling places with independent observers. The Federal Electoral Institute (IFE), the autonomous agency that oversees national elections, even designed new voting booths for the country's 112,500 polling stations to ensure the secrecy of the ballot.

These reforms have tipped the power balance between political parties and the poor in favor of the latter. However, clientelistic voting remains common, partly because people still have powerful affective ties to their leaders, and partly because many of the poor genuinely continue to support the PRI, but part of the answer also lies in the power of strong local networks. Even though it is objectively impossible for political parties or the government to know how individuals vote during elections, grassroots PRI organizations employ multiple strategies to create the perception among poor citizens that party leaders and the government can credibly monitor how individuals vote. Before the 1998 local elections, a local PRI group in Oaxaca distributed farm animals to anyone who gave the leaders a photocopy of their electoral identification card and signed a petition declaring that they were members of the PRI. The intention was to make people think that the PRI had their personal information and could use it to find out whether or not they had actually voted for the PRI.

These are not isolated instances. *The New York Times* reported that during the 1999 campaign to elect the governor of the state of Mexico, Mexico's most populous state, the governing party carried out a systematic campaign to collect photocopies of thousands of voters' electoral credentials.

> In some cases, the (PRI) campaign workers simply go door-to-door; some governing party workers said the party has promised them 150 pesos, about $16 (dollars), for each voting credential they copy. In other cases, teachers in primary and high schools administered by the state, whose current governor is a PRI member, have urged students to bring photocopies of their parents' electoral credentials to school. The party has also organized several giant raffles in which cars and stereos are to be given away after [the] vote; tens of thousands of tickets, bearing (Arturo) Montiel's [the PRI's candidate in the election] name and the party logo, have been distributed to state voters in exchange for copies of their voting credentials. (Dillon 1999)

Though not technically illegal, such tactics suggest to voters that the PRI has enough information to find out how they voted in the election. Given their general mistrust of the state and of politicians, the poor do not need much convincing. Approximately two-thirds of the people I interviewed believed there were ways for the PRI and the state to find out how people vote in elections. These opinions should not be dismissed as the result of some sort of false consciousness or political ignorance, especially since many of the people with whom I spoke have a high-school education and have long histories of political involvement. On the contrary, they mistrust the intentions of authorities because they know all too well what the party and state officials are capable of in order to control electoral results.[19]

INFORMATION CONSTRAINTS

These examples hint at the vital role that the manipulation of information plays in restricting the *perceived* choices Mexico's poor have for political participation and influence. In fact, the manipulation of information has been an important tactic used by the state and the PRI to preserve political stability and to enhance the regime's legitimacy. At the macro level, the state restricted political competition and the freedom of organization, thus reducing the diversity of information available to citizens. For many decades, the state was also able to control the content of the media's political coverage. Although the press has gained in freedom over the past decade and a greater number of independent sources are increasingly available, the Mexican state still exerts control over the information delivered on Mexican television.[20] This restriction on freedom of information affects the lower class the most since they receive the bulk of their news from television.[21]

This bias is reinforced at the micro level in the context of local and regional organizations affiliated with the PRI whose leaders—concerned as they are with political loyalty and delivering the vote—have strong incentives to find ways to control the information about political opportunities that filter down to rank and file members. This is easiest to accomplish within strong networks where contact with government officials and outsiders is mediated exclusively through them. This gate-keeping function often involves more than simply filtering or misinforming. The use of violence to keep rival organizers away from their "territory" and to prevent opposition parties from campaigning locally is a common tactic of community leaders to maintain the informational isolation of their constituents.[22] In short, the logic of Mexico's political system under PRI rule created powerful incentives for local leaders to encourage strong, dense ties among members and to discourage weak ties even to other PRI groups.

As a consequence, poor people's organizations in Mexico tend to be highly fragmented, with few if any horizontal ties across groups. Strong ties, while fostering local cohesion, exacerbate social fragmentation and information asymmetries that are at the root of the mistrust many of the poor have toward new leaders and new initiatives. When a new organization or political party comes on the scene, residents naturally adopt a conservative, show-me attitude, requiring new leaders to demonstrate that they are capable of delivering on the promises they make. This distrust makes the task of mobilizing people outside of PRI networks much more difficult because people discount heavily the potential gains promised by new organizations. This lack of interaction across groups, even groups nominally affiliated with the same party, breeds distrust, or *desconfianza*, makes cooperation for common goals more difficult, and contributes to the political marginalization of the poor. Though Solidaridad's leaders were not particularly repressive, for a time they did not need to be because their control over outside information kept their members dependent.

To succeed in combating clientelism and forging democratic opportunities, therefore, new organizations must not only promise material benefits, they must also find ways to establish ties to existing groups and increase the flow of information across groups. Without such bridging ties that allow members of strong networks to predict and affect the behavior of new leaders, members of strong networks are unlikely to develop trust in new leaders and will not participate in cooperative activities (Granovetter 1973: 1374).[23]

The power of strong ties in perpetuating clientelistic and apparently irrational behavior can be seen in the way Solidaridad's two networks reacted to the city's land titling program. One of the first and most important initiatives pursued by the new PAN administration was to establish a program so that people squatting on privately owned land could purchase legal titles.[24] Under the city's program, residents paid 21 pesos per square meter (about $400 dollars for an average plot of land) into an escrow account managed by a private bank. They had nine months to pay the full amount, after which time they would be given legal title to the land. Because it is a relatively small neighborhood and because the original owners of the land agreed to a settlement with the city, the initial pilot program was tested in Solidaridad.

The fact that the city, not the state government, had jurisdiction over land disputes in Solidaridad and the surrounding neighborhoods gave it the ability to drive a wedge between neighborhood associations and the PRI-controlled state government, and so encourage the defection of squatters from clientelistic organizations. With secure property rights, corrupt and authoritarian local leaders no longer have the leverage to make residents participate in community *tequios* or attend political events. As I mentioned earlier, however, out of a dozen neighborhood associations Solidaridad was the only one that signed up for the program, and even within Solidaridad, the PRI clique refused to participate. When the first deadline for participating in the program expired, less than fifteen percent of residents in Solidaridad had paid for their plot of land. After six years of putting up with bureaucratic red tape and broken promises, residents of the neighborhood were understandably skeptical and wanted evidence that this was not just another scam by local leaders. But once the city government distributed the first thirty titles to residents in Solidaridad, others gained confidence in the program and took advantage of an extension given to them by the city. Two years later, 150 of the 200 families had begun paying into the program and almost half of them had received their titles. It is revealing that most of the fifty families in Solidaridad that did not buy into the land-titling program belonged to the PRI clique.[25]

PRI-controlled neighborhood associations also refused to participate in the city's land tenure program. After two years and several extensions of city-imposed deadlines, only one other neighborhood besides Solidaridad had signed up for the program. The other ten or so leaders of neighborhood associations in the area—all affiliated with the PRI—refused to participate, withheld information about the program from residents, and even used sticks and stones to chase away delegations from the municipal government that came to the neighborhoods to talk directly with residents. The motivation of these neighborhood leaders is clear. They were holding out for a better deal from the PRI-led state government that would enhance their prestige and legitimacy with their constituents. Second, PRI leaders had little incentive to provide secure property rights to squatters since this was the main source of their leverage over residents' political participation. In a situation of electoral competition and proliferating organizations, squatters with secure property rights would be free to defect from the PRI and join rival organizations and parties free of sanctions. Thus, the incentives for authoritarian leaders to manipulate information, cultivate distrust of outsiders, and disseminate false information were strong since their ability to secure loyalty by providing patronage had diminished.

But why did settlers refuse to participate in a program that promised to grant them what they desired most, secure title to their land? The power of strong networks helps answer this question. Residents of PRI neighborhoods and of Solidaridad's PRI network were fed false information by party leaders, arguing that the land titles being distributed by the city were fake, cost too much, or that the state government would legalize the land holdings free of charge. As a result, the expectations residents formed about the best strategy to pursue were biased and inaccurate. Beginning around 1998, the local and state-level PRI organizations ran a campaign to discredit the municipality's program, suggesting to squatters that the land titles obtained through the municipal government were invalid. Instead, the PRI governor of the state proclaimed boldly at a rally that within five years he would award 10,000 squatters in the capital city legal title to their land, omitting the fact that the state government did not have jurisdiction over most of the land disputes within the city limits. As part of this campaign to misinform squatters, the president of the PRI municipal committee distributed *constancias de posesión*, or certificates of possession, free of charge to residents of several squatter settlements. Since a political party issued these certificates, they had no legal value and were designed to encourage squatters to seek legal title to their land through the state government rather than through the municipal program (Comité Directivo Municipal del PRI 1999). This confused members of the PRI clique in Solidaridad, some of whom dropped out of the municipal program believing that these certificates were actual land titles. Others began to express skepticism about the honesty of the COMVIVE leadership and of the city government, believing that they would make off with the money paid for the land. Though they wanted land titles above all else, they grew to distrust the PAN city administration and preferred to hold out for land titles granted by the PRI governor.

A focus on the different information constraints associated with strong and weak ties sheds light on the apparently irrational decision of the members of the PRI clique in Solidaridad not to participate in the city's land title program while residents affiliated with the COMVIVE joined in great numbers. On the one hand, because members of the COMVIVE group participated in weekly *tequios*, in community assemblies, in meetings with the mayor, and other joint activities organized by the COMVIVE, these residents established direct links to the new leadership and through them to the city government. These extended ties made it possible for residents to gain access to new information, become aware of new opportunities, and to trust the new administration. PRI members, on the other hand, have many ties with each other, some with other PRI neighborhood association, but almost none with their neighbors in Solidaridad. They get their information about politics and local issues from a common source (the local PRI hierarchy), they do not participate in weekly *tequios* or attend the community assemblies where decisions are taken and information is disseminated, and as a result they have few opportunities to interact with the COMVIVE or its leadership. Given their social isolation, they mistrust the COMVIVE leadership and give greater weight to the information they receive through their PRI contacts.

What appears at first glance to be irrational behavior by individuals in the PRI clique can thus be explained by the information constraints that exist within a strong network. Rather than bringing people together on behalf of emergent or contingent interests, the corporate and communal ties emphasized by PRI leaders divide citizens into insulated pockets that limit the flow of information. A lack of information about alternatives constrains the range—or perception of the range—of political strategies from which members of PRI groups can choose. They are reluctant to leave PRI organizations because they fear losing access to the scant resources they get and are uncertain about the ability of new organizations to deliver on their promises. It is not that their decisions are irrational, motivated by false consciousness or hegemonic ideologies. Rather, their decisions reflect the power of strong networks to create biased and inaccurate expectations among members about the best strategies to pursue.

This example also helps illustrate a more general point about the logic of clientelism. The poor are captured not only because of their dependence on the PRI for resources. They are also captured because of the structure of grassroots organizations that restrict information flows, monitor and punish efforts to work outside clientelist channels, and breed distrust of alternative organizations and leaders.[26] By constraining members' choice in these ways, strong networks help make clientelistic arrangements self-enforcing even when the benefits individuals receive from them are decreasing.

CONCLUSION

The case of Solidaridad parallels developments across Mexico, where clientelist politics stubbornly endure despite important changes in the links between the state and its citizens. If correct, my explanation should shed light on the enduring nature of clientelistic politics in Mexico despite important democratic and neoliberal reforms. First, the preceding analysis implies that pluralism, if pluralism means the spread of strong and tightly knit networks, will not necessarily enhance the participatory options of the poor in Mexico. Rather, the transformative capacity of grassroots organizations hinges on their ability to create extensive "weak ties" that bridge across strong clientelistic networks, allowing resources and information to flow more freely. Second, participation in extensive networks such as coalitions among squatter's groups, and/or links with human rights organizations or new political parties, allow the poor to tap into multiple sources of information about resources, repertoires, and political opportunities. Therefore, weak ties can play a potentially subversive role by counteracting the deleterious effects of restricted information flows, opening up choice, and spreading new models of collective action.

Third, my analysis suggests that the more sporadic government patronage becomes, the more the poor will cling to clientelistic networks in hopes that their loyalty will be rewarded with privileged access to declining state resources and benefits. In communities like Solidaridad, strongly tied residents tend to remain in clientelist organizations and continue to support the PRI in elections even as the benefits approach zero because their choice of organizations is constrained and information about new political opportunities is filtered. This explains the paradox of why the poor continue to support a political party that has failed to deliver benefits over the past two decades, namely that strong PRI networks at the grass-roots level control the information of what political opportunities are available to the poor. This effect is reinforced by a macro environment that still excludes the poor from the policy-making process.

The power of weak ties to overcome these constraints does not necessarily lie in their ability to make more resources available (though they may). Rather, their power derives from giving members more access to information about other opportunities and repertoires for action, alternative resources, and new political openings. This information reduces poor people's vulnerability to the sanctions of local leaders. In places like Oaxaca, where the PRI still controls most political, social, and media institutions, weak networks undermine information constraints, facilitate cooperation across groups, and diffuse information about political opportunities and repertoires to new publics. Whether poor individuals actually become more involved in politics is not certain, and actual political participation may not increase in all cases; but unlike before, the poor have the option to do so if they choose.

NOTES

1. *Tequios* are a traditional form of community service in Oaxaca with deep roots in indigenous culture. In Solidaridad, *tequios* usually focused on community improvement projects, such as building walkways and sidewalks and maintaining water tanks and the hoses that distribute water to houses, although on occasion residents would work together to repair the homes of needy residents. For more on the practice of *tequio* in indigenous communities see Aguirre Beltrán 1991; López Barcenas 1998; Nahmad Sittón 1994; Ríos M. 1994; Stephen 1991.

2. I should emphasize that the situation in local and congressional elections varies significantly across regions in Mexico. The PAN has electoral strongholds in the north and in major urban areas, but outside of these regions it has trouble recruiting candidates and mobilizing supporters. Similarly, outside its strongholds in Mexico City, Michoacán, Guerrero, and some regions of Oaxaca and Veracruz, the PRD has little electoral support and often is unable to run credible candidates for public office. The PRI still has greater organizational resources and is the only party in Mexico that truly has national penetration. The result is that many local elections are less competitive than they appear because of the local organizational weakness of the opposition parties.

3. The PRI is still able to exert significant political control over lower-class voters, who continue to supply most of the PRI's electoral support despite declining benefits and macroeconomic policies that threaten their economic survival. In the year 2000, the national daily *Reforma* published a series of articles analyzing the relationship between poverty levels and political support for the country's three major parties. The analysis showed that in 1997 the PRI candidates won congressional elections in 95 percent of the poorest electoral districts (80/84 districts) while only managing to win 37 percent (70/191) of congressional elections in districts with low socioeconomic marginality scores. Overall, PRI candidates received 55 percent of the vote in poor rural districts, compared with PRD candidates who received 26 percent and PAN candidates only 13 percent. By contrast, PRI candidates received only 31 percent of the vote in urban districts (Tuirán 2000). Moreover, in congressional elections of July 2003 the PRI once again emerged as the largest party in Congress.

4. For examples of more balanced case studies of the impact of organizations on political activism, see Cook 1996, Fox 1996, Levine 1992, and Oxhorn 1994.

5. Michels Iron Law of Oligarchy made the classic critique of organizations as vehicles for the political empowerment of the lower class (Michels 1962). Piven and Cloward have also argued that organizations can stifle mobilization and activism of lower class groups (Piven and Cloward 1979).

6. The sources of supposed political irrationality included lack of understanding of their political role, lack of political sophistication, cultural norms that emphasize deference to authority, parochialism, paternalism, machismo, authoritarianism, and a preference for personal ties. See Booth and Seligson (1978), especially pp. 13-16.

7. The actual population may be considerably higher since INEGI counts do not include many of the newer squatter settlements. According to city officials with whom I spoke, squatter neighborhoods in the *agencia* (akin to a city ward) of Santa Rosa Panzacola, where Solidaridad is located, may have as many as 30,000 residents who were not included in the last official census.

8. Despite the prevailing image of land invasions, Solidaridad's experience is probably much closer to the norm. See also Gutmann 2002 and Vélez-Ibañez 1983.

9. Though there were some reports of profiteering and hoarding of plots by leaders, which they later sold at a profit or gave to family members, the process seems to have been well organized, efficient, peaceful, and with little corruption.

10. This is an ongoing point of contention that divides current residents of Solidaridad. Founders of the *colonia* feel like they have a stronger claim over their land, since it was through their work and activism that the *colonia* was created. Their claim of ownership on the land is based on the work they put in to improve their plots and the community as a whole, while newer residents' claims are strictly monetary.

11. In Solidaridad, for example, the board of the neighborhood committee included officers in charge of

public works, legalization of land titles, public safety, arts and culture, ecology, and water supply.

12. Before 1995 the PRI had never lost a local election in the city of Oaxaca, ruling uninterrupted for six decades. As recently as 1992 it won local elections with more than 60 percent of the votes cast.

13. For additional studies of political activity and clientelism in poor neighborhoods in several Mexican cities, see Cornelius 1975, Eckstein 1977, Vélez-Ibañez 1983. Stokes (1995) and Dietz (1998) describe similar processes of incorporation of squatter groups in Lima, Peru, and provide an interesting comparison to the Mexican case.

14. COMVIVE is the acronym for Comité de Vida Vecinal, or Committee for Neighborhood Life.

15. PRI-leaders of many nearby popular *colonias* were able to block COMVIVES altogether, eschewing ties to the local administration and maintaining their corporatist linkages to local and state PRI organizations. This created a complex and sometimes tense environment in which participatory practices and political loyalties varied considerably across squatter neighborhoods. It exemplifies at a very local level the uneven spread of democratic practices and institutions throughout Mexico.

16. Many of the residents who remained attached to the PRI networks after the establishment of the COMVIVE were founding members of the *colonia* and had participated from the beginning in community improvement activities that required a significant degree of cooperation with their neighbors. As original settlers, many of them were directly involved in the affairs of the first neighborhood committee, before and after its leaders linked up to the local PRI organization. While this certainly created an identification with the PRI and predisposed them to maintain their links to the local PRI network, it does not explain why their political participation dropped off dramatically while the political activity of their neighbors who joined the COMVIVE increased.

17. The monitoring continues at the organizational level. Before leaving for the rally, the leaders of each organization make a list of all the individuals that attended. Members of PRI groups told me that during all-day events the leaders take roll almost every hour to make sure that "we do not leave in the middle of the demonstration to do our shopping or take care of other errands."

18. Doubts about the secrecy of the ballot in rural areas persist to this day. On the basis of reports from hundreds of electoral observers, Cazés concludes that violations of the secrecy of the ballot were among the most common electoral irregularities that occurred during the 1994 presidential elections (Cazés 1996).

19. Ironically, several respondents told me that they believed the technological innovations and new security features included in the new electoral identification card make it *easier* for the government to monitor people's vote.

20. This was true at least until the PRI lost the 2000 presidential elections to the PAN. See Levy and Bruhn (2001: 121).

21. See William Orme's *Culture of Collusion* for an insider's perspective on press freedoms in Mexico (Orme 1997).

22. In rural communities where illiteracy rates are very high, transportation infrastructures inadequate, and where the state is often willfully absent, local leaders are often the sole mediators between the community and outsiders (Bartra 1975). Nonetheless, such tight control over information was also common in urban areas. For example, delegations of city officials visiting squatter neighborhoods in Oaxaca to inform residents about the city's program to legalize land titles were chased away from two neighborhoods above Solidaridad by a stone-throwing mob linked to the local PRI neighborhood association (see also Cornelius 1975, Eckstein 1977, Vélez-Ibañez 1983).

23. In a recent article, Shefner (2001) demonstrates effectively how coalition work and alliances with outside organizations enabled community organizations in Guadalajara to combat clientelism by fighting the isolation that clientelism imposes on the poor.

24. Municipal governments only have jurisdiction over land disputes within municipal boundaries and where disputes involve privately owned land. If disputes are outside city limits or involve communal or *ejido* lands, then the state and federal governments must settle land disputes and award new land titles.

25. As of August 2004 these families were still holding out.

26. Sidney Tarrow (1998) described similar effects of strong ties in eighteenth-century Europe.

Chapter 6

CLAIM NETWORK ANALYSIS: HOW ARE SOCIAL PROTESTS TRANSFORMED INTO POLITICAL PROTESTS IN MEXICO?

Takeshi Wada

Contentious politics is central to citizenship and democratization (McAdam, Tarrow, and Tilly 2001). Citizenship, as mutually binding arrangements between state agents and the population, is constantly changing and contested (Tilly 2003a). State agents and social groups assert their preferred vision of citizenship—what constitutes rights and obligations and who are entitled to them—sometimes successfully, sometimes not. Thus, the current state of citizenship in any given country is a historical outcome of contentious claims making by citizens upon the state and the state's responses. These struggles for rights are part of the political process in established democratic states. In countries where democratic processes are emerging, these struggles are often frequent and intense. Therefore, studying the relationship between citizenship and popular contention is essential to understanding democratization processes.

There is, of course, a huge literature on popular contention and social movements. There is also a large literature on citizenship rights. However, as Foweraker and Landman (1997: 45) observe, these two bodies of research "do not usually 'talk to each other.'" A key premise of this chapter is that the cultural analyses of social movements—specifically frame and discourse analyses—can provide researchers with useful theoretical tools to link these two literatures. Cultural analyses suggest that widely shared beliefs and cultural understandings, or "master frames," have an important influence on the ways people make claims. I apply this insight to the authoritarian context of Mexico. Frame analysis, and in particular Noonan's (1995) idea of "cultural opportunities," have potential to explain claim-making activities under repressive political systems where political opportunity theories would predict few protest activities. In Mexico until the 1982 economic crisis, the relationship between the state and the population was characterized by durable institutional arrangements and cultural understandings that prioritized social and collective rights. If such broad cultural understandings or master frames had served as cultural opportunities for protest, there would have been a number of public protests even under the authoritarian regime, many of which must have framed their demands in terms of social and collective rights. In this chapter, I will examine this hypothesis empirically.

Mexico is a fascinating case for a study of citizenship and popular contention because neoliberal economic reforms in the 1980s triggered important disputes over the definition of citizenship. During this time, neoliberal technocrats and the private capital broke the traditional arrangements and understandings and tried to undo social and collective rights. This is an interesting moment because neither political opportunity theory nor cultural opportunity approaches give clear predictions of what kind of citizenship claims would prevail. While political opportunity remained closed for the most part, cultural opportunity based on the once dominant master frame of social and collective rights that predominated since the Mexican Revolution was disappearing. Were popular groups able to counter the neoliberal challenge? If they were, what alternative vision of citizenship did they assert?

Another way of posing these questions is through the lens of Sergio Tamayo's research (1999). By analyzing underground press and leftist party documents, he found a shift from social protests to political protests—a transformation of popular struggles from ones demanding social rights to struggles demanding civil and political rights in addition to social rights. The relevant questions then become why and how did claims for political and civil rights become prevalent, and what explains such a dramatic change in the patterns of claim making?

In this chapter, I employ a quantitative approach—protest-event analysis—to find answers to these questions. As Foweraker and Landman observe, "In the contemporary context, enquiries into collective action and citizenship are mainly confined to historical sociology and political theory, and their empirical base is at best a qualitative comparative history" (Foweraker and Landman 1997: 45). I intend to fill this gap by applying protest-event analysis to questions of culture, and make a quantitative contribution to the literature of cultural analysis of social movements where qualitative approaches are the norm.

I devise a method that allows me to differentiate between goal-oriented claims and strategic (means-oriented) claims. Goal-oriented claims convey the reasons *why* people engage in collective action. Strategic claims inform the ways *how* people try to accomplish their goals. I then trace whether Mexicans have made different kinds of claims (civil rights, political rights, social rights, material demands, etc.) in a goal-oriented manner or in a means-oriented manner. I discover that political rights—crucial claims for democratization—have become prominent not by supplanting previously dominant material demands and social rights claims as the principal goal-oriented claims. Rather, the real importance of political rights lies in the fact that protesters are more likely to make political claims *strategically* even when their main goal is civil rights, social rights, or other issues. In Mexico, citizens have come to identify their political representatives as the source of their problems during the neoliberal period. This finding advances our understanding of democratization: durable and powerful democratic movements like the one in Mexico will emerge when they are closely—i.e., strategically—tied to people's everyday economic and material concerns.

THEORY AND METHODOLOGY OF CLAIM ANALYSIS

Political opportunity theory explains the emergence, development, and outcome of collective action by the openness of political system. This influential theory, however, does not serve our purposes here because it is not sensitive to the actual content of claims. Favorable political opportunities will be conducive to protest activities making *any kind of claims*. Unfavorable political opportunities will likely shut down all sorts of claim makings. In this regard, frame and discourse analyses, which have enriched social movement studies by incorporating cultural and ideational factors (Gamson 1992; Johnston and Klandermans 1995; McAdam, McCarthy, and Zald 1996; Morris and Mueller 1992), give us more useful conceptual tools.

According to cultural framing theory, claim makers attempt to construct collective action frames that let people understand their circumstances, identify sources of their problems and discontents, and find strategies to address their problems (Snow, Rochford, Worden, and Benford 1986). These framing efforts are more likely to succeed when the collective action frames resonate with widespread ideas and visions, popular beliefs about justice and injustice, and systematic ideologies composed of cognitive images and moral evaluations (Oberschall 1996: 97; Snow and Benford 1988). Claims resonant with existing cultural schemata, or what Snow and Benford call master frames (1992), would legitimate and motivate collective action, mobilize potential adherents and constituents, garner bystander support, and demobilize antagonists. An implication is that researchers should be able to predict, to a certain degree, what kinds of claim will prevail by looking at a broader cultural scheme.

My research applies these ideas to a study of popular protests in an authoritarian context. While the cultural framing theory has been used mostly to account for contentious episodes in Western democracies, cultural framing can be more crucial in the authoritarian context of developing countries. In her study of women's movements in Chile, Rita Noonan finds that women were able to protest even under the military regime because only women were able to take advantage of the conservative ideology of traditional womanhood espoused by Pinochet himself (Noonan 1995). Broad cultural schemata and master frames may provide cultural opportunities by legitimizing—and thus protecting—certain types of claim. I will examine whether or not Mexican citizens were able to exploit such cultural opportunities in the face of unfavorable political opportunities.

Frame and discourse analyses commonly utilize qualitative approaches to textual data. In reviewing the literature, Hank Johnston finds that labor-intensive qualitative strategies tend to constrain research to case studies and preclude systematic examination of patterns over time and how they may vary according to other influences (Johnston 2002). To overcome this limitation, this study employs a quantitative event analysis, a popular method that has been used to examine a large number of popular contentions over a long period.

Studies using event analysis (Kriesi, Koopmans, Duyvendak, and Giugni 1995; Tarrow 1989) are typically guided by the political opportunity thesis and seek to relate the level of protest mobilization to shifting opportunities. It is surprising to find that event analysis of claim making has paid scant attention to the content of claims—that is, the reasons why people are protesting at all (Koopmans and Statham 1999: 216). It is as if the analysis of claims themselves is conceded to qualitative, political-discourse methods (Donati 1992). Thus, while there are plenty of event analyses of claim *making*, there are few serious analyses of *claim* making. Reasons for this may be that scholars perceive claims reported in newspapers as unreliable "soft news" biased by journalists' impressions. This assumption would preclude expending much effort to study an "unreliable" variable. Also, claim analysis is, simply stated, extremely difficult to study systematically. Expressions of claims are so rich and complex that they pose event researchers difficult problems such as how to code and quantify.

This study intends to elaborate and extend event analysis by applying its strengths to the discursive side of claim making. In so doing, it seeks to go beyond the artificial divide between studies of protest events addressing political opportunity issues and studies of political discourse addressing cultural framing issues.

NEOLIBERAL REFORMS AND VISIONS OF CITIZENSHIP IN MEXICO

The Mexican authoritarian state claimed as its historical legacy the Mexican Revolution of 1910, and legitimated itself according to the diverse political ideas derived from that bloody national upheaval. Among these ideas was so-called "revolutionary nationalism"—a fusion of assertions of national sovereignty and social justice—which played a crucial role in the popular identification with the regime. As a result, the ruling elite was more tolerant of demands focused on social aspects of citizenship than ones embracing civil and political aspects. True, Mexican social rights were often provided in a discretionary and paternalistic manner. The clientelist exchanges of material benefits and political support undermined political rights. Still, a broad sector of the population was able to expect a wide range of benefits including labor protection, land reform, government subsidies, public education, health services, urban infrastructure, and so on. In brief, the socioeconomic rights were conceived as legitimate claims in line with the revolutionary goals of social justice, and such broad cultural understandings consisted the master frame under the authoritarian regime.

Facing the debt crisis in the 1980s, the big business and the technocratic elites abandoned the import-substitution-industrialization model of economic development and, instead, sought solutions for the crisis in Mexico's economic integration into global markets. The "remaking of the economy" (Lustig 1992) was accompanied by a dramatic change in the prevalent vision of citizenship. The neoliberal vision was incompatible with the post-revolutionary citizenship arrangements that had placed emphasis on social and collective citizenship rights. The neoliberal elites attempted to restrict collective social rights while they protected individual civil rights, property rights in particular. When the elites made neoliberal claims and tried to withdraw traditional, post-revolutionary commitments to collective and social rights, the Mexican population responded to the breach. What kind of citizenship claims did they make when the once dominant master frame was no longer shared widely?

Sergio Tamayo's study of citizenship discourse from 1970 to 1994 (Tamayo 1999) gives us important insights into this question. Using a qualitative political discourse approach, he examines how political elites, economic elites, and social movements understood citizenship rights and tried to bring their visions into practice.[1] He uses presidential speeches, publications by business associations and the conservative National Action Party, and publications by left-wing parties, activists, and movements.[2] Though a brief summary will not do justice to his careful examination of a multiplicity of discourses, I will report his core findings on social movements' visions.

Tamayo presents table 6.1 as he summarizes his main findings. While economic elites were consistent in their vision of citizenship emphasizing individual civil and

	Vision and hierarchy of citizenship rights by actors	
Actors	1970-1982	1982-1994
Political elites	*Social*[b] Political - Civil	*Civil - Social* Political
Economic elites	*Civil - Political* Social	*Civil - Political* Social
Social movements	*Social* Civil - Political	*Social - Civil - Political*

[a] Adapted and translated from Tamayo (1999: 43)
[b] Italicized rights are given predominance.

Table 6.1. Actors' Changing Priorities of Citizenship Rights (1970-1994) from Sergio Tamayo's Political Discourse Analysis[a]

political rights, political elites sought to redefine citizenship in ways that would strengthen their control under changing circumstances. By comparing speeches given by different presidents, Tamayo finds a clear shift in the priority of citizenship rights from collective social rights to individual civil rights (private property, freedom of expression, and liberty of religious practices) in the age of neoliberalism.

Although Tamayo found that social movements' ideas of citizenship were not uniform, he was able to identify common tendencies. Until 1982, their main demands were mostly about social and labor rights obtained decades ago. These rights included land, credits, education, social security, and better salaries among others. Demands for the political rights were often derivative of social rights. Since union bureaucracy was seen as an obstacle to successful defense of social rights, political demands often took the form of a quest for union democracy and autonomy (Tamayo 1999: 268).

Economic crisis and neoliberal economic reforms changed this priority. Just when everyday economic hardships made the social rights even more valuable, the neoliberal elites were undoing social programs. People began to perceive a clear link between social and political issues. According to Tamayo, these processes led Mexicans to give social, civil, and political rights equal importance (Tamayo 1999: 44-45). The distinction between the individual rights (civil and political) and the collective rights (social) blurred. Social movements began to articulate these rights in their discourses.

Tamayo's analysis tells us a good deal about shifting emphases in citizenship claims by different actors. It is noteworthy that his findings are in agreement with Noonan's (1995) findings: (1) Cultural understandings could provide opportunities for protest even in the absence of political opportunities; and (2) the weakening of the once dominant master frame may open up ideological and political spaces that may lead to the creation of a new master frame (i.e., the rise of civil and political rights in this case). A major limitation is that, without quantitative measures, it is not possible from his description to verify his key assertions that Mexicans came to view the social, civil, and political rights with the same level of importance and that peoples' perception of a link between social and political issues lies behind such a shift. I will overcome this weakness by adopting a quantitative approach.

METHODS

This study employs protest-event analysis of newspaper data. I have gathered massive evidence on popular protests in Mexico from two contrasting sets of national newspapers, *Excélsior* on the one hand, and *Unomásuno* and *La Jornada* on the other. While *Excélsior* has assumed a political stance close to the elites, *Unomásuno* and *La Jornada* have taken an ideological stance sympathetic to the oppositions. In the discussion section, I will address how the problem of media freedom in Mexico may have influenced my findings.

I chose the issues published during the 29-day span around major election days (an election day plus two weeks before and after the election) from 1964 to 2000 as the sample.[3] A "major election" includes presidential elections (every six years) as well as mid-term elections for federal deputies and senators, both of which are scheduled on the first Sunday of July. I opted for this sample because the political opportunities around major elections are comparable. Before 1988, when presidential candidates from the official party, Institutional Revolutionary Party (PRI) won elections overwhelmingly, political conditions around election day would have been characterized by increased mobilizations, but would not have been tense or conflictful. A politically more crucial moment was when a president designated his successor—the PRI candidate—in the year prior to the election. However, as the presidential elections became more competitive among different political parties, it is arguable that political conditions around the election period would become marked by more claims making, a greater variety of mobilizations, and would be more tense and conflictful. The same can be said for the mid-term elections for federal deputies and senators. Examining protest patterns around these critical moments will be one of the intriguing ways to detect historical changes in Mexico's political system.

I searched the newspaper issues for protest events that included a disruptive public collective action. "A disruptive public collective action" is defined as an action that (1) was carried out by *collective actors* or a number of people (here, a minimum of ten) outside the government; (2) was undertaken in a *publicly* accessible place; (3) involved a *target*, or at least one person outside the protestors' own number who was the object of action; (4) involved *claims*, which if realized would affect the interests of the target; and (5) used *disruption* as a means to make the claims. This includes both nonviolent and violent protests such as public meetings, parades, marches, rallies, land invasions, property occupations, strikes, and lynchings, among others.

I employed the "Subject-Verb-Object (SVO) Triplet" scheme to extract the information from the articles. This approach is a product of recent methodological innovation in the field of event data analysis (Franzosi 1998, 2004; Shapiro and Markoff 1998; Tilly 1995). Franzosi exploits the fact that most news articles on protests are written in a simple grammatical structure, namely, Subject-Verb-Object (SVO) and their modifiers (Franzosi 1998). Subject identifies the actors who take an action, Verb the action, and Object the target of the action by the Subject. Modifiers give additional information on each SVO (e.g., time, location, or goal of an action represented by the Verb). In the database, I organized the basic elements of protest— "Who (subject) did what (action) to whom (object), why (claim), where (location), and when (time)?" This chapter focuses exclusively on the why element, the claims made in protests.

Episodes of protests were recorded at three spatial and temporal levels in the database: action, event, and campaign. Action is the smallest level and is equivalent to the SVO Triplet. Event is composed of a series of actions. When a group of individuals engage in one disruptive public collective action and this same group starts another disruptive public collective action in a continuous manner, these two actions (or two

SVO Triplets) are coded under the same event. Every event includes at least one action. Campaign, the largest level, and the primary unit of analysis in this study, is needed because events are not always independent of each other. Two or more events may be carried out for the same purpose, by the same actors, and/or against the same target. A campaign consists of a series of these related events. Two events belong to a campaign when they meet the following two conditions. First, two events should be coordinated beyond time and/or location by one or more actors. Second, two events should share principal goals or demands *in concrete terms*. For example, a demand for, say, "democratization of the electoral system" is too abstract to allow for the grouping of two events together. But, a demand for, for instance, "the resignation of the mayor of Oaxaca City for his electoral fraud" is concrete enough to classify two events claiming this goal as belonging to the same campaign. The analysis in this study will be done at the campaign level in order to keep "big" protests from determining trends in my data. If a 29-day sample span happens to include a few campaigns with many events, and if the analysis were done at the level of event, these campaigns would affect or even dominate the overall outcomes and our interpretations of the outcomes. The total number of protest campaigns is 638 in the Excélsior data set and 536 in the opposition press data set.

Concrete expressions of claims recorded in the database are aggregated into five abstract categories, which I call "claim spheres." These are civil conditions (civil rights), socioeconomic conditions (social rights), economic participation (economic demands), political participation (political rights), and social participation. It should be noted that socioeconomic conditions, not social participation, correspond to social rights. "Social participation" embraces claims about the ways by which important decisions are made in social organizations and institutions such as companies, unions, schools, civic associations, churches, social movement organizations, parties, etc. To put it differently, a social participation claim is related to democratization of social organizations and institutions. "Economic participation" is about claims related to participation in markets, that is, economic activities made by producers, workers, distributors, service providers, and consumers among others. Throughout the chapter, I will refer to these five claim categories by the terms "civil sphere," "socioeconomic sphere," "economic sphere," "political sphere," and "social sphere."

Finally, I divide the entire time frame of the study (1964-2000) into three periods: post-revolutionary (1964-1982), neoliberal transition (1983-1994), and neoliberal consolidation (1995-2000). The Tamayo study regarded 1982 as the key symbolic year dividing the post-revolutionary and neoliberal periods. The neoliberal period is further divided into two. The first is a period of transition toward the neoliberal regime under the strong initiative by two presidents, Miguel de la Madrid (1982-1988) and Carlos Salinas (1988-1994). When the neoliberal consolidation period began in 1995 with new president Ernest Zedillo (1994-2000), the neoliberal economic reforms had been more or less institutionalized.

RESULTS

Table 6.2 shows the relative frequencies of claims. The results are consistent with Tamayo's findings. During the post-revolutionary period, economic and socioeconomic (i.e., social rights) claims outnumbered other claims in both *Excélsior* (48 percent and 37 percent respectively) and the opposition press (46 percent and 37 percent). This supports framing theory's prediction that popular groups would likely

Newspaper	Excelsior			The Opposition Press		
Period	post-revolutionary (1964-1982)	neoliberal transition (1983-1994)	neoliberal consolidation (1995-2000)	post-revolutionary (1979-1982)	neoliberal transition (1983-1994)	neoliberal consolidation (1995-2000)
Claim Sphere						
Civil	21%	34%	30%	29%	35%	46%
Socioeconomic	37%	49%	51%	37%	42%	31%
Economic	48%	42%	38%	46%	41%	42%
Political	23%	30%	34%	28%	38%	42%
Social	19%	12%	17%	18%	14%	15%
Average campaign N per 29-day span	29	73	73	49	67	85
N	201	292	145	98	269	169

Table 6.2. Changing Claim Sphere Prevalence in Non-Electoral Protest Campaigns, 1964-2000

demand the social rights and material demands that resonated with the master frames. Citizens were reluctant to challenge the exclusionary political system as long as the regime appeared committed to the social aspects of citizenship. Civil and political claims increased their share considerably from around 20 percent to over 30 percent after 1982 according to *Excélsior* and from less than 30 percent to around 40 percent according to the opposition press. Social participation claims remained stable at a low level (less than 20 percent) for the entire period.

In talking about the changes, it is important to distinguish absolute and relative frequencies. While the *relative* frequency of economic claims in *Excélsior* has declined from 48 percent during the first period to 42 percent during the second period, the claims' *absolute* frequency has more than doubled from 13.9 protest campaigns per 29-day span (29 times 48 percent) to 30.6 campaigns (73 times 42 percent) respectively. The ability to make a distinction between these two figures is one of the advantages of the event analysis. It allows us to make subtle observations such as, "While economic claims had multiplied in absolute numbers, their prevalence in relative terms had actually declined during the neoliberal period."

Another reminder is that the table excludes protest campaigns whose main claims are related to electoral processes. These "electoral protest campaigns" are not included in this analysis because, otherwise, the sampling design—gathering data for a 29-day span around federal elections—would have overrepresented this kind of political claims. A series of massive post-electoral protests by the opposition parties after 1982 made Tamayo believe that the political citizenship rights had become a major agenda for social movements. My results are surprising because the number of the claims in the political sphere had expanded in both absolute and relative terms during the neoliberal periods *even after excluding the electoral protests*.

These basic findings are the same across newspapers regardless of political orientation. A major difference between them is that the establishment press deemphasized political aspects of protests and emphasized socioeconomic claims (social rights) compared with the opposition press. In other words, the opposition press was more politicized than the establishment press.

Claim Network Analysis: Standardized Degree Centrality (SDC)

Tamayo's political discourse analysis hinted at an important phenomenon by which political citizenship became a major claim in popular contention: Mexicans began to assert political claims even under the authoritarian context because they identified the political elites as those responsible for taking citizens' social and collective rights away. In this section and the next, I describe the method I devised to analyze this shift using my quantitative data.

To do this, it is necessary to distinguish whether a claim is expressed as an ultimate goal (ends) or as a strategic necessity (means). Let's call the first a goal-oriented claim and the second a strategic (means-oriented) claim. Goal-oriented claims convey the reasons *why* people engage in protests. Strategic claims inform the ways *how* people try to accomplish protest goals. I argue that it is possible to distinguish the two types of claims by using standardized degree centrality (SDC) statistics.

The analyses so far have treated claims as if they were independent of each other. They are not. The sum of the percentages far exceeds 100%, which indicates considerable overlaps among claim spheres. This means that citizens frequently make more than one claim at a time. This is not a surprise. For instance, so-called "democratic" social movements often address issues such as sustainable environment, gender equality, material well-being, union democracy, etc. in addition to democratization of the state institution. When two or more claims are made in the same protest campaign, I say that the claims are "linked" by the campaign. Campaigns with a single claim yield no linkage. Research designs that permit only one claim entry per campaign fail to detect linkages.[4] This research project has kept the information about linkages among claims and examines an issue that is rarely explored in protest-event analysis, that is, linkages among claims.

I borrow techniques from social network analysis to study claim linkages. I use the five claim spheres as unit (nodes) and create a five-by-five matrix that shows the number of protest campaigns that are "shared" by the row and column claim spheres. I call this matrix a "claim network." Once the matrix is created, centrality statistics can be calculated to measure the importance, power, or popularity of actors (nodes). The simplest definition of centrality is that "central actors must be the most active in the sense that they have the most ties to other actors in the network or graph" (Wasserman and Faust 1994: 178). This centrality statistic is called "degree centrality." An actor's degree centrality is obtained by counting the number of ties it has. In a network of five actors (nodes), the maximum degree centrality is four, and the minimum zero.

There is a technical problem, however. The degree centrality is meaningful for a binary graph (meaning a tie is measured dichotomously, whether it exists or not) but less so for a valued graph (meaning a tie is measured in a continuous scale). A claim network is a valued graph. The strength of the ties between spheres is measured by the number of shared campaigns. To make things more complicated, the total number of campaigns of each claim sphere affects its degree centrality. The higher the total campaign number of a claim sphere is, the higher the degree centrality of this sphere is likely to be. This property of the claim network leads to undesirable results as follows.

The civil and socioeconomic spheres have the same degree centrality score of 38 during the post-revolutionary period, according to *Unomásuno*. This means that the civil sphere shared campaigns thirty-eight times with the other four spheres, as did the socioeconomic sphere. Total campaign numbers of the civil and socioeconomic spheres are 28 and 36 respectively. Obviously, the civil sphere was linked to the other claim spheres more intensively than the socioeconomic sphere was because the former attained the score of 38 with a smaller number of campaigns. In order to make the degree centrality comparable across spheres and periods, I standardize it by dividing total campaign number of respective claim sphere. The "standardized degree centrality

Newspaper	Excelsior			The Opposition Press		
Period	post-revolutionary (1964-1982)	neoliberal transition (1983-1994)	neoliberal consolidation (1995-2000)	post-revolutionary (1979-1982)	neoliberal transition (1983-1994)	neoliberal consolidation (1995-2000)
Claim Sphere						
Civil	1.4	1.3	1.1	1.4	1.2	1.1
Socioeconomic	0.8	1.0	1.1	1.1	1.0	1.1
Economic	0.7	1.0	1.0	0.7	0.9	1.0
Political	1.5	1.6	1.5	1.5	1.4	1.4
Social	1.2	1.8	1.6	1.1	1.4	1.8

Table 6.3. Standardized Degree Centrality Statistics in Non-Electoral Protest Campaigns, 1964-2000

(SDC)" for the civil sphere is 1.4 (38/28) and for the socioeconomic sphere 1.1 (38/36). This standardization has a desired property. Like the degree centrality statistic for a binary graph, the maximum SDC is four, and the minimum zero.

Table 6.3 compares the SDC statistics for the five claim spheres. What does this table reveal? The nodes are not actors but claims. Rather than making a conventional interpretation of centrality statistics as a measure of importance, power, or popularity, I use them as a way to figure out whether a claim is expressed as an ultimate goal (ends) or as a strategic necessity (means). A low SDC indicates that claims in this sphere are often asserted alone. Such claims are likely to be the main goals and principal reasons that impel people toward collective action. In contrast, a high SDC implies that claims in this sphere are often made along with claims in the other spheres. The appearance of these claims is more dependent on the existence of the other claims. Popular groups make multiple claims simultaneously often because, in order to fulfill their main goals, they need to address other issues or obstacles.

A consistent pattern is found across the two sets of newspapers. The civil, political, and social spheres tend to have high SDC scores while the economic and socioeconomic spheres mostly have low scores. Look at the *Excélsior*'s first period. The SDC scores for the civil, political, and social spheres are 1.4, 1.5, and 1.2 respectively. In contrast, the scores for the socioeconomic and economic spheres are .8 and .7. Each claim in the political sphere shares a campaign with an average of 1.5 claims belonging to other claim spheres, while the claims in the economic sphere share a campaign with only an average of .7 claims in the other spheres. In Mexico, material demands (economic and socioeconomic) were likely to be goal-oriented claims while civil, political, and social participation claims tended to be employed strategically.[5]

In addition to the overall tendencies, table 6.3 shows three crucial changes. First, the SDC scores for the economic and socioeconomic spheres increased in the neoliberal periods, except the score for the socioeconomic sphere according to *La Jornada*. This indicates that it became increasingly difficult to satisfy material demands without touching the issues in the civil, political, or social spheres.

Second, the civil and political claims that were likely strategic in the post-revolutionary period became more goal-oriented in the neoliberal periods. The SDC for the civil sphere decreased substantially from 1.4 to 1.1 in both papers. It is likely that popular actors began to appreciate civil liberties and legal protections for their own sake, not as an "attachment" to other claims. A growing influence of human rights regime since the late 1980s may explain this shift in part. The same can be said for the political sphere. While the SDC score remained constant in table 3, it would have been much smaller if electoral protests had not been excluded from the analysis. Claims in the electoral protests belonged almost exclusively to the political sphere.

Third, the SDC score for the social sphere increased from 1.2, 1.8, to 1.6 according to *Excélsior* and from 1.1, 1.4, to 1.8 according to the opposition press. Social participation claims were employed even more strategically in the neoliberal periods than they had been in the post-revolutionary period. This evidence indicates popular groups' increased recognition that the undemocratic nature of unions, schools, peasant organizations, political parties, or social movements was the reason why they were unable to realize material or political goals. They were conscious that the incorporation of social groups into the regime was no longer a leverage but a serious hindrance to their successful claim making. They strategically addressed the issues of corporatism.

In sum, while popular actors had employed civil, political, and social claims strategically until 1982, they were more likely to make civil and political claims as the ends per se and social claims even more strategically after 1982. Socioeconomic and economic claims had been largely goal-oriented in the post-revolutionary period, but the recent increase in the SDC indicates that these claims were no longer likely to be made on their own. This analysis does not mean that all the claims in the economic and socioeconomic spheres should be interpreted as the real goals while all the claims in the social sphere were about strategic necessities. In many instances of claim making, it would be hard for a researcher to distinguish goal-oriented claims from strategic ones completely, even if he or she analyzes protesters' discourse in detail. Claim makers might not consciously make the distinction in practice. My research is a first step to demonstrate overall tendencies of and historical changes in the goal-oriented and strategic (means-oriented) claims. I believe that it is worth improving this measure further since the means-ends distinction is theoretically important, historically intriguing, and empirically hard to show.

Claim Network Analysis: Relative Degree

The previous analysis did not tell which claim spheres were closely related to each other. Figures 6.1 and 6.2 show such relationships. I decompose the SDC statistics reported in table 6.3 into four relative degrees. Each relative degree represents a claim sphere's likelihood of sharing a campaign with one of the other four spheres.

Take a look at the four relative degrees for the civil sphere from the *Excélsior* data (plotted in the middle-right graph in figure 6.1). The highest relative degree in a period between 1964 and 1982 is obtained by the political sphere (the circles) with a score of 0.50. This means that 50% of the campaigns involving civil claims also embrace political claims before 1982. The political sphere is followed by the socioeconomic (0.43), the economic (0.31), and the social (0.19). The sum of the four numbers yields the SDC statistic for the civil sphere (0.31 + 0.43 + 0.50 + 0.19 = 1.43) in the period between 1964 and 1982. The higher the relative degree, the more dependent the civil claim's occurrence is on the other claim's existence.

The most important finding in this analysis is "politicization of claim networks." Most of the claim spheres increased their dependence on the political sphere in the neoliberal periods, with an exception of the civil sphere whose degree of dependence on the political sphere was extremely high from the beginning. Compare the first and third periods. The relative degrees of the socioeconomic, economic, civil, and social spheres on the political sphere (lines with circles in the figures) had changed from .21 to .36, .21 to .35, .50 to .41, and .31 to .44, respectively, according to *Excélsior* and

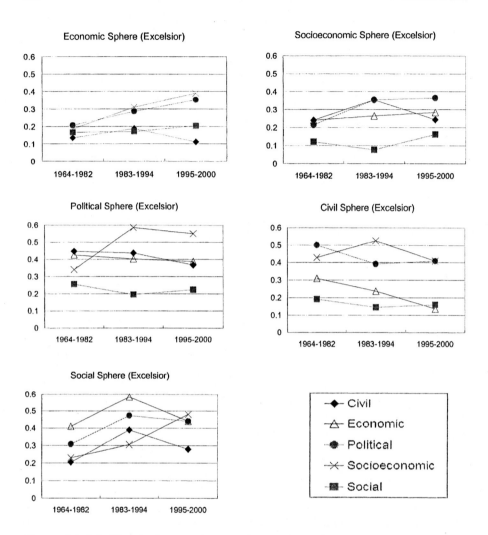

Figure 6.1. Likelihood of Two Claims Being Made in the Same Protest Campaign, Measured by the Relative Degrees of Claim Sphere, 1964-2000 (*Excélsior*)

from .36 to .44, .24 to .41, .46 to .46, and .22 to .52 according to the opposition press. I emphasize, in particular, that economic and socioeconomic claims, which used to have low relative degree scores—less than 0.30—in the first period, became highly dependent on political claims. Popular groups were more likely to associate material issues with political issues such as unaccountable politicians, corrupt bureaucrats, and exclusionary decision-making practices in the neoliberal periods than in the post-revolutionary period.

Another finding is a striking difference between the social and political spheres. While my previous analyses found both political and social claims as strategic, the analysis of the relative degree discovers a sharp contrast between the two kinds of claims. Continuing to compare the first and third periods, the political sphere's dependence on the other spheres remained constant at best, or even decreased if we take the effects of electoral protests into account, except for the socioeconomic sphere

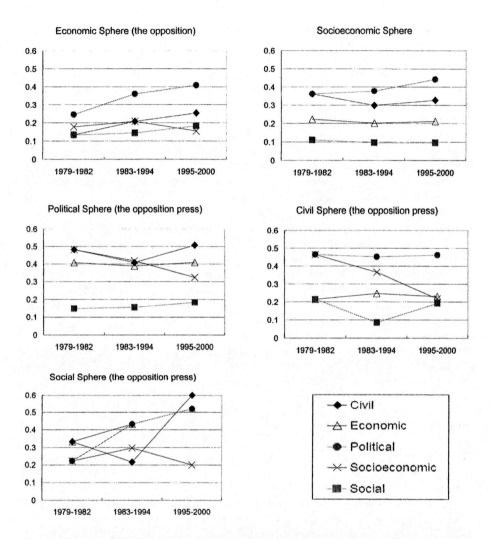

Figure 6.2. Likelihood of Two Claims Being Made in the Same Protest Campaign, Measured by the Relative Degrees of Claim Sphere, 1979-2000 (the opposition press)

according to *Excélsior*,[6] while the other claims' dependence on the political sphere increased except for the civil sphere for both *Excélsior* and opposition press, as I have just mentioned. In contrast, the social sphere's dependence on the other spheres increased while the others' dependence on the social sphere remained constant. This extreme imbalance implies a highly strategic nature of social claims. Popular groups demanded democracy within social organizations *mostly when* their organizations did not help them accomplish their principal claims in the other spheres. For instance, the rank-and-file workers might accuse their union leadership (social claim) when the latter did not defend their jobs (economic claim). Peasants might fight against their leader (social claim) when he favored family members when distributing government benefits (socioeconomic claim). Students might accuse a university rector (social claim) who attempted to quell their demands for democratization (political claim).

Will Mexicans continue to make social claims only strategically? Or, will they also demand democratization of institutions and organizations in civil society as the goal per se in the future? The two data sources suggest contradictory scenarios on this issue. The opposition press demonstrates that the social sphere's dependence on the other spheres continues to increase in the 1995-2000 period except for the socio-economic sphere (in the bottom graph in figure 2). *Excélsior* shows signs of decline in relative degrees during that period, again except for the socioeconomic sphere, indicating that this increase in the social sphere's dependence on the other spheres may be only temporary in the process of regime change (in the bottom graph in figure 1). Based on my finding about how the political claims have become prominent, I hypothesize that social participation claims will become more ends-oriented when the other spheres' dependence on the social sphere increases (i.e., "socialization" of claim networks). That is, social democratization demands will likely become a main focus of contention when citizens realize that their demands in the other spheres will not be satisfied unless they address the issues in the social sphere. Data on protests after 2000 are needed to inquire into this hypothesis.

In essence, figures 6.1 and 6.2 demonstrate the politicization of claim networks. In the neoliberal periods, when the state elites no longer committed themselves to the previously dominant cultural understandings emphasizing social rights and redistribution, citizens came to identify the political elites as the source of their everyday problems. As a result, people began to make political claims increasingly often even when they were in pursuit of other goals such as civil, socioeconomic, economic, or social claims. My quantitative data support this interpretation. In this sense, the political sphere has become central.

DISCUSSION

The idea of cultural opportunity helps us explain why certain types of claim making prevail even when political opportunities appear totally unfavorable. When political opportunities were not favorable during the post-revolutionary period, Mexicans were still able to carry out protest activities making economic and social claims because these claims resonated with the broad cultural understandings of the time.

I have also explored how popular actors framed their citizenship claims when, in the neoliberal context, the political and economic elites no longer shared the durable post-revolutionary master frame. I have done this by presenting a method to measure the degree of goal-orientedness and strategicness of claim. I find a tendency that claims in the socioeconomic and economic spheres were largely goal-oriented (the ends per se) while claims in the civil, political, and social spheres were more strategically employed (the means toward the ends). Given this overall tendency, this study has also detected an important change, which I called the "politicization of claim networks." People began to make political claims strategically when they were pursuing civil, economic, socioeconomic, or social claims. This new and innovative, "political democratization" frame emerged through Mexicans' everyday struggles over a multiplicity of needs, in which they came to realize that their demands for economic, civil, and social rights would not be satisfied without dealing with an undemocratic, non-representative, and corrupt political system.

The prominence of political claim makings in the neoliberal era can be attributed not only to the decay of the post-revolutionary master frame but also to a gradual opening of political opportunities. While I characterized political opportunity theory as insensitive to the actual content of claims, the theory is probably highly sensitive to *political* claims and explains the rise and decline of political claim making much better than other types of claim making, as Goodwin and Jasper suggest (Goodwin and Jasper 1999: 34-35). Favorable political opportunities will facilitate claim makings generally but encourage political claim makings more than others. An important issue here is that cultural and political opportunities are not independent of each other. Broad cultural schemes or master frames do not exist in vacuum but are shaped by political opportunity structure (Diani 1996). The post-revolutionary master frame that prioritized social and collective rights over political and civil rights was sustained by the unbalanced power relationship between state agents and citizens. More empirical research is needed in order to explore such complex relations between cultural and political opportunities as well as relations between these opportunities and protests.

How do qualitative and quantitative approaches compare with one another? On the one hand, Tamayo's qualitative analysis probably offers higher validity of the findings because "textual data come contextually embedded and are often gathered in ways that offer insights into their interpretation that are lost in survey techniques" (Johnston 2002: 63). On the other hand, my quantitative analysis offers higher reliability of the findings because it is easier to replicate. The procedure of data collection, coding, and analysis is transparent, and the findings are not likely to change dramatically by modifying coding of a small number of cases. One obvious advantage of the quantitative approach is that it yields numeric measures. While the use of statistics in this study was mostly descriptive, it is possible to associate these measures (frequencies of protests, SDC scores, and relative degrees) with other variables for further analysis.

Are the numbers constructed from media reports reliable? Since the Mexican media themselves have become increasingly independent of the government during the period under study (Lawson 2002), isn't it possible that politicization of claim making is a product of media transformation rather than a change in people's framing? Isn't it probable that censored media[7] abstained from reporting political claims during the post-revolutionary period, thus creating an impression that citizens wanted social rights more than political rights? This may have occurred, although I believe that changes in media coverage of protest events will likely reflect both changes in protest activities and changes in the media. In reality, it is unlikely that media effects can be completely separated out in order to gauge the "true" changes in popular protests. With any data set that falls short of the full universe of protest events, researchers must somehow deal with the biases inherent in their methods of measurement.

Recently it has been discussed that protest events reported in the media have their own significance as the object of study. Reported events are, as Tarrow explains, publicly "visible, not only to the observer, but, more important, to the elites, opponents, and potential supporters who make decisions and take actions about the movement" (Tarrow 1989: 28-29). By making their existence and actions public knowledge, protesters who hardly have any direct access to the polity may be able to garner public attention and support, accelerate policy controversies in front of the public, and encourage political debate and competition among policymakers in government (Kielbowicz and Scherer 1986; McCarthy, McPhail, Smith, and Crishock 1998: 113; Molotch 1979: 3; Oliver and Myers 1999: 38-39; Sampedro 1997: 201). Reported and unreported protests can be thought of as different classes of events, and both are worthy of attention. For those who are interested in the universe of protests, the quantitative finding from this study will still be useful because they are in a better position to estimate or guess the "true" numbers using their own knowledge of media influence.

How about the effects of my sampling strategy? Could it be that by choosing electoral moments, I captured the effect of political change too strongly? To remove the effect of electoral system changes, I excluded electoral protests from the analysis. It may be possible, however, that other protests unrelated to electoral issues might have framed their claims more politically than during non-electoral periods. I doubt if this is the case from my routine reading of Mexican newspapers, but new data sampling from non-electoral periods is necessary to test this possibility.

My overall conclusion—politicization of claim networks—will not likely change despite possible media influence and potential effects of my sampling method since it is also confirmed by Tamayo's political discourse analysis using underground press and party documents. At this juncture, I emphasize the importance of adopting multiple methods whenever possible since different methods—with their own strengths and weaknesses—often complement each other.

ACKNOWLEDGMENTS

Thanks to Charles Tilly, Francesca Polletta, Jorge Dominguez, Hank Johnston, Paul Almeida, Diane Davis, Patrick Heller, Douglas Chalmers, and Dana Fisher for helpful comments and conversations. Generous research support was provided in part by the National Science Foundation (SES-99-00867). An earlier version was presented at the 2004 American Sociological meeting in San Francisco.

NOTES

1. Tamayo's "social movements" category includes multitudes of popular organizations, socialist and communist parties, labor organizations, and civic associations.

2. Tamayo covered a broad range of archives. He used presidential archive (*Archivo Presidentes*) for political elites discourse. For the business elite discourse, he relied on *Transformación* (weekly journal by the National Chamber of Manufacturers, CANACINTRA), *Expansión* (business journal of Mexico), *Hombres de Negocios* (financial journal), and *La Nación* and *Memoria* (publication by the conservative National Action Party, PAN). For social movement discourses, he chose *Oposición* (Mexican Communist Party's publication), *Asi Es* (weekly publication by the Unified Socialist Party of Mexico, PSUM), *Bandera Roja* (newspaper by the Internationalist Communist Group), *Bandera Socialista* (newspaper by the Revolutionary Party of Workers, PRT), *Punto Crítico* (journal published by a political organization Punto Crítico), *El Pueblo* (journal linked to Maoist and revolutionary nationalist groups), and *Boletín del PRD* (publication by the leftist Party of Democratic Revolution).

3. Both *Unomásuno* and *La Jornada* did not exist in the earlier period under study. Journalists who were expelled from *Excélsior* founded *Unomásuno* in 1977. *La Jornada* was founded in 1984 by a group of journalists who left *Unomásuno* due to the differences over management and news policy (Sarmiento 1997: 34). I use *Unomásuno* from 1977 to 1984 and *La Jornada* afterward.

4. While it is important to keep this kind of relational information on claims, the research designs do not often permit it. Even one of the most sophisticated protest-event analyses chose not to gather the relational information. Their coding instruction says, "[Goals should] be coded from a prestructured list of some one hundred possible goals arranged into larger themes (peace, ecology, etc.). *If the action was directed at more than one goal simultaneously, the most important of these was coded*" (Kriesi, Koopmans, Duyvendak, and Giugni 1995: 266, italics by the author). Since one action is not allowed to have multiple goals, there is no overlap of goals, and the percentages of the goals add up to 100% (Kriesi, Koopmans, Duyvendak, and Giugni 1995: 20, Table 1.4).

5. A basic assumption in this analysis is that newspaper reporters tend to give a priority to goal-oriented claims more often than to strategic claims in writing news. When only one claim is found in an article, it is likely to be the goal of protest. My approach assumes that strategic claims can be found when two or more claims are reported. Of course, there is a chance that all these claims express challengers' goals. Still, it would be reasonable to interpret that a claim that is rarely asserted alone (like

those in the social sphere) is more likely than other claims to be strategic.

6. There is an inconsistency between *Excélsior* and the opposition press in the relative degree of the political sphere on the socioeconomic sphere. According to *Excélsior*, the score has increased from 0.34, 0.59, to 0.55. On the contrary, according to the opposition sources, it has decreased from 0.48, 0.42, to 0.32. This probably reflects the basic difference between the two sources we found in Table 2. The highly politicized opposition press tended to report those protests related to political issues while the press of the establishment downplayed the political protests and reported more socioeconomic claims especially during the neoliberal periods.

7. On different forms of the government influence over the Mexican press, such as "gasetillas" (article-disguised paid ads), government's financial "help" for journalists, government's disproportional advertisements, ties binding the press and the official party, PRI, etc., see Orme (1997).

Part III

Gendered Resistance and Neoliberalism

Chapter 7

THE MATURE RESISTANCE OF ARGENTINA'S MADRES DE PLAZA DE MAYO

Elizabeth Borland

On December 19 and 20, 2001, the days that mark the threshold of the recent era of protest in contemporary Argentina, the *Madres de Plaza de Mayo* (Mothers of the Plaza de Mayo, hereafter the Madres) joined throngs of protesters in the streets of Buenos Aires to bang on pots and pans and express their dissatisfaction with politicians. As women over seventy, wearing their well-known white headscarves, the Madres stood out in the crowds at the epicenter of the national protest in the Plaza de Mayo. By the end of the two days of protest, President De la Rúa had stepped down, 33 activists had been killed, and hundreds were wounded, including seven Madres. A few days later, the largest Madres group, the *Asociación Madres de Plaza de Mayo* (Association of the Mothers of the Plaza de Mayo), issued a press release about what they had experienced in the historic protest. They said:

> We Madres de Plaza de Mayo went out on the streets along with the people, banging pots and pans, bottles, and wastebaskets. We all yelled against De la Rúa, Cavallo, Menem, Duhalde, Ruckauf, and the other corrupt murderers...The people [killed] gave up their lives to protest that the corrupt ones should go, that they should stop paying the external debt, that the privileges of the judges and legislators should stop, that they should free political prisoners. We Madres de Plaza de Mayo say that the fascist right cannot keep governing us. We Madres participate in all social struggles, and last Thursday...we were gassed and attacked ferociously by murderers on horseback with [police] batons. (AMPM 2001)

This declaration was followed by a series of demands for the prosecution of those who killed activists and for the release of jailed protesters—both claims that reflect the Madres' long-standing concerns about state repression—but it also included demands for an end to the payment of the external debt and called for "dignified work for all."

Given their beginnings as a group of mothers looking for sons and daughters who were "disappeared" (called the *desaparecidos*, or disappeared ones) during the repression of Argentina's Dirty War—1976-1983—and the fact that they are now in their seventies and eighties, it may be surprising to some that the Madres were part of the 2001 street protests and that they have spent so much of their recent time and effort— sometimes putting themselves at physical risk, and often with great sacrifice—working on poverty, hunger, unemployment, and other issues that seem unrelated to their original human rights activism. However, to the Madres, these issues are intertwined with their earlier collective action against the dictatorship. They have framed their activism in the crisis through the lens of their experience as mothers of the disappeared, and by using this framing and their presence as aging veteran activists, they have expanded their work to encompass critiques of neoliberalism.

The activism of the Madres has made them one of the most studied and commented upon women's movements in Latin America over the last thirty years, but not much has been written about their recent activism (exceptions include Bosco 2004; Bosco forthcoming; Chejter 2004) or about how they have managed to expand their objectives to include such diverse issues as the external debt, hunger, unemployment, and corruption. Scholars of social movements are more familiar with the Madres as one of the most active human rights movements in Latin America (Bosco 2001) and as the prototypical model for women's mobilization within traditional gender norms, what Molyneux (1985, 1998) has called "practical" gender interests. Researchers have written about the Madres in myriad ways, exploring how they used motherhood as a tool of resistance (Bouvard 1994; Feijoo and Gogna 1987; Guidry and Sawyer 2003; Navarro 1989), how they can be seen as a peace movement (Hernandez 2002), how they use memory and grief (Foss and Domenici 2001; Schirmer 1994; Thornton 2000), and how they employ space and social networks (Bosco 2001; Bosco forthcoming; Rosenthal 2000), among other topics. Activists around the world have also held them up as models, and many women's groups have drawn on their work (Bejarano 2002; García-Gorena 2001; Ruddick 1994; Schirmer 1993). Most studies of the Madres have focused on their early actions, but now, more than twenty-five years after their sons and daughters had disappeared, the Madres continue to be important actors in Argentine politics, and they can still inform scholars of social movements, particularly those interested in modern resistance to neoliberalism in Latin America. Attention to how a long-standing movement, notably, one made up of old women[1], has embraced broad goals that address neoliberalism and has worked to build bridges with other activists, can teach us not only about trajectories of social movements, but about the impact of aging on activism.

These subjects are important for several reasons. First, although most of us recognize that age is part of a broader axis of inequality (Lorde 1984), aging and activism remains an understudied area of the literature on social movements. While there has been some research on activism over the life course in generational analysis inspired by Mannheim (1952), this work has included age as a way of comparing the political involvement of generational cohorts shaped by historical events (Johnston and Aarelaid-Tart 2000), and most often to follow the long-term life-course consequences of participation by youth in the U.S. civil rights movement (Cole and Stewart 1996; DeMartini 1983; Fendrich 1977; Whalen and Flacks 1989). Another way that age has appeared as important for social movements is in the literature on "biographical availability," where research finds that age is a central factor mediating recruitment to activism and that young people independent from parental authority are the most biographically available (McAdam 1986; Wiltfang and McAdam 1991). But these areas of the literature do not help us to understand how aging affects activism, beyond generational effects or initial recruitment into movements (Jennings and Andersen 2003), and it does not provide much leverage for understanding old activists. A focus on the Madres—vibrant veteran activists who call themselves "*viejitas*" (little old ladies)— can begin to address this gap in the social movement literature. Like other individual and collective identities, age is important for activism. Hunt, Benford, and Snow (1994) argue that framing processes can "proffer, buttress, and embellish identities" (185), so it makes sense that the Madres draw on their identities as old women as a reference point in their collective action frames, claims about the world that activists use to "activate adherents, transform bystanders into supporters, exact concessions from targets, and demobilize antagonists" (Snow 2004: 385). It also makes sense that their accumulated experience and changing vision of life and death will shape their approach to activism. How does the Madres' identity as *viejitas* and their aging affect their collective action?

Second, studying the evolution of the Madres can help us better understand goal expansion and related collective action framing processes. Shemtov (1999) defines goal expansion as a shift in the direction, geographic scope, or number of original goals held by a movement. In her work on NIMBY (not-in-my-backyard) environmental movements that start with narrow goals, Shemtov finds evidence of goal expansion and argues that when groups are able to take "ownership" of a social issue from authorities, they can solidify collective action framing and expand their goals successfully. Because goal expansion involves changes in the content of claims made by social movement actors, it is related to a framing process that Snow, Rochford, Worden and Benford (1986) call "frame alignment." Frame alignment is an ongoing process by which social movement actors link their claims to interested audiences, often to strategically construct more resonant and persuasive frames that will mobilize people. By focusing on the Madres, we can examine goal expansion in a long-standing social movement that began with narrow goals. How and why have the Madres expanded and changed their goals? As the Madres have used collective action frames to make connections between old and new goals, they have been driven by their activism to embrace new broader frames. Rather than consciously manipulating frames to broaden their base of support, the Madres have exercised their moral authority to respond to emerging political and economic grievances in Argentina. The case of the Madres reminds us that goal expansion and frame alignment are not driven only by strategic mobilization, but by moral authority in the face of changing structural conditions.

Finally, since the Madres are among the most prominent women's movements in Latin America, it is important to recognize their mature resistance. Calasanti and Slevin (2001) point out the lack of attention that has been paid to gender and aging in sociology, arguing that gender shapes the social organization of aging and affects how we treat (and study) the old. Feminist activist accounts signal that old age can override other forms of oppression that inspire activism (Macdonald 1983), and old women are often left outside of history (Smith 2001). This suggests that we should be attentive to the voices and experience of old women, people who are often made invisible. But the Madres are anything but invisible in Argentina. How have they remained relevant actors in politics?

This chapter seeks to address these questions by chronicling the contemporary work of the Madres and documenting their presence in the progressive movements organizing in modern Argentina. After describing how their activism has evolved, I show how they have broadened their goals over time, and then focus on their work in the recent crisis. Drawing on media reports, qualitative fieldwork about their activities in Buenos Aires in 2002-2003, published accounts, and organizational documents and publications, I chronicle how the Madres have expanded their goals to critique neoliberalism and its consequences. I show how they have used collective action frames related to their identity as aging mothers to draw connections between past and present, and to explain and support the expansion of their goals.

THE EVOLUTION OF THE MADRES DE PLAZA DE MAYO

To Argentine sociologist Atilio Borón, the activist longevity of the Madres represents the tenacity of people to fight for just causes and the capacity of resistance against oppression (Borón 2002). As the Madres approach 2007, the movement's thirty-year anniversary, their history is certainly one of tenacity and persistent resistance, but it also demonstrates an elasticity that has allowed for the evolution and expansion of their goals.

Now known throughout the world as pioneers for democracy and human rights, the Madres first came together in 1977 to find their missing sons and daughters who were seized, tortured, and murdered during the military regime's repression of the Left. Most were middle-aged housewives who had never been involved in politics, and they first made contact with each other as they waited in government ministries seeking information about their missing loved ones. Eventually they began meeting and marching weekly in the Plaza de Mayo, the central plaza in Buenos Aires that is the site of the cathedral, the presidential palace, and other important government buildings. Despite prohibitions on freedom of assembly, and the military government's labeling them *locas* (crazy women), their movement gained momentum and drew international media attention to the disappeared. A group of Madres with missing grandchildren branched off to form the *Abuelas de Plaza de Mayo* (Grandmothers of the Plaza de Mayo), and both the Madres and Abuelas groups grew (Arditti 1999, 2002; Bouvard 1994). When the dictatorship finally ceded to elections in 1983, the Madres were hailed around the world as heroines, and their activism flourished; there were Madres and support groups in over twenty cities in Argentina and abroad (Bosco 2001). The Madres pledged to remain separate from party politics, a decision they have sustained throughout their history. Investigations by the new democratic government revealed that as many as 30,000 people had been murdered during the Dirty War, and military tribunals tried and imprisoned high-ranking officers. However, by 1986, strategic and leadership disagreements led a group of women that included several of the founding members, the *Madres de Plaza de Mayo Línea Fundadora* (Founding Line), to split off from the original *Asociación Madres de Plaza de Mayo*; conflict between these two organizations has continued ever since (see Bosco 2004). Today, both organizations are important in the social movement sector in Argentina, and they continue to garner attention by speaking out for social justice. The history, differences, and conflicts between the two groups, while interesting, are mostly secondary to the goals of this chapter and I will only refer to them when necessary for clarity and accuracy.[2]

During the dictatorship and the early days of democracy, the claims of the Madres focused on the disappeared. When they first began marching in the Plaza de Mayo, the Madres slogans were "They took them away alive, we want them back alive" (*Con vida los llevaron, con vida los queremos*) and "Appearance with life" (*Aparición con vida*). They carried the photographs of their missing sons and daughters, and began to embroider their names on the white headscarves that became a symbol of their movement. After democracy was restored, they continued to insist that they wanted each disappeared person returned alive and the perpetrators of the repression punished.

As the movement developed, the Madres began to alter their claims to make them more communal. As Madre Esther Balestrina de Creaga put it, "It's useless to fight for only one child. We have to continue to fight for all the children" (cited in Bouvard 1994: 180). The *Asociación Madres de Plaza de Mayo*, writing about its history in 2002, said of this transition:

> Since 1986 we began a process of political definition that we call "the socialization of maternity." Each of us started searching for her own disappeared son or daughter. But slowly, we began to feel like the mothers of each of the disappeared ones, adding to our own the thousands that fell in the streets, in the mountains, in the jungles, fighting or teaching literacy. Little by little, in the Plaza de Mayo we divested ourselves of the photo of our own son or daughter, to carry the portrait of any other son or daughter. Then we went on removing the names and dates of disappearance of each of them from our own headscarf. (AMPM 2002b)

This shift toward a shared or "socialized" sense of motherhood strengthened the Madres' solidarity and reinforced the social networks that sustained their activism (Bosco 2001, 2004, forthcoming). As the quote suggests, the Asociación Madres has also included the felled leftist guerillas who fought in the 1970s among the disappeared (those that died "in the streets, in the mountains, in the jungles"). They emphasized the similarities between the disappeared, rather than remembering the details and individual differences. This was reflected in the symbols of their activism, such as their uniform headscarves without distinct names of the disappeared.

Although the Madres of the Línea Fundadora continue to include the names of their sons and daughters on their headscarves and have supported recognition for individual disappeared people in memorials, they too have emphasized life and embraced a shared view of motherhood. According to leader Nora Cortiñas, "Now we are not mothers of just one son, we are mothers of all *desaparecidos*. Our biological son was transformed into 30,000 sons and daughters" (Cortiñas, cited in Bellucci 2000: 282). Writing about their history in 2003, the Línea Fundadora said that the disappeared young people unite them: "We realized that each of us was looking not just for our son or daughter: all of us, together, were fighting to find all of our sons and daughters, and fighting against the dictatorship" (MPMLF 2003).

This transformation toward a broader vision of national motherhood facilitated the expansion of the Madres' goals during the new democracy to include broader demands for human rights. Both the Asociación and the Línea Fundadora have fostered network ties with other human rights groups around the world, and Madres often travel internationally to speak about human rights, bringing them into contact with activists concerned about similar problems. For instance, Hebe de Bonafini of the Asociación Madres met with women from the former Yugoslavia to speak out against the genocide there in 1999 (AMPM 2003a). In this type of work, the Madres frame the similarities between the situation of their disappeared loved ones and other victims of repression around the world. They also recognize the potential for human rights violations in democracies, and they have been vigilant about police and military actions in post-dictatorship Argentina, including in the recent protests. For example, in the annual 2002 march organized by the Línea Fundadora, activists displayed a long banner of fabric covered with photos of the *desaparecidos* and *desaparecidas*. The march began at the location where one of the victims of the December 2001 *Argentinazo* protests was killed by police with collective expressions of grief.[3] This action explicitly combined the goals of two seemingly disparate moments: the Madres during the Dirty War, concerned with their disappeared children, and the Madres of the new century, concerned also with broader aspects of human rights and social politics.

Extending their support for life and their opposition to military dictatorship, the Madres have also worked for peace and in support of demilitarization. They advocated cutbacks in military funding in Argentina, and spoke out against the Persian Gulf War in the early nineties. In 1997, two representatives of the Asociación Madres traveled to Israel to support efforts by Israeli and Palestine women for peace. Both groups of Madres mobilized against the U.S. war in Iraq and helped organize massive marches in Buenos Aires against the invasion of Iraq. In a February 2003 press conference, members of the Línea Fundadora gathered with the Abuelas and other women's groups to call for a peace march beneath a banner that read, "For life, no to war" (*Por la vida, no a la guerra*). They read a statement that said "we know the pain of the loss of the lives of our loved ones" and so they were "shouting out to the entire world, so that it will know that the women of Argentina are against the war."

Most recently, the Madres have expanded their activism to address the problems widely associated with neoliberal policy in Argentina. They have cooperated with other activists, including groups of unemployed people, neighborhood assemblies, workers who have "recuperated" their factories, women activists, and youth movements. They are recognized and often commended as important actors in national politics; one 2002 survey of female undergraduates even found that the Madres were the second most frequent answer to a question about public women they admired, after a more general answer that captured the crisis zeitgeist: "women who have communal kitchens for children" (COPUB 2002). However, the Madres' expanding goals and broadened activism have also brought criticism from some in the general public who say, "*se han politizado,*" (they have become politicized) suggesting that the Madres have corrupted or tainted the moral authority they derived from their heroism in the dictatorship.[4] This criticism can be seen partly as a response to the fact that the Madres break norms about gender and age—old women shouldn't "do politics"—but it is also a tacit recognition that the Madres are political actors in their own right.

EXPANDING GOALS AND SHIFTING FRAMES

One way to examine the expanding goals of the Madres is to study frame changes in their activism. This section presents two longitudinal analyses, one of Madres slogans and the other a media analysis of Madres coverage during the 1996-2004 period. Both analyses demonstrate that the Madres goals have expanded.

The Madres themselves have provided a way of analyzing these changes. Table 7.1 presents the slogans chosen by the larger of the Madres organizations, the *Asociación Madres de Plaza de Mayo*, to head the annual March of Resistance, a 24-hour march in the Plaza de Mayo held every December for the last 24 years (1981-2004). These slogans can be said to be measures of changes in how the Madres frame their activism. In each of these marches, the Madres of the Asociación endeavor to reflect the political context of the day and their role in it by choosing a thematic statement. Each year, they have extensive meetings to determine the slogan to lead the march, and the chosen slogan is published in the Madres newspaper and dispersed in the media (Gallego 2004; Vázquez 2004). It is significant that the Madres see these

Year	Slogans[a]	Dirty War	Rights	Neo-liberalism	Other[b]
1981	Appearance with life for the detained-disappeared.	✓			
1982	Appearance with life for the detained-disappeared. Restitution of the children to their legitimate families. Freedom for political prisoners.	✓			
1983	Against the amnesty law and for appearance with life for the detained-disappeared.	✓			
1984	Trials and punishment for the guilty.	✓			
1985	No to Final Stop. Jail for [those who carried out the genocide].	✓			
1986	No more *milicos!* [*milicos* is a depreciative term for military men]	✓			
1987	Against civil-military authoritarianism.	✓	✓		
1988	To resist is to combat disappearance, torture, death. It is also to combat injustice, repression, misery, corruption. . . . Let's resist together!	✓	✓	✓	
1989	We won't forget, we won't forgive.	✓			
1990	Rebellion to fight, courage to continue.				✓
1991	Always struggle, never turn back.				✓
1992	Solidarity and struggle or hunger and repression.		✓	✓	
1993	Clear head, solidary heart, combative fist.				✓
1994	Resistance and struggle today for the victory of tomorrow.				✓
1995	The only struggle you lose is the one you abandon.				✓
1996	Enough! Of impunity, of hunger, of unemployment, of freedom [for those who carried out the genocide], of persecution of political opponents, of misery, of corrupt unionists, of...of....	✓	✓	✓	
1997	Freedom for the world's political prisoners, jail for those responsible for hunger.		✓	✓	
1998	Against impunity and the lack of jobs, combat and resist.	✓		✓	
1999	Live combating injustice.				✓
2000	The future is here, help us to change it.			✓c	✓
2001	Resist and Combat State terrorism.	✓	✓		
2002	No to the payment of the external debt as the only way to end hunger.			✓	
2003	No to the payment of the external debt. For Latin American unity.			✓	
2004	To resist is not a crime, it is the obligation of all of us.				✓

Notes: [a] Recorded in Vázquez et al. 2004.
[b] These slogans typically use a general frame about resistance that is not specific to the Dirty War, human rights, or neoliberalism.
[c] This slogan ("The future is here") is somewhat obscure, but can be interpreted as an indirect reference to the economic problems that the Madres have associated with neoliberalism.

Table 7.1. Slogans for the Annual March

slogans as marking their work for the coming year and recognize that they are important because they are often taken up by other organizations (de Bonafini 2000). I coded each of these slogans according to the issues it addresses: "Dirty War" indicates claims stemming from the Madres' goals to recuperate the disappeared and to punish those responsible for the repression of the Dirty War; "Rights" indicates those related to human rights and peace in democracy; and "Neoliberalism" for claims addressing the

problems commonly associated with neoliberalism in Argentina (such as poverty, corruption, hunger, unemployment, and debt). The residual category, "Other," indicates
slogans with general statements about solidarity and resistance that cannot be catego-
rized in one of the other three categories, such as "The only struggle you lose is the one
you abandon" (1995), a theme that stresses solidarity.

The coding gives a rough approximation of the evolution of the claims made by
the Madres and documents the expansion of their goals, as expressed by the frames in
their slogans. In the first six years, the slogans created during the dictatorship and early
democracy claims focused predominantly on the Dirty War, often with frames emphasizing life. In 1987 and 1988, the Madres of the Asociación added claims about human
rights in democracy in their slogans for the March of Resistance. This was the year of
the military insurrection known as the Easter Rebellion and also a year in which the
Madres were attacked by police during a protest march (Bouvard 1994). In the first
half of the nineties, when President Menem came to office and started the privatization
policies that led to an initial economic boom, the Madres' slogans expanded to suggest
frames about solidarity, rebellion, and sustaining resistance (coded as Other in table
7.1). Frames about poverty and the effects of neoliberalism did not appear regularly
until the mid-nineties, when the boom of prosperity was ending. In contrast, over the
last eight years, a period of growing economic disparity in Argentina and a time when
most Madres were entering their seventies, frames about hunger, poverty, unemployment, and the debt have become more common in the slogans. The penultimate slogan, which included the phrase "For Latin American unity," reflects the Madres' 2003
meeting with Venezuelan President Hugo Chávez, who has spoken often about a new
Bolivarian unity, and indicates a new frame for the Madres. This frame captures the
turn to the Left that has been sweeping across Latin America and the desire to present a
united Latin American front against the international lending agencies that have advocated neoliberal policies.

To focus more closely on the neoliberal period, 1996-2004, I collected and coded
all articles that mentioned the phrase "Madres de Plaza de Mayo" in the electronic archive of the newspaper *La Nación* for the 1996-2004 period.[5] Overall, there were 740
articles that mentioned the Madres over the nine-year period, an average of 82 per year.
The annual number of articles mentioning the Madres has increased over the nine years
of news coverage, from a low of 22 mentions in 1996 to a high of 130 in 2003. There
was a spike in the number of articles mentioning the Madres in 1998, the year of the

	Dirty War		Human Rights		Neo-liberalism		Culture		International Relations		Other		Total
	%	(n)	%	(n)	%	(n)	%	(n)	%	(n)	%	(n)	(n)
1996	22.7	(5)	22.7	(5)	27.3	(6)	22.7	(5)	0.0	(0)	4.5	(1)	(22)
1997	24.1	(14)	13.8	(8)	20.7	(12)	31.0	(18)	5.2	(3)	5.2	(3)	(58)
1998	50.0	(60)	13.3	(16)	3.3	(4)	20.8	(25)	5.0	(6)	7.5	(9)	(120)
1999	31.3	(20)	15.6	(10)	0.0	(0)	43.8	(28)	3.1	(2)	6.3	(4)	(64)
2000	40.0	(22)	12.7	(7)	12.7	(7)	21.8	(12)	10.9	(6)	1.8	(1)	(55)
2001	19.6	(20)	11.8	(12)	23.5	(24)	31.4	(32)	8.8	(9)	4.9	(5)	(102)
2002	13.5	(12)	13.5	(12)	40.4	(36)	20.2	(18)	1.1	(1)	11.2	(10)	(89)
2003	23.1	(30)	33.1	(24)	15.4	(20)	18.5	(24)	6.9	(9)	3.1	(4)	(130)
2004	40.0	(40)	18.0	(18)	20.0	(20)	11.0	(11)	6.0	(6)	5.0	(5)	(100)
Mean	30.1	(25)	17.7	(15)	17.4	(14)	23.3	(19)	5.7	(5)	5.7	(5)	(740)

Table 7. 2. Mentions of the Madres in *La Nación*, by type and year

arrest of Alfredo Astiz, the notorious naval captain who infiltrated the Madres in 1978 and identified several Madres and their supporters to security units for disappearance. That year also saw extensive debate and protest over the creation of a memorial at the School of Naval Mechanics, site of a clandestine detention center during the Dirty War where many *desaparecidos* were tortured and killed (Bosco 2004).

I coded each article based on the type of activity or reference to the Madres, using six categories that expand on those used in the coding of the Madres' slogans (see table 7.2). In 30 percent of the news articles, the Madres were mentioned in relation to their traditional activism about the Dirty War. Protests, memorials, lobbying, and other activities directly related to the disappeared and the dictatorship were coded in this category. In about 18 percent of the articles, the references were about work for more general human rights or peace issues—the expanding goals that the Madres embraced in the new democracy. Many of these articles mentioned the Madres in relation to concerns about police repression or human rights violations in the democratic period, such as police crackdowns during protests and the killing of journalists and activists; this category also includes articles about peace marches and rallies. A third category includes mentions of the Madres in reference to a broader array of issues that have been seen as part of neoliberal policy in Argentina, including employment and unemployment; poverty and hunger; economic policy, trade, and the budget; corruption; the external debt; Latin American unity; and factories taken over by workers. It includes about 17 percent of all articles. The Madres were also mentioned frequently in articles about the arts and cultural events, such as concerts, plays, and art and movie openings. Some of these articles reported on events organized or attended by the Madres (such as a U2 concert in 1998 and a Sting concert in 2001), while others mentioned the Madres as cultural references by artists. This "cultural" category was surprisingly large, including about 23 percent of all articles. The fifth category includes articles mentioning the Madres as commentators or actors in international affairs—for instance, making reference to their support for the Zapatistas and other foreign movement groups in 2001 and recording their meetings with visiting dignitaries. It includes about 6 percent of the articles. The final category, a residual category, includes articles that did not fit into any of the other coding categories (5.7 percent).[6] The data show a large increase in the number of articles regarding claims or problems related to neo-liberalism during the

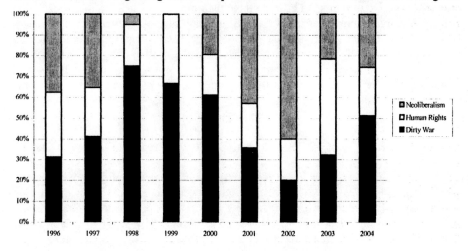

Figure 7.1. Percentage of Articles Mentioning the Madres

recent period of increased mobilization, from none in 1999, to 12.7 percent in 2000, to 23.5 percent in 2001, to a high of 40.4 percent in 2002.

Figure 7.1 compares the percentages of articles that refer to the Madres in the three framing-related categories that were identified in the previous analysis of slogans: the Dirty War, human rights, and neoliberalism. To examine the data related to these three frames, the figure excludes the articles with cultural references to the Madres, and references to the Madres' two smallest categories: "International Relations" and the residual "Other" category. The percentage of articles addressing general human rights has remained the most constant, while there has been fluctuation from year to year for references to the Madres related to the Dirty War and neoliberalism. Nevertheless, the general trend is that references to the Dirty War were gradually overshadowed by references to neoliberalism during the recent crisis, most notably in 2002. The last two years (2003 and 2004) indicate that this trend may have been temporary, and that it has reversed as Argentina's economy has stabilized and more progressive policies have been implemented during the presidency of Nestor Kirchner.

Both sets of analyses show that the Madres have not abandoned their earlier goals, frames, and activities; their demands for memory and constant reminders about the history of their activism are always present, but they have expanded them to renew the frames and make connections to the many concerns they share with others in Argentina and outside. The shifting frames that are recorded in annual slogans and reflected in newspaper articles mark the expansion of goals that parallels recent historical periods in Argentina: dictatorship, early democracy (and its fight for justice and truth, as well as punishment), and the modern struggles against neoliberalism and for peace, memory, and social change that extend the vision of the Madres' sons and daughters from the past into the future.

These patterns also show the elasticity of the Madres' goals, since they have expanded their arguments to make them more complex. Their political analysis is not just linked to motherhood and the dictatorship but it draws on the moral authority that the Madres have as people who stood up to the dictatorship, and the experience they have gained as politically savvy actors with years of activist experience to critique contemporary injustice. Rather than simply adding new social issues, the Madres interweave old and new, making their claims and critiques more complex and sophisticated, more "mature." This enables them to broaden their goals and to update them to address Latin American unity, neoliberalism, and the U.S. invasion of Iraq, as well as the problems of the economic crisis in Argentina. As citizen-activists, I suggest that they employ their identities as mothers and their experience in the Dirty War, but they are not "stuck in the past"—they simultaneously weave in new goals and frames into a sophisticated analysis that helps us to understand the continuity of past and present, as well as the complex reality of modern Argentina.

IN THE EYE OF THE STORM: MADRES CONFRONT NEOLIBERALISM

Examining the Madres' work in the 2001-2003 period, the height of the recent wave of protest, can help us to see how they have interwoven new and old goals to confront neoliberalism. During this period, the Madres were busy working with other activists to respond to the economic and political crisis. In addition to their weekly marches in the Plaza de Mayo, they participated in a variety of other protests, including: annual gay pride marches, a 2001 protest in support of striking Aerolíneas Argentinas workers, marches against poverty (including a 2002 sit-in and hunger strike by the Asociación

Madres at the Cathedral of Buenos Aires), protests at a beleaguered local hospital in support of doctors and nurses demanding wages and supplies, student protests at the city's university in 2002, and the ongoing weekly protests against corruption at the Supreme Court. Madres of the Línea Fundadora extended their criticism of U.S. support for the dictatorship during the Dirty War to a critique of U.S.-backed neoliberal policies, protesting the 2002 arrival of U.S. Treasury Secretary Paul O'Neill and the sale of Argentine lands to foreign businesses. The frames they used in these activities engaged with the crisis and the prevalent "master frames" of protest during the period, connecting past and present. A good example is the slogan the Asociación Madres used in their August 2002 march with the *piqueteros/as*—the unemployed road barricaders who have been important political groups in modern Argentina (Auyero 2003; Di Marco and Palomino 2004): "FIGHT FOR LIFE, AGAINST CAPITALISM!" This is an extension of the Madres' traditional framing of their activism as a struggle for life and against death that we see in "Appearance with life" (*Aparición con vida,* their traditional slogan), combined with a critique of capitalism.[7]

The Madres' annual protest activities in 2002 and 2003 also reflected the crisis and were a venue for making the connections between past and present. Among their many activities, the Madres hold rallies and marches each year to mark the junta's seizure of power (March 24), the commemoration of their first protest in the Plaza (April 30), and the annual 24-hour "March of Resistance" held each December. The following statement from a pamphlet distributed on April 30, 2003, by the Asociación Madres, is representative in how it amplifies the frame by linking state terrorism with capitalism:

> Lack of jobs is a crime. The businesspeople who leave millions of men and women without jobs are criminals. State terrorism is always organized by functionaries at the service of economic groups. They want to turn us into slaves. We *Madres de Plaza de Mayo* think that *desocupados* (the unemployed) are the new *desaparecidos* of the system. Dignified work is a right that no one can take away, and for which we should fight to the ultimate consequences. (AMPM 2003b)

This quote is remarkable because it equates the disappeared men and women who are at the heart of Madres activism, and who were and are the focus of their work during and about the Dirty War, with the *desocupados/as*—the often nameless and faceless but swelling ranks of men and women who have been victims of the economic crisis. By drawing this equation, the Madres dramatize the injustice of neoliberal capitalism ("a crime") and explain their presence in the protest. The public knows that the Madres are human rights activists, so by saying that "dignified work is a right that no one can take away" and that they are defending the *desocupados/as*, the Madres signal that these new goals are not so new or different after all.

A similar pattern can be seen in the Línea Fundadora's frames. They, too, have depicted their work for progressive social change in the face of neoliberalism as part of a broader struggle for human rights. According to leader Nora Cortiñas:

> We picked up the battle flags of our children and we learned that we had to defend all human rights. . . .What unified the madres, [although] we were from different social classes and educational backgrounds, was that the ideals of our children were the same. Today I understand that human rights are all rights, economic, social and cultural, civil and political, rights of women, of indigenous people, of homosexuals, of the disabled. (Cortiñas 2000)

This framing—that economic rights are also part of the framework of human rights—justifies the activism of the Madres on behalf of the poor. It also connects the struggles of the present with the struggles of the past made by the disappeared. The Madres have "picked up the battle flags" of their sons and daughters and modernized them, forced to reverse the usual generational order in the aftermath of dictatorship; Cortiñas frames her activism as inspired by the ideals of *los desaparecidos*, in a sense becoming the symbolic daughter inspired by her disappeared son.

In fact, both Madres groups have used the metaphor of birthing to explain this reversed chronology of inspired activism in their collective action frames, justifying their expanded goals with the language of maternity. The slogans "Give birth to rebellion" (Asociación Madres de Plaza de Mayo) and "Our children gave birth to us" (Línea Fundadora) use the language of birth to convey the source of the Madres' inspiration. When she speaks about the disappeared, Madre member Nora Cortiñas frequently explains that the Madres gave birth to their children physically, but the disappeared gave birth to the Madres in a political sense (Cortiñas 2002). This powerful metaphor uses the language of maternity to explain and inspire renewed resistance.

"MADRES *VIEJITAS*": GENDER, AGE, AND IDENTITY

Using words associated with pregnancy is paradoxical, because the Madres are long past physical childbearing. In fact, when I interviewed and accompanied the Madres, many of them told me, *"somos viejitas"* ("we are little old ladies"). Even when they started to march around the pyramid in the Plaza de Mayo, they were considered old— middle-aged mothers who were beyond childbearing, of an age when women are no longer seen as beautiful and vibrant in Argentina (Sutton 2004). Now, the Madres of the Línea Fundadora even call themselves *"ancianas,"* a word that roughly translates to mean "elderly women," and has an older and more fragile connotation than *viejas* (MPMLF 2005). What does it mean for the Madres to be activists who are *viejitas* or *ancianas*, and how does this identity inform the frames they use in activism?

If being women and mothers was a tool of resistance and a shield from repression for the Madres in the dictatorship (Bouvard 1994; Feijoo and Gogna 1987; Guidry and Sawyer 2003; Navarro 1989), perhaps now being *viejitas* functions in some similar capacity. Just as the Madres were able to subvert the traditional views about women's roles as mothers in patriarchy during the dictatorship, today they also indirectly challenge ageism. The fragility of being *viejitas* can be subverted as a strategic tool in the Madres' activist claims. They seem to use their identity as old women to shame opponents, as in this example of a quote from a sit-in occupation and hunger strike inside the Cathedral of Buenos Aires in protest of hunger in Argentina, in June 2002: "the [Cardinal's] secretary wants to throw us out of here, we who are a bunch of old ladies . . . but we are not going. We will stay here until tomorrow afternoon" (de Bonafini, as cited in "madres de Plaza de Mayo tomaron la Catedral Metropolitana" 2002). The quote is an interesting combination of courage and fragility, as it plays on the idea that old women should not be harassed, even as they challenge the powerful Catholic Church and commit courageous acts usually not associated with *viejitas* by engaging in a hunger strike.

Another aspect of the way that the Madres assert their age in frames is by speaking about their mortality in protest. For example, in a speech on April 30, 2002 in the Plaza de Mayo, Hebe de Bonafini of the Asociación Madres said that the Madres plan to be cremated and have their ashes dispersed in the plaza, so that they can continue to be there, even after they die. She even exclaimed, "We are going to be happy to keep being here!" As Madre Carmen de Guede told researcher Jo Fisher in the 1980s, "We always say that we're going to continue as long as our bodies allow us. We are going to lose some Mothers on the way, some who can't walk because they're too old or because they're too ill to carry on. But as long as there is some life left in us we'll continue marching in Plaza de Mayo" (Fisher 1989: 153).

"Losing Mothers on the way" is a problem that the Madres must contend with in their activism. Because the members of the Madres groups are mothers of people disappeared in the Dirty War, the membership of their organizations is limited. The passage of time means that the groups are destined to shrink as the Madres age and die. Secretary of Asociación Madres Evel Petrini explains:

> Well, there are about 200 of us left, and you have to consider that we are seniors, there are a lot of us that. . . . [hesitation] We unfortunately have some sick people, and some who have departed. . . . It is like a thing that does not have a successor. . . . Fortunately, because it would be terrible! [weak laughter]. (Petrini 2003)

Petrini sums up the irony of the situation well. Though they of course miss those "who have departed," the Madres do not lament their membership decay insomuch as it means that the era of disappearance and repression has ended. Nonetheless, the Madres are affected by the aging of their ranks. Many Madres complained to me about their ailments; one activist from the Línea Fundadora told me that in the past she could keep up with most Madres, but now she needs to pace herself and recognize her limitations (de Gropper 2005). Some of the Madres of the Línea Fundadora could not even climb the stairs to their borrowed office space, so they were relieved when they moved into a building with an elevator in 2001.

Despite, or perhaps because of, their age and their history, the Madres have a perpetual association with youth and young people, and this association also binds past and present, old and new. Their claims that we remember the disappeared youth forever connect the Madres to their sons and daughters (and all *desaparecidos/as*) whose lives were interrupted by the dictatorship. The Madres are always surrounded by the images of youth: the young faces that stare out from the photos of the disappeared—most of whom would now be in or around their fifties but are forever young, "icons to be venerated, legends to be lived up to" (Perelli 1994: 45). Thus the aging Madres remind people of the past. At the same time, the Madres' current activism puts them in daily contact with young people in other movements. Part of their work is to create connections with these young men and women, and they often speak about how they are "passing the torch" to the many young people active in contemporary protest, just as they "took up the battle flags" of their own sons and daughters. As Hebe de Bonafini says in an interview on her group's website:

> In general, mothers say: "No, don't go out, don't get wet, don't let anything happen to you, be careful." . . . We are the opposite, we say that you have to go out, when they pick up some kid [we say], "Let's go to the police station, let's face the *milicos* (the denigrating term the Madres use for the police or military), let's get him out". . . and the kids think, "Wow, I wish my mom was like that." More than anything, I am referring to the youngest ones, the ones who see us as friends, as *compañeras*. (AMPM 2002a)

Young activists work in both Madres headquarters and can be seen accompanying the Madres, facilitating their local travel, walking with them in the weekly marches in the Plaza de Mayo, and supporting them in their daily activities. By their relationships

with these "kids"—the new faces of protest in Argentina—the Madres are a bridge
between past and present resistance.

Just as young activists often support them, the Madres have also amplified their
maternity by nurturing fledgling movements during the crisis, extending motherhood
politically to protect and mentor young activists and organizations. They lend protection in protest, standing up for victims of repression as a human rights group with
moral authority and ready public recognition, demanding release of political prisoners,
and shielding activists in the front lines of protest. According to her grandson Pablo,
83-year old Línea Fundadora member Pepa de Noia tells him to leave the protests
when they are marching: "When things get rough, she kicks me out, and tells me she is
watching out for me [to keep me from] the police, but that she is going to stay" (Savoia
2002: 23). I heard similar stories from other young activists who were with the Madres
in protests with heavy police presence.

The Madres also lend legitimacy and tactical support to newer organizations.
Through their symbolic presence (in headscarves) at the events of other groups and by
endorsing the work of other organizations, the Madres lend the visibility of their organizations to others. Both Madres organizations regularly field calls from activists in
other local groups; I witnessed Madres of the Línea Fundadora talking with these activists on many occasions, to suggest they speak with specific media contacts or to offer
advice. Lawyers from the team that volunteers for the Asociación Madres even met
with the Brukman factory workers after the police tried to remove them from their "recuperated" factory in 2003, and the Asociación Madres began a formal market consulting program offered for free to workers of these factories.

The Madres use the language of motherhood in describing these activities, "giving
birth to rebellion" ("La resistencia tuvo hijos" 2002). They see it as a legacy for the
future that they recognize they will not live to see. "Our wish is that when the last day
arrives, we can look back and find a furrow planted with love, with resistance, and
watered with our tear. . . . It will be others who harvest, it will be others who retake our
path" (AMPM 1995). This legacy is clearly seen in the support both Madres organizations have shared with groups of sons and daughters of the disappeared. The most
prominent, H.I.J.O.S. (an acronym that stands for Children for Identity and Justice,
against Forgetting and Silence, and also a word that means children, or sons and
daughters), has become an important new human rights group in Argentina (Taylor
2002). By recognizing the generational line of protest—grandmothers, mothers, and
children—Madre activists foster ties that support their work. The Madres reach out to
young people, and the young people support them. As the Línea Fundadora explained:

> While we are alive, we will keep on going forward. The seeds of our disappeared
> ones are sprouting in a group of youth, still the minority, who are socially aware and
> happy, and who try to understand and remember what happened in order to really
> make *Nunca Más* (Never Again, a slogan of the early democratic period) a reality.
> (MPMLF 2003)

In turn, young people continue to be drawn to the Madres and Abuelas as a link to history and as a means to address the current crisis. As Diana Malamud, a young leader of
the group *Memoria Activa* (Active Memory), says, "They have been a great example of
struggle and also of constancy, it gives one strength to keep fighting, above all in difficult times like the ones we are living in now" (Malamud 2002).

CONCLUSION

While Argentina's disappeared may have been "frozen in time" by the violence of the Dirty War, the Madres are not stuck in the past. Their activism has not only addressed the dictatorship, but also the contemporary reality of Argentina. Nonetheless, scholarship on the Madres has generally left them congealed in time, and a fresh look at their recent activism highlights the dynamic aspect of their struggle and how it has changed as the Madres have aged. This study documents how the Madres have expanded and renewed their goals to address neoliberalism, and gives us insight into mature resistance.

Examining shifting collective action frames shows us that the Madres' goals have expanded due to changing contexts—political, economic, *and* the context of their increasing age and experience. Over almost thirty years of activism, they have weathered military dictatorship, the solidification of democracy, the hostility of the Menem presidency—when neoliberal policy transformed Argentina's economy, and Menem pardoned junta leaders and put an end to future tribunals—and now, a changed political climate in which the Supreme Court declared these amnesty laws unconstitutional (July 2005) and the current president Nestor Kirchner has often spoken in support of human rights. Over this time, they have gained activist experience, and they have become old women. This context of aging has affected their activism, and they assert their identities as *viejitas* and emphasize the link between past and present to explain and justify the expansion of their goals.

Studying aging and age relations among social movement actors is important, because age is a given in all activism, and often a contentious element. Getting older has an effect on the life course frames of activists, so we need to pay attention to aging in activism and how it can affect social movements: activists' strategies and tactics, collective and individual identities, goals and frames are likely to evolve as they age. As they grow older, activists' increasing physical limitations can affect the way they mobilize for collective action. For the Madres, this has meant needing to have office space with an elevator, asserting the fact that they are old women to shame opponents, and shaping their relationships with others—particularly the young supporters who help them in their daily work. They recognize their mortality and the finite future of their organizations, and this recognition has been an impetus for goal expansion. They have managed to modernize and expand their goals, linking old and new in a way that has enabled them to stay relevant, while they prepare to leave a legacy.

In fact, if culture is defined by interaction between generations, as Mannheim (1952) has suggested, then the Madres have an interesting position of using their aging motherhood to bridge between two *younger* generations—their disappeared children, and the young activists that are mobilizing against neoliberalism in contemporary Argentina. Long-term movements rely on generational passage of ideology, repertoires, and goals (Johnston and Aarelaid-Tart 2000: 672), and some movements make this inheritance an explicit part of their work. By paying attention to gender and age identities, we see how motherhood continues to shape the way the Madres frames the passage of their ideas: as old women and mothers, an important aspect of their activism is to work to build and nourish ties to young people and fledgling movements. This has been an extension of their mothering from their missing sons and daughters, to all the disappeared, to the young people active in protest, and finally to resistance itself. They see this as the work of their sons and daughters, the fruit of the sacrifice of the disappeared, and their own legacy. Thus, studying aging and activism can help us further understand how framing and collective identity are interconnected, an under-explored area of the literature on framing (Benford and Snow 2000). It can draw our attention to the way that changing life-course contexts shape the relationships that activists have with members of other generations, in the reversed chronology of the Madres' activism, or a more traditional generational passage.

ACKNOWLEDGMENTS

I thank Leslie Gates, Michael Mulcahy, Barbara Sutton, and Mary Nell Trautner for their comments on earlier versions of this paper, Nancy Ellis for her editorial aid, and Sarita Torres, Sarah Schoellkopf, and many Madres for their help in Argentina. I am also grateful to Joseph Garavente for his research assistance and to the College of New Jersey for a grant that supported this project.

NOTES

1. Few would object to using the label "young," but its opposite—"old"— is stigmatized. Following Calasanti and Slevin (2001), and the language that the Madres use when they call themselves *"viejitas"* (little old ladies), I use the term "old" to "naturalize and neutralize it" (10).

2. The conflict between the two Madres organizations can be traced to differences in political goals and strategy, as well as disagreements about decision making. The Asociación has been more confrontational with state authorities, rejecting state reparations and exhumations of the remains of *desaparecidos/as*, while the Línea Fundadora has held that each family should decide whether or not to apply for economic reparations. The Línea Fundadora also critiqued what they call "authoritarian attitudes in the leadership of the movement" (MPMLF 2003), and there are long-standing personal conflicts between leaders in the two organizations. The effects of the schism are still apparent today: though they march each week in the Plaza de Mayo at the same hour, the members of one group do not generally speak to members from the other.

3. The December 2001 *Argentinazo* was a period of protests that included rioting and looting which was sparked by freezing of bank accounts and other austerity policies.

4. Hebe de Bonafini, president of the Asociación Madres, has been criticized in this fashion. Her remarks in support of ETA in Spain and in celebration of the terrorist attacks on the World Trade Center have provoked widespread criticism, including from the Madres of the Línea Fundadora.

5. The sample excluded opinion editorials, letters to the editor, and Sunday magazine articles. *La Nación* is the second major newspaper in Argentina (behind *Clarín*), with an average weekly circulation of 630,000. I chose to use it because it has the longest and most accessible Internet archive, with complete issues since 1996. I do not contend that the newspaper captures all of the Madres activities; in addition to problems associated with media coverage (McCarthy, McPhail, and Smith 1996), *La Nación* is considered to be more politically conservative than other papers. Therefore, the sample is likely to be a conservative estimate for Madres coverage. However, when I compared the overall counts of articles mentioning the Madres in the top-selling *Clarín* for the dates in its web archive (1998-present) the number of articles was similar.

6. Most of the articles in this category mention Madres or people working with them without reference to their activities.

7. It is interesting to note that critiques of capitalism during the Dirty War were associated with the "communist subversives" who were the target of the repression. As mothers of the disappeared, the Madres' use of this language harkens back to the work of their sons and daughters. It is also notable because bold critiques of capitalism fell out of favor in the economic boom years of privatization, when neoliberal policy was being put into place in Argentina.

Chapter 8

A PLACE OF THEIR OWN? WOMEN ORGANIZERS IN THE MAQUILAS OF NICARAGUA AND MEXICO

Joe Bandy and Jennifer Bickham Mendez

Over the last thirty years, accelerated transnational flows of capital, people, and information have transformed social relations. A globalizing economy dominated by "neoliberalism"—free market ideology and policies of free trade, privatization, and export-oriented industrialization—has caused a global compression of social space and the exacerbation of uneven development within and across nations (Harvey 1990; Smith 1984). We also have witnessed challenges to neoliberal doctrine and the beginnings of a new global political space, or a "global civil society," as reflected in an explosion of transnational social movements (e.g., R. Falk 1993; Guidry, Kennedy, and Zald 2000). Transnational movements occur when groups from at least two different nations share information, organizational resources, strategy, and often but not always, political interests and values (Tarrow 2001; Fox 2000a). Such networks direct their opposition at "powerholders in at least one state other than their own, or against an international institution, or a multinational economic actor" (Tarrow 2001).

To date, most research on transnational movements has focused principally on their grievances, organizational forms, and structural constraints or opportunities (Rucht 1999; Smith 1998; Smith et al. 1997; McAdam, Tarrow, and Tilly 1996). However, to fully understand the transnationalization of movements, it is necessary to examine the local, spatial, and social dynamics by which movements participate in cross-border networks and negotiate place-based differences. Our analysis attempts to do this by comparing women workers' movements in Nicaragua and Northern Mexico that have mobilized in opposition to the abuses occurring within export-processing zones (EPZs) and their factories, or *maquiladoras* (*maquilas*).

GENDER, EPZs, AND RESISTANCE UNDER GLOBALIZATION

EPZs are a major component of neoliberal economic policies. Transnational capital accumulation has depended upon EPZs and their low-wage, young, female labor forces. The International Labor Organization (ILO 2003: 21) estimates that some 42 million people are employed in free trade zones (FTZs) around the world and that 90 percent of the workforce are women. Although the conditions and issues that maquila workers face vary across national and local contexts, there are common experiences and problems, reflecting a global and gendered division of labor (Sklair 1989: 170; Fernández-Kelly 1983: 8-9). Harsh work conditions, meager wages, and human rights violations are enabled by the devaluation of women's work and a discipline of women workers as "docile" employees with "nimble fingers"—a common discourse articulated by transnational corporate actors (Tiano 1994: 208-209; Safa 1990, 1998; Elson and Pearson 1981). In addition to low wages and speedups, maquila women have experienced sexual harassment and violations of their reproductive health and freedom, from toxic workplaces to firings for pregnancy (Human Rights Watch 1996: 27). And, changes in the geography of gender relations have given rise to tensions between men and women over workplace relations and access (in Sheridan 1999: 2). Such examples point to the complex ways in which the dynamics of globalization affect and are constituted by multiple spatial forms in everyday life (cf. Massey 1984).

Movements of women workers have mobilized for improvements in working conditions and to combat injustices in maquila factories, "forc[ing] a reconceptualization of the traditional terrain of class struggle and its privileged subjects" (Camacho 1999: 79; Rosa 1994; Mendez 2002). In this chapter, we examine the opportunities and obstacles that women workers' movements have faced, particularly surrounding gender differences, as they seek social change via national and transnational coalitions. Our focus will be gender tensions within transnational labor movements, highlighting the importance of place and locale in the articulations of strategies of resistance (Naples 2002: 268).

Our analysis is grounded in several years of research on each region. On the U.S./Mexico border, Joe Bandy conducted interviews with thirty labor activists, plus participant observation in multiple labor conferences, especially those of the Coalition for Justice in the Maquiladoras. In Nicaragua, Jennifer Bickham Mendez undertook participant observation as an international volunteer (*cooperante*) for the Working and Unemployed Women's Movement, María Elena Cuadra (MEC) in Managua. She also interviewed MEC founders, organizers, and participants.[1] We argue that, despite the compression of social space in the era of globalization, political contention over global capitalism's effects varies significantly and is locally embedded, calling critical attention to the very meaning of terms like "local," "global," and "place" (Cox 1997: 3; Massey 1994). Our cases demonstrate that local contexts are "not merely . . . effects but also . . . constitutive ingredients" of global processes (Freeman 2001: 1013).

In Nicaragua and Mexico transnational coalitions against export processing are fragmented along multiple fissures, including organizational resources, national or ideological interests, and strategies of opposition.[2] Of particular significance in our cases are the power relations between community-based women's organizations and male-dominated labor unions or NGOs. Such conflict is complicated by its spatial articulation across North/South, local/national, and private/public domains. Gender, along with power relations of race, ethnicity, and nation, compose persistent hegemonies that fracture the space of transnational civil society and constrain opposition to neoliberalism. In line with Hanson and Pratt (1995), we see the struggles of women workers' movements for a place of their own within transnational civil society as characterized by containment as well as border crossing and mobility.

BORDERING THE LOCAL AND THE TRANSNATIONAL: RESISTANCE ON THE U.S.-MEXICO BORDER

In 1965 the Mexican government loosened protectionist laws against foreign investment and created a free trade zone along its northern border. This zone was intensively industrialized, and eventually became the basis of NAFTA. The maquilas—ninety percent from the U.S.—manufacture anything from textiles to electronics, auto parts to plastics, and have found the border profitable due to $5/day average wages, deregulation, and low transport costs to consumer markets (La Botz 2001). In 1994, when NAFTA was implemented, maquila trade represented one-third of Mexican trade with the U.S. (Barry, Browne, and Sims 1994: 84), but between 1994 and 1999, the number of border maquilas rose from 2,157 to 3,143. Employment increased from 546,433 to 1,060,217 (INEGI in TwinPlant News 1999). In 1998, the maquila sector accounted for 40 percent of Mexico's total exports (CNIME in La Botz 1998), and one third of formal sector wages (Bayes and Kelly 2001: 166). The social changes associated with this rapid industrialization have been significant: shifts from subsistence agriculture to wage labor, migration, commercialization, and rapid urbanization (Sklair 1989: 11). Despite the closure of over 400 maquilas and the loss of almost 200,000 jobs since 2000 due to international competition (Sánchez in La Botz 2005), the social significance of the maquilas remains profound.

Contrary to the expectations of policymakers and maquila managers, the predominantly women workers in this ground zero for neoliberalism have not been mere passive or docile victims (Tiano 1994: 217-219). As Carmen Valadez of *Casa de la Mujer/Grupo Factor X* (CDM/GFX) proclaimed, "They thought we were passive, but from the beginning of the maquilas there have been struggles by women." Women worker's movements have sought to raise consciousness about local/global economic problems, and promote economic justice and human rights, from the home to the global economy. Maquila activism is growing in intensity and scope, due to the many social and spatial advantages of the border context: NAFTA and economic restructuring in both nations brought the attention of activists to maquila issues; border society is local and transnational simultaneously, allowing transnational networking; and border culture is binational and bilingual, allowing for closer and more frequent collaboration. In the words of Carmen Valadez (CDM/GFX), activism must focus on multiple spatial scales: "[We are] constructing networks of action, empowerment, and solidarity—local, national and international—between women."

Women labor activists on the border act as brokers, negotiating coalitions between workplaces and communities, between local and national organizations, and between workers of different nations and movement sectors. Most commonly, border coalition building at broad spatial scales occurs in worker-to-worker exchanges and conferences of North American labor and community activists, such as those of the CJM, a coalition of 120 member organizations. As both consciousness-raising and strategic planning events, these forums provide a political socialization for participants that helps develop shared values and identities, or what Snow, Rochford, Worden, and Benford (1986) would call "frame alignment." For example, Hortensia, an activist from a Tijuana community, expressed her appreciation for the CJM's coalition building and the new transnational vision it afforded her:

This gives us more confidence to continue with our struggle, for we see that we're not alone. . . . We hope each of you will continue forward with love, for your brothers and sisters, for communities like ours. This is the same struggle all around the world. (Hernández 1996)

U.S. and Canadian citizens have demonstrated similar shifts to a transnational identity of resistance, as Maureen Casey of the New York Labor-Religion Coalition reported about an exchange with Ciudad Juárez's *Pastoral Juventil Obrera*,

In all cases, people [from New York] have returned to their homes changed, knowing that "free" trade simply costs too much. They remain committed to working with people of vision and hope in Mexico to bring justice to the world of the maquiladoras and to the global economy. (*CJM Correspondence* 1999: 2-3)

This coalition building has improved practically every area of movement organizational capacity on the border. Financial resources have been shared and organizational capacity of community groups has grown. As movements collaborate on and beyond the border, their strategies have become more diverse in form, transnational in scope, and intense in militancy. These strategies may be grouped into four sequential categories, each succeeding the next over the past decade as contention escalated and as organizational networks expanded capacities.

First, labor organizations promoted "codes of conduct." Derived from the UN Universal Declaration on Human Rights, the International Labor Organization, the social charter of the European Union, and existent U.S. and Mexican law, these standards included adherence to U.S. and Mexican health and safety laws, livable wages, reasonable hours, rights to work without harassment or abuse, and rights to collective organizing (*CJM Newsletter* 1994: 4). Pursued in the early 1990s through shareholder resolutions, codes were essential to "frame alignment" among border organizations about labor rights, but since codes were voluntary, they had limited influence on foreign investors.

A second strategy was litigation against corporate violators of national labor laws in Mexico and the U.S. One successful example was the suit against John Shahid of American United Global (AUG) for sexual harassment after he demanded that women workers compete in a bikini contest at a corporate picnic, and for then closing the plant without notification. Because Mexican law possesses no civil sexual harassment law, the Support Committee for Maquiladora Workers (SCMW) and the *Asociación Nacional de Abogados Democráticos* (ANAD) sued in Los Angeles Superior Court on the basis of U.S. law—a possibility after NAFTA (Bayes and Kelly 2001: 167; Tong 1998). With pressure from the United Auto Workers who threatened to force automakers to cancel AUG contracts, the company settled with the workers (Tong 1998).

A third strategy was the use of trade law and international institutions such as NAFTA's National Administrative Office (NAO) to push for greater regulation of wages and work conditions. The NAO presented activists with a regulatory opportunity since it hears violations of NAFTA's labor side accords and can recommend "ministerial level consultations" between national labor authorities. By 2001, after twenty-two complaints, the NAO has found repeatedly that Mexican government agencies and U.S. corporations under NAFTA have failed to recognize collective bargaining rights and to provide healthy and safe work conditions (USDOL/NAO 2001). The NAO also recommended consultations and conferences in 1999 after a 1997 complaint against forty-three companies for pregnancy testing and firing of pregnant women

(USDOL/NAO 2001). However, the NAO has limited power. It has issued almost no fines, has no trade sanction authority, and has recommended few ministerial consultations. Pharis Harvey (International Labor Rights Fund) further argues that the NAO was patronizing to the claimants of the 1997 filing and allowed "no substantive participation by the non-governmental community" and yielded little social justice (*CJM Newsletter* 1999).

Thus, most border activists recognize a need for a fourth strategy of direct action and unionization. For instance, a corporation named in the 1997 complaint abandoned pregnancy testing only when it was confronted with protests and a shareholder resolution (*CJM Correspondence* 1998). In a more celebrated case, the workers at the Kukdong apparel plant in Atlixco, Puebla, with the assistance of the local *Centro de Apoyo al Trabajador* (CAT), the AFL-CIO, the Workers' Rights Consortium, and the United Students against Sweatshops, organized direct actions after multiple health/safety violations, harassment, speedups, low wages, and union-busting. The labor network demanded unionization, staged walkouts and protests, and sent faxes/letters to the Mexican officials and the parent company of Kukdong, Nike. Despite continuing corporate and government opposition, this strategy ultimately caused public relations problems for Nike. Therefore, Nike requested that Mexican officials step aside and allow contract negotiations, resulting in the official recognition of the union and eventually a contract. Currently, however, this is the only independent union with a contract in the maquilas.

However, as these transnational organizational networks and resistance strategies have developed over the last decade, women organizers have had to struggle to voice their perspectives and gendered critiques. In labor support and community organizations such as the *Comité Fronterizo de Obreras* (CFO) and the *Comité de Apoyo Fronterizo Obrera Regional* (CAFOR), women are more than half of the membership, and they occupy positions of great esteem and power. At the local community level, women *promotoras* have been among the most successful organizers, educating and empowering citizens with inclusive social movement agendas for economic justice. Whether they regard themselves as newly politicized maternal figures caring for their community, or feminist intellectuals fighting for gender equality in all areas of life, women activists in the borderlands display passionate vision. This has entailed building connections between a consciousness of labor and sexual exploitation in the factory and in the home; between analyses of productive and reproductive labor; between notions of class and gender; and between dilemmas of the workplace and community (Kamel and Hoffman 1999; Peña 1997; Dwyer 1995; Gabriel and MacDonald 1994; Tiano 1994). Through their organizing, *promotoras* have furthered a common belief that land rights, public services, environmental health, domestic violence, and violent crimes against women are all related to the denial of labor rights and economic deprivation under an exploitative and patriarchal form of export processing. Because of their influence, many predominantly male organizations, especially industrial unions, have become more inclusive of the methods and critiques of women organizers, expanding the diverse scope of national and cross-border coalitions. This is especially evident in organizations such as the *Frente Auténtico del Trabajo,* a progressive independent union in Mexico.

However, at times women's visions of justice have had trouble finding a voice in borderland labor activism, a recurring issue in interviews with women organizers. They have claimed that community-based concerns, particularly those of women workers regarding environmental health, reproductive freedoms, and workplace harassment have been slighted as larger industrial unions, predominated by men, have begun to shape the agendas of cross-border coalitions. They frequently have argued that authoritarian tendencies within labor organizations have accompanied a fraternal and masculine orientation of its organizers. One activist claimed these cadres of men are just like those in government, and that she was "tired of being treated as a second class organizer." In contrast, she and others have described their women-centered methods as more "authentic" due to their accountability to workers' communities. While these are not essential or absolute differences, they may be explained by several factors.

First, since NAFTA, unions have taken a greater interest in cross-border coalitions. In both nations, many unions have developed in patriarchal political cultures and in gender segregated labor markets, causing the traditionally powerful labor unions to be dominated by masculine identities and bureaucratic-industrial models of organizing developed in the 1930s and 1940s (Cobble 1993: 4). As these unions have had their power and membership threatened by industrial reorganization in North America, they have been the most active in organizing against maquiladora development, whether through protectionist self-interest or global solidarity. While many male unionists on the border have been effective feminist allies and have been transformed themselves by more multicultural and egalitarian models of border activism (Cobble 1993: 10), it is not uncommon to witness union tendencies toward macho bravado, paternalism, fraternal cultures of leadership, gendered divisions of labor in activism, and resentment for women's public voice and organizing styles (Needleman 1998: 153-4). These may be expressions of a "defensive masculinity," typical of moments in labor history when male power has been threatened by competition from women in workforces or unions, the threat of lost work or wages, and the financial independence of women (Brenner 1998: 44-50). It is this gendered division in union, if not class, solidarity that Mexican and U.S. women's movements have been challenging for decades (Lamas, Martínez, Tarrés, and Tuñon 1995: 327-328). As women's presence has grown in new labor markets, they have challenged unions to attend to issues such as maternity leave, second shifts, homework, discrimination, wage inequalities, low-wage work, reproductive health, and sexual harassment (Needleman 1998; Cook, Lorwin, and Daniels 1992).

Second, feminist activists frequently have struggled against hierarchical or less participatory organizational forms, and against grievances that privilege shop floor dilemmas over community concerns, or public (workplace) over private (home and community) spaces (Needleman 1998). On the border, some unions, but not all, have shifted attention from community organizing to workplace struggles and collective bargaining. Especially since the recent escalation of labor conflicts with repressive government unions and police, labor activists have increased demands for greater resources to be dedicated to strikes and factory elections. As unions assume more prominence in these conflicts, public attention and coalition resources are perceived by some to shift away from communities and women's issues—domestic violence, child care, education, and environmental protection. Also, perceived exclusion can be exacerbated by the relatively hierarchical structure of unions—with professional organizers and upper echelons comprised by legal and economic technicians, making many leadership roles inaccessible to many working class women (and men). This can result in a division of labor around private and public space, in which female activists and their community organizations are expected to occupy the *promotora* roles of educator or event coordinator, while male unionists work as spokesmen and strategists planning strikes, elections, and negotiations. This division risks disrupting labor solidarity and alienating not only community organizations, but also large numbers of women workers.

Third, traditional repertoires of industrial conflict common to both U.S. and Mexican unionists—strikes and litigation—are more easily adopted by male workforces.

Women workers are not unfamiliar with militancy, but men have been more willing to pursue confrontational tactics since they experience less physical or sexual coercion, and since their jobs are less susceptible to capital flight because they are typically more technologically intensive (Storper 1997: 195-199). Therefore, when unions search for militant workforces in public struggles into which they can invest resources, it is no accident that they tend to focus on those of male workers. These become the center-pieces of labor activism. When resources are limited, favoring one campaign over an-other can incite resentments and rivalries. Combine these tensions with those over various strategies and identities, and it is clear that gendered differences can be expres-sions of complex and multi-layered conflicts. Yet, as the transnational scale of labor coalitions has grown, women's community organizers have feared the marginalization of place-based social needs and the erosion of democracy.

NICARAGUA AND THE "MARÍA ELENA CUADRA" ORGANIZATION

As a post-revolutionary society, Nicaragua's political history makes it unique within the Central American region. Export-processing zones have only had a significant presence in Nicaragua in the last decade. With the 1990 victory of the National Oppo-sition Union over the *Frente Sandinista de Liberación Nacional* (FSLN), President Violeta Chamorro implemented tumultuous neoliberal reforms designed to stimulate growth. In addition to privatizations, reductions in public spending and dramatic down-sizing of the public sector resulting in massive lay-offs of workers, the Chamorro gov-ernment issued new legislation in 1991 to attract foreign investment via free trade zones. The state-owned free trade zone *"Las Mercedes"* opened the following year with eight factories in operation (Renzi 1996). Since the 1996 electoral victory of the Nicaraguan Liberal Alliance party, the government has continued in its neoliberal tra-jectory. Although Nicaragua has experienced some economic growth (9.3% average annual growth in GDP in 1998 and 7.3% in 1999) (World Bank 2000), according to recent UN statistics, 50.3% of the population continues to live below the national pov-erty line (UNDP 2000).

Privatization has had negative effects particularly for women workers (Babb 1996). In state-owned factories, women made up 70% of the textile workers (Alemán Pérez, Martínez, and Windmaier 1987: 5-7). Liquidization of these factories left some 10,000 workers unemployed—85% of the sector's jobs (Renzi and Agurto 1993: 41). Once unionized, in 1992 this work force became a part of a large and desperate labor pool available to the new foreign-owned assembly factories in the EPZ (Renzi and Agurto 1993.[3] At the time of this writing, there are fifteen factories located in Nicara-gua's state-owned FTZ and another twelve factories in the nation's privately operated zones, employing a total of 37,143 workers (Comisión nacional de zonas francas 2002).

The effects of structural adjustments on women prompted the Women's Secre-tariat of the Sandinista Workers' Central (CST), the largest trade union confederation in Nicaragua, to launch programs directed at women. The secretariat founded day-care centers, free women's clinics, and revolving credit funds for women's micro-enter-prises. As early as 1992 the secretariat was working to organize and support maquila workers, a sector ignored by the union federations of the CST until 1997.

Notwithstanding, as the 1990s wore on, it became increasingly obvious to the leaders of the Women's Secretariat that an autonomous women's organization was necessary. Gender-based conflicts between the secretariat and the CST (male) leadership developed and began to intensify. Women were actively prevented from attaining leadership roles in the National Executive Council of the CST, and often were excluded from decision-making processes, even with regard to the use of funding that they themselves had obtained. In 1994 a group of organizers from the Women's Secretariat formed an autonomous organization "by and for women" called María Elena Cuadra (MEC) with the goal of "making visible the role of women in all levels of society." MEC's efforts focus on organizing women workers in the FTZ and improving conditions in these factories. In addition, MEC's programs provide income-generating opportunities, job training, and micro-credit to unemployed women. Workshops sensitize women to gender issues such as domestic violence and reproductive health through education regarding their rights.

A major strategy of MEC has been to raise national, regional and international awareness regarding the situation of maquila workers and to lobby for pressure on factory owners to uphold workers' human rights and comply with local labor laws. MEC organizers have turned away from practices usually associated with the labor movement, such as unionization and strikes. In the words of Laura, a MEC founder: "We want to work with another more positive [*propositiva*] attitude in order to search for a more efficient path without having to arrive at holding a strike…We hold something in common that unites us: we are searching for alternatives to the problems that we live in the zone." MEC organizers have engaged in political lobbying and public awareness campaigns to achieve their objectives. Rather than organizing maquila workers on the shop floor, they work in communities and outside the work place, providing integral services to women workers and poor women. Thus, MEC organizers define MEC as an "alternative" to trade unions, typically stating, "We are not a unionist movement, nor do we have anything to do with unionism. They have their organizations and we have ours. We are offering an alternative by and for women."

In order to counter the mobility of transnational corporations, MEC has engaged in political strategies that span national borders. As a member of the Central American Network of Women in Solidarity with Maquila Workers (hereafter, the Network), MEC coordinates with other regional women's organizations to lobby state officials and negotiate with factory owners (see Mendez 2005). Further, MEC actively participates in a variety of transnational networks with NGOs and solidarity groups in Europe and North America, and is sustained through their financial support.

One of MEC's major strategic tools in its struggle has been the campaign for a code of ethics in the maquilas. MEC's campaign—"Jobs . . . Yes, but with Dignity!" —involved different scales of social movement action. MEC implemented the campaign locally, and wider regional and international campaigns were launched by the Network, with open financial support from Canadian and European NGOs. The transnational character of the Network gave MEC and the other local organizational members added leverage by drawing press coverage and spreading the word of the campaign in order to garner public support and pressure state and corporate actors. As the campaign's slogan suggests, MEC did not call for the removal of the assembly plants, as this would have left women workers jobless. Instead, it denounced cases of violence and unfair and harsh working conditions, calling for factory owners to respect national labor legislation and international conventions on workers' rights. The code of ethics protects pregnant women's rights to employment, payment of legal wages and overtime hours worked, the elimination of all forms of violence, and access to social security services. The demands in the code were drawn from Nicaragua's National Labor Code, the 1997 Apparel Industry Partnership Agreement (AIP), the Convention on the Elimination of All Forms of Discrimination Against Women (CEDAW), and the Universal Declaration on Human Rights.

By placing female maquila workers on the public agenda, MEC affiliates and organizers believe they have contributed to the drop in shop floor violence, sexual assault, and sexual harassment (MEC 1999). The campaign also resulted in an alliance with the Ministry of Labor, which endorsed the Network's code of ethics through the creation of a ministerial resolution that all FTZ factory owners subsequently signed. Through their entrée into the Ministry of Labor, MEC organizers gained access to factory inspections, to human resources administrators, to upper-level managers and factory owners, and to the FTZ itself. In addition, the public awareness generated by the campaign set in motion a bill to reform the legislation that establishes the FTZ and its operations (Anteproyecto de Ley 1999).

Despite these successes, MEC has faced obstacles in implementing its strategies, particularly those at the transnational level. MEC's campaigns and work within the FTZ has resulted in repeated encounters with the traditional labor movement. MEC's integrative approach, which addresses inequalities in both class and gender relations, challenges orthodox Marxist notions of the privileged revolutionary subject constituted solely by economic relations and, thus, goes against the traditional "separation of spheres" of popular organizations in Nicaragua. MEC's efforts challenge the Western distinction between private and public spheres, extending a focus on "labor issues" to sites beyond the workplace, reflecting a different spatial strategy for improving the situation in the FTZ—a strategy rooted in women's gendered experiences in their workplaces, homes and communities. Conversely, Sandinista-affiliated labor organizations often see factories and other workplaces as spaces that constitute their political domain, separate from the "community" sphere of "women's organizations."

It was only in 1997—five years after the formation of the FTZ—that the CST turned its attention to maquila workers. Labor federations, including the CST-affiliated textile and apparel workers' federation, led by Pablo Alvarez, have initiated several attempts to form unions—many of them successful, though it is difficult to gauge the size or level of activity of such unions. By 1999 the Ministry of Labor listed seven active CST-affiliated unions in the FTZ, which by 2000 had declined to two (Bellman 2003: 9). In the late 1990's Alvarez and others used the Sandinista media to publicize management's anti-union tactics and to threaten to shut down factories that were union busting. In addition, the federation tapped into long-standing transnational solidarity networks in the U.S. and Canada to support unionization. They waged several fax and email campaigns, targeting the Corporation of the Free Trade Zone, the Ministry of Labor, and the "home companies" that sell products assembled in the zone. Meanwhile relations with MEC deteriorated. In early 1997 rumors spread in MEC that the CST would send spies to infiltrate MEC's activities in an effort to destroy it and "take over" the factories. Several times, CST supporters confronted MEC organizers, challenging their intentions. In one culminating incident MEC promoters only narrowly avoided a physical conflict with Alvarez and a group of supporters at the entrance to the Free Trade Zone, hurling taunts like, "These women are trying to destroy syndicalism!"

MEC's contentious relationship with the Sandinista labor movement reflected different visions of social change as well as different spatial, political strategies. The Sandinista labor movement coupled nationally based strategies of "before"—strikes, collective bargaining, and unionization—with "new" transnational strategies—email and fax campaigns, using transnational networks to launch leafleting campaigns and direct actions at stores where products are sold in the North, and global media campaigns. The labor movement's strategies had serious implications for MEC, as organizers worried that the more militant and direct actions could have a negative impact on

MEC's delicate negotiations with factory owners and state agents.

In keeping with "jobs, but with dignity," MEC's strategies support a position of "self-limiting radicalism" (Cohen and Arato 1992), which at times limited the effectiveness of some transnational initiatives. Although MEC organizers acknowledge that the real power resides not in the factory subcontractors, but in transnational corporations like Gap and J.C. Penney, they adamantly refuse to support boycotts, as this could risk the loss of jobs when companies simply turn to other factories for their production needs. Indeed, this fear is not unfounded, as there have been several cases in Central America in which boycotted companies have withdrawn contracts, resulting in the closure of these factories (Molina and Quinteros 2000; Köpke 2000). Furthermore, MEC puts other direct actions, such as passing out flyers at the entrances of retailers in the U.S. as being on par with boycotts in terms of threatening their delicate and arduous negotiations with factory owners and sympathetic state agents.

MEC and Network organizers are conscious of the limitations of their strategies. As one participant put it, "We are asking for the minimum. We aren't even questioning the exploitation of workers." Although MEC has important and continuing relationships with Northern NGOs and networks of organizations active in the anti-sweatshop movement, the impact of these coalitions on working conditions in the FTZ is less discernible. In fact, a clear-cut plan of action for sympathetic individuals and groups in the North remains absent from MEC's public awareness campaigns. There also have been other obstacles in implementing transnational strategies. Organizers have wanted to present their code of ethics to the International Labor Organization (ILO), but because the ILO adheres to the model of tripartite negotiations—in which the participants are representatives of the state, management, and unions—autonomous women's organizations have been marginal to transnational labor rights forums.

The conflict between MEC and the Sandinista labor movement also has effectively excluded MEC from other transnational spaces. In November 1997, the New York-based National Labor Committee (NLC), with the help of a solidarity organization in Nicaragua and the Sandinista textile and apparel workers' federation, organized a visit of reporters from the television program *Hard Copy*. In a three-part series aired on national television, reporters used hidden cameras in the garment maquilas to expose working conditions. A national uproar ensued and public opinion was split. Maquila supporters, including neoliberal state agents, pointed to *Hard Copy's* dealings with the NLC and described the report as a plot by protectionist U.S. unions whose jobs are threatened by off-shore production. Meanwhile, Sandinista labor leaders called for the ouster of foreign-owned factories. Former Sandinista Minister of the Interior, Tomás Borge, wrote an editorial in the oppositional newspaper *La Barricada,* entitled "¡*Que se vayan!*" ("They should get out!"), and stated, "The benefit received by the country is insignificant. Our national dignity is of greater value" (Borge 1997: A4).

In response over 350 male and female workers marched at the Ministry of Labor calling for the factories to remain in operation. The Sandinista media portrayed workers as being manipulated by the Free Trade Zone Corporation in order to protect their jobs, while neoliberal state agents cited the march as evidence that Nicaraguans supported the FTZ (Barreto 1997; Meza 1997). Although Nicaraguan media sought MEC's view, organizers chose to remain silent rather than have their views distorted in the binary frame of the public debate. The more nuanced position of these women— that the factories remain in the country but respect the human and labor rights of workers—was not accommodated in public discourse. Approximately twenty workers, including everyone who appeared in the segment, were fired after the report aired. "Are *they* going to give these people work?," MEC organizers wondered of both state agents and the Sandinista labor movement.

It is important to note that MECs relations with organized labor in Nicaragua are complicated and shaped by a long history. Conflicts between MEC and the apparel and textile federation have subsided in recent years—although tensions still exist. Some organizers have even left MEC to return to the labor movement. Notwithstanding, perceptions of "gender blindness" within the Nicaraguan labor movement and its supporters in the transnational anti-sweatshop movement have prompted MEC to cultivate linkages with Northern women's and labor organizations that sympathize with the organization's "gender perspective" regarding the maquila issue, its rejection of boycotts, and its focus on negotiation, lobbying and legislation to effect change.

A PLACE OF THEIR OWN? GLOBAL-LOCAL RESISTANCE

These cases of mobilization against maquiladora injustices share many similarities that indicate a common set of economic and gendered relationships throughout export processing globally, a prominent space of globalization. Yet, they also possess many differences that demonstrate how movement organizations are shaped by places of their own—local structural opportunities and cultures of resistance.

In the twentieth and twenty-first century both Mexico and Nicaragua have been affected profoundly by pained and tumultuous relationships with foreign capital, and revolutionary conflicts between the imperatives of liberalization and redistribution. Throughout Latin America, the last thirty years have seen the growing hegemony of neoliberal doctrines (Veltemeyer, Petras and Vieux 1997: 2). The dominant discourse of development of the last twenty years has promoted export processing as the centerpiece of national development efforts and contributed to the spatial expansion of capital accumulation. Growth in productivity and foreign exchange has occurred largely within dependent export enclaves with little connection to national economies. And neoliberalism has brought to Latin America greater wealth polarization, volatility in currency and portfolio investments, declines in social services, increased natural resource use, and a colonizing culture of "Americanization" via U.S.-based commercialism (UNDP 1999; Veltmeyer, Petras, and Vieux 1997: 29-31).

If northern capital has encouraged liberalization and capital expansion to avoid crises of accumulation, resistance movements of recent years have undergone similar expansion to avoid the crises of disempowerment (Evans 2000). Women's movements in both Nicaragua and Mexico have sought improvements in their socioeconomic conditions through strategies that demand corporate and international institutions be accountable to local interests (Fox and Brown 1998: 12-17). Yet, while women workers in both regions have struggled for accountability, they also have sought to maintain the empowering elements of new political opportunities. They use various strategies to walk this tightrope—grassroots community organizing and education, consensus building around common moral claims or grievances, national and international lobbying efforts and legal actions, and direct actions of varying types.

As in other areas of the developing world, women's economic organizing in Nicaragua and Mexico publicizes the "private" and personalizes the "public," fostering gender solidarity and consciousness, while at the same time mobilizing resistance to neoliberalism (Marchand and Runyan 2000; Rowbotham and Mitter 1994). For instance, in educating about reproductive health and discrimination in the workplace, organizers for MEC or CDM/GFX acknowledge the common devaluation of both productive and reproductive labor under neoliberal development. Or, in educating about domestic violence, organizers claim there are common disciplinary effects of male violence on the shop floor and in the home. In so doing, these organizations enact a grassroots pedagogy that conceptualizes gender and class as mutually constitutive, rejecting essentialist views of political subjectivity. And as dialogue regarding gender and economics expands, place-based identities of resistance become trans-local and coalitional—with greater potential to transcend binaries of global/local, North/South, worker/woman and engage in a more radically democratic opposition to neoliberal globalization (Swyngedouw 1997: 144; Soja and Hooper 1993: 186).

This opposition has often yielded success. Networks' strategies in both nations involve factory monitoring, lobbying, media campaigns, and the development of fair trade principles and corporate codes of conduct. And, in both cases public attention has contributed to the elimination of some workplace problems and to more open public dialogue with powerholders regarding export processing. In Mexico, the successes extend to some precedent-setting legal victories against foreign investors in U.S. courts and the NAO, as well as independent unionization and even contract negotiations. In Nicaragua, successes tend to be reflected in national-level institutions such as the courts of the Ministry of Labor or within the National Assembly, as issues related to the maquilas are placed on the public agenda.

Common to both nations, women's labor movements have discovered that both national and transnational political spaces are highly gendered terrains. Contributing to the gendered dimensions of the transnational political landscape is the hegemonic association of women with private and men with public space. Public/private distinctions are constituted by discourses of a pragmatic, masculine class-reductionism in which established, professionalized, and often hierarchical unions are assumed to be the legitimate vehicles of organized resistance. This pragmatism is bolstered by the structural opportunities that privilege male-dominated labor movements. Established trade unions and labor federations in Nicaragua and Mexico have more resources, greater longevity, and more refined repertoires of public legal and direct action than do many women's organizations. Further, transnational solidarity organizations, government institutions, and even corporations are more accustomed to working or negotiating with unions and federations. Lastly, it is evident in women's stories of activism and domestic relations that there exists significant masculine resentment for women's economic power and involvement in political spaces. Many men perceive the feminization of industrial, especially maquila, workforces as a loss of traditional privileges in both the workplace and the home, an orientation that can potentially bolster union cultures of masculinity.

These factors can foster a gendered exclusivity in the national and transnational movement coalitions, producing conflict and contestation. Labor movements may reproduce gendered divisions of labor in which women and their organizations perform the least public and valued work, while men and unions assume public leadership roles. Consequently, women activists frequently regard male unionists as authoritarian interlopers with limited appreciation for local place. Labor coalitions also privilege shop-floor organizing models that push aside community-based organizing and popular mobilization around gender issues coded as private. Although women's organizations and others have endeavored to deconstruct private/public space and champion participatory agendas, masculine trade union models are persistent.

Despite the many commonalities between Mexican and Nicaraguan dynamics of contention over export processing, these cases demonstrate the locally embedded character of transnational resistance. First, Mexico's export industrialization was earlier and more extensive, which allowed women's maquila movements to develop over a longer period than in Nicaragua. Second, the border's "locational advantage" (Gertler 1997: 58) near the U.S. limits corporate mobility and offers opportunities to local resistance. Third, the implementation of NAFTA and its NAO creates a transnational political space not available in Nicaragua, for making claims against corporate and government abuses, thereby facilitating activist coalitions. Fourth, many U.S. allies have become interested in border workers because of their ties to U.S. immigrant communities and their economic significance for U.S. industry, especially after NAFTA. Last, as Chicana feminists have noted, border citizens live and work transnationally and negotiate differences through the construction of hybrid identities. Thus, activists of Northern Mexico possess a geographical advantage that opens material and cultural opportunities for transnational coalition.

On the other hand, Mexico and Nicaragua have contrasting political and economic histories. Nicaragua's popular revolution left in its wake a more highly politicized public sphere which has contributed to far less state repression of popular movements than in Mexico. The Sandinista Revolution in Nicaragua opened national political spaces of reform, presenting opportunities for organized initiatives opposed to aspects of neoliberal, political doctrine. The FSLN is still the largest political opposition in the country, and Sandinistas (and former Sandinistas) sympathetic to some anti-neoliberal causes hold positions of power in state institutions. Despite deep-seated tensions between the Sandinista party and MEC, social and political networks established during years of political work in the FSLN have actually enabled MEC organizers to access various levels of state institutions (Mendez 2005). Further, the popular politicizing effects of the more recent revolution and contra war has provided citizens with "cultural repertoires" of action (McAdam 1994: 43) which become oppositional tools for countering the effects of liberalization. By contrast, the Mexican revolution was consolidated into a semi-authoritarian state, and trade unions brought into state development policies. As dominant political parties have shifted to neoliberalism, official trade unions have done likewise, acting as agents of social control, constraining labor movements against liberalization. Despite the presence of anti-neoliberal movements such as the Zapatistas and El Barzón, labor militancy is highly limited.

Yet ironically, in Nicaragua, the same revolutionary culture that promotes labor consciousness and opposition to the hegemony of neoliberalism also contains a masculine nationalism and class reductionism that hinders development of a diverse and democratic civil society (Randall 1994). Polarized gender dynamics have been a contributing factor in MEC's development of a "self-limiting radicalism" that rejects unionism and militant direct actions, including international boycotts. Although revolutionary, class-based politicization is greater in Nicaragua than in Mexico, the gendered power dynamics of the FSLN and CST have led to a disunity of women's and labor organizations in Nicaragua that is also far greater (Criquillon 1995). Thus, a vibrant public culture nationally has been constrained by a masculine class politics, and this has affected the development of transnational civil society as well. In Mexico, gendered tensions are profound, but at least in some cases, the predominance of official unions has prompted an alliance between independent unions working with unorganized sectors, and women's community organizations. Combined with a greater diversity of foreign allies from the U.S., including women's organizations, Mexican women of the maquilas have had the opportunity to develop a more expansive civil society coalition than has Nicaragua's MEC—nationally and internationally.

CONCLUSIONS

It is obvious that access to systems of transnational governance and civil society varies across space, time, and social context. Even with the homogenizing features of economic globalization and the transnationalization of social movement practice, locally embedded social processes continue to affect the dynamics of contention. Material and cultural opportunities for resistance vary significantly across borders, presenting individual movements with an array of resources and obstacles in their search for social change. Civil society coalitions have mobilized in opposition to overlapping inequalities that neoliberalism has exacerbated. Yet, as movement coalitions, they face the monumental difficulty of confronting *internally* the profound historical differences that these power relations have constructed. The alchemy of multiple elements of domination—gender, class, race, nation, and empire—poses challenges to resistance movements, especially transnational ones, as they form bonds that are at once cooperative and differentiated, universal and particular, reciprocal and democratic.

Our comparative analysis illustrates the ways in which gendered power structures both affect and are reflected in the spatial workings of transnational politics. This comparison also deepens our understandings of the complex ways in which gender/class-based oppression, on the one hand, and women's agency, on the other hand, operate under conditions of globalization. As we have seen, groups of women in different local and national contexts have taken advantage of, created, reconfigured, and been excluded from differing spaces of resistance. These diverse experiences of resistance lend empirical support to the view that the realm of the so-called global cannot be understood as abstracted from historically situated localities.

In Mexico and Nicaragua, as transnational social movements resist global inequalities, they also face an awkward negotiation between, on the one hand modernist ingredients of labor internationalism, including a gendered separation of spheres and essentialist binaries of woman/worker and gender/class, and on the other hand, a more self-reflexive vision of transnational civil society that is both pluralist and radically democratic (Naples and Desai 2002). It is far from clear what the end of this negotiation will be, or what consequences the resulting form of resistance may have in the region. Yet, global capitalism's reliance on gendered divisions of power for its continued dominance raises important questions about the oppositional effectiveness of networks in civil society that reproduce these divisions. Further, civil societies that weaken the participation of diverse stakeholders only succeed in demobilizing a more inclusive and democratic alternative to neoliberalism, marginalizing many world citizens to places of their own.

NOTES

1. In our research in both nations, names of organizations have been left unchanged. Names of individuals have been changed to protect the anonymity of respondents, except when disclosure was authorized by them. All interviews were tape-recorded and transcribed. Translations from Spanish are our own. All uncited material is from field notes or from the interview transcriptions.

2. For more on conflict in transnational movements, see Bandy and Smith (2005) and Bandy (2004).

3. Although accurate data about the demographics of maquila workers is limited, studies have estimated that the percentage of women workers in the Nicaraguan Free Trade Zone has fluctuated around 80% (Organización Internacional de Trabajo 1996; Ramos 1996).

Part IV

The Moral Economy of Protest Participation

Chapter 9

THE MORAL POLITICS OF ARGENTINE CROWDS

Javier Auyero

Ten years ago, on December 16, 1993, approximately five thousand residents of the northwest city of Santiago del Estero looted and burned three public buildings (the Government House, the Courthouse, and the Legislature) and a dozen private residences of some of the most prominent local officials and politicians (notably, the homes of three former governors, a Supreme Court judge, and several members of the parliament). Described by the main Argentine newspapers as "hungry and angry people," the protesters were demanding their unpaid salaries and pensions (in arrears of three months) and voicing their discontent with widespread governmental corruption. During this episode, now remembered as the *Santiagazo* or the *estallido social* (social explosion), only a couple of commercial stores were looted. Two persons were injured during the brief police attempt to defend the crowd's first target, the Government House. Eighty-eight persons were arrested during the uprising, but were released without charges during the 72 hours following the episode.

Less than three years after the Santiagazo, another episode put the neglected Argentine provinces back into the headlines of newspapers and TV news programs. Between June 20 and June 26, 1996, the southern oil towns of Cutral-co and Plaza Huincul were blocked off by thousands of protesters (during the peak of the protest, there were 20,000 of them) who manned roadblocks on National Road 22 and Provincial Road 17. The piqueteros, as protesters in the barricades named themselves, demanded "genuine sources of employment" and called for the physical presence of the governor in order to personally discuss their claims with him. The sheer number of protesters intimidated the troops of the Gendarmería Nacional, who had been sent by the federal government to clear the National Road. On June 26, the

147

day after the repressive forces left town, Governor Sapag acceded to most of their demands in a written agreement he signed with a representative of the newly formed picketers' commission. During the *pueblada*, as this episode came to be known, nobody was arrested or injured, and no stores were looted.

It is hardly news by now that the last decade witnessed the emergence of new and unconventional forms of popular contention in Argentina. Sieges of (and attacks on) public buildings (government offices, legislatures, courthouses), barricades on national and provincial roads, and camps in central plazas (and more recently rallies including demands of food from supermarkets), became widespread in the south (the provinces of Neuquén, Rio Negro, Santa Cruz, Tierra del Fuego), center (Córdoba, Buenos Aires), and north (Jujuy, Salta, Santiago del Estero, Corrientes, Chaco, to name just a few) of the country. The *Santiagazo* and the *pueblada* are analyzed as founding events in the current cycle of protest in the country (Laufer and Spiguel 1999). They are interpreted in several ways: as main examples of the resistance to the implementation and outcomes of neoliberal adjustment programs (Iñigo Carrera 1999, Klachko 1999), as key cases that illustrate a changing repertoire of contention (Auyero 2001, Farinetti 1999, Villalón 2002), or as episodes that encapsulate the emerging modalities and meanings of protest (Scribano and Schuster 2001).

Estallidos (social explosions), road-blockades, country-wide rallies, or massive occupations of central plazas, are approached as variations of the same theme, i.e., as part of a wave, cycle, or repertoire of contention that, having its roots in the consequences of structural adjustment policies (Tenti 2000, Oviedo 2001), represents a rupture with traditional political practices (i.e., clientelism) and a novel form of popular politics (Dinerstein 2001). In many ways, scholarly accounts echo protesters' discourse. Many of the leaders and participants of insurgent organizations also mention the *Santiagazo* and the *pueblada* as founding episodes of their struggle: the 1993 *Santiagazo* inaugurated resistance against President Menem's neoliberal government; and the 1996 *pueblada* gave birth to the *piqueteros* phenomenon, which has swept Argentina since then and continues to this day (Kohan 2002; Cafassi 2002).

True, it would be hard to think of episodes other than the 1993 *Santiagazo* or the 1996 *pueblada* to better account for the nature of Argentine popular protest. However, the brief opening narratives attest to an undeniable fact: protesters in Santiago and Cutral-co acted in different ways. In this article, I reconstruct protesters' actions, collective beliefs, and shared self-understandings in both sites, using an approach that relies heavily on E.P. Thompson's and James Scott's notion of "moral economy." However, instead of inspecting the popular consensus as to what are legitimate and illegitimate market prices (the core meaning of the term for both authors), I here seek to dissect the shared beliefs as to what are right and wrong *political practices*, i.e., the actions of state officials and elected representatives. Contrary to more recent and fashionable conceptual vocabularies tackling the "culture" of contentious politics (like "framing" or "oppositional consciousness")[1], the notion of moral politics, like its economic counterpart, has the virtue of calling for *simultaneous* attention to the *content* of protesters' beliefs, to their *origin* and to their *impact* on the course of the events. In this article I argue that (1) popular grievances about unpaid wages in Santiago or rising unemployment in Cutral-co operated within *divergent moral politics*; (2) these moral politics are rooted in different political traditions (patronage in Santiago; populist welfare in Cutral-co); and (3) these moral politics influenced the crowds' behaviors in dissimilar ways (the targeting of wrongdoers in the first case; the public demonstration of collective determination in the second).[2]

CONTENTIOUS ARGENTINA

Less than a year after the *pueblada*, in April 1997, residents blocked access to the towns of Cutral-co and Plaza Huincul again, demanding the fulfillment of the previous promises by the governor. Three months later in Cutral-co, several hundred protesters besieged the government building and held provincial and municipal authorities hostage, asking for a raise in the amount of unemployment subsidies. In May, twenty-one roadblocks, organized by municipal workers and the unemployed, isolated the province of Jujuy for twelve days. The entire cabinet of Governor Ferraro resigned as a direct result of this massive protest.

Cutral-co and Jujuy might be the most memorable cases—they made the headlines of the three major national newspapers—but they are hardly the only ones. Between April and June of that same year, protesters barricaded National Road 3 in Trelew (Province of Chubut), residents and unemployed people organized by an umbrella organization called *Multisectorial* blocked traffic on National Road 38 in Cruz del Eje (Province of Córdoba), and municipal workers interrupted the traffic on National Road 11 in Capitán Bermúdez (Province of Santa Fe). During these three months, roadblocks on national and provincial roads took place in Catriel (Province of Rio Negro), Banda del Rio Salí (Province of Tucumán), and in the city of Neuquén (Province of Neuquén), while teachers, coming from the provinces and the capital, converged in the *Plaza de los Dos Congresos* and erected a huge tent (since then known as the *carpa blanca*) to object to their meager wages and poor working conditions. The governor of Salta, not exactly an ally of protesters, best synthesized what happened during this contentious cycle in his reference to the prolonged barricades organized by residents of oil towns Tartagal and General Mosconi on Route 34. He asserted that, "the roadblock is a political practice that is spreading throughout the country."

By November 2000, this form of protest had been learned and adopted in the entire country. Roadblocks cropped up in Isidro Casanova, Esteban Echeverría and Glew (Province of Buenos Aires), Plottier (Neuquén), Salvador Mazza, Tartagal, General Mosconi, Cuña Muerta, and Zanja Honda (Salta), Libertador General San Martín (Jujuy), Resistencia (Chaco), and Belén (Catamarca).

These events serve to summarize the recent emergence of new modalities of popular protest in Argentina. Among numerous observers (e.g., Schuster 1999, Scribano 1999), it is probably Marina Farinetti (1999, 2000) who best diagnoses these transformations. She characterizes the 1990s by five factors: (1) a shift in the locus of labor conflict from the industrial to the public sector; (2) a decrease in the demands for wage increases and an increase in the demands for arrears and job security; (3) a diminution in the number of strikes and an increase in the number of roadblocks (according to one count roadblocks swelled from 51 in 1998, to 252 in 1999, to 514 in 2000, and to 1383 in 2001)[3]; (4) the intensification of protest in the provinces, that is, outside the metropolitan region of Buenos Aires where an overwhelming proportion of roadblocks occur (relative to population)[4]; and (5) the increased centrality of provincial and municipal unions as main contentious actors (see also Schuster 2002; Giarracca et al. 2001).

Most of the students of protest in Argentina point to deproletarianization,[5] state-retrenchment,[6] and decentralization of state services[7] as the processes that lie at the root of the upsurge of contention, and they agree that these are the background conditions for the emergence of what they see as a form of protest that is discontinuous with routine politics. Lozano (2001), for example, asserts that insurgent organizations are autonomous from "traditional political structures." Dinerstein (2001) states that the road blockades "reinvent the forms of (doing) politics." Scribano and Schuster (2001), in turn, affirm that the "unaffiliated" are the main actors in this wave of social protest which constitutes "a mode of rupture with regular social order" (2001: 21). In the rest of this article, I will take a closer look at how the two episodes serve to question, first, the tendency to homogenize protest as emerging from similar causes and acquiring analogous forms; and second, the common proclivity to separate protest from routine politics—a standpoint, I should add, that goes against not only what we see on the ground, but also against much of what we know about the existing continuities between institutionalized politics and collective action (Goldstone 2003).

EL ESTALLIDO

On December 16, 1993, high school and university students, retired elderly, infor-mal-sector workers, and unemployed youth joined municipal and provincial govern-ment workers in the rally in front of the Government House of Santiago del Estero. Angry protesters threw bricks, sticks, bottles, and flat paving stones at the Govern-ment House while trying to enter the building. The police fired tear gas and rubber bullets at the crowd, who then backed off toward the middle of Santiago's main square. Soon, the police seemed to have run out of ammunition and abandoned the scene. The final sacking of the Government House began. Forty minutes later, the courthouse, just two blocks away, became the target. Hundreds of protesters broke windows and entered the building, where they took computers, typewriters, and court case files, and burned desks and chairs. The police report on the "riot" reads:

> [Around 1 PM, a] group arrived at the Congress and, making use of the same methods used in the previous two buildings, they entered, destroyed and burned different pieces of furniture and documentation, and looted different objects.

Here's how a protester describes to me what he calls "the procession" through downtown on the day of the *estallido*:

> When we were in the Government House, the public employees were clapping at the fire. It seemed natural to move on to the Congress. And, while we were going there, the feeling was that it had to be the same. It was at the Congress where the most anger had accumulated because legislators voted in favor of the *Ley Omnibus*[8]. . . . So it seemed natural to them that, having already settled the differences with the Government House and the Courthouse, the Congress was next.

Another protester talks about this "natural" character of the crowd's actions in terms of "necessity."

It was as if it was understood that it was necessary to go to the Congress, because there was still the anger caused by the repression that happened the day that they approved the *Ley Omnibus*.

Ley Omnibus [handwritten note]

After being in the legislature, some protesters return to their homes or go back to the main square, but "a very dynamic group begins to move around by mopeds and bicycles," another protester recounts. This "very dynamic group" arrives at a politician's home and is joined by neighbors in the burning and sacking. The residences that protesters attacked, sacked, and burned on December 16 had been, in a way, defined as targets in the previous months. The "precision" with which the crowd moved from one home to another (precision that officials and some of the press used as evidence of the presence of "subversive agitators") does in fact illustrate the previous process of reconfiguration of the city's geography in terms of the localization of the sources of corruption and suffering, sources who, in the words of another participant, "deserved to be burned down." "How do you decide where to go?" I ask Marilú, a public employee. He responds:

> Here, in Santiago, everybody knows each other and we know where people live. . . . Someone says, "Let's go there because he has also been stealing from us." Because that's how it is here in Santiago, we all know each other.

Although the great majority of the local political elite is considered corrupt in protesters' views, not everybody's house is looted. Some attacks are negotiated on the spot. According to one participant, Mariano, as hundreds of protesters reach the home of deputy Washerberg,

> [T]he guy is freaking out with his sons in the back part of the house. His wife comes out of the house to defend him, "Please, don't do it . . ." She is crying, kneeling in front of us. In any case, Washerberg opposed the *Ley Omnibus*, and he voted against it. So, after his wife cries so much, five gallons of tears, they don't enter his house.

Others, whose homes "deserve to be burned down," are spared for logistical reasons. Mariano continues his account. "The next target is the home of Corvalán, a union leader close to the government. They don't burn his house because he lives in a housing compound; they fear that his neighbors' houses will also be reached by the fire." And others, are (partially) saved from the attack because of the scattered police action: "We are trying to break into Lobo's house when the cops come," Raúl recalls; and Mario adds, pointing at the interaction between the size of the town and the intermittent repression in the making of the protesters' itinerary:

Corvalán union leader [handwritten note]

> *Santiago is a small town.* Everyone knows each other, everyone knows who's who. We leave the Congress and go to the governor's house. . . From there we take another street and go to [government official] Cramaro's house. It is a very nice house, with a lot of wood and many nice things inside. They enter and trash it. Some cops come in and take us out, running. We then take the Avenue . . . and the groups go to [former Governor] Juarez's house either by foot or by bike . . . [former Governor] Iturre's house is a spectacular house, with a swimming pool. . . . They also loot and burn it. After that, someone says we should go to [deputy] Granda's house. . . . He is inside, alone. They go into the house and don't

even touch him. But, again, they loot and burn it. They start to take things out, silver trays and tea pots. . . . *It is a moment of joy*. It is like stealing from the fellows that have abused power for so many years (my emphasis).

Through mutual signaling (signaling that comprised negotiation, logistics, and protection from potential repressive action) protesters move from one place to another. In this mutual signaling, local radio programs play a very important role by broadcasting the crowd's actions "as if it were a soccer match." The places that protesters attack have, indeed, different histories and meanings (while the plaza and the government house have long been centers of political life and thus of protest, the home of local politicians have become sites of contention only during 1993). On December 16, however, claims against corruption and wage demands get concretized in all of them, public buildings and private homes provide concrete representations to protesters' rage.

Routine politics is deeply imbricated in the itinerary of the crowd, after all, the route the protesters create involves the homes of the political bosses, the best-known political patrons, and homes that many protesters used to visit frequently. As Carlos tells me, in a comment that encapsulates the continuities between personalized political networks and contention:

> Here, in Santiago, there are gangs that serve many, many purposes. These gangs are formed by marginal youngsters. The Radical party or the Peronist party invite these youth for a barbecue, taking them for party rallies in exchange for food or money.... These youngsters know every single mechanism to get what they want from politicians, ministers, or members of the parliament. They are not Peronists or Radicals, they just go with everybody. They know the politicos' houses. They've been there, because the corrupt politician invites them to their residences, and they begin to figure out how politics work. These are the youngsters who attack the politicos' houses on December 16. They knew perfectly where they lived.

Fiesta

After an unsuccessful attempt to protect the Government House with tear gas and rubber bullets, the police leave the scene, showing up sporadically to protect some of the attacked victims. Protesters then have the chance to enjoy moments of amusement and joy, in contrast to the tension of the main square. When repressive controls relax, the "party" or "celebration" about which many of my interviewees talk about, then begins. "There are many interesting anecdotes. We laughed a lot. Do you want me to tell you those stories?" Roberto laughingly asks me. And Nana, another protester, adds: "We laughed like crazy. It was hilarious."

The main streets of Santiago become the stage for an unforgettable collective performance. "For once, Santiago was ours," Nana tells me. In participants' accounts, the observable spectacle merges with the experiential feast. There is both a "bond of sympathy" (Rude 1964) between those who join the crowd and those who line the sidewalks and/or sit in front of a TV set, as well as a constant exchange between the roles of spectator and active participant. As María comments, it is "a popular spectacle, a thing of the people, really spontaneous and comprehensible." In an interview with Manuel, another active participant, I mention the title of the newspaper report that describes the uprising. It is entitled "The Saddest Day." He responds: "No, not at all. It is a day of happiness and explosion. . . a lot of anger. . . It is a sad day *for them*, because the government palace and the legislature are burning." The uprising is lived as a pleasurable and amusing experience:

> At Casanegra's[9] house, the upstairs bedroom's windows have bars, and the kids already looted everything. They are starting to burn it, and you can see the flames going up. There are some kids left upstairs who are not going to be able to leave through the windows because of the bars. You can see them staying there, looking through [laughter]. And there is a crowd outside, all of them worried to see when the kids are going to get out. A woman raises her hand holding a beautiful pink shoe in it. Through the bars you can see a guy who knows her and is throwing her some stuff. She shows him the shoe and says "[I need] the other one!!" [laughter]. That guy is risking his life, and she is asking for the other shoe. How wonderful! We are laughing like crazy (Roberto).

Nana, at this time, is in the main square. She can't actually believe what is going on but takes pleasure in it. After running back and forth, after the stones and the tear gas, she is now wandering around, "enjoying the moment. . .We are celebrating, calm. . . . I never smoke a joint, but I think it is something similar to that." Another union activist, Andres, also compares his sensations at the time with "smoking pot or. . . at the time we are chatting with a friend and we are saying that it is as if we are making love to someone we *desire for a long time*." Newspaper reports mention in passing the applause and cheers of bystanders, describing the apparent happiness of protesters as a "contradiction":

> Given the critical moment in the life of the city . . . it might seem a contradiction that the persons who were observing the actions of demonstrators were, at the same time, celebrating, applauding protesters as they went by with their 'booty,' and showing a state close to happiness. (*El Liberal* 12/17/93:4)

In protesters' voices, the "celebration" takes center stage and is hardly perceived as a "contradiction."

A cluster of images of parody, open-air cursing, and degradation points to a carnivalesque dimension of the uprising. A man dressed in (Governor's Juarez's wife) Nina's clothes parades like a model in front of the former governor's mansion and leaves with his "trophies," another one sits in the governor's chair, his arms saluting the crowd from the balcony of the Government House. "That really impresses me," René says; "that is the image that strikes me the most," Juana states. Downstairs people are spraying the walls with curses and threats to established authorities: "Traitors. We'll kill you"; "God forgive me. Archbishop you are a son of a bitch;" (the Archbishop supported the approval of the *Ley Omnibus*) "Juarez, Iturre, Lobo, Mugica, *hijos de puta* (sons of bitches)." In these graffiti, protesters are not only identifying the objects of their claims and discontent, they are also putting forward an *understanding of who they are*: "In Santiago, there are no more sheep," someone sprays on the wall of the House capturing a general collective feeling. "No more sheep" means no more cowardly people, no more (stereotypically) calm and submissive *Santiagueños*. "No more sheep" means "We aggrieved, honest people, are not going to take it anymore, enough is enough." This statement was inscribed on the Government House walls, left by one protester for other protesters, for the elites, for the media, and for us, the analysts. It was one of those publicly available symbols in which the meanings of the protest and the self-understandings of protesters are embodied: the "honest *pueblo*" confronts the "corrupt *políticos*."

Episodes of ritual defilement, of comic degradation and inversion, and of passing suspension of boundaries, also abound. "This guy," Roberto describes, "pees all over Juarez's and Nina's bed . . . spread all over . . . so funny." And Toto, a policeman, adds: "There is this fool man, who goes into one of the homes, and comes out with a raincoat and a hat, a la Humphrey Bogart . . . people are laughing like crazy. It is a like a show, people are celebrating."

During this festive trashing, participants highlight the fleeting creation of a community of demonstrators. "One thing that catches my attention," Roberto says, "is that there are no fights among the people who are sacking those houses. Each person takes something, and no one bothers him." It is not a Hobbessian "war of all against all," because as Gustavo—at that time a journalist—recollects, "nobody even touched what someone else was stealing." For him, the protest is "a party, a catharsis, and a revenge." The transient community formed among protesters transforms fight and punishment into festive action, and, for one day, it turns the world of local hierarchies upside down:

> We see a huge fat man coming—very impressive—with a sofa, a jewel. It must be a unique piece, a beauty. The fat man is carrying it all by himself walking through the middle of the street, like the owner in his own house. And all of a sudden he turns around and sees a police car, filled with policemen from the infantry. It stops, and it is obvious that they have to put him in jail; the fat man can't deny he is stealing [laughter]. So the policemen surround him, make him put the sofa down and make him sit. The fat man doesn't really resist them. He uses the whole back seat of the car and sits down with his back facing the driver. And off he goes. When the car turns around, the people stop it and say: "Give us the fat man back, give us the fat man back!!" [laughter]. You know, they exchange him. The cops get the fat man out of the car and take the sofa. . . . People clapped [laughter].

For participants, December 16 has many elements of carnivalesque egalitarianism. That day is lived as "a privileged time when what oft was thought could for once be expressed with relative impunity," a special time that Peter Burke (1978) sees as characteristic of popular rituals, experienced as the "temporary suspension of all hierarchic distinctions and barriers," that Bakhtin defines as central in the carnivalesque (Bakhtin 1984: 15; Stallybrass and White 1986; Steinberg 1998). Far from being a space of forgetting, this *carnaval* allows protesters to vent their anger against clearly identified wrongdoers. It was lived at the time (and is remembered years later) as a "lesson for local politicians."

LA PUEBLADA AND LOS PIQUETEROS

Early on June 20, 1996, one of the main radio stations of Cutral-co, Radio Victoria, aired the bad news: The provincial government called off a deal with Agrium, a Canadian company, to build a fertilizer plant in the region. The radio station then, "open[ed] its microphones to listen to the people's reaction. . . . A neighbor called

saying that the people should show its discontent. . . . [Another one] said that we
should get together in the road," Mario Fernández, director and owner of the radio
station, recalls. All my interviewees mention those radio messages as central in their
recollections, not only in terms of the ways in which the radio called on people but
also in terms of the way in which the local radio publicly presented the cancellation
of the fertilizer plant project. On Radio Victoria, the former mayor Grittini and his
political ally, the radio station owner and director Fernandez, depicted the cancellation of the deal with Agrium as a, "final blow to both communities," as the "last
hope gone," and as an "utterly arbitrary decision of the provincial government."
Daniel remembers, "There was a lot of anger. . . . The radio said that we should go
out and demonstrate; they were saying that it was the time to be courageous." "I
learned about the blockade on the radio. . . . They were talking about the social situation," Zulma says.

The radio broadcast, "the ire that we felt," to use Daniel's words. On the
airwaves were calls that the people congregate on Route 22 at *Torre Uno*—where a
memorial of the discovery of oil in the region was located. Taxicabs brought people
there free of charge. Was this a sudden eruption of indignation? Were radio reporters
and taxi drivers merely the first to spontaneously react? Hardly so. The factionalism
within the governing party, the MPN (Movimiento Popular Neuquino), and
particularly, the actions of the former Mayor Grittini who had been waging his own
personal fight against Mayor Martinasso and Governor Sapag,[10] are at the root of
rapid spread of the "bad news" and the quick mobilization of resources that
followed. In an interview that he preferred I not tape, "because the truth cannot be
told to a tape recorder," Martinasso tells me, "Grittini backed the protest during the
first couple of days. How? Well, in the first place buying a couple of local radio
stations so that they call people to the route . . . that's how politics work in Cutral-
co." Grittini and his associates' efforts (Radio Victoria's owner Fernandez being a
key figure at this stage) did not end there. Although there is not conclusive evidence,
many sources (journalists, politicians, and protesters) indicate that he also sent the
trucks that brought hundreds of tires to the different pickets and some of the
bulldozers to block the traffic. According to many residents I talked to, he also was
behind the free distribution of food, gasoline, firewood, and cigarettes at the
barricades. Some even say that Grittini paid fifty dollars per night to hundreds of
young picketers and that his associates provided them with wine and marijuana.

Thus, while the radio aired its angry messages, tires were brought to the pickets,
food, cigarettes, and other essentials were distributed free of charge. "We even got
diapers for the babies!" many women protesters recalled. News and resources did
not, however, circulate in a vacuum but rather via well-established political
networks. Resources and news, furthermore, mushroomed in conditions that were
ripe for a large-scale protest namely, the skyrocketing unemployment in the area and
the ensuing rapid process of collective inmiseration.

At Risk

Plaza Huincul and Cutral-co were born of and developed through oil activity.
Since their inception in 1918 and 1933 respectively both towns grew with the rhythm
of (and became highly dependent on) the benefits provided by oil production and by
the activities of the state oil company, Yacimientos Petrolíferos Fiscales (hereafter,
YPF, the first government company founded in 1922). With the discovery of
petroleum in the area came the territorial occupation and settlement carried out under

the aegis of state action. The rapid population growth of both towns reflects the expansion of YPF's activities. From 1947 to 1990, the total population increased from 6,452 to 44,711, an impressive growth by all accounts (Favaro and Bucciarelli 1994). The cradle-to-grave enterprise welfare of YPF benefited its workers with higher than average salaries, modern housing serviced by the very same company personnel ("anything that was broken in the house was fixed by YPF," I was repeatedly told by former YPF workers), access to a very good hospital and health plan, and paid vacations ("once a year, we had free plane tickets and two weeks in a hotel in Buenos Aires or anywhere in the country"). YPF's welfare extended well beyond the confines of the company: The whole social and economic life of the region was boosted by its presence. YPF built entire neighborhoods, provided others with sewers and lighting, erected a local high-quality hospital, a movie theater, a sports center, and provided school buses for most of the population. In other words, YPF "was everything for both towns: work, health, education, sports, and leisure" (Costallat 1999: 6).

In less than two years an economic system and a form of life that had lasted more than four decades was literally shattered. The privatization of YPF was passed as law by the National Congress on September 24, 1992, and soon enough, the devastating effects were felt in the region. YPF not only cut back its personnel from 4,200 employees to 600 in less than a year (Favaro, Bucciarelli, and Luomo 1997); it also ceased to be the welfare enterprise around which the life of both towns revolved (the company even moved its headquarters out of Plaza Huincul), and became an enclave industry functioning under strict capitalist guidelines. Headlines of the major regional newspaper captured the general mood as the first effects of the privatization began to be felt in Cutral-co and Plaza Huincul: "Uncertain future awaits Cutral-co and Plaza Huincul" (*Rio Negro* 1/21/1992), "Alarming unemployment in the oil region" (*Rio Negro* 5/6/1992), "The struggle against becoming a ghost town" (*Rio Negro* 3/26/1994). As massive layoffs were taking place, the articles described a "general feeling of uncertainty" about the beginnings of the process that is now in its mature form: hyper-unemployment. In Cutral-co, 30 percent of the economically active population (25,340 residents) was unemployed (1997). More than half of the population of both towns now lives below the official poverty line (Favaro, Bucciarelli, and Luomo 1997).

En la Ruta

In a few hours, hundreds of residents mobilize on the *Torre* to express their discontent at what they perceive as an arbitrary decision by the governor. As the day comes to an end, some protesters decide to stay on the road (coordinating their actions through local radio) to blockade the access to both towns with burning tires, barbed wire fences, old machines, cars, stones, and their own bodies. After a day on the barricades, the initial organizers (linked to the MPN) call a meeting at the *Torre Uno*. At this meeting, some of the local notables express their disgust with the governor's decision and call for his resignation. Others, mainly those with little or no political experience and who have stayed on the picket lines during the previous night, are strangely left out of the public discussion. This meeting looks pretty much like a well-attended political rally during an electoral campaign. As Rubén recalls: "When I went to the *Torre*, I realized that it was like a political rally, there were, as always, three or four politicians making promises. . . ." The only difference is that, instead of returning home, participants go back to the barricades. A group of them

Committee of Pickets Representative

convene a meeting at another barricade (the barricade at the airport) where they give birth to their own organization, the "Committee of Pickets' Representative." Laura Padilla is one of its spokespersons, and the presence of the governor "to give us solutions (i.e., jobs)" emerges as their main claim. Four years after the episode, a picketer named Jote tells me,

> The first day, they, the politicians, secretly organized the whole thing. But on the second day, talking among ourselves, in the picket, we realized the protest was a political maneuver. And so we began to organize, saying that politicians should stay outside, and stressing that we only wanted to talk to one politician, the governor himself.

pol. trying to profit for this

In the meeting at the airport, on the protest's second day, the picketers agree that politicians are trying to use the protest for their own purposes. "At the meeting," Laura tells me, "we all had a common feeling: they, the politicians, were using us, they ignored us at the *Torre Uno*." Laura's, Jote's, and others' private disgust for local politicians soon became the basis for a self-understanding shared by most protesters.

The next day, the local TV channel broadcasts Laura's first appearance. She read a communiqué from the recently formed Committee of Pickets' Representatives: "Yesterday, when they called us to the assembly, we felt disappointed because we couldn't speak up. That's why we called a meeting. We agreed on the following: 'We, the *self-convened neighbors*, demand the governor. . . .' And she continued with a long list of demands including jobs, support for the unemployed, cheap credit for local businesses, reactivating the fertilizer plant project, and moratoriums on local taxes, electricity, and gas bills.

As I said, the postponement of the construction of the fertilizer plant was the protest's precipitating event. However, the dynamics of the following days push that claim to the background—so much so that the picketers hardly mention the plant thereafter (it reappears as the last item in the agreement signed with the governor, almost as an afterthought). Although protesters never cease to demand "genuine sources of employment," after the third day blocking the road, the claims lose specificity ("we want the fertilizer plant") and become more general ("we need jobs") but, at the same time, more urgent ("We want Governor Sapag to come here, now"). Every chance they get to speak to a local radio or TV channel, residents of Cutral-co and Plaza Huincul voice the same determination: "Sapag should come here and listen to us," "What we need here is the governor's presence. We need him to come and talk with us. After that we'll see if we cease the protest."

Nowhere is the making of the picketer's self-understanding more patently reflected than in the notebook carried by Laura, the picketers' spokesperson. In her recorded minutes of several picketer meetings during the protests, she notes the organizational tasks that the *piqueteros* devote most of their time to: "place labels on vehicles," "call for a meeting with the lawyers association," "machines to block roads," "retirees are in charge of food." On one of the pages, the notebook has the phone numbers of TV and radio stations, and one phrase: "Utilize the media." "Use the media," Laura explains to me, "so that someone pays attention to us." Her annotations and comments show the protesters' profound awareness about the key role the media can play in making the protest visible beyond the confines of the two towns, and even beyond the limits of the province. In her statement, however, this concern with visibility is not merely a strategic need. It is also an expression of the

postponed area of fert. plant project fueled this

dialogical basis of the identity picketers are by now defending; if they, with the help of the media, are taken into account, the Governor will pay them due attention. "He will realize that the whole people are here," Laura recalls.

The media at the time, along with my interviews years later, record this need to be listened to. At a time when both Cutral-co and Plaza Huincul are perceived, by locals and outsiders alike, as rapidly becoming ghost towns, the crowd's emphasis on "being heard," "being noticed" by the "governor in person" can be read as a cry against the threat of disappearance. As Marcelo, a picketer, recalls, "We obstructed traffic because it was the only way in which we could be listened to. . . ." Or as Mary, her eyes on the verge of tears, clearly puts it,

> My son asked me why we were in the road. And I told him: 'Look son, this *pueblo* needs to be heard. The people in this town need to be aware of the things we are losing, of the things that the government is taking away from us.' I understood it that way; I lived it that way.

Listening to Mary, Marcelo, Mónica—who angrily tells me, "We won't move from the road because we are here, in Cutral-co, to stay . . . . Why do I have to leave if I love this place. . . . I grew up here"—and to many others, I would even venture that the social world of blocking the road offered residents and picketers alike, for seven days, that which they most lacked as inhabitants of a place-in-danger: a justification for existing. Being at the barricade rescues them from official oblivion; it offers them the chance to emerge from the indifference of the state.

Who is this "we" that wants to be seen, acknowledged, and recognized? Brief as the phrases that Laura scatters in her notebook are, they synthesize the picketers' (relational and dialogical) claims and self-understanding.

> 50,000 residents. No, coup d'etat. . . . Before privatization, they didn't get the people ready. The richest soil, the poorest people. An unarmed people, 20,000 people. Picketers-Citizens. Unemployment. . . . 4100 unemployed. . . . Joy-People. United. Expelled from the economic system. . . . The representatives of the pickets inform the people; we are having meetings, we are more determined than ever. The governor has (in front of him) a people demonstrating that it is united, that it will not give up, and that it wants to have a dialogue.

How did protesters define themselves? As many a crowd before this one, this crowd described itself as united (saying, "The whole people [*el pueblo*] is here"), numerous (asserting, "We are thirty thousand, not five thousand"), committed to one goal (claiming, "We want jobs. We want Governor Sapag to come here and give us a solution"), worthy (insisting, "We provide the gasoline, the oil, to the rest of the country"), and lacking leaders (shouting, "There are no politicians here"). What does *el pueblo* mean? What are the roots of this collective self-understanding? On the one hand, *el pueblo* refers to location, to the fact that entire towns are present in the road. In residents' minds, theirs is a very special *pueblo* because it provides energy (natural gas and petroleum) to the rest of the country. Among residents, there is a widespread belief (itself rooted in a deeply entrenched nationalist rhetoric) that the region's mineral resources belong to them. As a young picketer remarked just a couple of feet away from the gendarmes who came to town to "clear the road" (and it was repeated several times during those days in the road), "We provide gasoline, oil, and electricity to the rest of the country and . . . is this the pay we get?" In other words, the collective self-understanding that was forged during those days has its roots (its material bases, I would say) not only in the current plight of Cutral-co and Plaza Huincul as towns at risk of disappearing but also in the memories of the "golden times" of YPF and in the deeply held conviction concerning the ownership of natural resources. In this way, residents' collective memories of a semiwelfare state gave them a powerful sense of solidarity that provided an impetus to fight for what they saw as their cities' interests.

There is, however, another crucial connotation of the term *pueblo* implicit in the roar of the crowd. Protesters constructed their identity and their demands in democratic terms against what they saw as politicians' obscure dealings and constant attempts to "use the people." From the picketers' point of view, who the protesters were and what they were shouting about had as much to do with the devastation provoked by state-retrenchment—expressed in the privatization of the state-run oil company—as with the ruin brought about by politicians' self-interested actions (a striking, if paradoxical, identity development given that this protest, as many others, began as part of an intraparty fight). Picketers identified themselves against one main actor—the political class. It is, without the usual representatives (or, rather, in spite of them), that residents were able to broadcast their discontent about the towns' rapid decay to the whole country. "For once," Laura and many picketers told me, "politicians couldn't use us."

THE MORAL POLITICS OF THE CROWDS

In a now classic article, E.P. Thompson asks a simple but still essential question: "[B]eing hungry, what do people do? How is their behavior modified by custom, culture, and reason?" (1993: 187). Paraphrasing the English historian, we could ask a parallel question about the crowds in the south and north of Argentina: Being unpaid or unemployed, what do residents in Santiago and Cutral-co do? How are their contentious actions modified by local history and prevailing political routines and beliefs? The primary stimulus of collective suffering is indeed present but do the contentious behaviors of thousands of protesters not contribute toward a more "complex, culturally mediated function, which cannot be reduced . . . back to stimulus once again?" (1993: 187). In this essay, I proposed the following answer: Pretty much like in the collective actions of the English eighteen-century silk-weavers (Steinberg 1999), the twentieth-century Burmese and Vietnamese peasants (Scott 1977), or, more recently, the Chinese students (Calhoun 1994) and workers (Lee 2000), we can detect among protesters in different sites in contemporary Argentina diverse moral politics, different notions as to what are legitimate and illegitimate *political* practices, as to what local officials and politicians should and should not do—notions themselves grounded in traditional views of the role that the state is supposed to fulfill. It was outrage to these deeply held political beliefs that drove much of the protest and shaped the behavior of protesters. This chapter sought to describe these dissimilar moral politics, unearth their differential origins, and examine how they impact the unfolding of contentious events. To put it simply, I intended to answer these three questions: Who did protesters in Santiago and Cutral-co think they were, what did they think they were doing, and to what ends did they think they were doing it? Where did the two sets of beliefs that animated these protests come from? How did they influence protesters' actions?

What did they do? In 1993, protesters paraded through town and attacked the residences ~~of wrongdoers and the~~ symbols of public power in what reminded close observers of carnivalesque celebrations (see also, Farinetti 2000). In 1996, insurgents blocked off roads and halted the movement of people and goods while attempting to forge an autonomous mobilizing organization (see also, Klachko 1999; Oviedo 2001). Well-established clientelist networks determined much of the itinerary of protesters during the 1993 *estallido*; party politics, not strictly clientelist, were deeply involved in the origins of the 1996 *pueblada*.

What did they believe? Protesters not only behaved in differing ways and had different kinds of relations with established political actors; they also understood themselves differently. In Santiago, protesters thought of themselves as the "honest pueblo" that fought against a "corrupt political class." In Cutral-co, although contempt for the local politicos was indeed present, contentious actors saw themselves as part of a "threatened town," a "pueblo" endangered by a set of national and provincial policies.

Where did these moral politics come from? The rootedness of contention in local context gives protest its power and meaning. The *Santiagazo*, the deeds and beliefs of the crowd and the emphasis protesters placed on their "honesty" vis-à-vis the corrupt political class and on the personalized character of the punishment they were administering, have to be understood in a context such as the Santiago of the 1990s in which widespread public nepotism and patronage politics were the prevailing way of conducting government affairs. Local sociologists refer to the *modelo juarista* (in reference to the five time governor Carlos Juarez) as a system of power based on the distribution of jobs in the public sector (46 percent of wage earners in the province are public employees) and public housing carried out through well-oiled clientelist networks (Tasso 1999b).[11] In a context in which politics take such a personalized character it should not come as a surprise that collective insurgency took the form it did on December 16. Prevailing political routines give the *Santiagazo* its character; they also provide the crowd with a set of beliefs as to what are right and wrong political practices and who is to be (personally) blamed for their plight.

Matters were quite different in the Cutral-co and Plaza Huincul of the 1990s. The actions and roar of the crowd, the emphasis protesters placed on their citizenship, visibility, and worthiness have to be understood in the context of an entire region threatened in its very existence. Since the 1992 privatization of YPF and the subsequent explosion of joblessness and poverty, the specter of the "ghost town" haunted old and young residents. Memories of functioning welfare state policies informed protesters' demands to a great extent. Party politics was indeed present in the origins of the protest (and contempt for it shaped much of the course of the episode) but the *pueblada* was not a personalized protest. Although the governor becomes the object of protesters' claims, what is right and what is wrong take on a different meaning here. It is more related to policy decisions than with the doings or undoings of this or that official.

And finally, *how did these moral politics influence their actions?* E. P. Thompson's crowds limited their demands for redress to preexisting traditions (traditions, he argues, very much infused by paternalism) by, for example, paying bakers and millers the established (and considered fair) prices. Existing, durable worldviews also influenced the actions and claims of the Argentine crowds. Together with the previous existence of patronage networks, a simple but intensely lived moral boundary, provided the crowds in Santiago with an object and a reason: Those thought to be responsible for their plight had to be punished *in situ*. In Cutral-co, the road blockades were intricately related to a shared self-understanding as an endangered town that was once created and supported by the state: they stayed on the road to be seen and recognized at a time when the risk of collective disappearance is a common and pressing concern. They were showing their collective determination against policy decisions that, taken elsewhere, were confining them to a ghost-like existence.

CODA

The "culture" of contentious collective action has been the object of much recent scholarly scrutiny. The main task of this chapter was to examine the different sources, forms, and impacts of protesters' shared representations during two contentious episodes. At a more modest level, however, I sought to suggest that those interested in the cultural dimensions of protest might, rather than continuing to come up with new concepts and terms, have a lot to gain from a critical translation of the concept of moral economy to the realm of politics.

NOTES

1. On framing and its critics, see Snow and Benford (1988, 1992), Benford and Snow (2000), Steinberg (1998), Polletta (1998a); on oppositional consciousness see Mansbridge and Morris (2001).

2. Fieldwork for this chapter was carried out during the summers of 1999 and 2000, and during January through April of 2001. It is composed of archival research, in-depth interviewing, informal conversations, and photo-elicitation. Archival research included the reading of every issue of Santiago del Estero's main local newspaper (*El Liberal*) for the years 1993 and 1994, selected issues of *El Liberal* and *El Nuevo Diario* of subsequent years, every issue of *La Mañana del Sur* for the years 1995 through 2000, and selected issues of *Rio Negro*. Archival research also comprised content analysis of three major national newspapers (*La Nación, Clarín,* and *Página12*) for the year before and the year after the uprisings. I also read leaflets, press communiques, police records, and court case files to the extent that they were available. To ensure the representativeness of informants in Santiago, I interviewed people from different unions, with different levels of participation during the months prior to the event, and with diverse itineraries during the day of the uprising. In Cutral-co, I interviewed people with different levels of participation during the uprising (female and male picketers who stayed in the blockades round the clock, residents who only participated during the day, etc.). In both cases, some names have been changed to protect anonymity, but many people did not mind (in fact, many insisted) that their real names be used.

3. Centro de Estudios para la Nueva Mayoría (www.nuevamayoria.com).

4. While 48 percent of the population is concentrated in Buenos Aires and the Federal Capital, they had 38 percent of the roadblocks between 1997 and 2000. For the same time period, the provinces of Jujuy, Tucuman, Neuquén, Santa Fe, Cordoba, and Salta with 27 percent of the total population registered 42 percent of roadblocks.

5. From 1988 to 1998, the industrial heartland of Argentina (known as the *Conurbano Bonaerense*) lost 5,508 industrial plants, and industrial jobs decreased from 1,381,805 in 1985 to 1,082,600 in 1994 (a 22 percent loss in manufacturing jobs over nine years). Argentina's current, record-high unemployment rate is 19.5 percent. Rising poverty results from this veritable hyper-unemployment (Iñiguez and Sanchez 1996). As economist Ricardo Aronskind (2001: 18) summarizes: "21.5% of the population was poor in 1991, 27% at the end of 2000. Indigents were 3% of the population in 1991 and 7% in 2000. At the beginning of the 1990s there were 1.6 million unemployed, at the end of the 2000 there are 4 million unemployed."

6. The retrenchment and dismantling of the welfare component of the populist state, caused by the resolute adoption of structural adjustment policies, makes the risks involved in situations of material deprivation, and the inequalities, even greater. The last decade has witnessed a constant degradation of the public school system and the health system, while public support for low-income housing has become negligible (see Auyero 1999). The privatization of public companies (phone, mail, aviation, waterworks, energy, oil, train, and gas) comprised a central dimension of the process of state retrenchment and has dramatically impacted employment levels. Between 1989 and 1999, close to 150,000 workers lost their jobs as a direct

consequence of the privatization process.

7. Starting in 1989, administrative responsibilities and financial liabilities for education (mainly high schools) and health services (mainly public hospitals) were transferred from the federal to state and municipal levels. Decentralization of education and of health services has deepened the crisis in both sectors because already deficient provincial administrations confront the new financial burden with meager funds. Provincial governments, incapable of providing resources, maintaining buildings, and paying their personnel, have become targets for the claims of the now "provincialized" state employees.

8. Ley Omnibus is the name given to the local adjustment law that the parliament passed on November 12, 1993, and that implied the layoff of hundreds of temporary workers, the reduction of public administration wages, and the privatization of most public services. In a province where close to half of wage-earners are public employees, such a law was destined to provoke massive protests.

9. Casanegra was the former public works minister. His house was among those most damaged by the protesters.

10. Months before, in the party primaries current Governor Sosbich allied with Cutral-co former Mayor Grittini against then Governor Sapag. Sapag won the primaries and Mayor Martinasso, who initially sided with Sosbisch-Grittini, switched factions and joined Sapag's group.

11. "El Tata" Juarez, "the only successful endeavor in a province plagued by frustrations and failures," (Tasso 1999a:5) is undoubtedly the ultimate *caudillo*. His first term as governor was when Perón was at the peak of his power in 1949. He was re-elected governor in 1973, in 1983, in 1995, and, for the last time in 1999. Now in his eighties, he publicly admits that he is "condemned to this job" (as governor). In the last election his running mate (and the current governor) was his wife Nina Aragonés who, as I was repeatedly told by journalists, union leaders, and residents of Santiago, is the one "who now gives the orders." She is the leader of the powerful Peronist Women's Branch, a group of her followers that controls access to public jobs, attendance to rallies, distribution of public housing and of other goods and services provided by the government.

Chapter 10

FAMILIES, FIELDS, AND FIGHTING FOR LAND: THE SPATIAL DYNAMICS OF CONTENTION IN RURAL BRAZIL

Wendy Wolford

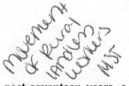

Over the past seventeen years, a movement that began with 400 people in southern Brazil has grown to become "the most dynamic, best organized, and effective social movement" in the history of the country (Petras 1997: 18). Founded in the belief that "land belongs to those who work it," *O Movimento Dos Trabalhadores Rurais Sem Terra* (the Movement of Rural Landless Workers, or MST) organizes the landless poor throughout Brazil to enter (occupy) "unproductive" estates and demand title to the property. Since 1984, the MST has organized over 250,000 such occupations throughout the country and won land for almost 300,000 families. In a country where a handful of landowners control the vast majority of land, the potential benefits of joining the MST are clear. Individual decisions to join the movement, however, are not made easily. People leave everything familiar behind in order to engage in activities that will set them against large segments of both state and society. They live in squatter camps without access to basic services, and they are regularly subjected to psychological and physical pressure by outsiders (CPT 2000). So why do they do it?

In the literature on the MST, academics and movement leaders alike have attributed the movement's explosive rise to three factors (Navarro 2000; Stedile 1997). First, agricultural restructuring in the countryside during the 1970s created a large landless class, and organization became necessary for economic survival. Second, the return to democracy in 1985 after twenty-one years of military rule provided the political opportunity for organization. Third, movement members found institutional support in progressive religious centers located throughout rural Brazil. These three factors—agricultural restructuring, the transition to democracy, and institutional support—are referred to so consistently that they now form the heart of

163

what I call the MST's "Official Genesis Story." The story parallels three "classic" fields in social movement studies: grievance theories, political opportunity theories and resource mobilization theories.

Although the Official Genesis Story is convincing at the macro level, it does not actually explain why people decided to join the MST, because it does not locate the act of resistance in either people or place. The different elements of the story are correct, but in focusing on these particular correct pieces, the official story mistakenly assumes a direct link between broad structural changes and mobilization. The Official Genesis Story does not explain who, out of all the people affected by agricultural restructuring, political transition, and religious organization, constituted the small minority that joined the MST. What did they hope to accomplish? And why didn't more people join? Did everyone who joined the MST even want land? The Official Genesis Story cannot answer any of these questions because it is, as Sherri Ortner would say, "thin"— "thin on the internal politics of dominated groups, thin on the cultural richness of those groups, thin on the subjectivity—the intentions, desires, fears, projects—of the actors engaged in these dramas." (Ortner 1995: 190)

The "thick" questions of why people engage in contentious activity are too often left out of the research on social mobilization. The aspatial and ethnographically thin question —"why do movements form?"—is regularly privileged over the question— "why do people decide to form movements in particular places and times?" This is particularly problematic in studies of social movements, because they are almost by definition operating outside of the social and political center. As a result, movement members are often eager to present their own genesis stories in ways that legitimate marginal(ized) identities and strategies.[1]

In their ambitious attempt to frame a new research agenda, McAdam et al. (2001) suggest a way forward that turns on the spatial dynamics of mobilization—or the political importance of place—although they do not phrase it as such. The first step toward incorporating the spatial dynamics of mobilization is to embed actors in their particular material and symbolic environments.[2] The second step is to examine how different actors negotiate the spaces of resistance and domination produced by political, social, and economic forces. The third step is to acknowledge diversity (instead of trying to explain it away in defense of a particular theoretical framework) and use comparisons of diverse groups in order to understand how notions of community, place, and tradition shape mobilization—sometimes facilitating it, sometimes discouraging it—in different environments.[3]

In this chapter, I analyze the spatial dynamics of MST mobilization by comparing two very different groups within the movement—former small family farmers in the southern state of Santa Catarina and former rural plantation workers in the northeastern state of Pernambuco.[4] In both places—the South and Northeast of Brazil—the way in which social relations were embedded in particular spatial contexts was critically important to the decision to join the MST. In southern Brazil, small farmers who decided to join the MST were tied into a spatially expansive form of production that they valued as a part of a broader community. Family and community ties that were forged and reforged through everyday practices working on the land helped to lower the threshold for participation in the MST.[5] In the Northeast, on the other hand, the MST found it very difficult to mobilize new members because social ties on the sugarcane plantations were too weak to facilitate mobilization and the culture of private property and hierarchy made MST's methods of land occupation appear illegitimate. The MST was only able to generate support in the region when political restructuring precipitated a massive economic crisis and joining the movement became a more attractive option. At that time, community bonds actually raised the threshold for participation—the people who chose to join the MST during the economic crisis were the ones who had the weakest ties to family and community and as a consequence had the least to lose from violating social norms.

In what follows, I outline in detail the "Official Genesis Story," then describe the case-study communities in the South and the Northeast. This research is based on one year of fieldwork conducted in 1998-1999. I interviewed approximately 100 MST settlers in Santa Catarina and 100 settlers in Pernambuco, as well as many MST leaders, local politicians, small farmers in the regions surrounding the settlements, agrarian reform agents and agricultural day-laborers living in urban peripheries.[6]

THE OFFICIAL GENESIS STORY IN THE MAKING

The Official Genesis Story is useful for understanding the broad context in which the MST was formed. In 1964, the Brazilian military seized executive power. Two of the military's primary goals were to quell unrest in the countryside and modernize large-scale agricultural production. To quell unrest, the military relocated "men without land to a land without men," sending people from troubled areas in the Northeast and South to the as yet untamed areas of the Northwest—the Amazonian frontier. These resettlement schemes were notoriously unsuccessful, and most of the people who accepted land in the remote rainforest region left within years of their arrival. To modernize agricultural production, the military provided the largest landowners with generous incentives and resources in the hopes that production increases would generate foreign currency and lower the cost of living for urban workers (Delgado 1985; Müller 1985).

The modernization of agriculture, part of the military's overall industrial development plan, was surprisingly successful. Between 1967 and 1973, Brazil experienced such rapid economic growth that the period was dubbed the "economic miracle" (Burns 1993).[7] Despite the overall economic advances, the gap between social classes grew, and a large part of the country's population was left out of the economic miracle altogether.[8] Mechanization of agricultural production altered labor requirements in ways that spawned massive unemployment and generated an exodus from the rural areas into the cities (Graziano da Silva 1982).[9] The out-migration from the countryside exacerbated the inequitable distribution of land, and by 1985 just over 10 percent of the landowners in the country controlled almost 80 percent of the land (IBGE 1990). Movement leaders and academics have argued that this rapid modernization of agriculture was one of the most important factors underlying MST's formation (Poletto 1997; Robles 2001; Stedile and Fernandes 1999; Veltmeyer 1997). This materialist explanation of movement formation parallels the school of "grievance theories," which argues that arduous economic conditions push people to resist their circumstances (Eckstein 1989; Edelman 1996, 1999; Migdal 1975; Paige 1975; Slater 1985).[10]

MST's Official Genesis Story also emphasizes the importance of religious organizations in the movement's initial moments. As a result of the 1968 Latin American Bishops' Council held in Medellin, Colombia, the Catholic Church officially strengthened its "preference for the poor," creating *Comunidades Eclesiais de Base* (Ecclesiastical Base Communities, or CEBs) to be run by lay priests in previously unserviced areas (Mainwaring 1986). These CEBs spread throughout rural Brazil and provided important meeting places at a time when oppositional political parties and trade unions had been largely shut down by the military government (Lehmann 1990). Many of the first MST leaders came directly out of the Church (Petras 1997; Schwade 1992). Social networks created by members of Catholic and Lutheran churches in Brazil have been characterized as "institutional hosts" (cf., Houtzager 1997) that fostered movement formation among the rural and urban poor throughout the 1970s and 1980s. This emphasis on institutional support is theoretically situated within the resource mobilization perspective, which argues that social movements form where and when particular groups can organize sufficient institutional, financial, and cultural resources (McCarthy and Zald 1973; Morris 1984).

The third and final component of the Official Genesis Story is the political opportunity provided by the withdrawal of the military government. The military began a process of *abertura* (political opening) in 1978-1979, and in 1982 civilian elections were held for the first time in eighteen years. At that time, trade unions (Houtzager 1997; Houtzager and Kurtz 2000), religious organizations (Mainwaring 1986), student groups, and social movements (Medeiros 1989) all organized to participate in the transition to democracy (Sader and Silverstein 1991). Even "peasants began to lose their fear of fighting against the government" (Stedile 1997: 70). Political crises and transitions—such as the democratic transition in Brazil—have been optimistically viewed as uniquely fertile spaces for movement formation (Dominguez and Lowenthal 1996; O'Donnell and Schmitter 1986; Oxhorn 1991) because "people engage in contentious politics when patterns of political opportunities and constraints change" (Tarrow 1998: 19).

PUTTING THE OFFICIAL GENESIS STORY IN ITS PLACE(S)

The Official Genesis Story and its associated social movement theories have contributed greatly to our understanding of organized resistance, and they highlight important elements of the context surrounding MST's formation. But none of them gets to the heart of the question "who joined MST and why," a spatially specific, actor-oriented question crucial to understanding how movements come together. The Official Genesis Story and the theoretical frameworks in which it operates assume a fairly unproblematic link between context and action based on the hypothetical ideal of rational, well-informed actors (see Miller 1992). In what follows, I go beyond the Official Genesis Story to explain why certain actors made the decision to join the MST in the context of agricultural modernization, political transition, and religious mobilization.

Santa Catarina

Vento is an MST land reform settlement located in the southern state of Santa Catarina.[11] Most of the families (82 percent) interviewed in Vento were small farmers who owned or rented land in western Santa Catarina before joining the MST. Eighty families were given land in Vento after spending several years in MST squatter camps, while seventeen families were given land because they had worked on the property. Once they had settled in Vento, each household received use rights to eighteen hectares of land.[12] The question, "why did these settlers join MST?" is a fundamentally spatial one because both production and social reproduction for small

demographic Cycle

family farmers turned on access to adequate land, generating a spatially expansive "cultural toolkit" (Swidler 1986). The small farmers lived off their land, and by custom their children searched for land of their own in order to begin a family, creating a generational dynamic that Alexander Chayanov (1966) has called the "demographic cycle" (see also Cazella 1992; Paulilo 1996).[13] Even before joining the MST, Vento settlers had moved an average of two times in search of land, most of them escaping the demographic pressures on land in the southernmost state of Rio Grande do Sul by moving northward into the relatively open areas of western Santa Catarina. By the early 1970s, available land in western Santa Catarina had become increasingly scarce. Over the next decade, 70,000 people would leave the area (Testa et al. 1996: 22). The diminishing availability of space was a function of multiple pressures: the expansion of highly capitalized soy and wheat farms, the arrival of new migrants from the southernmost state of Rio Grande do Sul, and the subdivision of household plots due to the need for new land to begin a family. In addition, worsening environmental conditions effectively reduced the amount of land for cultivation.[14] As one former resident of the region said: "In western Santa Catarina, the land has been abandoned because it is so bad. Full of insects, little bugs."[15] According to another settler, years of planting corn and beans on steep inclines had led to deteriorating soil conditions and lower yields: "there were so many rocks, and it seemed like there were more every year."

diminishing availability of space and land

As productive land became harder to find, small farmers increasingly planted on land that was not their own. Between 1975 and 1980, the number of farms worked by either a renter or a sharecropper increased by almost 50 percent from 9,918 to 13,659 (Testa et al. 1996: 57; also see Cazella 1992: 19). MST settlers argued that renting land was a distasteful alternative to owning your own, because farmers always had to work the landlord's worst land (Cazella 1992: 33). Landowners often dealt the harshest with those tenants whose hard work might have entitled them to a legal

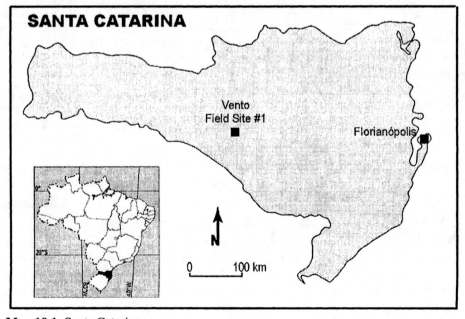

Map 10.1. Santa Catarina

claim on the land.[16] One settler commented: "You can't really survive by renting land in the countryside. The rent is so high and just when you start to do well, the landlord kicks you off."

As available land in western Santa Catarina dwindled, there were several possible responses. Many small farmers left the area for industrial jobs or agricultural daywork that could be scraped together from the peripheral areas of large cities. Only a small percentage decided to join the MST; they did so because they saw a chance to create a new frontier—a *political* frontier instead of a *spatial* one. "*Spatial* frontiers" are areas represented as (and perceived to be) relatively "empty," although they are usually inhabited by people who do not possess the political voice to make themselves seen (Slater 2002). The Amazon region in Brazil is the best known spatial frontier in the country (Amado at al. 1990; Schmink and Wood 1984). By contrast, "*political* frontiers" are areas that have been opened up for access by political contestation or negotiation (Burns 1995). When the MST occupies private or public property, movement members represent that space as "empty" and resolve their need for land by creating a political frontier—in a sense, employing their own spatial fixes to counteract the intrusions of landed capital. The new frontier makes sense to the settlers because their traditional mobility in search of land, combined with the historical existence of an open spatial frontier in the region, created an imaginary of unlimited land that rightfully belonged to anyone who worked it. The settlers in Vento saw geographic mobility as a "right"—a respectable solution to limited land, degraded soil, and rental conditions they considered unfair.

The people who saw the MST as an opportunity to produce a new frontier had emotional or social ties to working the land—where the land represented tradition, subsistence, social reproduction, and community—and a determination to stay on the familiar soils of Santa Catarina. To one young settler, having land meant "citizenship, and the dignity to be able to produce. Land is life." The settlers' strong association of property ownership with household sustainability helped them legitimate claims to new land while simultaneously delegitimating claims made by wealthy absentee landowners. MST's characterization of wealthy landowners as thieves fit with the small farmers' sense that the "right" to land was earned through work and overseen by God, not awarded through position and overseen by politicians.

In addition to providing an understanding of space that made joining the MST thinkable, the spatialized practices of reproduction in western Santa Catarina also provided the social relations that helped to make joining the MST *possible*. Many parents who were unable to give their children land from their own farm helped them survive during the occupation. One settler who regularly brought his two sons food and money while they were living in an MST encampment said he told them: "[your mother and I] can't give you land, but we will help you until you do manage to get land of your own. When you have land, then you are on your own." For parents, MST continued the demographic cycle in which young families obtained the land needed to raise their own children: "Through the struggle for agrarian reform, our kids have gotten married and gone after their own land." When some settlers saw their brothers and sisters win land, they joined an occupation to "stick with" the family and "see what would happen." Sometimes, one person endured the trials of the occupation and called his or her family only when it looked as though they might soon receive land. In other cases, the whole family—wife, husband, and children— would pack up their belongings and head to an occupation together. In this way, several brothers and sisters, mothers, fathers and children settled the same land.

Strong familial bonds among small farmers in western Santa Catarina created what I call a "social multiplier effect," whereby one person's decision to join the movement was multiplied by his or her influence on family members who also decided to join. The households of Vento averaged four relatives living in them or in the MST settlements somewhere in the state. Without this "social multiplier effect," people probably would still have chosen to occupy land, but their decisions might not have created a movement.

The farming communities that dotted the landscape of western Santa Catarina also provided important material resources for mobilization. Communities were certainly not free from conflict, but community centers—usually a church or a school—provided relatively safe spaces for families to learn about the MST. Information spread rapidly through community networks. Many of the settlers heard about the MST by talking to their neighbors: "At that time, no one knew anything about the movement and these occupations. Then it began with some people who lived there and they were the first. And then one person began to pull on the other and pretty soon everyone went." Familiarity made it easier to withstand the uncertainty and fear involved in an occupation, and large groups facilitated logistical preparations. Local leaders also played important roles as mediators between the radical ideas of mobilization and resistance and the settlers' own desires for change. As one settler recounted, "In the beginning, it wasn't MST, it was just community leaders."

The small farmers who joined the MST used the tools of their traditions to carve out a new form of frontier. The *political* frontier was created by occupying private property that had been preserved for several hundred years through powerful traditions of domination. Small farmers represented this land as both "a gift of God" and a right that every impoverished Brazilian citizen deserved. Although these acts of resistance might have been more difficult without the transition to democracy and resources provided by the Catholic church, the MST never would have been formed without the small farmers who needed land and saw occupations as a legitimate means to an end.

For all of the reasons outlined above—the spatial mobility of small farmers, the demographic cycle, the "social multiplier effect," the geographically extensive community ties, the cultural attachment to land, and the historical perception of occupation as noble—the Official Genesis Story is insufficient to explain MST's formation in southern Brazil. By decontextualizing causal mechanisms the official story points to the most obvious explanations for contentious activity, but overlooks the specific ways in which resistance was produced by the symbolic and material relationships between people and their environments.

Ironically, the genesis story of economic restructuring and political transition does work as an explanation for the movement's success in the coastal sugarcane region of Pernambuco, a state in Northeast Brazil. The MST did not develop a significant presence in this region until the mid-1990s. Even then it was never as strong as in the South, nonetheless, it is there that economic modernization and political opportunity overcame community preferences and provided the impetus for organized resistance.

The Sugarcane Region of Pernambuco

Flora is an MST land reform settlement located in the northeastern state of Pernambuco.[17] Flora was originally a sugarcane plantation, but it had not produced cane for over three years when the MST members occupied the property in 1996. Thirteen families affiliated with the MST were given access to land when Flora was expropriated in 1997, and the rest was distributed among the thirty-three families formerly associated with the plantation (referred to as *moradores*, or residents). According to federal law, everyone who worked or lived on the plantation and who did not own (or rent) land elsewhere was eligible to receive land. Incredibly, this allowed a wide range of social classes including the former *patrão* (plantation boss) to remain on the settlement.[18] Regardless of their former social standing, each family received use rights to approximately nine hectares.

A major factor inhibiting participation in the MST before the 1990s was the social construction of space on sugarcane plantations in northeastern Brazil. Plantation owners manipulated labor relationships in ways that separated workers from both the land and each other (Sigaud 1979). As a result, the MST struggled to convince workers that land was necessary for either production or reproduction. Plantation workers were occasionally allowed to plant subsistence crops by their houses if they lived inside the plantation grounds, but permission was always at the discretion of the *patrão* (c.f., Sigaud 1979). When the price of sugar or alcohol was high, the plantation owners exercised their right to reincorporate the land and plant cane wherever they could. According to one former plantation worker, "when you left your house, you opened the door, and you were already right on top of the cane." Many plantation owners simply refused to allow their workers access to land. One settler described the near total control of the mill owners: "This mill where we were working never gave anyone land to plant, no, never. Even the trees that the workers planted, the mill owner would knock them all down. They planted cane and threw the workers out. The mill didn't want to give anything to the worker, because they thought that the worker would take over their lands."

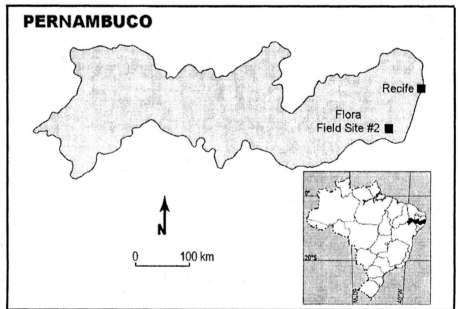

Map 10.2. Pernambuco

In addition to the workers' physical separation from the land, cultural notions of space and property discouraged occupation of "someone else's property." Plantation workers generally found it very difficult to accept MST's strategy of land occupations as morally justified by either the Brazilian Constitution or the Bible. No historical process of settlement legitimated occupations, because there had not been an open frontier in the region since the early 1500s.[19] The plantation owners who did provide their workers with land did so as a *dom* (gift), and "the workers were not—and perhaps are still not—accustomed to considering land as a right equal to other rights" (Sigaud 1979: 84). Plantation workers believed that private property was an institution to be respected. While they may have wished for access to land, many insisted that they wanted it only if, as one settler said, the government "gave it to [them] without any problems." As one of the former *moradores* who received Flora land said, "If the head of MST came and settled people inside some area, I would be in favor of this. But just to invade, when they don't even know if it is possible for them to get that land, I am against this." Even a settler who had joined in the MST occupation said that, "right up to when we entered the area of the [plantation], I didn't know that it was an invasion, I didn't know anything about this, I knew that it was to get land and so I joined up."[20]

As a result of material and cultural separation from the land, few plantation workers were experienced in family farming, and most preferred paid employment to landed production (see also Maybury-Lewis 1994). The culture of work-as-paid-employment created a dependence on money, and people relied on their regular income to purchase groceries at the weekly *feira* (market). Without their salary, they were nervous about how they would continue to pay their bills and feed themselves. An MST activist in the region explained:

> When you go to [the plantation workers] with an idea about [joining an occupation]…they measure the time [that they would spend in an occupation] against the time that they would spend employed. If they started a job today, in five days they would already have money in their pockets. And so if you go to them and ask if they want land or a job, they are going to say a job.

At the same time, the spatial segregation of laborers on the plantation generated extremely tenuous community ties. Social relations mirrored the hierarchical nature of the labor process and were reflected in style and quality of housing. The production process on the plantation required a few skilled *empregados* (employees) and many unskilled *trabalhadores* (workers). Employees managed the estate and oversaw the work crews. Workers cut the cane, weeded the fields and loaded the trucks.[21] Most common *trabalhadores* lived on the plantation in small, one-room houses connected by side walls, while more important workers either lived in larger stone houses in the center of the plantation or further out on *sitios* (small farms) allotted to them by the plantation owner.[22] Workers who did not live on the plantation were contracted seasonally (often without their legal working papers) and occupied the most insecure, unstable positions on the plantation. Such pronounced labor segmentation left little room for the sort of mutual assistance that took place in southern communities. None of the people on Flora participated in the MST occupation with members of their original community. People from the same community did join the MST, but they had made their decisions independently and did not consciously maintain social ties after receiving land. Community ties were further weakened by the high rate of mobility among workers. Unlike their counterparts in southern Brazil who saw mobility as a way of continually expanding or shifting the spaces of their own authority, plantation workers saw mobility as an individual survival strategy in a system that offered them few rights.[23] Working contracts on the plantation were usually informal and open to interpretation. Exit was often the most effective response to difficult working conditions perceived as unfair. One former worker described mobility as a welfare maximizing strategy: "At that time, there wasn't anything holding you in one place....I would spend two or three years in one place and when that started to get bad, I was already leaving for somewhere else."

Given the many factors discouraging rural workers from joining the MST, it is initially unclear how the movement was able to build its membership in the region. The answer lies in the changing calculus of what was deemed necessary and possible when the sugarcane industry entered a severe crisis in the early 1990s. After thirty years of relative prosperity, plantation and distillery owners in the Northeast found themselves with fewer markets and less government support. The global market for sugarcane had become more competitive due, in part, to the presence of new competitors in global sugar production and increased use of artificial sweeteners.[24]

The market crisis was exacerbated in the northeastern state of Pernambuco, because the new post-1985 civilian governments deregulated the sugarcane industry and revised regional legislation that had previously protected the northeastern producers (Buarque 1997: 3). Although national cane production increased significantly between 1982-1983 and 1994-1995, the contribution by northeastern producers fell from 30.1 percent to 19.4 percent (MEPF 1998: 3). In 1995, 44 percent of the sugarcane refining distilleries in Pernambuco were classified as "paralyzed or functioning with difficulty" (Lins 1996: 2).

The regional sugarcane crisis forced rural workers in Pernambuco to reevaluate the desirability of joining the MST. Land previously subordinated to sugarcane was opened up, or "diverted" (*detournement*) in Lefebvre's (1991 [1974]) words, for new purposes such as agrarian reform or tourism.[25] On most settlements, as on Flora, there were two groups of people who decided to join the movement: families who had occupied the plantation with the MST and families who had previously worked on, or somehow been associated with, the plantation (the *moradores*).

The MST families defied the broader community's social norms regarding space and property, in large part because they had tried everything else and had no other option. According to one settler, "Today, sugarcane is finished...and so, the way we were living, if it hadn't been for agrarian reform, we could say that we would have been dead. There were no jobs, there was no work—how were we going to live?" In general, the people most affected by the crisis were ones who had no permanent residence in the interior of the plantations and were living in poor conditions *na rua* (in the small rural cities of the plantation region). One Flora settler described her husband's discovery of the MST and their subsequent decision to join the movement: "A man came and asked my husband if he wanted a piece of land, you know? And [my husband] said that he did, because he lived working for others and paying rent [in the city]. One day it was here, the next day there, living in the stables because we didn't have a house to live in. It was too much suffering." Many of these workers were contracted seasonally as *clandestinos* (uncertified workers) and did not receive any of the public or private benefits that come with legal registration.[26] As uncertified, seasonal workers, their positions were unstable. They often had to do the most menial tasks of the harvest for a fraction of the pay they were promised. They had little recourse to complain, however, if they wished a work contract the following year (Maybury-Lewis 1994; Pereira 1997; Sigaud 1979).

The second group of people living on Flora joined the MST for different reasons. They did not *have* to join the MST in order to receive land. Rather, they became settlers simply by virtue of their association with the plantation at the time of its expropriation. Unlike the people who occupied the plantation, they insisted that as residents they had a *right* to be there. A woman who worked for the *patrão* in the *Casa Grande* (Big House) explained: "I got [land] because I lived here on the [plantation]. It was a right, because I was working legally and so I got the land by right, I tried not to invade land or anything, it's just that this invasion came and INCRA (the National Institute for Colonization and Agrarian Reform) bought the land."

Over time, however, all of the former plantation residents decided to join the movement, because they could no longer rely on the plantation boss or the local trade union to provide economic or political support. Although the former *patrão* still lived on Flora, he was not in a financial or social position to provide for the workers. And the local trade union was itself greatly weakened as a result of the high unemployment generated by the sugarcane crisis.[27] MST's aggressive organizing efforts offered the settlers an alternative political voice—the settlement association.

As a land reform settlement, Flora was required to form an association that would meet regularly and be responsible for such things as collecting official documents from the settlers, disseminating information, and regulating conflict. On Flora, the movement virtually controlled the association. In the words of one settler, "Listen, it's like this, I live here inside the settlement. What they say I have to pay, and what they tell me I have to do with the association, these things, I do it." For a group of people as marginal to the political process as plantation workers, the opportunity for institutional entrée was extremely significant, even though it was sometimes unwelcome. One former *morador* who had worked as an administrator on the plantation said: "Whether I want to or not, I have to be part [of the movement] because we arrange things within the movement."

One of the settlers on Flora who had been a resident on the plantation before the movement said that he did not support the occupation: "[The MST people] sent for us and told us to go there and pressure the mill owner too. But I said, I am not going, I am a resident here." Three years later, however, he decided, "I am part of the movement, because if not the movement, what is ours? We only get things through the movement." The movement was considered responsible for forcing the government to disburse money for housing as well as credit for planting.

As the settlers adjusted to life in the new regional economy, ongoing participation in the movement was justified in the context of life on the plantations. Membership in the MST did not necessarily indicate resistance to the political system as it had in Santa Catarina, because Flora settlers did not necessarily see the system as flawed. Instead, participation in the MST improved their position by using rules with which the settlers were already familiar. They considered the MST an institution comparable to a trade union, an organization that would help them navigate the political waters, not redirect them. In this sense, the MST was seen as a service organization that *represented* the settlers rather than a social movement of which they were members. As one settler said, "I think it's good, they are always doing marches and things, and it's to help us, isn't it?"

CONCLUSION: THE ONGOING SPATIAL DYNAMICS OF RESISTANCE

What are the benefits of trying to understand MST's formation from a spatially in-formed perspective on contentious actors rather than contentious action? Three main benefits are evident. First, we go from explaining *what* conditions facilitated the formation of the movement to explaining *how* those conditions facilitated the forma-tion of the movement. In Santa Catarina, political opportunity and institutional re-sources would not have been translated into action if they had not resonated with the spatial dynamics of local norms and practices. Small farmers needed to employ the tools of their traditions to embrace the aggressive act of occupying land. The politi-cal frontier the settlers created was unfamiliar, but the *process* of dislocation, relo-cation, and land occupation this new frontier required was very familiar. Rural work-ers in the Northeast, on the other hand, found it difficult to reconcile their notions of private property with MST's tactics. In this case, the MST was unable to build a sig-nificant membership in the sugarcane region because of the workers' very different spatial dynamics of production. The social construction of space on the sugarcane plantations generated a preference for money over land, and weak family and com-munity bonds made it difficult for the rural workers to imagine occupying "someone else's property." Not until economic crisis hit did people began to join the MST. As the crisis deepened, severely affected workers began to view the MST more favor-ably. When the state expropriated more plantations and gave land to former workers living on the property, more settlers joined the movement because they perceived membership to be a legitimate means of accessing government assistance.

Second, if we examine who joined the MST and why, we gain an implicit under-standing of who did not join the MST and why. In Santa Catarina, the people who joined MST were small farmers whose mode of production and reproduction clashed with capital's "spatial fix" and resonated with the movement's messages. In most cases, these were not the poorest people in the countryside or even the ones most affected by capitalist land appropriation. Many small farmers who joined the MST still had a plot of land in western Santa Catarina where they came from. They were not in the same dire straits as the rural workers who left for the cities and contracted out their labor on a daily basis. But the small farmers needed the land they had—and more—in order to continue their spatially expansive way of life. At the same time, people who had fewer ties (social, material, and cultural) to the land were more likely to move to new spatial frontiers or urban areas with enticing possibilities for wage work.

The third benefit of a spatially informed perspective on contentious actors is un-derstanding what people wanted to gain by joining the movement. MST members throughout Brazil invoke the movement's name when they march together through the streets, but with very different understandings of what it means to be part of the movement. These understandings have been forged in the diverse places where MST members have lived, both before and during participation in the movement. Evolving relationships between people and place continue to shape movement dynamics even after land has been won and settlements created. Despite MST's rhetorical coherence at the national level, the regional constitution of people and place has created very different movement actors across the country. If studies of mobilization are to be-come more dynamic as McAdam et al. (2001) rightfully encourage, we need to have some basis for understanding whether members will stay with a movement or drop out when the context changes. In the case of the MST, the common analytical focus on agricultural restructuring, political opportunity, and religious organization has hidden the fact that a significant portion of movement members desperately tried to *avoid* joining. This attempted avoidance is an important component of mobilization dynamics because those members are likely to leave the movement as soon as the context in which they joined changes (see Wolford forthcoming a).[28]

Theoretically locating actors within spatial structures, and analyzing how the two are mutually constituted, is a useful way of incorporating actors *and* actions, as they are embedded in agency and structure, contingency and context, space and time. Comparing the formation of resistance in two distinct spatial contexts, like southern and northeastern Brazil, provides a clearer understanding of how the spatial constitution of social life shapes people's ideological and material practices and how, in turn, people shape socio-spatial practices through resistance.

NOTES

1. In MST's case, the attribution of mobilization to the depredations of capital fits neatly with the movement's ongoing critique of capitalism (see Wolford forthcoming b).

2. This would highlight the social mechanisms described by McAdam et al. (2001: 24-27) and generate a dynamic, relational analysis that moves away from explication of structural characteristics and toward understanding how people engage with those structures (see particularly p. 47).

3. For a critique of theoretical partisanship see McAdam et al. (2001: 312-313).

4. These two regions, Santa Catarina in southern Brazil and Pernambuco in northeastern Brazil, were chosen because they represent very different economic and political frameworks and are strong areas of MST activity.

5. Thanks to Byron Miller for suggesting the idea of a "lowered threshold."

6. The interviews varied in style, but most included an extensive tour of the settler's property, lunch, and a two to three hour open-ended interview. Upon returning to Berkeley, I transcribed a significant portion of the interviews, which were coded and analyzed with the help of a qualitative research program called Filemaker Pro. A return trip to Brazil in the summer of 2001 helped me to solidify my arguments.

7. The country's Gross Domestic Product (GDP) increased at an astonishing annual rate of 11.2 percent per annum during this period (Fausto 1999: 291), and inflation fell from 58.2 percent in 1965 to a low of 16.4 percent in 1970 (Skidmore 1999: 178).

8. In 1960, the wealthiest 5 percent of Brazil's economically active population earned 27.7 percent of the country's total income. In 1990, the wealthiest 5 percent earned 35.8 percent of total income (see Skidmore 1999: 198).

9. Between 1960 and 1980, the population of Brazil's largest city, São Paulo, rose from 4.7 million to 12.6 million, and real urban wages fell by two-thirds from 1960 to 1976 (IBGE 1990). From 1960 to 1985, the Brazilian population went from being predominantly rural to predominantly urban.

10. Jeffrey Paige's (1975) work on rural resistance in Latin America was one of the seminal pieces in the field of grievance theory in relation to Third World (agrarian) social movements. He argued that rural groups in the most precarious positions would be the likeliest to form resistance. Joel Migdal (1975) also suggested that the increasing level of peasant organization throughout the 20th century resulted from the shock of deepening imperialism.

11. Not the community's real name.

12. In each state, local officials with the National Institute for Colonization and Agrarian Reform (INCRA) calculate the amount of land considered sufficient to support a family of four (called a "module"). This amount varies from place to place depending on factors such as quality of soil and topography.

13. Chayanov's analysis of the peasant economy in early 20th century Russia turned on the so-called "demographic cycle," whereby a household's access to land was determined by the number of people that needed to produce and consume within the household. When a peasant couple had children, the family would acquire more and more land, so that a large family would seemingly have a considerable amount of land. As the children grew older, however, they would take pieces of their parents' land in order to begin households of their own. This demographic cycle has been the most contested—and the most enduring—component of Chayanov's analysis.

14. In 1996, a government-sponsored report (Testa et al. 1996) judged that 41.5 percent of the former

agricultural land was totally inappropriate for cultivation due to soil loss, hillside slope, and prevalence of rocks.

15. Unless otherwise noted, all direct quotes come from the author's fieldwork.

16. Land law in Brazil is notoriously contradictory, because the Federal Constitution upholds both the sanctity of private property and the need for land to fulfill a "social function." Land titles are so often fraudulent that ownership can be challenged, often on the grounds of possession (see Holston 1991 for an excellent summary of what he calls the intentionally vague laws surrounding land ownership in Brazil).

17. Not the community's real name. Names have been changed in order to further protect the identity of interviewees.

18. The Patrão himself did not receive land because he was renting another plantation down the road but his wife and son both received plots.

19. The Northeast of Brazil was the first area to be settled and land in the region was considered a gift of the Crown. Land was both "nobody's" and "already somebody's," depending on the person's position in society.

20. MST occupations are often referred to as "invasions," although generally by people who do not support the movement and wish to cast the idea of occupying land in a negative light.

21. Although the workers planted and cut cane side by side, their daily production quotas were established on an individual basis.

22. The importance of a worker was determined both by occupation and by the favor of the plantation owner. Plantation owners often rewarded good service with a sitio, or offered one to a worker whom they hoped to entice to work on their plantation.

23. Lygia Sigaud's (1977, 1979) work is an excellent source of information on working conditions in the sugarcane economy of the Northeast. She outlines the ways in which owners used segmentation, insecurity, and job switching to push workers off the plantation.

24. Between 1975 and 1985, the industrialized countries increased their sugar exports from 20 percent of the world's total to 43 percent (De Souza et al. 1997: 2).

25. Diversion is defined as a situation where: "An existing space may outlive its original purpose and the raison d'etre which determines its forms, functions, and structures; it may thus in a sense become vacant, and susceptible of being diverted, reappropriated and put to a use quite different from its initial one" (Lefebvre 1991).

26. According to Pernambuco state law, plantation owners are expected to sign working papers for every person employed on the plantation. Papers are intended to insure that the workers receive their rights, that they are eligible for union membership, and that they have their years of service counted in the interests of receiving their state benefits.

27. The unions were hurt badly by the region's economic crisis, because unemployment meant that people did not pay union fees. The unions' fate was connected to sugarcane production, and union leaders were highly ambivalent about supporting the MST. An MST activist said, "In seven or eight cities around here, it's the mill owner who controls the unions, so the president of the union does whatever the boss says." In the municipality of Agua Preta, union leaders were trying to bring in settlers. Although the MST leaders argued that the union was unnecessary, union leaders tried to convince the settlers that they needed the political support traditionally provided by unions.

28. This is in fact what happened in Flora. When I returned in 2001, the price of sugarcane had risen due to a drought in southern Brazil, and the settlers were planting cane again, essentially becoming contracted wage workers for the sugar plantations and distilleries. They seemed somewhat embarrassed when I mentioned the MST, and the movement's presence was considerably less visible than it had been in 1999.

Part V

Transnational Dimensions of Latin American Social Movements

Chapter 11

THE ZAPATISTAS AND
TRANSNATIONAL FRAMING

Thomas Olesen

The Zapatista movement has caught the attention of activists, scholars, and media since its uprising in 1994.[1] One of the reasons for this is that the Zapatistas represent a unique way of weaving together local, national, and transnational levels of activism. Through an innovative transnational framing of their claims, they have inspired the formation of what I call a transnational Zapatista solidarity network—the focus of this chapter.[2]

In the twelve years that have passed since the uprising began on January 1, 1994, the Zapatista movement has helped redefine two important and related agendas. First, activists disillusioned with the identity crisis of the Left after the end of the Cold War were inspired by the Zapatistas to think about resistance against neoliberalism in transnational terms. The idea of international resistance is not new, of course—it was a staple of leftist discourse for decades. What *is* new is the way the Zapatistas have departed sharply from leftist traditions of vanguardism and working-class internationalism to emphasize respect for difference, democracy, and the local. Second, for scholars working in the field of social movements, the Zapatistas and the transnational solidarity network that coalesced around them seemed to confirm a growing suspicion that popular activism in the 1990s was becoming more and more transnational. This made the Zapatistas an inspiration for many of the pioneering works on social movements and globalization in the mid- and late-1990s and today the Zapatistas are a recurring element in this constantly expanding literature.

Much of what is written and passed along about the Zapatistas and their transnational connections is anecdotal or focused only on some aspects of the movement. The latter problem is especially evident in the Zapatistas' much trumpeted use of the

179

Internet. But the Zapatistas and their transnational solidarity network are about much more than the Internet. To grasp the broader picture of the movement we need to assume a more systematic and encompassing analytical perspective than what is typical of past studies. The aim of this chapter is to specify the conditions and activities that underlie the transnational framing process that have facilitated the formation of the transnational Zapatista solidarity network in the period from 1994 to 2001.

A BRIEF HISTORY OF THE TRANSNATIONAL ZAPATISTA SOLIDARITY NETWORK

The Zapatista uprising on January 1, 1994, in the Mexican state of Chiapas, immediately posed a challenge to students of Mexican politics. The appearance of an armed movement, mostly consisting of indigenous peasants and representing demands ranging from land and housing to democracy and justice, was a surprise to the Mexican political establishment and scholars alike. The Zapatistas at first seemed almost anachronistic in the post-Cold War setting of the 1990s when the "end of history" had recently been proclaimed. It soon became clear, however, that they were not simply a continuation of Latin America's historical experiences with armed movements. Or perhaps more accurately, the Zapatistas quickly realized that the prospects for an armed uprising at this historical juncture were not very promising. After twelve days of armed confrontations between the Zapatistas and the Mexican army the Zapatistas embarked on a new course in which the weapons played an increasingly symbolic role, shifting the terrain of their struggle from the battlefield to the level of words and ideas. In doing so, they became a key actor in the process of democratic social change that Mexico has been undergoing since the late 1980s.

But the impact of the Zapatistas does not stop at the borders of Mexico. In fact, one of the most salient aspects of this movement is its resonance *beyond* Mexico. The transnational interest generated by the Zapatistas is probably matched by no other movement in the post-Cold War period.[3] Despite the obvious physical, social, and cultural obstacles, an extraordinarily large number of civil society actors, mainly Europe and the U.S., have initiated solidarity efforts in support of the Zapatistas, leading to the formation of what I called the transnational Zapatista solidarity network. This network has been characterized by flux and reflux over the past twelve years, but it has never disappeared. Instead, it has shown a capacity for reinvention and remains vibrant to this day.[4] The development of the network may be divided into five phases that cover the period from 1994 to 2001. This is the period analyzed in this chapter. In the conclusion I present some speculations as to the present state and future of the Zapatistas and the solidarity network.

Phase 1 (January 1994-February 1995): The incipient solidarity network is formed already in January 1994 when transnational activists protest the armed confrontations in the wake of the uprising. The network does not have an independent infrastructure at this time, and activities build on already existing networks and movements.

Phase 2 (February 1995-summer 1996): In this phase, the network starts to develop an infrastructure of its own. The very intense activities of the network are mainly aimed at monitoring the human rights situation in Chiapas following the Mexican army's invasion of Zapatista territory in February 1995.

Phase 3 (summer 1996-December 1997): In this period, the network becomes more politicized and begins to overlap with other transnational networks. The politicization is largely a result of the Zapatistas' call for the First Intercontinental Encounter for Humanity and against Neoliberalism in Chiapas in 1996 (see the section below on neoliberalism for more details on this event).

Phase 4 (December 1997-mid-1998): Following the Acteal massacre in Chiapas in December 1997, the network undertakes probably its most intense period of activities. The major concern once again becomes the human rights violations in Chiapas and the militarization of Chiapas after the Acteal massacre.

Phase 5 (mid-1998-April 2001): This period was characterized by silence on the part of the Zapatista leadership. Initiatives mainly targeted Mexican issues. Network activities protested the Mexican government's refusal to fully accept the so-called San Andrés Accords on indigenous rights.

THEORIZING TRANSNATIONAL FRAMING

Framing is a process that aims to maximize the public resonance of a movement's claims to generate interest in and sympathy for the movement (Snow et al. 1986; Snow and Benford 1988, 1992; Noakes and Johnston 2005). Social movements do not do this simply by pointing to objective facts, although there must be an element of empirical credibility about the frames in order for them to be successful. Frames are about interpretation and, as the concept implies, this means that as social movements present themselves publicly, certain things are downplayed or left out and other things are emphasized in order to portray events and situations in a way that attracts maximum attention from the public, the media, and politicians.

Most work in the framing tradition has focused on national contexts (McCarthy 1997; Smith 2002). In what follows I attempt to elaborate the processes of *transnational* framing whereby socially, culturally, and physically dispersed actors develop a degree of common understanding that enables them to act together in some form. Put differently, transnational framing is about the bridging of distance. A successful transnational frame links grievances at various local and national levels with each other in such a way as to promote shared actions and interpretations of social and political problems. Drawing on the corpus of framing theory, I suggest that four key concepts are central to understanding the Zapatista's transnational framing efforts.

1. A Master Frame of Democratic Participation. Frames are expected to be more successful when they are derived from a master frame. Master frames are the general interpretive medium through which social actors legitimate action and formulate alternatives (Snow and Benford 1988, 1992). In other words, master frames are socially and culturally dominant ideational reservoirs from which social movements construct their own and more action-oriented frames. I argue that the development of the Zapatista's solidarity network drew upon an especially potent master frame, namely, the proliferation on a transnational scale of democracy as a goal of social change. By drawing on the democratic master frame, it is relatively easy for a "democratic" movement to demonstrate how its claims are relevant to people in socially, culturally, and physically diverse settings.

2. Frame Extension: From Insurgency to Diversity. Frame extension is the attempt by social movements to encompass new ideas and values that have not so far been part of the social movement's frame, but are considered to have resonance with potential constituents and sympathizers (Snow et al. 1986). Early in the Zapatista uprising, leaders realized that armed revolt was a severely limited way to characterize their movement to potential supporters outside Chiapas and moved to extend the frame by which their struggle is defined to embrace diversity, flexibility, dignity, and dialogue.

3. An Injustice Frame of Neoliberal Restructuring. An injustice frame defines a problem and proposes a solution to it (Gamson, Fireman, and Rytina 1982: 123; Snow and Benford 1988). It is complex task to invoke injustice transnationally in a way that resonates across social, cultural, and physical distances. But the process of neoliberal restructuring since the 1970s and 1980s, I argue, has affected large parts of the world's population in a more or less similar way. This condition enhances the potential for constructing injustice frames that resonate transnationally. It creates, in other words, a common point of reference in the interpretation of what is wrong and what should be done about it.

4. Experiential Commensurability through the Internet. A successful frame must establish a degree of commensurability between the everyday experiences of senders and recipients in the framing process. In other words, a frame must have empirical credibility (a fit between the frame and actual events) and experiential commensurability (resonance with the experiences of potential target groups) (Snow and Benford 1988). The transnational framing process is highly dependent on the availability of means of communication as it is, in essence, a communicative process taking place across considerable physical, social, and cultural distance. I argue that the Internet makes it easier for today's distant actors to exchange information and share everyday experiences and thus to verify empirical credibility and construct experiential commensurability. These "small" stories are the kind of stories that rarely make it through the mass media, concerned as it is mainly with "large" issues.

THE DEMOCRATIC MASTER FRAME

A key element of the Zapatistas' transnational resonance and formation of its transnational solidarity network is the way they have anchored their claims in a democratic master frame. Democratic participation has been a dominant legitimizing principle since the early twentieth century and especially since the end of the Cold War it has become the banner of many social movements—especially what I call radical democracy (Olesen 2005a). On the one hand, social movement frames that demonstrate an adherence to democratic ideas stand a better chance of generating transnational resonance. This is because democracy has a strong degree of universalism at its theoretical core. Democratic claims, in other words, are relatively easy to universalize and therefore have a strong potential for generating support among socially, culturally, and physically distant actors. On the other hand, the Zapatistas' critique of neoliberalism cannot be seen in isolation from their approach to democracy. This is because their critique of neoliberalism, in large part, is formulated in what I will refer to as radical democratic terms. The Zapatistas' engagement with democratic ideas, therefore, does not simply involve acceptance of but liberal democracy characteristic of the advanced Western states,[5] but extends to a radical critique of liberal democracy that has found an echo with many activists around the world.

It is possible to synthesize three broad lines of thinking on democracy that are evident in the contemporary master frame: broadening, delegation, and deepening. The *broadening* of democracy refers to the extension of democratic principles to more and more societal areas (Mouffe 1993). The *delegation* of democracy refers to the creation of autonomous spaces with authority to govern independently from the state. This view mainly entails the aspirations of minorities who feel excluded or repressed by the state (Esteva 2001). The *deepening* of democracy refers to the empowerment of civil society through social action. This perspective rests on a normative ideal that an active civil society should be a vital part of democracy (Lummis 1996). These dimensions of radical democracy all represent links of Zapatista ideology with the democratic master frame.

Broadening of democracy. The Zapatista definition of democracy revolves around the concept "to rule by obeying" (*mandar obedeciendo*). This vision is to a large extent influenced by the traditions of decision making within Zapatista indigenous communities (Harvey 1998a: 208-209) and differs from liberal democracy in that it is based on continuous consultation and debate aimed at the establishment of consensus. Thus, "to rule by obeying" means that there is a strong relationship between the governed and those who govern whereby the decisions of the community—arrived at by exchange among equals—are respected by those in authority.

The delegation of democracy. The major efforts of the Zapatistas have gone in the direction of securing a degree of autonomy for the indigenous people in order to establish a legal recognition of indigenous practices of government and decision making sketched above. This effort has revolved around the so-called San Andrés Accords signed by the Zapatistas and the Mexican government in February 1996. The San Andrés Accords have not yet, however, resulted in the constitutional changes desired by the Zapatistas.

The deepening of democracy. The concept of civil society is vital to understanding the Zapatistas' radical democratic vision. The main difference between liberal and radical democracy is that the latter views civil society not only as a terrain but also as a target of action (Cohen and Arato 1992). This reflects a cultural politics, which focuses on the politicization of civil society and the promotion of debates on what counts as political (Alvarez, Dagnino, and Escobar 1998). All major Zapatista initiatives since 1994 have been aimed at the politicization of civil society.[6]

The Zapatistas' radical democratic ideas have been an important source of inspiration for activists trying to redefine leftist politics after the Cold War. David Martin (2000), an activist in the Denver Peace and Justice Committee, puts it this way:

With the example of the Zapatistas you can talk about grassroots democracy and local control and local democratic practices . . . and I think that is what we are trying to do in terms of organizing coalitions for economic justice, we are saying we need to get the power into the hands of grassroots organizations and have more democratic forms of government . . . what we are trying to do is create . . . grassroots democratic structures so that we can start building momentum to even have more influence politically, but also practice democracy amongst our own groups before we try to exercise power.

In Austin, Texas, the Zapatista solidarity organization Acción Zapatista has also tried to apply Zapatista ideas to their local setting:

We wanted to introduce this whole strategy of *coyuntura* . . . It is a strategy of analysis that allows for everybody in the room to make a contribution . . . and develop a strategy that . . . everybody feels a part of. . . . And the other thing we want to introduce is the notion of councils, which we weren't very clear on, we had this vague notion of how councils were operating in Chiapas . . . so we are kind of testing it on ourselves, experimenting what we vaguely have a sense of is happening in Chiapas. (Callahan 2000)

This quote demonstrates that solidarity activists consider that the Zapatista ideal of radical democracy has origins in indigenous communities. The perception of how democracy works in the indigenous communities seems to fit well with the anarchist and new social movement currents already present in activist circles, especially in the U.S. and Europe.

Looking beyond the Zapatista solidarity network to the global justice movement we also find that democracy plays a central role. This explains why the Zapatistas have become such an important symbol and source of inspiration for activists outside Mexico. Speaking of the global justice movement, Jackie Smith (2001a: 16) notes that:

> If one had to identify a common thread among the demands of activists in this movement, it would be a demand for democracy. As governments seek to coordinate policies at the global level, they have systematically excluded ever greater numbers of people from decision-making. Against this exclusion, activists call for greater access to information about the free trade agreements that governments are negotiating.

This emphasis on the extension of democracy as a social change strategy is also reflected in the ideas that have inspired the world social forums held since 2001. The forums are open to everyone critical of neoliberalism and in many ways continue the ideas and spirit of the intercontinental encounter held in Chiapas in 1996:

> The World Social Forum is a plural, diversified, non-confessional, nongovernmental and nonparty space that, in a decentralized, networked fashion, interrelates organizations and movements engaged in concrete action at levels from the local to the international to build another world. . . . The World Social Forum asserts democracy as the avenue to resolving society's problems politically. As a meeting place, it is open to the pluralism and to the diversity of activities and ways of engaging of the organizations and movements that decide to participate in it. (World Social Forum 2001)

The WSF's approach puts more emphasis on democracy within and between groups and organizations, and less on the democratization of what is largely considered to be illegitimate international institutions. It is interesting that a radical democratic vision is generally shared by the WSF, the global justice movement, and the Zapatistas. The similarities here are not so much in the *deepening* and *broadening* of democracy but rather in the question of autonomy and *delegation* of democracy defended by the Zapatistas.

To sum up, the Zapatistas' transnational resonance owes much to the way they have anchored their claims in the democratic master frame and elaborated it with the radical democratic vision. The Zapatistas' vision of radical democracy contains elements of democratic broadening, delegation, and deepening and has been flexible enough to generate resonance among diverse leftist positions around the world.

FRAME EXTENSION: DIGNITY, FLEXIBILITY, AND DIALOGUE

An important framing strategy of the Zapatistas was their unwillingness to define themselves clearly and authoritatively in terms of a fixed identity and ideology, portraying the movement as highly flexible and accessible for a wide range of people and movements. Closely related to this tactic was the Zapatistas' refusal to play the role of a vanguard cadre for social change characteristic of former Latin American revolutionary movements. In an interview with Gabriel García Márquez and Roberto Pombo (2001), Subcomandante Marcos (spokesman of the Zapatistas) emphasizes how the Zapatistas' anti-vanguardist position entails a radical departure from both previous and existing armed movements in Latin America, as well as a rather ambiguous relationship with their own weapons:

> Our army is a very different army because it is proposing to cease being an army. . . . If the EZLN persists as an army, it is destined for failure. . . . And the worst that can happen . . . is that it comes to power and installs itself as a revolutionary army. For us, this would be a failure. What would have been a success for a political-military organization in the 1960s and 1970s . . . would be a failure for us. We have seen that in the end these victories are failures or defeats hidden behind their own disguise. . . . This is an oppressive power that decides for society from above. . . . The world and Mexican society are made up by differences, and the relationship between these differences has to be constructed with a basis in respect and tolerance, things that did not appear in the discourses of the political-military organizations of the 1960s and 1970s.[7]

Social change through armed struggle is thus seen as an authoritarian and undemocratic dead end. This partly explains the Zapatistas' constant emphasis on civil society as the main engine of social change. To the extent that the Zapatistas envision a role for themselves in changing Mexican society, it is as a force that opens spaces for the empowerment of civil society (Bellinghausen 1999). The abandonment of the armed path to social change was, according to Subcomandante Marcos, a consequence of the encounter between the Zapatistas and what he refers to as *zapatismo civil* (Le Bot 1997: 307); that is, the civil society solidarity efforts directed at the Zapatistas from within and beyond Mexico that called for a peaceful solution to the conflict. Marcos explains this in an interview with Carlos Monsiváis and Hermann Bellinghausen (2001):

> The EZLN prepared for January 1 [1994; the first day of the uprising], but not for January 2. . . . The EZLN appears on January 1, starts the war and realizes that the world is not what it was thought to be, but something else. Anyway, since then the virtue of the EZLN, if we can call it that, has been the ability to listen. . . . In this moment, the EZLN says: "here is something we do not understand, something new," and with the intuition that the leadership of the EZLN had we said, "Let us detain ourselves, here is something that we do not understand, that we did not foresee, and for which we did not prepare." The most important thing is to talk and listen more.

The focus on listening and talking is captured in the Zapatista phrase "asking as we walk" (*preguntando caminamos*). This principle defines a process and a method rather than an end goal; it makes it impossible to predefine the path of social struggle or revolution and to think of a defined point of arrival (Holloway 1998: 165). The focus here on the lack of self-definition does not imply that the Zapatistas do not define long-term strategies and concrete goals (as evidenced for example in the struggle for constitutional reform in the area of indigenous rights). In the words of one observer, this definition is something that consistently moves forward:

> [It] overflows, thematically and politically. The definition of indigenous rights is seen not as an end-point, but as a start, as a basis for moving on into other areas of change, but also as a basis for taking the movement forward, a basis for breaking out. (Holloway 1998: 173)

Had the Zapatistas limited themselves to the quest for indigenous autonomy, the scope of their frame extension would probably have been much less conspicuous. The aim of the Zapatistas, in other words, is not to create a new identity or affirm an old identity in a negative manner by establishing a us-versus-them dichotomy. The Zapatistas and the indigenous people of Chiapas are instead framed as a universal symbol of exclusion.

This symbolic role of the Zapatistas is expressed, for example, in the circulation of expressions such as "We are all Marcos" and "We are all Zapatistas." These expressions, used by solidarity activists, are inspired by Subcomandante Marcos, who refers to himself not as a person, but as a figure and a symbol, an interpretation evident in his now famous response to a question concerning his sexuality:

> Marcos is a gay in San Francisco, a black in South Africa, an Asian in Europe, a Chicano in San Isidro, a Palestinian in Israel . . . a peasant without land, an underground editor . . . a doctor with no office, a non-conformist student. . . . In other words, Marcos is a human being in this world. Marcos is every untolerated, oppressed, exploited minority that is resisting and saying "Enough!" (quoted in Holloway and Peláez 1998: 10-11)

The concept of dignity (*dignidad*) is a recurring theme in the Zapatista discourse regarding the oppression of the indigenous people. At the same time, they also use it to articulate their struggle in a national and transnational perspective. The concept of dignity comes not from the urban intellectuals (among them Subcomandante Marcos) that formed the Zapatista movement in the early 1980s, but from the indigenous communities and their century long tradition of resistance (Bruhn 1999: 49). In the formulation of the Zapatistas, dignity is about more than the right to defend and define one's own identity. During the March for Indigenous Dignity in February/March 2001, the Zapatistas gave a number of speeches en route to Mexico City. In a message delivered in Puebla, they presented the following definition of dignity:

> Dignity is a bridge. It needs two sides that, being different . . . are united in the bridge without ceasing to be different and special, but ceasing to be distant. Dignity demands that we are us. But dignity is not that we are only us. In order for dignity to exist, the other is necessary. Because we are always us in relation to the other. . . . Dignity is thus recognition and respect. Recognition of what we are and respect for what we are, yes, but also recognition of what the other is, and respect for what the other is. . . . Dignity should be a world, a world in which many worlds fit. (EZLN 2001)

In their references to dignity the Zapatistas thus transcend the community-based particularity of the indigenous people and link their struggle to the global consciousness master frame. This is accomplished on at least two levels: abstractly, through references to humanity and dignity as in the above quote; and concretely, through universal demands, for example, housing, food, and health (Ceceña 1996). Both aspects are captured in this interview with Mario Galván (2001), a U.S.-based Zapatista solidarity activist in the National Commission for Democracy in Mexico:

> The issues that the Zapatistas address are not specific to Mexico. When they speak of human dignity, their message is universal. When they list their specific demands, they address the basic needs of every human being: food, shelter, medical care, education, equal protection of the law, etc. . . . Their emphasis on the dignity of every

human being bridges issues and borders and opens the door to a worldwide movement for humanity.

To sum up, the Zapatistas' ability to extend their collective action frame from revolutionary insurgency to encompass principles of flexibility, civil society, diversity, and dialogue universalized their claims so as to make them relevant and intelligible to other actors who may be separated from them by social, cultural, and physical distances. This does not mean erasing or downplaying the particular aspects of their claims and problems. Rather, it involves an effort to show how the particularities of their struggle are in fact not particularities at all, but something that can be found in a similar or almost similar form elsewhere in the world.

THE NEOLIBERAL INJUSTICE FRAME

At the root of the injustice frame lies the empirical fact that since the late 1970s neoliberal policies have extended world-wide. This has created a shared transnational experience that the Zapatistas have been able to tap into by portraying neoliberalism as the main cause of their and the world's social and political problems. The Zapatistas' use of the concept of neoliberalism is visible on two levels. First, the neoliberal injustice frame is rooted in the national and regional contexts of Mexico and Chiapas; second, it is broadened to the transnational arena.

On local and national levels the Zapatistas' use of neoliberalism is anchored in a critique of the loss of national sovereignty. This loss has been associated by the Zapatistas with the inauguration of NAFTA (North American Free Trade Agreement) on the day of the uprising (January 1 1994) and with the neoliberal reforms of the PRI government since the 1982 debt crisis. In criticizing this situation, the Zapatistas make use of notions of history and nation. According to Subcomandante Marcos,

> The neoliberal project demands this internationalization of history; it demands that national history is erased and made international; it demands the erasing of cultural borders. . . . Neoliberalism's main error is to think that one can go against history. (Blixen and Fazio 1995)

The transnational level has been most visible since 1996 when the Zapatistas convened an Intercontinental Encounter for Humanity and against Neoliberalism. In July and August, the encounter gathered more than 3,000 activists from around the world in Chiapas' Lacandon Forest to discuss and analyze neoliberalism, but without the aim of producing a common manifesto or a united political front. The diverse and dialogical nature of the Chiapas encounter has been a major source of inspiration for the later development of the social forum form (see also the section on the democratic master frame).

The encounter broadened the Zapatista injustice frame but did not discount the national dimension. Rather, the two dimensions remained simultaneously present. Nor does the transnationalization of the Zapatista injustice frame after 1996 mean that the Zapatistas had not given its injustice frame a transnational dimension before this time. The very coincidence between the Zapatista uprising and the coming into force of NAFTA in fact enabled such an analysis at a very early point and provided a transnationally recognizable link for what might otherwise have been seen as a local or national conflict (Bob 2001).

anti-neoliberal struggs

links btwn neoliberal and its threats to humanity

La Realidad

But while NAFTA provided an early connection between the Zapatistas and critics of neoliberalism outside Mexico, the International Encounter changed the position of the Zapatistas. It moved them from being an object of solidarity to becoming a transnationally recognized source of inspiration in anti-neoliberal struggles. The Zapatistas wanted the encounter to establish a link between neoliberalism and its threats to humanity (as evident in the gathering's name—Encounter *for* Humanity and *against* Neoliberalism). To enforce this point, the First Declaration of La Realidad spoke of neoliberalism as a *world* war against humanity:

> During the last years, the power of money has presented a new mask over its criminal face. Disregarding borders, with no importance given to races or colors, the power of money humiliates dignities, insults honesties and assassinates hopes. Renamed as "Neoliberalism," the historic crime of the concentration of privileges, wealth, and impunities, democratizes misery and hopelessness. A new world war is waged, but now against the entire humanity. (EZLN 1996)

The resonance of this expanded Zapatista injustice frame must be considered in the light of the timing of the uprising. The almost paradoxical appearance of the Zapatistas, only a few years after the end of the Cold War, is a common thread in many accounts of the echo they quickly found beyond the borders of Mexico. Accounts of this type often refer to Francis Fukuyama's (1989) famous insistence on the end of history, which seemed to leave little room for alternatives to liberal democracy and neoliberal capitalism. Justin Paulson (2001), webmaster of the pro-Zapatista Ya Basta! website (see also the section on the Internet) thus situates the importance of the Zapatista uprising in a post-Cold War setting with a radical Left on the retreat and without promising alternatives to the end of history:

> In terms of time, the EZLN sprang into public view three years after the collapse of the USSR. [T]he "End of History" had been declared; the Labor Movement was relatively weak, especially in the United States; NAFTA was being enacted; etc. For both the activist Left and the academic Left, the early 1990s was a period of retreat and of resigned capitulation to neoliberalism. What was so surprising about the Zapatistas was that they weren't supposed to be there! What's a National Liberation Army doing when there aren't supposed to be any more National Liberation Armies? . . . The EZLN has reminded people that there is still reason to struggle. I think for a lot of people, seeing indigenous women armed only with sticks opposing heavily-armed soldiers and tanks, was something of a wake-up call: "If they can do it, I can do it too."

social struggle still possible

The quote suggests that, apart from presenting an analysis of neoliberalism as a transnational phenomenon, the main inspiration coming from the Zapatistas is that social struggle is still possible in the post-Cold War era. However, when it comes to solutions to the problems the Zapatista injustice frame is rather silent. The absence of concrete solutions (beyond radical democracy as a method) points back to the earlier discussion of the Zapatistas' anti-vanguardist position. In fact, the Zapatistas consider variation in the forms of resistance to neoliberalism to be valuable:

> Not only in the mountains of South Eastern Mexico is there resistance and struggle against neoliberalism. In other parts of Mexico, in Latin America, in the United States and Canada, in the Europe of the Maastricht Treaty, in Africa, in Asia, and in Oceania, the pockets of resistance multiply. Each one has its own history, its differences, its similarities, its demands, its struggles, its accomplishments. . . . This is a

model of pockets of resistance, but do not pay too much attention to it. There are as many models as there are resistances. . . . So draw the model you prefer. In regard to the pockets, as well as in regard to the resistances, diversity is richness. (EZLN 1997)

In a seemingly paradoxical manner, the Zapatistas' insistence on the diversity of social struggles has given them considerable influence in the global justice and solidarity movement after Seattle in 1999. As suggested above, the 1996 inter-continental encounter in Chiapas thus heralded a situation where the Zapatista soli-darity network started overlapping with other transnational networks and movements:

> International solidarity increased in 1996 with the [first intercontinental encounter], which placed the EZLN in the vanguard of the just-beginning-to-burgeon anti-globalization movement. Suddenly, the Zapatistas were players on a much larger battlefield and Chiapas became a mandatory way stop on the road to the new resistance that first exploded in Seattle, 1999. (Ross 2001)

The influence of the Zapatistas is clearly visible in two of the main actors in the global justice and solidarity movement; the Peoples' Global Action (PGA) and the Italian Ya Basta group.[8] The PGA was officially formed in February 1998, but traces its lineage to the intercontinental encounters in Chiapas in 1996 and in Spain 1997,[9]

> The sense of possibility that this uprising gave to millions of people across the globe was extraordinary. In 1996, the Zapatistas, with trepidation as they thought no one might come, sent out an e-mail calling for a gathering, called an *encuentro* (encounter). . . . This was followed a year later by a gathering in Spain, where the idea for the construction of a more action focused network . . . Peoples' Global Action (PGA), was hatched. . . . (Peoples' Global Action 2000)

Another example of the lines of diffusion between the transnational Zapatista solidarity network and recent transnational protests is the Italian Ya Basta group:

> The Zapatista movement is a popular resistance movement, which aims to defend the right to survival and self-determination of the indigenous peoples of Chiapas. In the summer of 1996 thousands of people from all over the world gathered in the rebellious South East of Mexico . . . to take part in the global meeting . . . known as the First Intercontinental Meeting for Humanity and Against Neoliberalism. A group of Italian delegates decided to establish an association that would be a useful tool for supporting the Zapatistas' fight in Chiapas and their struggle against neoliberalism in Europe. (Ya Basta 2001)

Today the Ya Basta group is closely associated with the so-called White Overalls who have played a significant role in the global justice and solidarity movement. The White Overalls use foam padding and helmets to protect themselves in clashes with police during demonstrations and have become a powerful and visible symbol of the worldwide protests against international institutions. What is interesting about the Ya Basta group is not just that it was formed in response to the Zapatista uprising. Rather, it has become one of the most vociferous actors in the transnational protest wave in recent years, thus expanding its activities much beyond those first related to the Zapatistas. During the Zapatista March for Indigenous Dignity in February and March 2001 to Mexico City, the Zapatistas were accompanied by White Overalls (Petrich 2001). This return of the Ya Basta group to Chiapas and

Neoliberalism is at the center of Zapatismos injustice frame

Mexico in the form of White Overalls illustrates the reciprocal relationship we increasingly find between local, national, and transnational levels of organization and action.

To sum up, the concept of neoliberalism has been at the center of the Zapatistas' injustice frame. By tapping into a social and political critique of neoliberalism—both in poorer countries and the West—the Zapatistas have been able to link their claims and problems with a diverse range of people and movements around the world. The Zapatistas' anti-neoliberal injustice frame acquired a definite transnational dimension with the Intercontinental Encounter for Humanity and against Neoliberalism in Chiapas in 1996, an event which became an important part of the transformation of the Left after the end of the Cold War and precursor for the social forums of recent years.

THE INTERNET AND THE MEDIATION OF EVERYDAY EXPERIENCES

Internet bring groups together

The Internet has played a crucial role in the Zapatista's transnational framing and the formation of its transnational solidarity network. A frame must have empirical credibility (a fit between the frame and actual events) and experiential commensurability (resonance with the experiences of potential target groups). Verifying empirical credibility and constructing experiential commensurability are always complex tasks, but even more so in a transnational context where social, cultural, and physical distances are at play. The Internet provides a qualitatively new form of communication media with a significant potential for establishing transnational forms of social interaction. This potential is especially evident in the Internet's ability to facilitate exchange between the everyday experiences of physically, socially, and culturally separated senders and recipients in transnational framing processes.

Harry Cleaver, a Zapatista solidarity activist and theorist on the use of the political use of the Internet draws out the main advantages of the Internet.

> The way I put it now is that it took six years to build the antiwar movement in the sixties, it took six months to build the antiwar movement in the Gulf War, and it took six days to build an anti-Mexican government movement in 1994. . . . It is quite clear that the Internet is making possible a level of organization, a speed of organization, that we have never seen before. . . it is a qualitative difference that has to do with a quantitative change . . . just like the Zapatista mobilization against the Mexican government, in Mexico 200,000-300,000 people would gather at the Zócalo, but around the world it was happening in forty countries and 100 cities, and it was having an effect, and it would not have been possible without the Internet. (Cleaver 2000)

The reception of information via the Internet is rarely an isolated action. It takes place in an already existing social space marked by the traces of prior activities and with a stable presence in the form of listservs, archives, and websites. The Internet, accordingly, cannot be sufficiently understood simply as a tool for communication. Cleaver (2000) puts it this way:

> My position is that we are the Internet, it is not the computers, it is not the wires, it is the communications that flow and change, we are the Internet, so it is not a tool. I don't like the term virtuality, because there is nothing virtual about working the Internet, the Internet . . . is the people who are communicating with each other and we construct that, so I think of the Internet as a space. . . . Every time you send a

new email linkage it's a new space, a new website is a new space. . . . There is nothing virtual about that, it is real people setting up computers, talking to each other, and that interacts with the rest of their lives, just like going to a demonstration interacts with the rest of their lives.

The Internet blurs the sender-recipient dichotomy that dominates traditional mass media such as newspapers and television. Such media are mass media where the distribution of information does not take place on a personalized level and where the recipients of information are only abstractly defined. Information distributed through mass media communication does not reach its audience before it has passed through a filter where news is subsumed to specific standards of what is newsworthy and what is not (Slevin 2000: 73-75). In the worst case, this may lead to the distortion of information. In most cases, though, it simply means that news is left out. The Internet also enables forms of mass communication, but it does so differently—mainly that it allows a high degree of unmediated communication. The Internet is the first communication media that enables distributors of information to reach a large undefined audience (as do traditional mass media) but without having to conform simultaneously to conventional mass media standards. It is here that the Internet has the greatest potential for social movements.

There is no evidence that the early Zapatistas had direct access to the Internet through modem or cellular phones.[10] Hosting the Zapatistas' information on the Internet, then, is carried out by solidarity activists (Mexican and non-Mexican) and by Mexican newspapers and magazines:

> It is important to note that the EZLN has played no direct role in the proliferation of the use of the Internet. Rather, these efforts were initiated by others to weave a network of support for the EZLN. Although there is a myth that EZLN spokesman Subcomandante Marcos sits in the jungle uploading EZLN communiqués from his laptop, the reality is that the EZLN and its communities have had a mediated relationship to the Internet. (Cleaver 1998: 628)

Central actors in the distribution of Zapatista documents and information have been (and continue to be) the Ya Basta website and the Mexican newspaper, *La Jornada*. Justin Paulson (interview 2001), administrator of Ya Basta recalls the early phases in the creation of the website and the special role played by *La Jornada*:

> As it turned out, it became the earliest (as far as I know) use of the web in support of an insurgency anywhere in the world. . . . It started slowly, but in November of 1994, I was asked by *La Jornada* to help them develop a website . . . and in return I would not only have access to their paper before it even hit the newsstands in Mexico . . . but I also had permission to reprint news articles and graphics. Since *La Jornada* was also the first place EZLN communiqués were printed, this vastly increased the amount of information I had at my fingertips, and I was able to much more quickly and thoroughly add news and communiqués to the webpage as soon as they became available. This became especially important when the government offensive began in February 1995; at the time, the Mexican government had no significant presence on the internet, and the Ya Basta site contributed, along with several other websites, email lists, etc., to successfully countering the misinformation being spread by the Mexican government. The offensive ended unsuccessfully a short time later, and although I question to what extent this was due to Internet activities, I'm sure they played some role.

There has been a high level of violence in Chiapas since the 1994 uprising. This state of intimidation and violence is the result of heavy military presence in Chiapas in the form of the Mexican Army but also in the form of numerous paramilitary groups. The mainstream media rarely report on this low intensity warfare. Seen from the point of view of the indigenous people in Chiapas, the greatest advantage of the Internet is that it allows them to find an audience for this type of information without having to pass through the filters of mainstream media. *Denuncias* (denouncements) issued by the indigenous communities of Chiapas are not directly uploaded to the Internet. In general, they are passed on to the Internet through the listservs of Mexican-based and Zapatista-related organizations such as the FZLN (Frente Zapatista de Liberación Nacional, or the Zapatista Front of National Liberation, the civil branch of the Zapatistas) and *Enlace Civil*, an organization sympathetic with the Zapatistas that works in Chiapas to establish links between the Zapatista communities and the world around them. The *denuncias* all reflect the problems that the indigenous communities in Chiapas face on a daily basis.

The distribution via the Internet makes it possible to reach a wide audience around the world in a very short time, potentially just a few hours after the incidents have taken place. This is obviously also possible in the case of phone and fax communications. But as stated earlier, information distributed via the Internet has the potential of reaching a much larger number of people at the same time, at a much lower cost, and with a considerably smaller effort in terms of working hours and technical knowledge. Moreover, information distributed via the Internet does not only end up at the immediate recipients. Information via the Internet is easily passed on, for example through forwarding of emails.

Denuncias distributed through the FZLN and Enlace Civil primarily originate in indigenous communities that are direct Zapatista support bases. Other actors such as Indymedia-Chiapas provide an outlet for the indigenous communities of Chiapas in general. The communication efforts of Indymedia-Chiapas are mainly Internet based. In the words of an anonymous representative of Indymedia-Chiapas (2001), the media center more precisely tries to:

> Open a space where the indigenous people, social and civil groups, solidarity groups, may have access to publish and present information on their struggle, and on how they are affected by the conflict created by the government and the paramilitaries. In the sense that we do not censor information, and open doors to Zapatista support bases, as well as many other social organizations, in order to create autonomous media, directed and maintained by the people themselves, we have similar objectives as the Zapatistas.

This vision obviously rests on an understanding of the mainstream mass media as being of limited value in regard to increasing transnational awareness of the situation in Mexico and Chiapas. Incidents of violence and intimidation are serious and disturbing for the people who live under these conditions on a daily basis. But from a mainstream-media perspective they are still small incidents, the likes of which occur every day in a number of countries around the world. In other words, these small stories are rarely sufficiently newsworthy to make it through the filter of most mainstream mass media, and even when they do they are rarely presented in the words of the people involved.

To sum up, the Internet has played a vital part in generating the transnational resonance surrounding the Zapatistas. The Internet provides an unprecedented opportunity for people to get acquainted with the everyday lives and experiences of people living thousands of miles from their own homes through unfiltered and personal accounts. The potential for creating a direct link between senders and recipients of information in transnational framing processes is probably the major achievement of the Internet, at least seen from the perspective of activists working on issues of social change and transnational solidarity. The Zapatistas, however, are not directly on-line. Instead they rely on solidarity activists, newspaper and organizations in and outside Mexico for the distribution of information about the uprising and conditions in Chiapas.

CONCLUSION

This chapter has analyzed the transnational framing processes underlying the formation of the transnational Zapatista solidarity network in the period from 1994 to 2001. Four elements were singled out as central to this process. First, it was shown how the Zapatistas have been able to locate their movement in a democratic master frame, which drew upon widely accepted cultural resources to extend their movement's support network. Second, the Zapatista tactic of frame extension was documented whereby their particular and local/national struggle for indigenous rights was broadened by embracing the values of civil society, dignity, dialogue, and flexibility. Third, the chapter discussed how the concept of neoliberalism has been used by the Zapatistas as an injustice frame with transnational applicability and resonance. Fourth, it was argued that the Internet provided the Zapatistas with new technological opportunities for making their struggle known to a much larger audience than would have been possible without it.

There are three broader implications arising from this study. The first has to do with the much-debated globalization concept. What the analysis of the Zapatistas shows is how globalization, rather than denoting an erasure of the local and national boundaries, points to an interweaving of the local, the national, and the transnational. As I suggested in the introduction to the chapter, the Zapatistas are interesting, to activists and scholars alike, precisely because they are able to frame their struggle in a way that connects local, national, and transnational levels of action and analysis.

The second implication concerns the current state and future of progressive politics and the Left. Contemporary transnational interactions, such as those surrounding the Zapatistas, are quite reciprocal in the sense that they involve actors from both developing and developed countries. The problems faced by physically, socially, and culturally distant actors are increasingly interpreted as aspects of the same processes. We should not, however, draw too rosy a picture. Important differences between developing and developed countries persist in social and economical terms. These inequalities will obviously continue to be reflected in transnational interactions (Smith and Bandy 2005). Despite growing participation by people and organizations from developing countries, the overwhelming majority of participants in transnational activism still come from the U.S. and Europe.

The third implication follows from these concerns. The case of the Zapatistas demonstrates the benefits for social movements, especially movements of the poor, subaltern, and dispossessed, of framing their grievances and strategies in ways that give them transnational resonance. In other words, the attraction of support and resources, and sometimes even survival, hinges on this ability. But generating transnational resonance is no easy task, especially for movements with few resources in terms of technology and education. The Zapatistas have benefited significantly from the communication skills of Subcomandante Marcos, who has a cosmopolitan and educated background that makes it easier to connect to a non-Mexican audience than it would have been, for example, for an indigenous peasant leader with little education and experience outside Mexico and Chiapas. When social movements' chances of developing and having their demands met become more and more dependent on their ability to "market" their struggles transnationally, two problems seem pertinent. First, it can potentially create a kind of transnational movement hierarchy with media savvy and cosmopolitan oriented movements at the top. Second, movements may, precisely for this reason, be tempted to speak the language that transnational audiences want to hear, leading them to play a double game where they have one role locally and another transnationally. This can create serious conflicts, either in relation to their local constituencies or their transnational supporters, and potentially erode legitimacy.

Finally, let me say a few concluding and speculative words about the present state and future of the Zapatistas and the transnational solidarity network. Following the March for Indigenous Dignity in February/March 2001, the Zapatistas fell silent after disagreements with the Mexican government over the issue of indigenous rights. As a consequence, transnational activities also began to wane. In November 2002 the Zapatistas broke the silence with an initiative regarding the conflict between the Spanish state and the Basque separatist group ETA and initiated a period of renewed transnational activity. This intensified in 2003 as the tenth anniversary of the uprising on January 1, 2004, approached. However, levels of attention and activity have appeared not to match that of previous periods. There seem to be two reasons for this. First, the Zapatistas have been relatively inward-looking in this period and engaged in internal processes of restructuring. Second, the events of September 11, 2001, created a more hostile environment for contentious politics and shifted attention to other issues.

When looking at this ebb and flow of the transnational Zapatista solidarity network it seems fair to suggest an analytical distinction between two networks that are, in reality, intertwined. The first network consists of activists and organizations whose activities are closely connected to actual events in Chiapas and Mexico and/or to specific initiatives launched by the Zapatistas. This network is, to some extent, dormant, and is activated primarily when events in Chiapas and Mexico seem to require attention. The second network is more stable and also more political. Its origins are found mainly in the intercontinental encounter arranged by the Zapatistas in Chiapas in 1996. The activists involved in this network find important inspiration for their own local and national political activities in the Zapatistas and its radical democratic critique of neoliberalism. This core network is consequently also less dependent on specific events and initiatives in Chiapas and Mexico than the first network.

At the time of writing this the Zapatistas are working on a major political initiative to create a nationwide social movement consisting of those sectors of Mexican society most affected by the neoliberal policies of the Mexican government.[11] The aim of this initiative is to intervene in the presidential election in Mexico in 2006, not as a political party or coalition, but as a space for critical debates and alternatives. This new outward-looking initiative seems to have revitalized the transnational Zapatista solidarity network, but it remains to be seen whether it can reactivate the network to its former level of activity or if mobilization will be limited mainly to the core network.[12] In the first years of the Zapatista uprising the solidarity network was crucial for the survival of the Zapatistas. The global exposure by solidarity activists of the conflict put a limit to what the Mexican government could do militarily to quell the uprising. Today, it seems unlikely that the government would opt for a military solution. The Zapatistas today are a much more established movement nationally and globally than they were ten years ago. But even if the Zapatistas do not need the solidarity network for protection in the same way as in the early years they still need it as way of increasing the pressure on the Mexican government to respond to claims about social, cultural, economic, and political reforms. The Zapatistas will continue as a national movement for social justice even in the absence of the solidarity network, but from the point of the Mexican government the disappearance or dimming of the global spotlight will make it far less politically costly to ignore them. Striking an effective balance between their national and transnational dimensions is the main challenge for the Zapatistas in the coming years.

ACKNOWLEDGMENTS

This chapter is based on a book-length study of the Zapatistas and the transnational solidarity network surrounding them (Olesen 2005a). For a recent collection of articles on the Zapatistas see the *Humboldt Journal of Social Relations* 29 (1), 2005.

NOTES

1. The official name of the Zapatistas is EZLN (Ejército Zapatista de Liberación Nacional, or the Zapatista Army of National Liberation). The Zapatistas take their name from Emiliano Zapata, a prominent peasant leader during the Mexican Revolution (1910-1919). The name EZLN is used in some of the quotes in the chapter as well as in references to Zapatista documents.

2. Not all actors engaged in Zapatista solidarity work are necessarily direct supporters of the Zapatistas. Many activists dissociate themselves from the armed element of the movement, while they sympathize with its social and political demands. Zapatista solidarity activists may thus be defined as those actors who (1) have an interest in the impact of the Zapatista uprising, (2) share some of the Zapatistas' political views, and (3) engage in information distribution, material-aid delivery, human-rights observation, and lobbying efforts in relation to the Zapatistas and Chiapas.

3. Used with reservation, a webpage count (Google, March 9, 2002) gives a measure of the comparable "popularity" of the Zapatistas. Coupled with the search word "solidarity" these Latin American movements turned up the following number of webpages: EZLN: 5,620; FARC (Fuerzas Armadas Revolucionarios de Colombia/Revolutionary Armed Forces of Colombia): 3,760; MST (Movimento dos Trabalhadores Rurais Sem Terra/Landless Workers' Movement) of Brazil: 3,540; MRTA (Movimiento Revolucionario Tupac Amaru/Tupac Amaru Revolutionary Movement) of Peru: 2,320; EPR (Ejército Popular Revolucionario/ Popular Revolutionary Army) of Mexico: 720.

4. A survey from March 2002 found at least 42 organizations in Europe and the USA currently active on Chiapas and Zapatista related issues. These organizations all devote large parts or all of their time to Chiapas and the Zapatistas. The survey thus excludes the large number of organizations that work on Chiapas and the Zapatistas only on an occasional basis. Moreover, the survey was carried out partly by following the hyperlinks of central Chiapas and Zapatista related websites, and as such excludes organizations without Internet presence. This means that large European and U.S. based organizations are probably overrepresented, while smaller organizations and organizations in Latin America are underrepresented.

5. It should be made clear that the Zapatistas do not dismiss elections and other central elements in liberal democracy as important for a functioning democracy.

6. The most important activities have been (1) the 1994 National Democratic Convention (CND) in Chiapas; (2) the 1995 National Consultation for Peace and Democracy; (3) the First Intercontinental Encounter for Humanity and against Neoliberalism in Chiapas in 1996; (4) the visit of 1,111 civilian Zapatistas to Mexico City to celebrate the formation of the FZLN in 1997; (5) the National Consultation Concerning the Legal Initiative on Indigenous Rights of the Commission of Concordance and

Pacification and for an End to the War of Extermination in 1999; and 6) the March for Indigenous Dignity in 2001.

7. Translations from Spanish-language documents are mine, except when otherwise indicated.

8. This should not be confused with the U.S.-based website Ya Basta (www.ezln.org), which has published Zapatista communiqués since the early days of the uprising.

9. The encounter in Spain in 1997 was a follow-up to the intercontinental encounter in Chiapas in 1996, but was not arranged by the Zapatistas.

10. This may be changing, however. During the 2001 March for Indigenous Dignity, a so-called Zapatista Information Center was established. The center was not run by the Zapatistas themselves, but it did provide a more direct outlet for their messages, and came close to an actual Zapatista presence on the web.

11. The initiative is outlined in the Sixth Declaration of the Lacandon Forest, June 2005.

12. This chapter focuses on the first five phases; that is, the period from 1994 to 2001.

Chapter 12

WHEN LOCAL TROUBLES BECOME TRANSNATIONAL: THE TRANSFORMATION OF A GUATEMALAN INDIGENOUS RIGHTS MOVEMENT

Julie Stewart

Carlos Chen Osorio and Jesús Tecu Osorio would like to forget what happened in 1982 in their village of Río Negro. They are tired of the nightmares and headaches that accompany their memories. But the severe poverty and ongoing repression of their community forces them to remember, as they struggle for legal justice, equitable development, and respect for indigenous rights. Their story begins in 1982, during Guatemala's brutal internal conflict.

On March 13, 1982, Jesús was eleven years old and living in a rural river valley in central Guatemala. That morning, a group of government soldiers and a local paramilitary troop entered the Maya village and demanded that everyone congregate. The soldiers claimed to be looking for guerrillas and were enraged when they found only women and children. Undaunted, they accused them of being guerrilla collaborators and forced everyone to march up the mountain. After walking several hours, the soldiers told the community that it was time for it to pay for its sins. They divided the children from the women and began to systematically kill everyone, first the women and then the children.

For reasons still unknown to him, Jesús survived that day. After witnessing the brutal murder of his family, a soldier told Jesús he would spare his life if he would agree to live with him and work for his family. Jesús agreed, and was virtually enslaved to the murderer of his family for over two years.

Carlos and several other men were in hiding that day. Because of the internal conflict, and official suspicion regarding poor, indigenous men, they knew they were at risk. They had no idea that women and children would be targeted. But when rumors reached them of what happened, they returned immediately. As Carlos related in his personal testimony:

> When I arrived, I didn't realize what had happened. But when I saw, I wanted to wake from the horrible dream. Maybe it wasn't true what my eyes were seeing: my loved ones mutilated, beheaded, throats slit, tortured, raped. . . . I asked God to help me. I wanted to be dead in the place of my brothers and sisters. That day was silent, so silent that not even the birds sang.

Carlos lost seventeen family members that day, including his pregnant wife and two children. Fearing that he, too, would be killed, he went into hiding for several years. In the late 1980s, Carlos returned to the region, and found Jesús, who had been liberated from his captors. They joined with survivors of the four government massacres in and around Río Negro—which killed 444 people—to try to comprehend this tragedy and its national and international context.

Today, Carlos is the representative of a regional NGO that promotes respect for indigenous rights, equitable community development, and reform of international financial institutions (IFIs). He has spoken to audiences throughout North America and Europe, and once received a standing ovation at the World Bank. Jesús works as a key advocate for the prosecution of local war criminals. He received the Reebok Human Rights Award in 1996 for his activism, and has appeared on U.S. television. While unique and personal, their stories reflect the broader transformation of the Rio Negro tragedy into a transnational issue. How did this occur? How did a relatively powerless group of Maya Indians launch a challenge to local authorities that eventually reached the World Bank? How did a local tragedy in a remote village become the center of a transnational activist network and the focus of international media? The Río Negro massacre and its subsequent translation into a transnational issue represent an important case to help understand an important contemporary development in social movement mobilization: a local to global shift. This article examines in depth the birth of the local movement and its subsequent development into an integral member of a global movement as a means of testing, elaborating, and focusing a theory of transnational activist networks.

TRANSNATIONAL ADVOCACY NETWORKS

First coined by Keck and Sikkink, transnational advocacy networks—or TANs— refer to nongovernmental organizations (NGOs), social movements, philanthropic foundations, the media, churches, and members of the government that work internationally on an issue. They are bound together by shared values, a common discourse, and dense exchanges of information and services (Keck and Sikkink 1998a: 2, 3, 8, 200; Keck and Sikkink 2000: 52). Rather than replacing social movements or international NGOs, TANs contain them (Tarrow 2001). In contrast to movements motivated mainly by material concerns, TANs are "distinguishable largely by the centrality of principled ideas or values in motivating their formation" (Keck and Sikkink 1999: 89). TANs represent *ideas* more than *constituencies*, and so are more flexible and less geographically bound than many social movements (Keck and Sikkink 1998b).

In this age of globalization, international boundaries blur, domestic and global arenas become intertwined, and national social movements may become less relevant (Smith 2001b; Tarrow 2001; Hamel et al. 2001) while the fluid and flexible transnational network may become more important (Keck and Sikkink 1998a). As capital, people, goods, services, and ideas move more quickly, transnational linkages can mobilize like never before. Tarrow argues that the international NGOs which are so central to TANs constitute "the most rapidly growing sector of trans-national politics today" (Tarrow 1998: 188). Appadurai (2000: 15) similarly suggests that TANs are "the crucibles and institutional instruments of the most serious efforts to globalize from below." He argues that TANs are uniquely constituted to challenge the negative aspects of globalization. Finally, although McAdam, Tarrow and Tilly (2001: 332) argue that most contentious action "never outgrows [its] local, categorical or institutional context," they note that the exceptional cases of scale shift are seen in Keck and Sikkink's work on TANs.

The Boomerang Model

While Keck and Sikkink describe several conditions for TAN emergence, they emphasize a *boomerang model*.[1] This model predicts that blocked channels of grievance articulation between domestic groups and the government spur activists to look elsewhere for support. When networks successfully develop between domestic actors and their international allies, activists can more effectively pressure their target, usually the state. The authors coin the term *boomerang model* to describe transnational activists drawing on international allies to pressure the state for change (Keck and Sikkink 1998a, 1998b, 1999, 2000). Much of Keck and Sikkink's work focuses on human rights abuses and state repression, and highlights two corollaries of the boomerang model. First, state repression externalizes domestic human-rights struggles because the very institution to which citizens would normally turn for protection or redress is their principal human-rights violator. This spurs activists to form alliances with their counterparts abroad. Second, state repression also generates diasporas. People fleeing repression to live in exile are a crucial source of information about the home country, adding legitimacy to a cause (Keck and Sikkink 1998b).

While suggestive, the boomerang model is problematic in three ways. First, it fails to accurately explain or predict when movements remain local and when they go global. Why did state repression in El Salvador and Guatemala spark tremendous transnational activism, while serious human rights abuses in Honduras rarely received international attention?[2] Keck and Sikkink's emphasis on blockage may be misplaced due to the overwhelming generality of this condition in Latin America—the region on which their human rights chapter focused. Repressive states were common in Latin America. According to one survey, fifteen of the seventeen Latin American states were designated as repressive in the early 1980s (Ball 2000). If we focus solely on repressive states, where channels for claims making are likely to be closed, then there are many more repressive states than movements that have gone global. A repressive state may be a necessary condition for transnational activism, but it is not sufficient.

Second, an exclusive focus on state blockage overlooks important global influences on state power and local grievances. It assumes that when claim-making channels are not blocked, collective grievances and their redress principally occur within the nation state. This underestimates a key element of transnationalized activism: *the nested nation* whereby the nation state must be understood in the context of its relationships with international financial institutions, multinational corporations, intergovernmental organizations, and the transnational capitalist class (Sklair 1995). This implies not only that there are more actors relevant to TAN emergence, but also that the qualities of key actors may be more complex than Keck and Sikkink suggest.

Third, the boomerang model provides little room for activist agency and dynamism. Do people, movements, and the networks merely respond to changes in the transnational arena, or do they also shape it in fundamental ways? A boomerang focus fails to capture how people interpret their situations, define grievances, mobilize communities, and form strategic alliances and goals. To be sure, the cases upon which Keck and Sikkink build their theoretical models are descriptively rich, but the theoretical emphasis moves too far away from actors. A more helpful approach would look at the myriad ways that people form movements, and movements form networks in order to enter transnational public space. As Tarrow (2001: 15) argues, we need to better understand how "nonstate actors with weak resources and opportunities in their own societies can develop transnational ties that can boomerang on behalf of their own claims." Put another way, my criticisms follow McAdam, Tarrow, and Tilly's (2001) theoretical preference for specifying the mechanisms of contentious politics: namely, that the boomerang model is poorly specified in terms of mechanisms. I argue that a key mechanism in this case is grievance transformation. By engaging in the transnational sphere, local grievances are transformed, which in turn transforms transnational processes. That is to say, this process "renders the global and the local mutually transformative" (Guidry, Kennedy, and Zald 2000: 12). Rather than viewing actors as statically responding to changes in the global economy, a focus on activist agency renders the process reciprocal and transformational. Local troubles become transnational when domestic and international activists gather, exchange information, strategize, and redefine the problem and its solution. This in turn often transforms the activists themselves, how they view themselves and their place in the world.

Division of Labor in TANS

The emergence of transnational activism usually relies on a specific division of labor. As Caniglia (2001) and J. Smith (2001b) have argued, actors from the global North tend to have privileged access to official documents (whether from international financial institutions, multinational corporations, international foundations, or national governments), and can thus function as key sources of information for activists in the global South. Also, international actors often have more influence on governments of the global South than domestic activists. Northern activists are identified with power (Lewis 2000). Further, as Millie Thayer has argued in her discussion of "traveling feminisms"—a case study of how feminist discourse in Brazil has changed as a consequence of new linkages with feminists from the global North—discursive innovations often travel from North to South but are then selectively appropriated for the needs and interests of domestic actors (Thayer 2000). This means that actors from the global South do not passively receive information, but rather provide irreplaceable knowledge about the local dimensions of a global issue while also crucially contributing to the legitimacy of transnational campaigns. Thus, when knowledge of the "global" combines with local legitimacy, the conditions are ripe for TAN emergence. But this still leaves the question of motive. The motive is found in the economic, political, and cultural contours of globalization.

The division of labor within transnational activism can best be thought of as a network of partners who draw from their respective comparative advantages to contribute to collective action. It follows that transnational relationships will be horizontal—as Keck and Sikkink themselves suggest—rather than hierarchical, with each member contributing material resources, knowledge, emotions, and practical know-how in a way that continually transforms the issues and actions. Because of globalizing processes and the growing insight that many social problems cannot be contained with territorial boundaries, the potential for TAN emergence is great.

The Efficacy of TANs

Keck and Sikkink suggest that TANs experience their greatest success when they mobilize around "issues involving bodily harm to vulnerable individuals, especially when there is a short and clear causal chain (or story) assigning responsibility" (Keck and Sikkink 1998a: 27). Basic concerns over human rights, they argue, resonate across cultures and often provide specific targets. In their studies of the Central American peace movement in the U.S., Smith (1996) and Nepstad (1997, 2001) similarly argue that key human rights abuses—such as the assassination of El Salvador's Archbishop Oscar Romero, or the testimonies of Guatemalan survivors of politically motivated torture—catapulted North Americans into activity in the 1980s. The "moral shock" which accompanies the revelation of human rights abuses is often key for mobilization.[3] It can move people out of complacency and into action. I agree that fundamental human rights abuses attract attention and demand transnational responses. However, this does not fully explain why some human rights movements are more effective than others.

I argue that the bodily harm/short causal chain argument is a key predictor of mobilization—certainly a prerequisite of movement success. But to understand how and why activists move from protest to proposal, from outrage to action, frequently activists lengthen the causal chain and analyze human rights abuses as part of a larger problem, embedded in economic and political institutions and shaped by international structures. This means that the short causal chain must be elongated and that the simple target becomes more complex. The idea of object shift—an "alteration in relation between claimants and objects of claims" (McAdam, Tarrow, and Tilly 2001: 144)—partially captures this dynamic in that the importance of the initial target may recede as activists learn more about the chain of command relevant to their issue and find a target more able to remedy their problem. Even greater success is likely when the dynamic is more dramatic, combining object shift and upward scale shift. The latter idea involves a "change in the number and level of coordinated contentious actions leading to broader contention involving a wider range of actors and bridging their claims and identities" (McAdam, Tarrow, and Tilly 2001: 331; Tarrow 2005b).

In sum, the bodily harm/short causal chain argument better explains mobilization than success. Exposure to information about an ongoing tragedy often provokes the moral shock necessary to make people act. But few social problems have a simple cause and effect. By locating domestic grievances within an international structure, activists forge common cause with global actors while locating targets with greater capacity to redress those grievances. As this case study demonstrates, an innovative pairing of blatant human rights abuses and destructive economic development policies explains the success of this solidarity effort. Without the broader, structural perspective, the movement headed by Carlos and Jesús would likely have dwindled rather than grown exponentially following the end of Guatemala's internal conflict.

RESEARCH METHODOLOGY

The data for this article mainly come from my experience working in Guatemala with Witness for Peace (WfP)—a U.S. nongovernmental organization whose mission is to change economic and foreign policies that contribute to poverty and oppression in Latin America. In early 1994, I began working with WfP to document the community effects of U.S. involvement in the region. For over two years, I spent substantial periods of time in Pacux, Río Negro, and other Guatemalan communities, working with people whose experiences are featured in this chapter. I met with local activists, pastors and priests, other international human rights advocates, and the citizens whose labor and courage created this movement. I participated in community activities, attended organizational meetings, and lived with local families. I also conducted dozens of semiformal interviews with people involved in this community movement.

WfP's initial interest in working in Pacux was prompted by the community's efforts to document the region's violent past. This work entailed considerable risk, prompting WfP to provide international accompaniment to local activists. However, once we became better acquainted with the communities, it became clear that many of the problems we were documenting stemmed not only from the war, but also from the disastrous effects of a World Bank-sponsored development project during the region's genocidal period. Almost all of the forty-five testimonies that I and the WfP team gathered mentioned the Chixoy dam, a project that in people's minds was inextricably combined with forced disappearances, death, displacement, and poverty.

The constant mention of the Chixoy dam led WfP activists to more fully investigate the World Bank's role in the project. This investigation resulted in the publication of *A People Dammed*, a report that highlights the World Bank's role in a failed development project while suggesting that the Bank may have hidden the project's connection to the genocidal regime in power during construction. This publication and the activities organized around its release provided entrée to more international activist involvement. These events also began the transformation of a local movement into a member of a transnational network.

At this point, my role in the story also changes. While the data come from my work as an activist, I later revisited it as a researcher to study the dynamics of transnational activism. I supplemented the original data with additional visits to Guatemala during the summers of 1998 and 2003. Although I remain involved in this issue on many levels, my primary goal here is to present a detailed and accurate case history of this movement's mobilization trajectory to better understand questions of TAN emergence and efficacy. Walton observes that the strength of case studies is their ability to challenge accepted wisdom about causal processes (Walton 1992). This case study demonstrates that the received wisdom about the emergence and outcomes of transnational activism is not universal.

THE POLITICAL HISTORY

Most scholars of contemporary Guatemala trace the origins of its internal conflict to the emergence of four leftist opposition movements in the early 1960s. Formed to challenge the military dictator Ydígoras Fuentes, these groups sporadically attacked Guatemalan military outposts. After a decade of minor skirmishes, the movement expanded to the rural interior, attempting to recruit indigenous followers. At its height, the movement boasted having a million supporters. The Guatemalan government countered this guerrilla threat with counter-insurgency strategies that targeted its leadership, and later its supposed base of support. This latter strategy materialized into a genocidal campaign that demolished indigenous communities in the highlands in the early 1980s. After decades of conflict and years of stalled negotiations between the Guatemalan

National Revolutionary Unity (URNG) and the Guatemala government, a final peace accord was signed on December 29, 1996. During the war, 200,000 civilians were killed or disappeared, 250,000 fled the country, and one million people were internally displaced (Jonas 1991; Barry 1992; CEH 1999).

Although the roots of Guatemala's conflict are complex and contested, key statistics on social exclusion reveal the depth of the grievances that motivated ordinary Guatemalans to challenge the status quo. Primary amongst these is economic inequality. Guatemala is one of the most economically unequal countries in the western hemisphere, where the gross domestic product of the richest 20 percent of the population is 30 times greater than the poorest 20 percent. Maintaining this division of wealth requires coercive labor systems and mandates the withholding of goods and education that promotes social mobility. Less than 40 percent of the population has access to health care, running water, and electricity; 70 percent of the population is functionally illiterate, and 78 percent live in poverty. When the indigenous population is considered in isolation, the statistics on social exclusion increase by as much as 20 percent. Guatemala also has one of the most unequal land tenure systems in the Americas: less than 3 percent of the population owns over 65 percent of all arable land (Black 1998; CEH 1999).

Structural poverty preceded the internal conflict, facilitated rivalries during the war, and remains omnipresent in the post-conflict era. In many respects, the Rabinal region, the area where the Río Negro massacre survivors ultimately resettled, is a microcosm of Guatemala. Located within the department of Baja Verapaz, in north central Guatemala, *Rabileños* have seen their quality of life deteriorate in the last several decades.[4] Although historically, *Rabileños* relied on subsistence agriculture for survival, soil degradation, and inadequate land have rendered this strategy untenable (EAFG 1997). Consequently, nearly half of the population periodically migrates in search of seasonal agricultural jobs or work in the capital. But poverty is increasing, currently encompassing approximately 87 percent of the population (Alecio 1995: 26; EAFG 1997: 28).

Not only is the Rabinal region one of the poorest in Guatemala, it was also devastated by the internal conflict. Located along a strategic axis between three geographically important departments (El Quiché, Alta Verapaz, Baja Verapaz), Rabinal was an early target of both guerrilla and military intervention. Although the guerrilla presence was ephemeral, violent military actions developed in the early 1980s that left an estimated 4,000 to 5,000 people—almost a fifth of the local population—dead (EAFG 1997: 179, 314).

Adjoining the municipality of Rabinal is the lush Chixoy river valley, where residents, like the Río Negro villagers, farmed the fertile flood plains and enjoyed a higher standard of living than most *Rabileños*. Survivors of this period believe their objection to the Chixoy dam—a massive hydroelectric project funded by the World Bank—made them a target of government repression. One resident remembers life before the violence:

> Life was hard, but it was good. Everyone lived nearby, we all knew each other, and we lived peacefully. But when they began the construction, many strangers came to our community. The army arrived, the guerrillas arrived, and then the violence started. (interview with author, January 1995)

First, several community leaders were killed en route to a meeting concerning the dam with local officials in 1980. Two years of negotiations with government officials followed, but the residents of Río Negro refused to leave their ancestral home. Their resistance was met with more repression, culminating in the four brutal massacres of 444 villagers in 1982 (of a total population of 800). The survivors fled, and in late 1982 when the dam was completed, the Chixoy river basin began to fill, flooding the village of Río Negro.

Eventually Río Negro survivors returned to the region and settled in Pacux, the resettlement community built in 1983 for those displaced by the dam. Pacux—a community of small cement houses organized into a grid of regimented rows—adjoins Rabinal's regional military garrison. In contrast to their previous village, the land around Pacux is rocky and impoverished, insufficient both in quantity and quality to feed the resettled population. Because the regional employment opportunities are scarce, most people migrate regularly, live on the edge of poverty, and are constantly reminded of the violence.

Despite persistent poverty and the pressure of living in the military's shadow, Pacux residents began to organize in the mid-1990s. Organizing was facilitated by the beginning of civilian rule in 1985 and a gradual process of political liberalization that permitted both local and international human rights groups to openly operate in the country. A small group of massacre survivors formed to denounce the violence of the 1980s and to demand justice. The resultant Widows and Orphans Committee (Comité de Viudas y Huérfanos) sought the exhumation of the mass graves of its loved ones, a public burial, and the construction of a monument honoring the dead. They enlisted support from national human rights groups and international NGOs to secure the services of a forensic team and to fund the construction of a monument (Witness for Peace (WfP) Guatemala Team 1996: 15-20).

Witness for Peace (WfP) was one of the first international organizations to support the committee. Initially, its interest in Pacux was prompted by the community's effort to document the region's violent past. After nearly ten years of living in a shroud of silence, community members mobilized to denounce the violence, bury their dead, and initiate an investigation and criminal justice procedures. In its earliest phase of mobilization, the Widows and Orphans Committee focused on one objective only: to rescue its dead from the clandestine cemetery in Río Negro and properly bury them. This was a concrete and achievable goal that met one of the most basic needs arising from the internal conflict: to publicly grieve for lost loved ones. With much effort and international support, they met that goal.

In November 1993, the Guatemalan Forensic Anthropology Team (EAFG) unearthed the remains of 177 women and children who were killed in one of the more significant Río Negro massacres, the one in which Carlos lost his pregnant wife and children. In April 1994, the surviving family members publicly buried their loved ones and erected a small monument. Written on the monument was a dedication to Río Negro's martyrs, those "who gave their life for peace, whose blood fertilizes our land and represents the seed of truth, justice and hope" (WfP Guatemala Team 1996: 19). As the first public burial of its type in the country, this act attracted national media attention and the attendance of Nobel Peace Prize recipient Rigoberta Menchú. However, two weeks later, the small monument was destroyed and many of the graves were overturned. Because of the cemetery's proximity to the Rabinal military base— the garrison literally overlooks the cemetery—most people believe the military was involved. Such an action could not have occurred unseen by the soldiers on constant vigilance and thus sent an unequivocal message to local activists. According to Russell (1995: 1), "The killers did not want the truth told about what they did. Publicly telling the truth was the first and most important step in breaking the wall of impunity."

Undaunted, Pacux activists began to organize internationally to seek funding for a new memorial. They contacted groups such as Peace Brigades International, the Campaign for Peace and Life, Witness for Peace, and Amnesty International. The threats that activists received and the monument's destruction added legitimacy to their movement and helped attract greater international support. The committee held frequent community meetings to plan the construction of a bigger, better monument. One local leader commented, "We are going to build this monument so big and strong that they will need a tank to destroy it" (WfP Guatemala Team 1996: 19). Although there was considerable apprehension within Pacux during the planning, the community collectively built the monument.

On March 12, 1995, the community dedicated a new monument—this one a seemingly indestructible twelve-ton concrete and steel structure. The monument stands over twelve feet tall and is topped by an enormous cross. The story inscribed on the monument's face recounts the massacres, lists all those who died, and accuses the Guatemalan army of genocide. Borrowing imagery from the Bible, it talks of the "Christs of Río Negro—those martyred for peace." At the dedication one activist made the movement's objectives very clear. She said,

> We build this monument so that our children will know what happened during the violence. We write the names of 177 murdered women and children so that everyone will know who died. We will not let our past be forgotten, nor will we let it be repeated. (Pacenza 1996: 11)

These activities were just the inception of the committee's political life. Next, Pacux residents began meeting regularly to pursue their legal case against those responsible for the massacres and to plan economic development projects. Its first successes included acquiring the support of the Center for Human Rights Legal Action (CALDH), a Guatemalan human rights NGO, to prosecute its case against the Guatemalan army and its paramilitary branch for ethnic genocide.[5] They also acquired international financing for several community development initiatives. As the movement grew in numbers and in scope, however, it became clear that other factors required consideration to fully understand the past. So what began as a relationship of international accompaniment to offset the dangers of domestic activism developed into a richer relationship of North-South information exchange and investigation into the extralocal forces behind the violence in Río Negro.[6]

LOCAL TROUBLES BECOME TRANSNATIONAL ISSUES

Almost from the beginning of our work in Pacux, people dated the start of their troubles to the planning of the Chixoy dam. As one community member notes, regional violence was nonexistent before the onset of the dam construction in 1977. He states, "I'll tell you the real reason for the violence: they wanted our land for their cursed reservoir and dam, and we were in the way" (author interview with Pacux resident, January 1996). Although the construction of the dam coincided with the most brutal period of the counterinsurgency campaign, it seemed worthwhile to investigate whether the linkage between the two was coincidental or causal. In the following months, WfP activists investigated the Chixoy project, interviewing pastors, journalists, and government officials, doing government archival research, and searching decades' worth of newspapers. This directed us to the financial role played by the World Bank and the

Inter-American Development Bank. Through connections with the International Rivers Network (IRN), we were able to acquire confidential papers from World Bank archives that suggested the bank's role in the violence.[7] These World Bank documents include audits, project completion reports, and policy guidelines concerning resettlement. The objective of this report is not to reanalyze these documents, but rather trace the local-transnational linkages of the movement. The documents are presented in the WfP report, *A People Dammed* (1996).[8]

In February 1975, Guatemala's National Institute of Electrification (INDE) unveiled the Chixoy hydroelectric project as the solution to the energy crisis plaguing Guatemala. The project's principal objective was to provide a sustainable source of cheap and abundant energy, and the government solicited funding from the World Bank and the IADB. Together, the IADB and the World Bank provided $177 million in initial loans, approximately 65 percent of the project's estimated total cost. As it turned out, the Chixoy dam was inefficient, unreliable, and unsustainable.[9] The incontrovertible failure of this project is widely accepted. Even the World Bank acknowledges that the project was an "unwise investment." However, it denies responsibility for the failure of the project despite decades of intimate involvement with the Guatemalan electricity sector. More damning, however, are statements about the bank's knowledge of human rights abuses that occurred during the project planning and construction, and the direct role that INDE played in the Río Negro massacres. As one Río Negro survivor argues, "INDE knew about and collaborated in the violence against our village because we were refusing to leave Río Negro." He speculates that it was easier to label the community as a guerrilla stronghold and eliminate the opposition to the dam than to negotiate a fair settlement with the people who would be displaced. A Catholic priest who has worked in the area for more than thirty years elaborates:

> The project was a gold mine for INDE and the army generals. There was so much money coming in that as the project progressed, so did the violence, the disappearances, and finally the massacres.

Further, a construction worker who worked on the dam between 1977 to 1982 asserts:

> Of course INDE knew about and condoned what was happening in Río Negro because they stood to gain from it. Dead or terrorized peasants aren't going to demand their rights. The generals, politicians, and INDE people pocketed all those cash payments. Everybody knew about the corruption and the violence, but we were all too terrified to say anything. (author interview February 1996)

Finally, according to a journalist who worked in the region for many years, one of the heads of security at the Chixoy project was the brother of a high-ranking army official in nearby Cobán. He asserts that "There's no doubt that INDE encouraged and benefited from the massacres." This resonates with the testimony of many massacre survivors who explain that when the second Río Negro massacre took place on May 14, 1982, the assassins were driving an INDE truck.[10]

The final question relating to the Chixoy dam is how much the World Bank knew about the violence. World Bank documents indicate that bank personnel worked in supervisory capacities at the Chixoy site for up to three months each year from 1979 to 1991. In 1984, the bank even hired an "expert on resettlement policy to assist in the supervision function of resettlement." Despite this expert presence, none of the bank's Chixoy reports mention the Río Negro massacres. Instead, they occasionally make oblique references to insurgency activity in the area, and note delays in resettlement and compensation. Nevertheless, in 1985, three years after the Río Negro tragedy, the bank granted a supplemental loan of nearly $45 million to the Chixoy project. If the bank knew about the massacres, then giving an additional loan to the project was at best a calculated coverup and at worst an act of complicity in the violence. If the Bank did not know about the slaughter, then it was guilty of negligence.

In light of these revelations, committee members began intensely lobbying the Guatemalan government to comply with the resettlement promises associated with the Chixoy project. To pressure the international financiers of the dam—principally the World Bank—three committee members toured the United States with Witness for Peace representatives to tell their story of the pairing of genocide and "development." During this speaking tour, committee members spoke to thousands of people across the country, distributed several thousand copies of *A People Dammed*, and received mainstream media coverage. The highlight of the tour was a press conference in which Carlos condemned the World Bank for funding the Chixoy project and demanded reparations.[11] Sponsored by both Witness for Peace and the International Rivers Network, this press conference generated enough public outrage that the World Bank could no longer ignore the issue.

In response to this publicity, the bank initiated an internal investigation of the project. World Bank President James Wolfensohn informed the executive directors of WFP and IRN that the Bank would send a delegation to Guatemala to investigate. In the letter Wolfenson wrote, "Although we may not subscribe to all the specific points in the publication, we certainly share the distress you express over the kind of violence which existed in the Guatemalan highlands and, in particular, in the vicinity of the Chixoy Dam Project. . . .Such actions have no place in a civilized society and certainly should not be any part of any project associated with the World Bank."[12] The World Bank delegation went to Rabinal in July of 1996 to investigate the bank's involvement in the project. After visiting Pacux, the bank agreed to facilitate a financial package that included cash payments, land and home titles for Pacux residents, and the purchase of several farms (Euloff 1998: 8). While still denying knowledge of the connection between the massacres and the dam, in a follow-up letter to WFP and IRN, Wolfensohn acknowledged that "Our recent mission to all the major resettlement areas has revealed that many commitments to the relocated people have yet to be met." In his conclusion, Wolfensohn states, "I am very grateful to Witness for Peace for having brought these allegations to our attention."[13]

This victory provided new hope for the committee. The key leaders began to broaden their efforts to work with a regional, rather than a local constituency. With the assistance of the Group for Mutual Assistance (GAM)—a national human rights organization formed in 1985—the committee opened an office. Simultaneously, international relationships formed during the exhumation/burial process deepened, leading to several more international tours. Of particular importance was the relationship forged between local leaders and Rights Action (formerly Guatemala Partners) – an international NGO that works in Central America and the Caribbean in pursuit of a wide range of social justice and human rights goals.

Through Rights Action's efforts, Jesús Tecú Osorio—the child survivor of a Río Negro massacre with which we opened this report, and key committee activist—won the Reebok International Human Rights Award in 1996. In addition to its international prestige and broad media coverage, this award brought $25,000.[14] These funds allowed the committee to build its own office, start paying salaries to leaders, establish a scholarship fund to educate young people from Pacux, and pursue economic development projects.

For Rabinal's social movement trajectory, 1996 was a watershed year. The earlier mobilization around a relatively narrow human rights agenda transformed into the center of a transnational network. Whereas previous mobilization targeted the Guatemalan government and military, the revelations about the involvement of the World Bank and the IADB changed the orientation of this movement and created the potential for more direct involvement of international allies. Critically, this happened in 1996, the year the peace accords were signed between the URNG and the Guatemalan government. For many international observers, this signaled the end of military intimidation and suggested a reduced need for international observers. Instead, a transnational network formed out of this issue at precisely the time when more traditional human rights work seemed less pressing.

Since the blossoming of this transnational network in 1996, activism around the Chixoy issue has multiplied. At present, a minimum of eighteen international NGOs (representing activism in eight countries) are working on the Chixoy case, work that is loosely coordinated by Rights Action staff.[15] For example, COHRE (Centre on Housing Rights and Evictions) is currently drafting reports on the Chixoy case for United Nations entities such as the UN Special Rapporteur on Housing and Property Restitution and the UN Committee on Economic, Cultural and Social Rights. COHRE also plans to issue a petition to the Inter-American Commission on Human Rights, the first step toward a trial in the Inter-American Human Rights Court. The Chixoy case was also one of six projects featured by the World Commission on Dams in a series of international conferences and direct actions, largely due to the efforts of International Rivers Network and the Reform the World Bank Campaign—Italy. Academic groups such as the American Anthropological Association, the American Association for the Advancement of Science, and the Princeton Working Group on Multilateral Institution Accountability have studied the Chixoy case and issued reports in the interests of public policy scholarship. For example, the Princeton group ultimately submitted its findings to the UN Commissioner for Human Rights. And the history of Rio Negro was recently made into a film—*Discovering Dominga*—which aired on PBS in the U.S. and on HBO-Olé throughout Latin America during the summer of 2003. It was featured as one of public television's annual award-winning showcase films for independent documentaries.

Despite different organizational identities, strategy preferences and goals, the Rio Negro/Chixoy case has provided common ground for transnational coordination. The pairing of human rights and sustainable development issues allows for groups to engage in education, advocacy, lobbying, and direct action. Some groups are more concerned with community reparations, while others see it as a springboard to demand the reform of international financial institutions.[16] While some want to educate people about Guatemala, other groups see it as a microcosm of failed policy in the global South. Rights Action—in conjunction with many transnational organizations—has publicized the Chixoy case broadly and has offered it as an illustration of failed development policy in numerous international protests, including the April 2000 anti-WTO uprising in Seattle, the September 2000 rally against the World Bank and International Monetary Fund in Prague, the April 2001 demonstrations against "free" trade during the Summit of the Americas meeting in Quebec City, and the semiannual protests in Washington, D.C., against the Bank and the IMF.[17] The agreement on core values facilitates coordination, but as the network concept implies, there is no strict hierarchy, so each group has the freedom to work on this issue given its own ideological disposition, strategy preferences, and overall goals.

It is important to note that the flowering of this TAN did not come at the expense of local activism. Due to new resources in terms of networks, information, and money, the Pacux-based committee that formed in the early 1990s also transformed, becoming the Association for the Integral Development for the Victims of the Violence in the Verapaces Maya-Achí (ADIVIMA). ADIVIMA is broader in both mission and membership than its predecessor. Its approximately 800 members are residents of thirty-five Rabinal villages. Attendance at the bi-monthly meetings is between 50 and 75. Its new mission statement highlights three areas: post-conflict legal justice, cultural vindication, and economic development.

As mentioned earlier, in 1995 Río Negro massacre survivors initiated legal proceedings against those responsible for the massacres in the 1980s. After multiple trials and frustrating reversals, three paramilitary members were found guilty for the Río Negro massacres and were sentenced to fifty years in prison (Bodeau 1999; Russell 2000a). This was the first guilty verdict ever pronounced against the participants of the hundreds of massacres committed in Guatemala.[18] ADIVIMA's legal work gained momentum with the 1999 opening of a legal clinic, the *Bufete Juridico Popular*, which provides lawyers to help local people file requests with the district court, press charges, file complaints about intimidation, or resolve property disputes. Jesús, the 1996 Reebok Human Rights Award Recipient, has been a full-time employee of the *Bufete*, working closely with the broader Rabinal community (Russell 2000b).

Regarding its second focus area, ADIVIMA coordinators say cultural vindication is central to their work. One leader says, "We were targeted because we are indigenous. Here in Rabinal [proper] there was very little violence because they are all *ladino*. The *ladinos* blame us for the violence, so our work answers that accusation by exposing the truth."[19] For ADIVIMA activists, this means they clarify who were the victims and who were the perpetrators of the violence. Another goal of ADIVIMA activists is to preserve indigenous culture by providing both educational scholarships for indigenous youth and workshops on domestic indigenous and human rights.[20] Inspired by a visit to the Holocaust Museum in Washington, D.C., during one of his tours to the U.S., Carlos has founded a museum to honor the history and current struggles of the Maya-Achí (Russell 2000b).

Although the legal and cultural work is crucial, ADIVIMA activists are prioritizing economic development projects. According to one leader, "Although the massacres are over, another type of violence continues, the violence of poverty. Poverty is a massacre of economics, in which children and babies die because they don't have enough to eat, because there are no jobs, no money for anything."[21] ADIVIMA's economic development projects include a regional carpentry workshop, business training for local entrepreneurs, several village irrigation systems, a petition for agricultural inputs to benefit dozens of communities, a handicrafts workshop, and a housing project.

CONCLUSION

While the boomerang theory predicts that transnational activism emerges from state blockage, it is important to remember that the state is subsumed within a global political economy. Ayres (2001), Lewis (2000), Rothman and Oliver (1999), and Kriesberg

(1997) argue that "nested" international political opportunities must replace an overly domestic gaze if we are to understand how and why transnational activism develops. This idea is perhaps most forcefully argued by Smith, Pagnucco and Chatfield: "Increasing global dependence, coupled with the emergence of institutions that move decisions of relevance further from local populations, forces social movements and other actors to target political arenas beyond those of single states" (Smith, Pagnucco, and Chatfield 1997: 68). Moreover, Smith states that "as political authority moves towards global institutions, we should expect similar changes in social movement repertoires that Tilly observed with the rise of nineteenth-century national polities" (J. Smith 2001b: 9). In short, as Jenkins observes, "social movements are not just prisoners of their national boundaries, but are profoundly shaped by their international environments" (1995: 33). As this case demonstrates, international financial institutions such as the World Bank and the IADB can play a key role in local events. The Río Negro-Chixoy case also demonstrates how a local movement principally targeting state actors can develop into a transnational network as new information regarding the international dimensions of a local grievance become apparent.

When the role of international financial institutions in Guatemala's internal conflict became clearer, the possibility for transnational activism became more pronounced. The information exchange between domestic and international activists dramatically altered the way they viewed local troubles and potential solutions. Rather than seeing the Guatemalan military as the principal antagonist, activists extended culpability far beyond Guatemala's territorial borders. Armed with this new information, *Rabileños* became embedded in a transnational network in 1996 that far exceeded the traditional parameters of the Guatemalan solidarity movement. This dynamic is reflected both locally and transnationally. On the local level, the Widows and Orphans Committee became ADIVIMA, a transformation that captures the enlargement of the group's mission and membership. Perhaps even more important, participation in the campaigns of the mid-1990s provided both the financial resources and the organizational capacity for Guatemalan activists to initiate urgent economic development projects. Narrowly defined grievances and the strategies to counter them became more complex and created the possibility for transnational alliances. International activists were similarly transformed. WfP's narrow goal of accompanying local activists grew into an investigative role that finally challenged powerful international institutions. In this way, local problems became transnational issues.

This transformation relied upon a delicate division of labor between local and international activists. While Northern activists often have more information and greater access to institutionalized sources of power, their Southern counterparts can provide the local knowledge and poignant personal testimonies that lend legitimacy to transnational networks. This partnership implies a mutual dependency. In their study of an anti-dam movement in southern Brazil, Rothman and Oliver argue that "International networks and movements need active local groups just as much as local groups need external resources. Their exchanges are bilateral, interactive, and strategic, with both agency and reactivity occurring on both sides" (Rothman and Oliver 1999: 43-44). This echoes Brysk's work on opposition to multilateral development bank projects in Latin America. Brysk argues that transnational networks that actively partnered with indigenous groups had better access to local knowledge, ultimately leading to more successful campaigns against such actors as the World Bank (Brysk 1996). Similarly, in explaining the differential outcomes of two indigenous rights movements pursuing similar policy goals in Latin America, Maney suggests that one reason the San Blas Kuna in Panama were successful while the Yanomani in Brazil were not was because the former strategically allied with scientists and activists in formulating ecological preservation goals, while the latter's relationship with international actors was plagued by patronage, ultimately undermining their goals (Maney 2001b). Thus, transnational alliances that bridge cleavages—whether economic, racial, ethnic, or cultural—potentially bring pitfalls.

Three general dangers of transnational alliances can be identified. First, there is an eminent danger that TANs engender dependence. Whether financial, organizational, or ideological, the resources that actors from the North provide can create an unhealthy reliance on them. Second, as Shefner demonstrates in his study of community movements in Guadalajara, Mexico, international stratification can develop between Northern allies and their Southern counterparts when disagreements arise over strategies and goals. Shefner found that local community activists felt obliged to pursue partisan tactics at the urging of their sponsor organization. He argues that "when the sponsor pushed electoral participation, the [local] leaders acquiesced out of feelings of obligation and dependence. The leaders paid the price" (1999: 386). Third, outright cooptation can occur. Some observers of transnational activism such as Bob have argued that "NGOs are strategic actors who seek first and foremost their organizational survival (Bob 2002: 7). Bob identifies the dangers of cooptation and argues that pressures to conform to the needs of international NGOs can undermine the original goals of a local movement.

While I believe these three fears are warranted, a genuine convergence of interests is also possible within transnational networks. When asked about these triple dangers of transnational activism, Grahame Russell, the executive director of Rights Action responded,

> For us, we are always aware of the long-term perspective of our activism. Some microenterprises we fund, for example, may fail in a year or two, but the organizational learning that occurred is irreplaceable. A short-term "failure" often becomes a long-term success. So this long-term perspective really changes how we view our role in international activism and the alliances we make with people in countries like Guatemala." (author interview June 2003)

As this case study demonstrates, this local movement grew in membership, material resources, and tactical repertoires as it was incorporated into a transnational network of nearly twenty INGOs. And while the initial proximate goals changed—for the local activists and WfP —it was in a mutually beneficial way.

This brings discussion to the question of efficacy. While Keck and Sikkink favor the bodily harm/short causal chain argument, I suggest that a better predictor of mobilization is a moral shock that prompts them to protest fundamental injustices. In their depiction of the emergence and efficacy of Amnesty International and Oxfam, Ennals (1982) and Stamp (1982) both concur that concern about human rights abuses forms a solid platform upon which to build a meaningful movement. However, mobilization does not always breed efficacy, nor is the most direct target always the best target. Instead, activists must often elongate the causal chain (or even engage in object shift) to identify the targets that share responsibility and have the capacity to address grievances. The Río Negro-Chixoy case suggests that a simpler story must become more sophisticated for mobilization to translate into results. This observation seems to be supported by Maney's discussion of indigenous rights movements (2001b), Rothman and Oliver's description of environmental struggles in Brazil

(1999), and Thayer's assessment of the Brazilian women's health movement (2000), and deserves greater research focus in the future.

These same studies also demonstrate that international connections can lead to more effective results. This may be because these international connections help uncover new targets that have both a greater capacity to redress grievances and a greater vulnerability to criticism because of their status as international agents. Further, the identification of international targets potentially enlarges the base of support for a local movement, especially among "conscience constituencies" with deep pockets. Many people may feel no connection to or responsibility for human rights abuses committed by a local or even a national government. But when an international target enters the equation—whether an international financial institution or a multinational corporation—people far from a grievance may feel compelled to become part of its solution.

One of the reasons why the Río Negro-Chixoy became a magnet for transnational activism is because over ten million people were forcibly displaced by World Bank-supported dams in the 1970s and 1980s (Russell 2000c). And, as in this case, such displacement has frequently coincided with repressive state practices. Further, the World Bank is particularly vulnerable to criticism due to its policy of obliging impoverished nations to pay off debts for failed projects from loans made to corrupt and repressive governments. The Río Negro-Chixoy case embodies these problems in the international arena.

As for local activists in Guatemala, along with their international allies, they have identified important targets like the bank, broadened their goals, forged ties with like-minded groups, and developed more sophisticated strategies. If this movement had remained local, it is likely that when Guatemala's internal conflict ended in 1996, the fight for justice in Rabinal would have dwindled. At that time, the threat of local repression had diminished and the national government had pledged its commitment to human rights. But instead of dwindling, 1996 signaled the beginning of a transnational mobilization with Rabinal activists at the center. Uncovering the World Bank's role in Guatemala's internal conflict allowed for a confluence of actors who shared a criticism of economic development strategies favored by powerful international financial institutions. To this day, the bank's lack of responsiveness and its continued role in large development projects harmful to indigenous peoples keep it as a central target that unites activists from the North and the South. The Río Negro-Chixoy case demonstrates how transnational networks can transform movements, change the way people view the world, and thus challenge the structures and relationships that permit injustices to flourish.

APPENDIX: COMMUNITY HISTORY

February 1975	INDE (National Institute of Electrification) announces plans to build the Chixoy Hydroelectric Project.
Late 1976	INDE informs Río Negro of upcoming displacement.
June 1978	World Bank approves a $72 million loan for the Chixoy project.
March 1980	INDE's Military Police kill seven Río Negro residents.
July 1980	Río Negro community leaders murdered en route to INDE.
February 1982	73 Río Negro men and women killed in Xococ.
March 1982	177 Río Negro women and children murdered in Pacoxóm.
May 1982	84 Río Negro residents killed in Los Encuentros.
September 1982	35 Río Negro children murdered in Agua Fría.

Late 1982	Filling of the Chixoy Reservoir begins, Río Negro is submerged.
Mid-1980s	Massacre survivors from Río Negro relocate to Pacux.
March 1985	World Bank approves additional $44.6 million loan for the Chixoy.
Late 1992	Massacre survivors denounce violence, demand investigation, and initiate legal proceedings.
November 1993	EAFG (Guatemalan Forensic Anthropology Team) excavates the Pacoxóm massacre site.
March 1994	Río Negro survivors bury their dead. First gravesite is destroyed.
March 1995	Río Negro survivors inaugurate a new Monument to Truth.
May 1996	*A People Dammed* is published, Río Negro activists tour the U.S.
July 1996	World Bank investigative team comes to Rabinal.
December 1996	Jesús Tecú Osorio receives the Reebok Human Rights Award.
November 1998	Three paramilitary members sentenced to 50 years in prison for role in Río Negro massacres.
March 1999	Río Negro survivors receive partial land compensation from the World Bank.
1999 – Present	Río Negro activists attend international protests for IFI reform.

NOTES

1. Keck and Sikkink suggest that TANs also emerge when political entrepreneurs believe networking will further their mission and when international conferences create new arenas for network formation (Keck and Sikkink 1998a). In a later elaboration on transnationalism, Sikkink *et al* introduce the spiral model of transnational emergence, which extends the boomerang model to better explain the divergent effects of TANs (Risse and Sikkink 1999). While the spiral model represents an important theoretical innovation, it has not produced scholarly commentary in the same way that the boomerang model has.

2. Walter LaFeber estimates that a minimum of 10,000 Hondurans died between 1979 and 1991 in the regional conflicts (LaFeber 1993: 362), yet these abuses provoked little international concern. It is worth noting, however, that Honduras experienced nowhere near the level of state repression of its Central American neighbors. As Goodwin has extensively documented, a guerrilla insurgency movement did not develop in Honduras in part because state repression was less extreme (Goodwin 2001).

3. Jasper (1997: 106) argues that "moral shocks" are frequently the first step toward recruitment into movements. His working definition is "when an unexpected event or piece of information raises such a sense of outrage in a person that she becomes inclined toward political action, with or without the network of personal contacts emphasized in mobilization and process theories."

4. To further clarify the area's geography, Rabinal is the municipality which includes the large village of Rabinal plus seventy-four nearby villages. Survivors of the Río Negro massacres eventually resettled in Pacux—a military-controlled community that borders the village of Rabinal.

5. CALDH was started by a Guatemalan exile, Frank LaRue. CALDH is one of the leading groups sponsoring exhumations and prosecutions of the authors of the counterinsurgency campaign. The first community development projects included a communal vegetable garden and a chicken breeding project for local consumption, as well as a peanut cultivation project for regional sale. Both Amnesty International and the Campaign for Peace and Life funded these projects.

6. As Coy (1997) argues, social movement histories richly document this strategy. Perhaps the most famous examples come from the U.S. Civil Rights Movement. In essence, the participation of northern, white elites in campaigns such as Freedom Rides and Freedom Summer was partially inspired by the insight that the presence of whites would deter attacks against black activists in the South. See McAdam (1988) and Halberstam (1998) for excellent descriptions of this strategy. This same strategy is also fundamental to the WfP's philosophy. Some of the first foreigners to visit Nicaragua during the Contra war in the 1980s were told by civilians that their presence in the war zone deterred Contra attacks against their villages. This inspired these visitors to return to the U.S. to form an organization, WfP, to provide international accompaniment in Nicaragua's war zones.

7. IRN is a nongovernmental organization located in Berkeley, California, that specializes in re-

search and advocacy around opposition to large hydroelectric projects.

8. This discussion that follows draws upon the WfP team research. See the 1996 WfP publication for full bibliographic references regarding World Bank activities.

9. Among its many failures, the Chixoy hydroelectric project was 521 percent more expensive than anticipated, required frequent and costly maintenance, has never operated above 70 percent of its capacity, and could cease to function in as little as twenty years. For more information on the Chixoy dam, see Witness for Peace Guatemala Team (1996), coauthored by the author.

10. The interviews cited in this paragraph were conducted between January 1995 and February 1996 by the author and other members of the WfP Guatemala team in the process of researching *A People Dammed*.

11. The author participated in WfP speaker's tour/World Bank reform campaign in May-June 1996.

12. Quotations extracted from a letter written by James Wolfensohn on June 18, 1996, to Paul Sciré of WfP and Owen Lammers of IRN.

13. Quotations extracted from a letter James Wolfensohn wrote on July 27, 1996, to Paul Sciré of WfP and Owen Lammers of IRN. It should be noted that failure to provide reparations to populations displaced by World Bank-funded hydroelectric projects is a constant allegation made against the Bank. World Bank-funded dams have displaced over ten million people worldwide and population displacement was one of the decisive factors in successfully halting the famous Sardar Sarovar Dam in India (Sklar and McCully 1994; Shrivastava 1996).

14. The Reebok award ceremony was a star-studded event including Michael Stipe of R.E.M and Peter Gabriel; excerpts appeared on MTV.

15. Based on interviews conducted with Rights Action staff in April 2004 and my own investigations, I found the following NGOs have worked or are working on the Chixoy issue: Advocacy Project, Amnesty International, Campaign to Reform the World Bank (composed of 41 organizations), Center for Economic Justice, Center for International Environmental Law, Centre on Housing Rights and Evictions, Chixoy Dam Reparations Team, Guatemala News and Information Bureau, International Rivers Network, Movimiento Mundial por los Bosques Tropicales (World Movement for Tropical Forests), Network of People in Solidarity with Guatemala, POV, Probe International, Red Latinoamericana de Represas, Rios y Poblaciones (Latin American Network of Dams, Rivers, and Communities), Reform the World Bank Campaign—Italy, Rights Action, Witness for Peace, World Commission on Dams.

16. For example, although the people of Rio Negro lost 2,469 acres due to the Chixoy dam, they only received 780 acres in compensation. They also demanded that survivors receive reparations for the seventeen years of lost income due to lack of access to land and lost family support resulting from the murder of dozens of household heads.

17. Interview conducted by the author with Rights Action Director Grahame Russell in June 2001.

18. This important legal victory is tempered by the fact that at least 15 other paramilitary members and ten soldiers who participated in the Río Negro massacres have not been prosecuted (Russell 2000a).

19. Interview conducted by the author with ADIVIMA leader in Rabinal in June 1998. *Ladino* is the term used in Guatemala to describe non-indigenous people or those who have tried to conceal their indigenous ancestry in favor of European dress, language, and customs.

20. Specifically, the workshops focus on the Comprehensive Human Rights Accord and the Accord on the Identity and Rights of Indigenous Peoples—both part of the 1996 peace accords (Byrne 1997; Palencia 1996).

21. Interview conducted by the author with local activist in Rabinal in May 1998.

Chapter 13

TRANSNATIONAL LABOR MOBILIZING IN TWO MEXICAN MAQUILADORAS

Victoria Carty

There is a vigorous debate underway regarding how the global economy should be governed; who should govern it, and whose interest it should serve (Faux 2002). Campaigns to improve workers' rights in export processing zones (EPZs) are politically at the center of this debate. Scholars and activists interested in understanding and bettering working conditions in developing countries must come to terms with two major trends in the global economy. One is the increasing subordination of state-centered development by powerful supranational institutions and trade agreements, which dictate the rules for countries integrating into the global economy. The state is often unwilling or unable to direct foreign capital in a way that benefits local industries and workers, as global arrangements are altering domestic political structures and constraining state decisions. Another concern is that multinational corporations (MNCs) are closing manufacturing plants in the United States at an unprecedented rate and relocating production sites overseas in EPZs. According to many critics, these zones are notorious for substandard working conditions, low pay and anti-union behavior.

The recent accelerated economic integration, the growing numbers of international institutions and treaties, the increasing power and autonomy of MNCs, and emerging issues that transcend national borders have increased transnational contentious politics (Rucht 1999). To counteract some of the ill effects of global economic arrangements on local populations, non-state actors are mobilizing from below to challenge the authoritarianism and practices of states and international institutions (P. Falk 1993; O'Brien et al. 2000).

This article uses two case studies of labor struggles in Mexican maquiladoras to examine forms of resistance to corporate global capitalism. It explores some of the strategies and organizing tools participants are employing to enhance international network building and information sharing. It specifically analyzes attempts to increase wages and improve working conditions through unionization at two plants in the maquila industry in Mexico.

Although Tarrow (1998) points out that globalization and transnational activism are not new, there is growing research interest in transnational advocacy networks (TANs) and international political opportunity structures (POSs). This analysis utilizes these frameworks to conceptualize the internationalization of grassroots efforts among workers, activists, and other political actors to pressure MNCs and host governments to respect labor laws included in international trade agreements, national standards, and self-mandated corporate codes of conduct. The case studies contribute to our theorization of transnational social movement activity by shedding light on how activists mobilize around local issues in transnational networks. By framing their claims globally, activists have been able to gain support from transnational networks, coalitions, and NGOs in local struggles. This research demonstrates the important role nonstate actors can play in domestic and international politics when they are able to operate outside national borders to simultaneously target the local, national, and international level.

RECENT TRENDS IN THE GLOBAL ECONOMY

The past few decades have brought about intensified processes of globalization under which neoliberal strategies emphasize market-oriented approaches to economic development (Strange 2000; Mann 2000; Dicken 1998). The term globalization loosely refers to an increase in the scale, scope and velocity of flows of information, technology, and trade (Castells 1989). These changes make national economies increasingly susceptible to international pressures, as international organizations have assumed greater power over global economic forces and local political processes (Smith and Johnston 2002). The ability of host governments (as well as labor) to regulate and control trade and foreign investment is constrained by an increasing matrix of commitments to trade agreements and other international actors (Faux 2002; Dicken 1998). Trade agreements such as the North American Free Trade Agreement (NAFTA) tend to be controlled by the wealthy, industrialized nations that set the agenda to protect the interests of foreign investors and the mobility of capital in supply chains, but do little to protect the interests of labor (Basu 2001; Connell 2001).

Another major constraint for states and labor under global economic restructuring is that MNCs now play a dominant role in the new economic order (Sklair 1998, 1995). As the power of MNCs steadily increases, the ability of the state in lesser developed countries to pursue national goals such as local economic and human development are diminished due to insufficient leverage over global corporate actors (Dicken 1998). Because MNCs tend to subcontract manufacturing where labor costs are lowest, low-income countries must compete with one another to attract foreign investment and to attain employment opportunities (Boswell and Chase-Dunn 2000; Dicken 1998). One way that countries attempt to undercut their competitors is to create EPZs. Foreign investors are attracted to the zones for tax incentives, lax environmental standards, and a guaranteed cheap and compliant workforce (Korten 2001; Rodrick 2000). In some EPZs minimum wages are suspended, unions are forbidden, and benefits, job security, and working conditions are very poor (Sklair 1995; Bailey et al. 1993). Many critics refer to this process as the "race to the bottom" (see Collingsworth 1998; Spar and Yoffe 1999).

Though there is an ongoing debate as to what extent states or global markets are in control of socioeconomic life, there is a general consensus that globalization offers great opportunities for human advance, but only with strong governance (for a detailed discussion, see Dicken 1998). In EPZs, however, MNCs enjoy an advantage in the balance of power due to particular arrangements under which the interests of workers and governments are compromised in comparison to other sectors of the economy.

Different proposals have been suggested as to how to balance the interests of MNCs with those of labor. Some propose that self-regulation by foreign investors themselves is the best solution because business executives have the leverage to convince host governments to address human rights issues. Others argue that global mechanisms, such as international accords on labor standards, are needed to guarantee basic labor rights. Still other strategies proposed advocate regulation at the national and local level whereby host governments would force foreign investors to obey national laws.

To date, neither the goals nor the enforcement of any of these proposals have been systematically accomplished. What small victories have been won were achieved through the internationalization of grassroots mobilization that persuaded international, national, and/or corporate actors to recognize and enforce legislation protecting workers' rights.

MOBILIZATION FROM ABOVE

In the 1990s allegations involving the use of sweatshop labor by major brand-name retailers received a lot of attention in the mainstream media and in academic circles. By the late 1990s there was evidence that consumers were willing to express their dissatisfaction with corporate labor abuses through their retail purchasing decisions. According to a 1999 study conducted by Marymount University's Center for Ethical Concerns, 75% of respondents said that they would avoid shopping at a retailer who is known to sell garments made in sweatshops. Eighty-six percent stated that they would pay an extra dollar on a $20.00 garment if they were sure that it was not made in a sweatshop (Fung, O'Rourke, and Sabel 2001). Increased popular pressure against sweatshop labor in part gave rise to two adaptations in labor practices that fall under the rubric of mobilization from above.

Self-Regulation: Codes of Conduct

Several MNCs took the initiative to legislate working conditions by establishing codes of conduct to which they demand their subcontractors adhere. Despite the initial popularity of these measures among retailers, by the mid-1990s there was widespread agreement that the individual company-mandated codes were seriously flawed (Greenhouse 1997). Workers tended to have little if any knowledge of the codes and subcontractors rarely enforced them. Even when subcontractors did attempt to adhere to them there was no mechanism to do so. To establish more comprehensive reform leaders of the apparel and footwear industries and representatives from human rights and labor rights organizations came up with standard regulations that subcontractors must recognize and enforce. In 1997 they released the Apparel Industry Partnership (AIP) Code of Conduct, which included guidelines on worker rights along with general health and safety regulations (Greenhouse 1997). A subsequent agreement established the Fair Labor Association (FLA) to enforce and monitor the AIP code.

Task force members representing labor and human rights groups soon began challenging the FLA's endorsement of a minimum rather than a living wage. It also condemned its monitoring strategy for being one of corporate governance; under which apparel manufacturers select their own accounting firms to conduct internal and secretive inspections (Featherstone 2002). Overall, opponents of the FLA charged that compliance with the weak standards as implemented by the FLA was merely a public relations tactic designed to defray public interest in sweatshops rather than construct systemic change.

In the late 1990s student participation in the movement began to grow. United Students Against Sweatshops (USAS) formed in 1998 to ensure that their college and university names and logos would not be associated with sweatshop labor (Featherstone 2002). Students organized across the country to pressure administrations to uphold the manufacturers of collegiate footwear and apparel to a code of conduct. In 1999 when labor, human rights groups, and NGOs dropped out of the FLA, these groups together with USAS established the Workers Rights Consortium (WRC). The WRC attempts to help the indigenous worker-allied groups develop their capacities to participate effectively in the monitoring system (Featherstone 2002). The WRC adopts a process of spot checks in response to worker complaints to ensure compliance with national law and codes of conduct. Monitoring is carried out by WRC members in conjunction with local NGO and labor organizations.

Institutional Solutions Through Trade Agreements

Another mobilization-from-above option is for the international community to standardize worker rights in foreign-owned factories, and that trade agreements contain and provide the same enforcement mechanisms as for other commercial provisions (Connell 2001). As an alternative, some see it as the exclusive role of the ILO to constitutionally set and deal with labor standards.

Currently, neither of these has been vigorously pursued, and the interests of business continue to enjoy advantages over those of workers, the environment, and human rights. Advocates for the inclusion of human-rights guarantees in trade agreements note that supranational institutions and trade agreements such as the WTO entail specific terms of trade and operate according to ground rules that favor corporate and financial interests and that protect trade, investment, and intellectual property rights (Winston 2002). However, corporations are not subject to any binding regulations or formal sanctions for failure to respect human and labor rights (Faux 2002; Winston 2002). The limited clauses that do address labor issues are weak and/or not enforced.

Monitoring is also problematic. One example is the WTO contracts with Social Accountability International (SAI), an organization that administers a code to monitor contractors. It has a commission that can recommend trade sanctions if conditions do not meet the prescribed standards to which it holds subcontractors. However, its standards can bypass ILO standards of freedom of association. For example, in 1998 the SAI clause was used to implement guaranteed normal trade status with China despite its ban on independent unions and collective bargaining by mandating that factory managers can appoint government worker representatives to act on behalf of workers' interests (Gilley 2001). Governments, of course, can also be highly selective in their ratification of ILO labor standards. Reliance on ILO conventions in general has substantial drawbacks because the ILO operates on the basis of consensus among labor, management, and governments, and therefore, its actions are necessarily limited to what can be agreed upon by all three actors (Winston 2002).

Another example of how business interests trump labor rights under corporate globalization is the side agreement in NAFTA. It allows workers and interested third parties in the U.S., Mexico, and Canada to file complaints when a government fails to enforce its own labor legislation (Fung, O'Rourke, and Sabel 2001). However, it does not allow for similar motions against corporations for labor rights violations, or address the problem of weak and deteriorating labor standards in national legislation. Though there have been dozens of complaints filed against both Mexico and the U.S. charging an unwillingness to enforce workers' rights, not a single independent union has been able to negotiate a contract as a result of any NAFTA ruling (Bacon 2001). Also, MNCs can easily evade international or national standards by moving their production facilities elsewhere (Winston 2002).

A final problem is that there is much resistance to universal labor standards in developing countries themselves. Many governments fear that such standards and monitoring efforts will serve as an instrument of protectionism for the North to impose arbitrary and inflexible trade sanctions on Third World countries (Basu 2001).

MOBILIZATION FROM BELOW

The concerted grassroots efforts of workers and activists in host countries, in conjunction with those at the transnational level, have in a few cases successfully pressured governments, brand producers, and their subcontractors to adhere to labor laws and codes of conduct. The following case studies illustrate the importance of targeting local, national, and international levels to improve working conditions in EPZs, and how these different spheres can be mutually reinforcing. A decisive factor in each case has been whether or not the host government can be forced to take a proactive role in helping to resolve conflicts between foreign capital and labor.

Labor Mobilization at the Kukdong Plant

In January 2001, 9,800 workers went on strike at the Korean-owned Kukdong factory in Puebla, Mexico. The strike was in reaction to a host of substandard conditions including the use of child labor, failure to pay the minimum wage, and the firing of union leaders (Kepne 2000; Verite 2001). Also, workers were forced to sign with the government-mandated CROC (Revolutionary Confederation of Workers and Peasants) union in order to be employed. After a three-day strike a police crackdown ensued and state police attacked the workers guarding the factory. Fifteen workers were hospitalized, and five organizers of the strike were fired (Bacon 2001). Nike Corporation was one of the largest manufacturers doing business with Kukdong, producing sweatshirts for many big-name universities.

A diverse network of support for the workers mobilized among student, labor, and other human rights groups across the North and South. The workers used the power of the growing anti-sweatshop movement in the United States to reinforce their efforts. They contacted the Mexico City office of the AFL-CIO, which helped

Kukdong workers publicize their case on U.S. and Canadian campuses (Bacon 2001). Across the country, at universities that had contracts with Nike, students pressured administrators to threaten Nike with termination of these contracts if they did not help to rectify the situation. They used creative forms of resistance to raise awareness about the issue. They organized speaking tours for Kukdong workers across the country, held sit-ins and occupied administrative offices, leafleted on campus and outside NikeTowns, staged rallies, and held mock fashion shows sporting Nike gear with information about where and under what conditions the footwear and apparel was being made (Featherstone 2002). Representatives of USAS and the WRC, in conjunction with WRC's monitoring agency Verite and the International Labor Rights Fund (ILRF), also went to the Kukdong factory and verified the workers complaints (CLR 2002)

Support was also provided by the Workers Support Centre (CAT) in Mexico, students at the Autonomous University of Puebla, the AFL-CIO, and Campaign for Labor Rights (CLR), the United States Labor Education in the Americas Project (US/LEAP), Sweatshop Watch, the European Clean Clothes Campaign, Global Exchange, the Maquila Solidarity Network (MSN), and the Korean House for International Solidarity.

Thus, the mobilization to sustain the workers' campaign was a multilevel, multi-task strategy targeting the local, national, and international levels. At the local level, the workers staged a walkout to disrupt the accumulation of capital at the level of production. At the national level, in solidarity with the workers, activists pressured the Labor Secretary in Mexico and the Mexican Cabinet Secretary. And globally, they pressured the Global Director for Labor Practices at Nike, Kukdong International (Mexico), and Kukdong Corporation Korea (Korea) to resolve the dispute. Their demands also cut across the local national and international dimensions. They insisted that management comply with Mexican labor laws, Nike's code of conduct, the respective universities' codes of conduct, and the international agreement regarding the right of freedom to organize.

NGOs played an instrumental role in the organization and information-sharing aspect of the campaign, most of which was done via the Internet. MSN, Global Exchange, and CLR in particular were fundamental in organizing the broad network of activists. CLR's action alerts that circulate on the Web requested that concerned citizens send letters to Nike demanding the corporation support a fair negotiation process between the workers and the factory management. CJM and Global Exchange also had frequent updates on their websites and published these on various labor-oriented listservs and email listings.

After receiving letters from over 6,000 people from seventeen countries, in a unique move Nike declared it would not abandon production orders at Kukdong but preferred the situation be rectified between management and workers, and that management meet their legal responsibilities (Maquila Solidarity Network 2001). Nike released its plan outlining the corrective actions and a timetable for Kukdong to comply with Nike's code of conduct. Through letters and contact with Mexican government officials, Nike urged respect for freedom of association and requested an expedited review of any forthcoming application for an election of a new union (WRC 2002).

However, the conflict was not solved easily or quickly. Weeks of intimidation ensued at the factory and managers refused to allow organizers of the strike to return to work. Eventually, management did succumb to pressure from local and international protestors and pressure from Nike. The organizers of the strike were eventually allowed to return to work and charges were finally dropped against two of the five leaders as demanded by Nike. After a nine-month strike, workers successfully established their own union and negotiated a contract with the Korean owners. At Kukdong, now renamed Mexmode, an independent union replaced the CROC union and workers received a wage increase of 10 percent, a 5 percent increase in cash benefits, and attendance bonuses (Kidd 2001). Workers now make up to 40 percent more pay than they were making under the old contract. In addition, the Mexico City office of the ILO conducted freedom of association training and provided technical assistance to the factory at Nike's urging (Kidd 2001).

International solidarity at the grassroots level unequivocally played a significant role in the success of this campaign. Speaking at the University of Michigan, Marcela Muñoz Tepepa, a seamstress at the Kukdong factory who helped to initiate the work stoppage stated, "Without the dialogue at the University of Michigan it would have been impossible to win the struggle. This is one of the reasons we continued to struggle . . . because we knew we had your support" (Schrader 2002).

Maria Eitel, vice president and senior advisor on corporate responsibility for Nike Corporation, also credits the protesters' actions for bringing these issues to Nike's attention and the ultimate concessions. She states, "I don't think Nike would have made the kind of progress it has made if we hadn't been attacked" (Cave 2002). Additionally, Dusty Kidd, the vice president of Nike, sent a letter to universities that partook in the monitoring process. He stated,

> We believe collaboration can yield positive, successful results for workers in delicate situations like Kukdong/Mexmode. Companies like Nike . . . can make an immediate impact in reaching resolution because we have the ability to place or terminate orders which can affect the factory's ability to be profitable and attract other buyers. (quoted at http://www.nikebiz.com)

Thus, the case of Kukdong supports the idea that corporations can have a positive impact on forcing host governments to abide by certain standards regarding labor and human rights. However, it was only the intense and constant pressure put on Nike that led the corporation to urge government officials and its subcontractors to take action, and led to change at least at the factory level.

The overall success for the workers was due to organizing, solidarity, and corporate campaign strategies in enforcing concessions among retailers, their subcontractors, and local governments to respect workers' rights. The combined efforts of students, university administrations, NGOs, unions and labor rights organizations created sufficient democratic space for the workers to organize and win their independent union. While pressure on Nike was crucial in helping workers achieve their victory, and lobbying of the Mexican government helped win the registration of the independent union, ultimately it was this transnational grassroots networking that empowered the workers and enabled them to have a voice in the decision-making process. The Kukdong struggle is therefore an excellent example of how globalization from below can be an effective strategy in at least slowing the race to the bottom.

On the other hand, this case also illustrates the limitations of the social clause in the NAFTA agreement that does not allow workers to challenge MNCs directly. Organizers had to operate outside the legislative realm of any established trade agreement. It also highlights some of the flaws in the corporate-driven self-monitoring process. Although Nike's social responsibility department currently employs 100 people, and it has tripled its budget since 1998 and spent $500,000 on global reporting initiatives (including those produced by the FLA), it was only through independent verification monitoring mechanisms that workers' rights came to be respected (Cave 2002).

Mobilization at the Duro Plant, Río Bravo, Mexico

In June 2000 workers at the Duro plant in Río Bravo went on strike to establish an independent union and force the reinstatement of their elected leaders who were illegally fired (CLR 2000). Duro produces gift bags for retailers such as Hallmark, Neiman Marcus, and the Gap. In August 2000, Mexican government officials granted official registration to the Duro workers independent union. This was the first independent union to win registration in decades in the state of Tamaulipas and forced a representation election. Like the union at Kukdong, this independent union competed with the government-controlled CROC union. With the help of the FAT (Authentic Workers Front) the workers presented over 400 signatures on a petition for the election to the Conciliation and Arbitration Board (CAB) in Mexico City on September 28, 2000 (Bacon 2001).

Elections to vote on union membership were held in March 2001, but were conducted in the midst of threats of violence and reprisals by the company and CROC "enforcers" (Bacon 2001). Out of 1,400 workers, only 502 voted and the four workers who voted for the independent union were fired (Bacon 2001). Workers had been escorted to the voting area by CROC organizers and were forced to verbally declare their choices. While campaigning for president, Vicente Fox promised reforms to establish secret-ballot union elections (MHSSN 2001). Not only was this right neglected, but during the ensuing firings, intimidation, and physical abuse the government did nothing to protect the workers' rights.

In October 2001 the union was taken over by members of the CROC union, which conducted a secret election of the independent union's Executive Board without the knowledge or participation of the union's members (CLR 2001). The CROC move, backed by local government authorities, was designed to prevent the independent union from contesting the March election as a violation of the workers' right to a secret ballot election (MHSSN 2001). This was in direct violation of the Joint Declaration signed by the labor ministers of Mexico and the United States (as part of the NAFTA agreement), in which Mexico pledged to promote "the use of eligible voter lists and secret ballot elections in disputes over the right to hold the collective bargaining contract."

Again, NGOs and their links with other grassroots organizations coordinated efforts to play an essential role in the struggle. CLR organized letter-writing petitions to Hallmark to uphold its code of conduct, which ensures freedom of association (Bacon 2001). It also sent out action alerts asking people to email, call, fax, and write the CEO of Duro Bag Manufacturing Company and tell him to reinstate the workers, pay all workers their due amount of severance pay according to the Mexican Federal Labor Law, and improve conditions at the Duro factory (CLR 2001).

Duro workers were also supported from the North by the Coalition for Justice in the Maquiladoras (CJM). This NGO has over 100 member organizations, including North American unions, churches, and community organizations; and serves as a bridge between workers, researchers, and activists in all three NAFTA countries. The CJM coalition demonstrated with signs and banners demanding that the right to freedom of association be upheld wherever Tomas Yarrington, the governor of

Tamaulipas, made a public appearance. They also confronted police outside the plant where the workers were striking, and camped out in Río Bravo's main plaza when police physically removed them from the factory. When CJM activists were arrested for refusal to leave, the coalition sent hundreds of letters, emails, and faxes to media outlets and NGOs regarding the abusive behavior of Duro company officials (Bacon 2001).

In addition, CJM arranged for the Mexican Association of Democratic Lawyers to provide legal counsel and for the Transnational Information Exchange to sponsor a speaking tour in the U.S. and Canada for a former Duro worker. It then incorporated the assistance of the Interfaith Committee for Corporate Responsibility and the Marin Interfaith Task Force to arrange a meeting with executives of Duro clients to press the company to abide by the Mexican Labor Board's resolution and to reinstate the Duro workers with back pay or severance pay. CJM members also sent letters to all Duro Company clients to pressure the Duro Company into abiding by the CAB resolution that secured legal recognition of the independent union (CLR 2003).

In March 2003, the company finally agreed to meet the workers' demands during a conference call between the Duro Company, CJM, and Hallmark, one of Duro's most important clients. The legal battle lasted almost three years, but Duro workers were able to establish an independent union, and those that were illegally fired received full severance pay and back wages (CLR 2003).

The situation at Duro again shows the effectiveness of mobilizing from below, and the inability of treaties like NAFTA to provide sufficient mechanisms to protect workers' rights. Although the labor ministers of the United States and Mexico signed an agreement ensuring secret ballot elections, this agreement was not respected. It also demonstrates the lack of state support for national labor laws and the tendency among national and state governments to appease MNCs in an effort to promote investment under neoliberal reforms at the expense of the legal rights of workers to unionize (Bacon 2001). As was the case at Kukdong, it was only through consistent organization at the micro level across the North and South that activists gained sufficient leverage to press retailers and government officials to respond to the workers' demands and to obtain policy change. The disruptions at the local level and at the site of production, combined with networking at the national and international levels gave the workers the leverage they needed to have their demands met.

GLOBALIZATION AND PROTEST STRATEGY AT KUKONG AND DURO

McAdam, McCarthy, and Zald define mobilizing strategies as "those collective vehicles, informal as well as formal, through which people mobilize and engage in collective action" (1996: 3). The success or failure of these strategies is influenced by the available political opportunity structures (POSs) at the specific historical juncture, which either constrain or provide incentives for collective action (Tarrow 1998, 2001). These POSs operate at both the domestic and international level.

Recent social movement research has begun to recognize the implications of globalizing trends and how they affect collective action (Smith et al. 1997; Keck and Sikkink 1998a; della Porta and Kriesi 1999). Smith and Johnston (2002) argue that since globalization brings with it substantial changes in the types of contemporary social relations, the ways that people engage in collective political action is transformed as well. These changes have been accompanied by emerging political institutions that create both opportunities and constraints for activists. As globalization continues to reduce the state's ability to act on its own behalf, transnational social movement organizers are now directing more of their resources toward international linkages and partnerships (Guidry, Kennedy, and Zald 2000).

Therefore, much of the current research on social movements is incorporating the literature on international relations—particularly the branch that explores the dynamic intersection of domestic politics and the international system. Social scientists have begun to analyze more vigorously how international pressures influence domestic POSs, how social movements operate in both a domestic and international environment, and the importance of international networks in local mobilization (Rothman and Oliver 1999; Tarrow 1998). Scholars of contentious politics that work within the tradition of international relations have made some important advances in improving social movement theories about global integration and its effects on political contention both nationally and transnationally (Smith and Johnston 2002).

The maquiladoras in Mexico are an excellent example of how globally mandated neoliberal strategies are fast shaping domestic politics. They have also created new institutional mobilizing structures and opportunities for transnational allies to mobilize across borders against common targets (Ayres 2001). The explosion of transnational social movement activity highlights the challenges to the neoliberal doctrine and the beginnings of a new global political space (P. Falk 1993; Guidry, Kennedy, and Zald 2000). The activists in the struggles in the Mexican maquila industry, for example, were able to identify links between new social structures and new forms of collective action. The response by CJM, CLR, MSN, and Global Exchange are good representations of how new institutional opportunities are being created in response to the global race to the bottom. These NGOs provided an overarching forum for the exchange of information and communication among activists that helped expedite the campaigns and enhance coalition building.

The success of the Kukdong and Duro campaigns shows that the state does not have to be directly or solely targeted, but it can be forced to respond to civil society's demands through other mechanisms. Michael Mann (2000: 13) describes how new solutions to social problems are developing in what he calls "interstitial locations." These consist of the "nooks and crannies in and around the dominant institutions." He argues that groups that are marginal and blocked by the prevailing institutions can link together and cooperate in ways that transcend these institutions. Such movements create "subversive invisible connections across state boundaries and the established channels between them. . . . These interstitial networks translate human goals into organizational means" (p. 13). The actors engaged in the mobilizing strategies in the maquiladoras were forced to make use of such interstitial locations because they were locked out of the international and national dialogue regarding trade regulations.

Global forces have altered the domestic political climate in Mexico in a number of ways. As a result, there is much resentment toward international trade agreements such as NAFTA among much of the local population. For although a significant number of jobs crossed the border since the inception of NAFTA, real wages in Mexico have steadily decreased in the maquila industry. Part of this is due to an abundant labor supply. One of the concessions the government made when signing the NAFTA agreement was to rescind Article 27 of the Mexican Constitution that guaranteed the use of communal lands to the indigenous population. This land is now being sold to foreign corporations and is forcing many subsistence farmers to look for employment in the manufacturing industry. Also as a result of NAFTA, the

United States is free to export cheap, subsidized corn to the Mexican market. The result is that farmers can no longer afford to grow corn in Mexico. As the bottom drops out of the agricultural sector, farmers are forced from their land and again end up migrating to the overcrowded cities along the border. In response, the groups affected are using contentious politics by working outside the legitimate political structure to create their political opportunities. The Zapatista uprising is indicative of this. The rebellion in 1994 was in direct response to the signing of NAFTA, as the Mayan Indians in Chiapas foresaw the damaging impact the neoliberal agenda would have on their local communities. With institutional channels of claims making closed, armed insurgency was their response.

In the manufacturing sector, a similar uprising is happening. There is a growing realization that the wealthy elites in the North and South set the agenda for all others through these types of trade agreements—typically at the expense of labor, environmental, and human rights concerns. Therefore, while NAFTA strengthens the ability of those in power to impose their will on more marginalized groups, it has also enhanced the connection between workers in the North and South as they came to recognize that they share a common enemy in their respective struggles. Jobs have been exported from the North to the South on an unprecedented scale. This means jobs for workers in Mexico, but under exploitative conditions. This has negative consequences for workers in both countries. To combat these forms of abuse workers are collectively focusing their anger on what they understand to be the collusion between the elite representatives of MNCs and governments that work on behalf of business interests rather than on those of their citizens. Thus, the treaty served to create and/or recharge a number of international support groups and coalitions, such as CJM, CLR, LRC, and Global Exchange that have carved out a political space to make claims against MNCs and government abuse (see Bandy and Mendez's chapter 8 in this volume).

This convergence is occurring because globalization is creating common interests (respect for environmental, worker, and human rights) that transcend both national and interest-group boundaries. By facilitating flows of information across national borders, organizations with transnational ties helped cultivate movement identities, transcend nationally defined interests, and build solidarity with a global emphasis (J. Smith 2001b).

According to McAdam, McCarthy, and Zald (1996), another factor that increases the likelihood of protest is a decrease in the capacity or propensity of repressive states to intimidate workers and activists. Mexico had one of the oldest one-party governments in the world, which took the form of a semiauthoritarian state. Like many developing countries, it historically combined repressive production sites with political exclusion in order to secure a safe environment for foreign investment (see Bandy and Mendez's chapter 8 in this volume). The government-controlled CROC acts as a typical corporatist union—a method of social control to constrain workers while protecting the interests of MNCs. At the factories in Kukdong and Duro, the domination of the CROC union made independent unionization virtually impossible. The expansion of the neoliberal global agenda and the signing of NAFTA further increased pressure on the Mexican government to maintain a controlled workforce.

However, over the past few years Mexico has in some other ways become more democratic. In 2000 the 71-year rule of the Institutional Revolutionary Party (PRI) lost the Mexican presidential elections. This trend toward democratization enhanced the ability of workers to organize, which is a quintessential component of any democratic society. In comparison to other Latin American countries, POSs are now more open in Mexico because as Maney (2001a) points out, Mexico began its export-led industrialization much earlier. This allowed an independent workers' movement to develop over a longer period of time. Also, the border's location offers opportunities to local resistance in that there is an increased likelihood of international support (see Bandy and Mendez in this volume).

These case studies illustrate how a combination of open and closed POSs can sometimes be simultaneously at play, which can work to the advantage of workers and activists. When domestic groups have open domestic POSs and governments that are responsive to its citizens, they do not seek out international institutional access regardless of the source of their problem (Tarrow 1995). They will try to influence their own governments to represent their interests in the international arena. But, when there is a high level of repression, authoritarianism, or both, social movement actors bypass their own target states and look to the transnational arena for international support. The outcome is similar if activists view the government to be unconcerned with their demands, or are working in collusion with international actors at the expense of its own citizens. Seidman states, "Activists who view their national states as relatively powerless in the international arena or unresponsive to a particular issue may stress global identities, hoping to attract international support for issues that in a different context have been considered a purely local affair" (2000: 347). This was clearly the case with the labor struggles at Kukdong and Duro. Workers felt that President Fox was more interested in appeasing the MNCs and adhering to stipulations in trade agreements than upholding national laws and responding to legitimate worker grievances. They therefore sought out international support on a number of different levels.

The combination of closed domestic POSs and an open international POS initiates what is referred to as the "boomerang effect" (Keck and Sikkink 1998a; Risse and Sikkink 1999). To understand the dynamics of external-internal movement linkages, Rothman and Oliver (1999) argue that we must recognize the nature of "nested POS." The dynamics of contention concerning workers' rights in the Mexican maquiladoras can refine our understanding of these processes because they demonstrate the local embeddedness of transnational resistance.

The main source of contention initially was at the factory level, and the main targets of the workers' hostility were the managers and subcontractors at these two plants. However, when workers were denied their legal rights and shut out of any legitimate negotiating process, they began to channel their grievances toward the national and international level. The target then became their government for its failure to enforce nationally established labor laws, MNCs for their unwillingness or inability to uphold their own codes of conduct, and international trade agreements and global institutions that do not provide safeguards for worker rights. Though the source and demands of the campaign began at the local level, in both instances they soon became transnational. The immediate outcome was that workers won the right to bargain collectively at each plant and secured financial rewards in their efforts. However, locally embedded struggles such as these necessitate a global perspective and transnational mobilizing.

As the workers realized how global forces were imposing on their everyday lives, they began to interpret their local experiences in terms of international forces. In response, they sought resolution to their domestic problems beyond the nation-state. When social movement actors are able to make this connection they can transcend local and national identities and interests to oppose state and corporate elites (J. Smith 2001b). In the cases of Kukdong and Duro, activists formed networks to advocate for a stronger governmental role. They simultaneously demonstrated an increased organization in civil society at the local, national, and international level. International and national standards such as freedom of association and minimum wage laws were respected only when non-state local actors linked transnationally with other civil actors to assure their enforcement.

In these types of labor struggles the ultimate goal is to change international policy by shaping individual state decisions. Participants are urged to target their own states in order to push the overall movement's agenda forward (J. Smith 2001b; Guidry, Kennedy, and Zald 2002). Activists appeal to the transnational community with the hopes that they can act back on their states and force them to induct policies and institutional change. The case studies examined here did not lead to this outcome, but an increase in these types of victories may eventually lead to institutional change at the national or international level.

Keck and Sikkink (1998a) perhaps most accurately describe the type of mobilizing strategies used in the Kukdong and Duro struggles. They use the term "advocacy networks" to describe similar emerging types of organizations that are voluntary, and through which there are "reciprocal and horizontal patterns of communication and exchange," "operating beyond national boundaries and motivated primarily by shared principled ideas or values. These are based on informal types of action and the actors involved may include NGOs as well as local social movements, the media, churches, trade unions, consumer organizations, intellectuals, parts of regional and international governmental organizations, and parts of the executive and/or parliamentary branches of governments" (1998a: 8, 30). Advocacy networks take on an international dimension when they consist of groups from at least two different nations that share information, resources, strategies, and at times political interests and values (Tarrow 2001; Fox 2000b). Such networks direct their opposition at power holders in at least one state other their own, or against an international institution or economic actor. These networks are very flexible and the main bond among the various individuals and coalitions is that they maintain similar values and visions. This flexibility among social movement actors allows them to reach wide and heterogeneous audiences that can organize from different angles to form broad coalitions across various movement domains (Rucht 1999).

One of the primary goals of TANs is to create, strengthen, implement, and monitor international norms (Khagram and Sikkink 2002). These international norms are sometimes part of the resources and POS actors use them to draw others to the cause and to develop their collective beliefs. Preexisting international norms can act as pull factors to facilitate the emergence and growth of the TANs, as NGOs act as facilitators by appealing to international norms to legitimate local grievances. The fact that the AFL-CIO's mandated right to organize was not being respected (in addition to national and local labor laws) drew sympathy from multiple coalitions concerned with various aspects of social justice to support the workers' struggle.

As an alternative, transnational networks, coalitions, and movements may attempt to transform their collective beliefs into international norms (Khagram and Sikkink 2002). The exchanges among activists can often shape new identities and activist frames (Smith and Johnston 2002). Frames are ways of packaging and presenting ideas and are used as a source of persuasive communication to convince others to join a particular struggle (McAdam 1996b). When social movement actors build on already existing norms to expand the domain to which these norms apply, it is called "frame bridging" (Snow and Benford 1988). This can also draw others to a cause in that the appeal for justice is put forth in a much more generalized sense. For example, for those involved in the anti-sweatshop campaign and resisting the race to the bottom, framing workers' rights (or the ability to unionize) as human rights issues can attract groups or individuals that share a similar vision but work on different social justice campaigns.

Also, NGOs and other transnational advocates use information, persuasion, and moral pressure to change international institutions and governments (Khagram and Sikkink 2002: 11). They do this by displaying or publicizing norm-breaking behavior to embarrass neglectful political officials or corporations to get them to conform to norms—using what is referred to as the "mobilization of shame." This was an effective tactic in getting retailers, university administrators, government officials, lawyers, and the consuming public to acknowledge and to respond to the workers' grievances. It may have also persuaded NGOs and other coalitions that do not deal specifically with labor issues to join the cause.

In the Kukdong and Duro struggles, social movement actors combined conventional and novel forms of repertoires and protest. They petitioned governmental officials, wrote letters to retailers and other significant parties, boycotted certain brand-name retailers, and held strikes, walkouts, and sit-ins. The multilevel, synergistic, cross-border organizing demonstrated some innovative strategies as well. Those involved in the mobilization targeted multilateral institutions and individuals. The variety of tactics that they engaged in displayed an awareness of the local/global connection. This was enhanced by "global witnessing" regarding the effects of global economic policies. As Smith's (2002) research also suggests, the AFL-CIO sponsored speaking tours informed the public about economic globalization, the race to the bottom, and its effects on local policies and democratic institutions. The use of this pedagogical style allowed workers in the North to recognize that workers in the South were also victims of NAFTA, and to humanize the conflict. It also created awareness that the struggle is clearly global in scope, and that therefore solidarity across borders would be pertinent in forging resistance in the form of a "globalization from below."

Another more novel repertoire, as well as an aspect of globalization that has enhanced the international POS, was the use of innovative technology—the Internet. Smith (2002) argues that electronic activism has in fact been essential for the high level of success among NGOs carrying out their activities. Internet sites, electronic listservs, and alternative electronic media networks rapidly disseminate up-to-date information about resistance, which helps to empower a more democratic (online) community (Ribeiro 1998). One of the most hotly debated political topics on the Internet discussed among cyberactivsts is the debate between capitalist interests versus community needs (Ribeiro 1998). The websites and action alerts maintained by the NLC, CLR, CJM, and Global Exchange were essential in providing links to educate citizens about international trade agreements, facilitating the dissemination of information, and organizing resistance. Also, for many participants in the Kukdong and Duro labor struggles, the fastest, easiest, and perhaps only way to express their concerns to retailers, government officials, subcontractors, or university administrators was through online petitions and email contacts.

This phenomenon, by which amorphous groups of NGOs link online and can descend on a target, has been labeled an "NGO swarm" by David Ronfeldt and John Arguilla in a recent RAND study. They argue that the swarm is incredibly effective because "it has no central leadership or command structure, it is multiheaded, impossible to decapitate. And it can sting a victim to death" (cited in Brecher et al.

2002). This has been an important tool in the globalization from below movement in that these networks lack the funds that their opponents have readily at their disposal. Also, with so much information circulating and organizing happening instantaneously online, it is very difficult for MNCs to effectively do what they do best when faced with public criticism—damage control.

CONCLUSION

Justice for maquiladora workers is still a long way off as the political apparatus in developing countries continues to protect foreign investors at the expense of labor rights. The case studies provided in this research offer insights into the effects of global forces on the anti-sweatshop campaign. They further illustrate how global processes affect social movement repertories that are forged primarily through local or nationally oriented contention.

Actors in civil society are increasing their capacity to influence policy to try to strike a fairer balance between global capital and workers' rights. Though there is no anti-systemic movement rapidly emerging upon the scene, numerous interconnected movements and networks are negotiating spaces to democratize the global economy. As this research shows, NGOs in conjunction with other groups are becoming increasingly threatening to foreign investors and the political apparatus that protects them.

The successes at Kukdong and Duro were due to the coordination and reinforcement of different synergistic strategies between different agents and coalitions. These cut across national boundaries to link activist groups in developed countries with labor and community groups in the global South. Cross-national networks of solidarity that linked grass roots organizers in the factories with students, labor, and human rights groups achieved the greatest success in pressuring brand-name retailers, local manufacturers, and local authorities to improve wage levels and working conditions. Grassroots efforts were far more effective than alternative "top-down" mechanisms such as corporate codes of conduct or supranational initiatives such as NAFTA or the WTO. However, they succeeded only when the state was forced to play a proactive role in protecting worker rights. Thus, the ultimate goal must be to ensure workers have a democratic space to pressure their governments to enforce their rights. Both a stronger governmental role and increased organization in civil society are needed to ensure that workers' rights are upheld.

In the future, the empowerment of local and national communities and politics will require a degree of global regulation and governance because they are interdependent. For example, unless the ILO standards of freedom of association are respected by national governments, MNCs, and international trade agreements, workers will have no power to even attempt to make demands. Once their grievances are aired democratically, and perhaps resolved, this resolution may some day be institutionalized and respected more broadly at the national and international level. Thus, making the local/global connection is essential for social movement actors involved in the labor struggles in EPZs. It was only by establishing greater control over global capital that the workers were able to establish greater control over their own economic lives. If we want to establish a democratized type of globalization from below in a true sense, institutions at the local, national, and global level must be made accountable to those that they affect.

REFERENCES

Aguilar, Maria Angela, and Estela Vazquez. 2000. "De YPF a La Ruta: Un Acercamiento a Tartagal." Pp. 327-345 in *Trabajo y Población en el Noroeste Argentino*, Marta Panaia, Susana Aparicio, and Carlos Zurita, eds. Buenos Aires: Editorial La Colmena.

Aguirre Beltrán, Gonzalo. 1991. *Obra Antropológica IV: Formas de Gobierno Indígena*. Mexico City: Fondo de Cultura Económica.

Albro, Robert. 2005. "'The Water Is Ours, Carajo!': Deep Citizenship in Bolivia's Water War." Pp. 237-248 in *Social Movements: An Anthropological Reader*, June Nash, ed. Malden, MA: Blackwell.

Alecio, Rolando. 1995. "Uncovering the Truth: Political Violence and Indigenous Organizations." Pp. 26-45 in *The New Politics of Survival: Grassroots Movements in Central America*, Minor Sinclair, ed. New York: Monthly Review Press.

Alemán Pérez, Paola, Diana Martínez, and Christa Windmaier. 1987. *Fuerza laboral feminina en la rama textil-vestuario: Segregación, salarios y rotación*. Managua: Oficina de la Mujer, Ministerio de la Presidencia.

Almeida, José. 2005. "The Ecuadorian Movement and the Gutiérrez Regime: The Traps of Multiculturalism." *PoLAR: Political and Legal Anthropology Review* 28 (1): 93-111.

Almeida, Paul D. 2002. "Los Movimientos Populares contra las Políticas de Austeridad Económica en América Latina entre 1996 y 2001." *Realidad: Revista de Ciencias Sociales y Humanidades* 86 (Marzo-Abril): 177-189.

———. 2003. "Opportunity Organizations and Threat-Induced Contention: Protest Waves in Authoritarian Settings." *American Journal of Sociology* 109 (2): 345-400.

Almeida, Paul D., and Mark I. Lichbach. 2003. "To the Internet from the Internet: Comparative Media Coverage of Transnational Protests." *Mobilization* 8 (3): 249-272.

Almeida, Paul D., and Linda Brewster Stearns. 1998. "Political Opportunities and Local Grassroots Environmental Movements: The Case of Minamata." *Social Problems* 45: 37-60.

Alonso, Jorge, ed. 1986. Vol. 1 of *Los Movimientos Sociales en el Valle de México*. Mexico City: Centro de Investigaciones y Estudios Superiores en Antropología Social, Ediciones de La Casa Chata.

———, ed. 1988. Vol. 2 of *Los Movimientos Sociales en el Valle de México*. Mexico City: Centro de Investigaciones y Estudios Superiores en Antropología Social, Ediciones de La

Casa Chata.

Alonso, Jorge, Alberto Azis, and Jaime Tamayo, eds. 1992. Vol. 3 of *El Nuevo Estado Mexicano: Estado, Actores y Movimientos Sociales.* Mexico City: Nueva Imágen.

Alvarez, Sonia E., Evelina Dagnino, and Arturo Escobar. 1998. "Introduction: The Cultural and the Political in Latin American Social Movements." Pp. 1-29 in *Cultures of Politics and Politics of Cultures: Re-visioning Latin American Social Movements,* S. Alvarez, E. Dagnino, and A. Escobar, eds. Boulder: Westview Press.

Amado, Janaina, Walter Nugent, and Warren Dean. 1990. "The Frontier in Comparative Perspective: The United States and Brazil." Working Paper No. 188 of the Latin American Program of the Woodrow Wilson International Center for Scholars.

Amenta, Edwin, and Neal Caren. 2004. "The Legislative, Organizational, and Beneficiary Consequences of State-Oriented Challengers." Pp. 461-488 in *The Blackwell Companion to Social Movements,* David Snow, Sarah Soule, and Hanspeter Kriesi, eds. Malden, MA: Blackwell.

Amenta, Edwin, Neal Caren, and Sheera Joy Olasky. 2005. "Age for Leisure? Political Mediation and the Impact of the Pension Movement on U.S. Old-Age Policy." *American Sociological Review* 70 (3): 516-538.

Amin, Samir. 1976. *Unequal Development.* New York: Monthly Review Press.

Aminzade, Ronald. 1995. "Between Movement and Party: The Transformation of Mid-Nineteenth-Century French Republicanism." Pp. 39-62 in *The Politics of Social Protest: Comparative Perspectives on States and Social Movements,* J. Craig Jenkins and Bert Klandermans, eds. Minneapolis: University of Minnesota Press.

AMPM (Asociación Madres de Plaza de Mayo). 1995. "Declaración."

———. 2001. "Declaración del 22 de diciembre de 2001," retrieved May 20, 2001, http://www.madres.org/documentos/contenido/11222declaracion.htm

———. 2002a. "Hebe a fondo," retrieved June 4, 2005 from http://www.madres.org/asp/contenido.asp?clave=793

———. 2002b. "Un recorrido de 25 años: Comunicado de las Madres de Plaza de Mayo." Press release, September 5.

———.2003a. *Historia de las Madres de Plaza de Mayo.* Buenos Aires: Ediciones Madres de Plaza de Mayo.

———. 2003b. "Nuestras Consignas." Buenos Aires.

Anteproyecto de Ley. 1999. "Proyecto de Ley de Reformas y Adición al Decreto No. 46-91. Denominado Zonas Francas Industriales de Exportación." Managua, Nicaragua.

Aoki, M. 1990. *State Space Modeling of Time Series.* Heidelberg: Springer-Verlag.

Appadurai, Arjun. 2000. "Grassroots Globalization and the Research Imagination." *Public Culture* 12 (1): 1-19.

Arditti, Rita. 1999. *Searching for Life: The Grandmothers of the Plaza de Mayo and the Disappeared Children of Argentina.* Berkeley: University of California Press.

———. 2002. "The Grandmothers of the Plaza de Mayo and the Struggle against Impunity in Argentina." *Meridians: Feminism, Race, Transnationalism* 3: 19-41.

Armbruster-Sandoval, Ralph. 2005. *Globalization and Cross-Border Labor Solidarity in the Americas.* New York: Routledge.

Aronskind, Ricardo. 2001. *¿Más cerca o más lejos del desarrollo? Transformaciones económicas en los '90.* Buenos Aires: Libros del Rojas-Universidad de Buenos Aires.

Auvinen, Juha. 1996. "IMF Intervention and Political Protest in the Third World: A Conventional Wisdom Refined." *Third World Quarterly* 17 (3): 377-400.

Auyero, Javier. 1999. "This Is Like the Bronx, Isn't It? Lived Experiences of Slum-dwellers in Argentina." *International Journal of Urban and Regional Research* 23(1): 45-69.

———. 2001. "Glocal Riots." *International Sociology* 16(1): 33-53.

———. 2002. *La Protesta: Retratos de la Beligerancia Popular en la Argentina Democrática.* Buenos Aires: Libros del Rojas-Universidad de Buenos Aires.

———. 2003. *Contentious Lives: Two Argentine Women, Two Protests, and the Quest for Recognition.* Durham and London: Duke University Press.

——— .2004. "When Everyday Life, Routine Politics, and Protest Meet." *Theory and Society* 33

(3-4): 417-441.

Ayres, Jeffrey M. 2001. "Transnational Political Processes and Contention Against the Global Economy." *Mobilization: An International Journal* 6 (1): 55-68.

Babb, Florence E. 1996. "After the Revolution: Neoliberal Policy and Gender in Nicaragua." *Latin American Perspectives* 23 (1): 27-48.

Babb, Sarah. 2001. *Managing Mexico: Economists from Nationalism to Neoliberalism.* Princeton, NJ: Princeton University Press.

———. 2005. "The Social Consequences of Structural Adjustment: Recent Evidence and Current Debates." *Annual Review of Sociology* 31: 199-222 .

Bacon, David. 2001. "NAFTA's Side Agreements Fail." *In These Times.* April 16.

Bailey, Paul, Aurelio Parisotto, and Geoffrey Renshaw. 1993. *Multinationals and Employment: The Global Economy of the 1990s.* Geneva: International Labour Office.

Bakhtin, Mikhail. 1984. *Rabelais and His World.* Bloomington: Indiana University Press.

Ball, Patrick. 2000. "State Terror, Constitutional Traditions, and National Human Rights Movements: A Cross-National Quantitative Comparison." Pp. 54-75 in *Globalizations and Social Movements: Culture, Power, and the Transnational Public Sphere,* John A. Guidry, Michael D. Kennedy, and Mayer N. Zald, eds. Ann Arbor: University of Michigan Press.

Banaszak, Lee Ann. 2005. "Inside and Outside the State: Movement Insider Status, Tactics, and Public Policy Achievements." Pp. 149-176 in *Routing the Opposition: Social Movements, Public Policy, and Democracy,* D. Meyer, V. Jenness, and H. Ingram, eds. Minneapolis: University of Minnesota Press.

Bandy, Joe. 2004. "Paradoxes of a Transnational Civil Society in a Neoliberal World: The Coalition for Justice in the Maquiladoras." *Social Problems* 51 (3): 410-431.

Bandy, Joe, and Jackie Smith. 2005. *Coalitions Across Boarders: Transnational Protest and the Neoliberal Order.* Lanham, MD: Rowman & Littlefield.

Barreto, Pablo Emilio. 1997. "Porátil ante el MITRAB." *La Barricada.* November 25.

Barry, Tom. 1992. *Inside Guatemala.* Albuquerque, NM: Inter-Hemispheric Education Resource Center.

Barry, Tom, Harry Browne, and Beth Sims. 1994. *The Great Divide: The Challenge of US-Mexico Relations in the 1990s.* New York: Grove Press.

Bartra, Armando. 1996. *Guerrero Bronco: Campesinos, Ciudadanos y Guerrilleros en la Costa Grande.* Mexico City: Ediciones Sinfiltro.

Bartra, Roger. 1975. *Caciquismo y Poder Político en el México Rural.* Mexico City: Siglo XXI Editores.

Basu, Kaushik. 2001. "The View From the Tropics." Pp. 59-64 in *Can We Put an End to Sweatshops?* Archon Fung, Dara O'Rourke, and Charles Sabel, eds. Boston: Beacon Press.

Bayes, Jane H., and Rita Mae Kelly. 2001. "Political Spaces, Gender, and NAFTA." Pp. 147-170 in *Gender, Globalization, and Democratization,* Rita Mae Kelly, ed. Lanham, MD: Rowman & Littlefield.

BDEBP. 2003. *Base de datos El Bravo Pueblo.* Caracas, Universidad Central de Venezuela, Proyecto CENDES-FACES-CDCH 26-50-4047-2000.

Bédoyan, Isabelle, Peter Van Aelst, and Stefaan Walgrave. 2004. "Limitations and Possibilities of Transnational Mobilization: The Case of EU Summit Protesters in Brussels, 2001." *Mobilization* 9 (1): 39-54

Bejarano, Cynthia L. 2002. "Las Super Madres de Latino America." *Frontiers: A Journal of Women's Studies* 23: 126-150.

Bellinghausen, Hermann. 1999. "La sociedad civil, protagonista en la búsqueda de un país mejor: Marcos." *La Jornada,* March 11.

Bellman, Mary. 2003. "Factory Unions in Garment Industry Maquiladoras: Lessons from Central America." Presented at annual meeting of the Latin American Studies Association, Dallas, TX.

Bello, Walden, D. Kinley, and E. Elinson. 1982. *Development Debacle: The World Bank in the Philippines.* San Francisco, CA: Institute for Food and Development Policy.

Bello, Walden. 2001. *The Future in the Balance.* Oakland: Food First.

Bellucci, Mabel. 2000. "El Movimiento de Madres de Plaza de Mayo." Pp. 266-287 in *Historia de las mujeres en la Argentina: Siglo XX*, vol. 2, F. G. Lozano, V. S. Pita, and M. G. Ini, eds. Buenos Aires: Taurus.

Benford, Robert D. 1997. "An Insider's Critique of the Social Movement Framing Perspective." *Sociological Inquiry* 67 (4): 409-430.

Benford, Robert D, and David A. Snow. 2000. "Framing Processes and Social Movements: An Overview and Assessment." *Annual Review of Sociology* 26: 611-639.

Bennett, Vivienne. 1992. "The Evolution of Urban Popular Movements in Mexico between 1968 and 1988." In *The Making of Social Movements in Latin America: Identity, Strategy, and Democracy*, A. Escobar and S. Alvarez, eds. Boulder: Westview Press.

Black, James. 1998. "Scorched Earth in a Time of Peace." *NACLA Report on the Americas* 32 (1): 11-15.

Blixen, Samuel, and Carlos Fazio. 1995. "El neoliberalismo: La abolición de la patria y la propiedad. El subcomandante Marcos habló del neoliberalismo al analizar el tema de la tierra en el contexto de las luchas campesinas," *Brecha* 11, no. 517, October 27.

Block, Fred. 1977. *The Origins of International Economic Disorder: A Study of United States International Monetary Policy from World War II to the Present*. Berkeley: University of California Press.

Blustein, P. 2001. *The Chastening: Inside the Crisis that Rocked the Global Financial System and Humbled the IMF*. New York: Public Affairs.

Bob, Clifford. 2001. "Marketing Rebellion: Insurgent Groups, International Media, and NGO Support." *International Politics* 38 (3): 311-333.

———. 2002. "Merchants of Morality." *Foreign Policy* 129 (March/April): 36-45.

Bodeau, Jean. 1999. "First-Hand Account: Day Three of the Río Negro Massacre Trial." *Solidaridad: News and Analysis from Central America* January 20: 4-5.

Booth, John A., and Mitchell A. Seligson, eds. 1978. *Political Participation in Latin America: Citizen and State*. Vol. 1. New York: Holmes and Meier.

Booth, John A. 1995. "Introduction: Elections and Democracy in Central America: A Framework for Analysis." Pp. 1-21 in *Elections and Democracy in Central America, Revisited*, M. Seligson and J. Booth, eds. Chapel Hill: University of North Carolina Press.

Booth, John A., Thomas Walker, and Christine J. Wade, eds. 2006. *Understanding Central America: Global Forces, Rebellion, and Change*, 4th ed. Boulder, CO: Westview Press.

Borge, Tomás. 1997. "¡Qué se vayan!" *La Barricada*. November 21, A4.

Borón, Atilio. 2002. "Formidable tenacidad." *Página 12*, April 30.

Bosco, Fernando J. 2001. "Place, Space, Networks, and the Sustainability of Collective Action: The Madres de Plaza de Mayo." *Global Networks: A Journal of Transnational Affairs* 1: 307-329.

———. 2004. "Human Rights Politics and Scaled Performances of Memory: Conflicts among the Madres de Plaza de Mayo in Argentina." *Social and Cultural Geography* 5: 384-402.

———. In press. "Embeddedness, Emotions and Social Movements: The Madres de Plaza de Mayo and Three Decades of Human Rights Activism." *Annals of the Association of American Geographers*.

Boswell, Terry, and Christopher Chase-Dunn. 2000. *The Spiral of Capitalism and Socialism: Toward Global Democracy*. Boulder, CO: Lynne Rienner.

Bouvard, Marguerite Guzmán. 1994. *Revolutionizing Motherhood: The Mothers of the Plaza de Mayo*. Wilmington, DE: Scholarly Resources, Inc.

Bradshaw, York W., and J. Huang. 1991. "Intensifying Global Dependency: Foreign Debt, Structural Adjustment, and Third World Underdevelopment." *Sociological Quarterly* 32: 321-342.

Bradshaw, York W. 1987. "Urbanization and Underdevelopment: A Global Study of Modernization, Urban Bias and Economic Dependency." *American Sociological Review* 52: 224-239.

Brecher, Jeremy, Tim Costello, and Brendan Smith. 2002. *Globalization from Below: The Power of Solidarity*. Cambridge, MA: South End Press.

Brenner, Johanna. 1998. "On Gender and Class in U.S. Labor History." Pp. 41-56 in *Rising from the Ashes? Labor in the Age of "Global" Capitalism*, Ellen Meiksins Wood, Peter Meiksins, Michael Yates, eds. New York: Monthly Review Press.

Brubaker, Rogers, and Frederick Cooper. 2000. "Beyond Identity." *Theory and Society* 29: 1-47.

Bruhn, Kathleen. 1999. "Antonio Gramsci and the *Palabra Verdadera*: The Political Discourse of Mexico's Guerrilla Forces." *Journal of Interamerican Studies and World Affairs* 41 (2): 29-55.

Brysk, Alison. 1996. "Turning Weakness into Strength: The Internationalization of Indian Rights." *Latin American Perspectives* 23: 38-57.

Buarque, Sergio C. 1997. *Proposta de Re-Estruturacao do Setor Sucro-Alcooleiro e Negociacao da Divida por Terra para Assentamento de Reforma Agraria.* Recife, PE: National Institute for Colonization and Agrarian Reform.

Burke, Peter. 1978. *Popular Culture in Early Modern Europe.* England: Wildwood House.

Burns, E. Bradford. 1993. *A History of Brazil.* New York: Columbia University Press.

———. 1995. "Brazil: Frontier and Ideology." *Pacific Historical Review* 64 (1):1-18.

Burstein, Paul. 1979. "Public Opinion, Demonstrations, and the Passage of Anti-Discrimination Legislation." *Public Opinion Quarterly* 43: 157-172.

Burstein, Paul, and April Linton. 2002. "The Impact of Political Parties, Interest Groups, and Social Movement Organizations on Public Policy: Some Recent Evidence and Theoretical Concerns." *Social Forces* 81 (2): 380-408.

Burstein, Paul, Rachel Einwohner, and Jocelyn A. Hollander. 1995. "The Success of Political Movements: A Bargaining Perspective." Pp. 275-295 in *The Politics of Social Protest: Comparative Perspectives on States and Social Movements,* J. Craig Jenkins and Bert Klandermans, eds. Minneapolis: University of Minnesota Press.

Byrne, Hugh. 1997. *The Guatemalan Peace Accords: Assessment and Implications for the Future.* Washington, DC: Washington Office on Latin America.

Cafassi, Emilio. 2002. *Olla a Presión. Cacerolazos, Piquetes y Asambleas sobre Fuego Argentino.* Buenos Aires: Libros del Rojas-Universidad de Buenos Aires.

Calasanti, Toni M., and Kathleen F. Slevin. 2001. *Gender, Social Inequalities, and Aging.* Walnut Creek, CA: Altamira Press.

Calderón, Fernando. 1995. *Movimientos sociales y política: La década de los ochenta en Latinoamérica.* Mexico City: Siglo Veintiuno Editores.

Calhoun, Craig. 1994. *Neither Gods nor Emperors: Students and the Struggle for Democracy in China.* Berkeley: University of California Press.

Callahan, Manuel. 2000. Interview in Austin, TX, October 5.

Camacho, Alicia Schmidt. 1999. "On the Borders of Solidarity: Race and Gender Contradictions in the 'New Voice' Platform of the AFL-CIO." *Social Justice* 26 (3): 79-102.

Camarasa, Jorge. 2002. *Días de Furia. Historia oculta de la Argentina desde la caída de De la Rúa hasta la asunción de Duhalde.* Buenos Aires: Sudamericana.

Campaign for Labor Rights (CLR). Various years. Online, http://www.clrlabor.org.

Canahuí, Enrique. 2005. "Protestas dejan pérdidas por Q85 millones." *SigloVeintiuno,* March 16, p. 4.

Canel, Eduardo. 1992. "Democratization and the Decline of Urban Social Movements in Uruguay: A Political-Institutional Account." Pp. 276-290 in *The Making of Social Movements in Latin America,* A. Escobar and S. Alvarez, eds. Boulder: Westview Press.

Caniglia, Beth Schaefer. 2001. "Informal Alliances vs. Institutional Ties: The Effects of Elite Alliances on Environmental TSMO Networks." *Mobilization: An International Journal* 6 (1): 37-54.

Carr, Barry. 1986. "The Mexican Left, the Popular Movements, and the Politics of Austerity, 1982-1985." In *The Mexican Left, the Popular Movements, and the Politics of Austerity,* Barry Carr and Ricardo Anzaldúa Montoya, eds. La Jolla, CA: Center for U.S.-Mexican Studies.

Carrillo, Silvia E., and Octavio Enríquez. 2005. "Desprecio a Usarios." *El Nuevo Diario,* March 30, 2005.

Castañeda, Jorge E. 2000. *Perpetuating Power: How Mexican Presidents Were Chosen.* New York: The New Press.

Castells, Manuel. 1989. *The Informational City.* Oxford, UK: Blackwell.

————. 1997. *The Power of Identity.* Vol II of *The Information Age: Economy, Society and Culture.* Oxford, UK: Blackwell.

Cave, Michael. 2002. "Just Change It." *Australian Financial Review,* June 14.

Cazella, Ademir A. 1992. *Assentamentos Rurais e Cooperação Agrícola: Políticas Conflitantes.* Master's Thesis, Center for Research in Agriculture and Development, Federal Rural University of Rio de Janeiro. Rio de Janeiro: Federal Rural University of Rio de Janeiro.

Cazés, Daniel, ed. 1996. *Memorial de las Elecciones de 1994.* Mexico City: La Jornada Ediciones, Centro de Investigaciones Interdisciplinarias en Ciencias y Humanidades.

Ceceña, Ana Esther. 1996. "Universalidad de la lucha zapatista: Algunas hipótesis," *Chiapas* 2.

CEH (Comisión de Esclarecimiento Histórica). 1999. *Guatemala: Memoria de Silencio.* Guatemala City: United Nations.

Centeno, Miguel Angel. 1997. *Democracy within Reason: Technocratic Revolution in Mexico.* University Park, PA: Pennsylvania State University Press.

Chalmers, Douglas A., Scott B. Martin, and Kerianne Piester. 1997. "Associative Networks: New Structures of Representation for the Popular Sectors?" Pp. 543-582 in *The New Politics of Inequality in Latin America: Rethinking Participation and Representation,* Douglas Chalmers, Carlos M. Vilas, Katherine Hite, Scott B. Martin, Kerianne Piester, and Monique Segarra, eds. Oxford: Oxford University Press.

Chase-Dunn, Christopher. 1992. "The Comparative Study of World Systems. *Review* 15: 313-334.

Chase-Dunn, Christopher, and Thomas Hall. 1993. "Comparing World Systems: Concepts and Working Hypotheses." *Social Forces* 71: 851-886

Chayanov, Alexander V. 1966. *The Theory of Peasant Economy,* Daniel Thorner, Basile Kerblay, and R.E.F. Smith eds. Homewood, IL: AD Irwin.

Chejter, Silvia. 2004. "Argentinian Women Survive Economic Crisis." *Signs* 29: 534-539.

CJM Correspondence. 1998. San Antonio (October-November): 4-5.

————. 1999. San Antonio (February): 2-3.

CJM Newsletter. 1994. "CTM Finds Basic Market Basket Is Beyond the Reach of 8.7 Million Workers." 4 (3): 7.

————. 1999. 9(1): 10.

Cleaver, Jr., Harry M. 1998. "The Zapatista Effect: The Internet and the Rise of an Alternative Political Fabric." *Journal of International Affairs* 51 (2): 621-640.

————. 2000. Department of Economics, University of Texas at Austin. Interview in Austin, TX, October 4.

Cobble, Dorothy Sue. 1993. "Introduction: Remaking Unions for the New Majority." Pp. 3-18 in *Women and Unions: Forging a Partnership,* Dorothy Sue Cobble, ed. Ithaca, NY: ILR Press.

Cohen, Jean L., and Andrew Arato. 1992. *Civil Society and Political Theory.* Cambridge, MA: MIT Press.

Cohen, Robin, and Shirin M. Rai. 2000. "Global Social Movements: Towards a Cosmopolitan Politics." Pp. 1-17 in *Global Social Movements,* Robin Cohen and Shirin M. Rai, eds. London: Athlone Press.

Cole, Elizabeth R., and Abigail J. Stewart. 1996. "Meanings of Political Participation Among Black and White Women: Political Identity and Social Responsibility." *American Psychological Association* 71: 130-140.

Collingsworth, Terry. 1998. "An Enforceable Social Clause." *Foreign Policy in Focus* (3) 28: 1-3.

Collins, Jennifer. 2004. "Linking Movement and Electoral Politics: Ecuador's Indigenous Movement and the Rise of Pachakutik." Pp. 38-57 in *Politics in the Andes: Identity, Conflict, Reform,* J. Burt and P. Mauceri, eds. Pittsburgh, PA: University of Pittsburgh Press.

Comisión Nacional de Zonas Francas. 2002. http://www.czf.com.ni.

Comissão Pastoral da Terra (CPT). 2000. *Assassinatos no Campo Brasil 1985–2000: Violência e Impunidade.* Goiânia, MT: CPT Press.

Connell, Tula. 2001. "Maquila Melee: Death Threats and Plant Closings Threaten Workers Rights in Guatemala." *In These Times.* Dec. 7.

Comité Directivo Municipal del PRI. 1999. "De cara al 2000." Oaxaca: CDM del PRI.

Cook, Alice H., Val R. Lorwin, and Arlene Kaplan Daniels. 1992. *The Most Difficult Revolution: Women and Trade Unions*. Ithaca, NY: Cornell University Press.

Cook, Maria Lorena. 1996. *Organizing Dissent: Unions, the State and the Democratic Teachers' Movement in Mexico*. University Park: Pennsylvania State University Press.

COPUB, (Centro de Opinión Pública de la Universidad de Belgrano). 2002. "Perfil de las mujeres estudiantes universitarias." Buenos Aires: Universidad de Belgrano.

Cordero Ulate, Allen. 2004. "Los Movimientos Sociales y lo Local." Working Paper. FLACSO-Costa Rica.

Cornelius, Wayne A. 1974. "Urbanization and Political Demand Making: Political Participation among the Migrant Poor in Latin American Cities." *American Political Science Review* 68 (3): 1125-1146.

———. 1975. *Politics and the Migrant Poor in Mexico City*. Stanford, CA: Stanford University Press.

Coronil, Fernando, and Julie Skurski. 1991. "Dismembering and Remembering the Nation: The Semantics of Political Violence in Venezuela." *Comparative Studies in Society and History* 33: 288-335.

Cortiñas, Nora. 2000. "Las Mujeres en la Lucha por los DDHH y en contra del neoliberalismo." *Brujas* 19: 16-18.

———. 2002. Remarks from a panel discussion held at the University of Buenos Aires, School of Psychology, October 15.

Costallat, Karina. 1999. "Efectos de las Privatizaciones y la Relación Estado-Sociedad en la Instancia Provincial y Local: El Caso Cutral Co-Plaza Huincul." Buenos Aires, INAP. Unpublished Manuscript.

Cox, Kevin R. 1997. "Spaces of Dependence, Spaces of Engagement and the Politics of Scale, or: Looking for Local Politics." *Political Geography* 17 (1): 1-23.

Coy, Patrick. 1997. "Cooperative Accompaniment and Peace Brigades International." Pp. 81-100 in *Transnational Social Movements and Global Politics*, Jackie Smith, Charles Chatfield, and Ron Pagnucco, eds. Syracuse, NY: Syracuse University Press.

Criquillon, Ana. 1995. "Farmers' organizations and agrarian transformation in Nicaragua." In *The New Politics of Survival: Grassroots Movements in Central America*, Minor Sinclair, ed. New York: Monthly Review Press.

Cuadernos del Cendes. 1989. Special issue on the *Caracazo*, No. 10.

Davis, Diane. 1999. "The Power of Distance: Rethinking Social Movements in Latin America." *Theory and Society* 24: 589-643.

de Bonafini, Hebe. 2000. "Resistir con sueños y esperanzas." *Locas, cultura, y utopias*, December.

de Gropper, Margarita. 2005. Personal interview conducted on March 9, Buenos Aires.

De Souza, Hermino R., José F. Irmão, and Tacisio P. de Araujo. 1997. *Cana de Açúcar e Cacau: Re-Estruturação Produtiva e Mercado de Trabalho na Zona da Mata do Nordeste*. Recife, PE: INCRA.

Delgado, Guilherme C. 1985. *Capital Financeiro e Agricultura no Brasil: 1965-1985*. Campinas, SP: Editora UNICAMP.

della Porta, Donatella, and Hanspeter Kriesi. 1999. "Social Movements in a Globalizing World: An Introduction." In *Social Movements in a Globalizing World*, Donatella della Porta, Hanspeter Kriesi, and Dieter Rucht, eds. London: Macmillan.

della Porta, Donatella. 2005. "Making the Polis: Social Forums and Democracy in the Global Justice Movement." *Mobilization*: 10: 73-94.

DeMartini, Joseph R. 1983. "Social Movement Participation, Political Socialization, Generational Consciousness, and Lasting Effects." *Youth & Society* 15:195-223.

Di Marco, Graciela, and Héctor Palomino. 2004. "Presentación de los resultados de la investigación sobre movimientos sociales emergentes." Pp. 27-43 in *Reflexiones sobre los movimientos sociales en la Argentina*, G. Di Marco and H. Palomino, eds. Buenos Aires: Jorge Baudino Ediciones.

Diamond, Larry. 1999. *Developing Democracy: Toward Consolidation*. Baltimore, MD: Johns

Hopkins University Press.

Diani, Mario. 1996. "Linking Mobilization Frames and Political Opportunities: Insights from Regional Populism in Italy." *American Sociological Review* 61 (6): 1053-1069.

Dicken, Peter. 1998. *Global Shift: Transforming the World Economy.* New York: Guilford Press.

Dietz, Henry. 1998. *Urban Poverty, Political Participation and the State.* Pittsburgh, PA: University of Pittsburgh Press.

Dillon, K. Burke, and Gumersindo Oliveros. 1987. "Recent Experience with Multilateral Official Debt Rescheduling." Washington, DC: IMF.

Dillon, Sam. 1999. "Reports of Coercion in a Mexican Election." *New York Times,* July 4.

Dinerstein, Ana. 2001. "El Poder de lo Irrealizado. El corte de ruta en Argentina y el potencial subversivo de la mundialización." *OSAL* Septiembre: 22-35.

Domínguez, Jorge I., and Abraham F. Lowenthal. 1996. *Constructing Democratic Governance: Latin America and the Caribbean in the 1990s.* Baltimore, MD: Johns Hopkins University Press.

Donati, Paolo R. 1992. "Political Discourse Analysis," In *Studying Collective Action,* Marco Diani and Ron Eyerman, eds. London: Sage.

Dwyer, Augusta. 1995. *On the Line. Life on the US-Mexican Border.* London: Latin American Bureau.

Eckstein, Susan. 1977. *The Poverty of Revolution: The State and the Urban Poor in Mexico.* Princeton: Princeton University Press.

———, ed. 1989. *Power and Popular Protest: Latin American Social Movements.* Berkeley, CA: University of California Press.

———. 2001a. "Power and Popular Protest in Latin Amceria." Pp. 1- 60 in *Power and Popular Protest: Latin American Social Movements,* 2nd edition. Susan Eckstein, ed. Berkeley: University of California Press.

———. 2001b. "Epilogue. Where Have All the Movements Gone? Latin American Social Movements at the New Millennium." Pp. 351-406 in *Power and Popular Protest: Latin American Social Movements,* Susan Eckstein, ed. Berkeley: University of California Press.

Eckstein, Susan E., and Timothy P. Wickham-Crowley. 2003. "Struggles for Social Rights in Latin America: Claims in the Arenas of Subsistence, Labor, Gender, and Ethnicity." Pp. 1-56 in *Struggles for Social Rights in Latin America,* Susan Eckstein and Timothy Wickham-Crowley, eds. London: Routledge.

Edelman, Marc. 1996. "Reconceptualizing and Reconstituting Peasant Struggles: A New Social Movement in Central-America." *Radical History Review* 65: 26-47.

———. 1998. "Transnational Peasant Politics in Central America." *Latin American Research Review* 33, 3: 49-86.

———. 1999. *Peasants against Globalization: Rural Social Movements in Costa Rica.* Stanford, CA: Stanford University Press.

Edwards, Sebastian. 1995. *Crisis and Reform in Latin America: From Despair to Hope.* Oxford: Oxford University Press.

Efron, Bradley. 1987. "Better Bootstrap Intervals (with Discussion)." *Journal of the American Statistical Association* 82: 171-200.

Ellner, Steve. 1995. *El sindicalismo en Venezuela en el contexto democrático, 1958-1994.* Caracas: Editorial Tropykos.

Elson, Diane, and Ruth Pearson. 1981. "'Nimble Fingers Make Cheap Workers': An Analysis of Women's Employment in Third World Export Manufacturing." *Feminist Review* 7: 87-107.

Ennals, Martin. 1982. "Amnesty International and Human Rights." Pp. 63-83 in *Pressure Groups in the Global System: The Transnational Relations of Issue-Oriented Non-Governmental Organizations,* Peter Willetts, ed. New York: St. Martin's Press.

Entel, Alicia. 1997. *La Ciudad Bajo Sospecha. Comunicación y Protesta Urbana.* Buenos Aires: Paidos.

Equipo de Antropología Forense de Guatemala (EAFG). 1997. *Las Masacres en Rabinal: Estudio Histórico Antropológico de las Masacres de Plan de Sanchez, Chichupac y Rio Negro.* Guatemala City: EAFG.

Escobar Salom, Ramón. 1997. Personal interview conducted in New York, May 23, 1997.

Esteva, Gustavo. 2001. "The Meaning and the Scope of the Struggle for Autonomy." *Latin American Perspectives* 28(2): 120-148.

Euloff, Jonathan. 1998. "An Unfulfilled Package: The World Bank and Pacux—An Addendum to *A People Dammed*." *Witness for Peace Newsletter* 15, 1: 8-12.

Evans, Peter. 2000. "Fighting Marginalization with Transnational Networks: Counter-Hegemonic Globalization." *Contemporary Sociology* 29(1): 230-41.

Evrensel, A. 2002. "Effectiveness of IMF-Supported Stabilization Programs in Developing Countries." *Journal of International Money and Finance* 21 (5): 565-587.

EZLN. 1996. "Primera Declaración de la Realidad," online at *www.ezln.org/documentos/1996/19960130.es.htm*.

———. 1997. "Siete piezas sueltas del rompecabezas mundial," online at *www.ezln.org/documentos/1997/199708xx.es.htm*.

———. 2001. "Palabras del EZLN el 27 de febrero del 2001 en Puebla, Puebla," online at *www.ezln.org/marcha/20010227b.es.htm*.

Falk, Peter. 1993. *Global Visions: Beyond the New World Order*. Boston: South End Press.

Falk, Richard. 1993. "The Infancy of Global Civil Society." Pp. 219-234 in *Beyond the Cold War: New Dimensions in International Relations*, Geir Lundestad and Odd Arne Westad, eds. New York: Oxford University Press.

Farinetti, Marina. 1998. "Cuando los Clientes se Rebelan." *Apuntes de Investigación del CECYP* 2/3: 84-103.

———. 1999. "¿Qué Queda del Movimiento Obrero? Las Formas del Reclamo Laboral en la Nueva Democracia Argentina." *Trabajo y Sociedad* 1 (1): 2-45.

———. 2000. *El Estallido: La Forma de la Protesta*. Unpublished manuscript. Buenos Aires.

Fausto, Boris. 1999. *A Concise History of Brazil*. New York: Cambridge University Press.

Faux, Jeff. 2002. "Corporate Control of North America." *The American Prospect* 3(4). Online edition, http://www.prospect.org/web.

Favaro, Orietta and Mario Bucciarelli. 1994. "Efectos De La Privatización De YPF: La Desagregación Territorial Del Espacio Neuquino?" *Realidad Económica* 127: 88-99.

Favaro, Orietta, Mario Bucciarelli, and Graciela Luomo. 1997. "La Conflictividad Social en Neuquén: El Movimiento Cutralquense y Los Nuevos Sujetos Sociales." *Realidad Económica* 148: 13-27.

Featherstone, Liza. 2002. *Students Against Sweatshops*. New York: Verso.

Feijoo, María del Carmen, and Mónica Gogna. 1987. "Las Mujeres en la Transición a la Democracia." Pp. 129-187 in *Ciudadania e identitad: Las mujeres en los movimientos sociales latinoamericanos*, E. Jelín, ed. Geneva: Instituto de Investigaciones de las Naciones Unidas para el Desarrollo Social (UNRISD).

Fendrich, James M. 1977. "Keeping the Faith or Pursuing the Good Life: A Study of the Consequence of Participation in the Civil Rights Movement." *American Sociological Review* 42: 144-157.

Fernandes, Bernardo M. 1999. *MST, Movimento dos Trabalhadores Rurais Sem-Terra: Formação e Territorialização*. São Paulo: Editora Hucitec.

Fernández-Kelly, M. P. 1983. *For We Are Sold, I and My People. Women and Industry in Mexico's Frontier*. Albany, NY: State University of New York Press.

Figueroa Ibarra, Carlos. 2002. "Democracia precaria y rebelión en América Latina." *Política y Cultura* 17: 143-163.

Fisher, Dana R., Kevin Stanley, David Berman, and Gina Neff. 2005. "How Do Organizations Matter? Mobilization and Support for Participants at Five Globalization Protests." *Social Problems* 52 (1): 102-121.

Fisher, Jo. 1989. *Mothers of the Disappeared*. Boston: South End Press.

Foss, Karen A., and Kathy L. Domenici. 2001. "Haunting Argentina: Synecdoche in the Protests of the Mothers of the Plaza de Mayo." *Quarterly Journal of Speech* 87: 237-268.

Fourcade-Gourinchas, Marion and Sarah L. Babb. 2002. "The Rebirth of the Liberal Creed: Paths to Neoliberalism in Four Countries." *American Journal of Sociology* 108(3): 533-579.

Foweraker, Joe. 1995. *Theorizing Social Movements*. London: Pluto Press.

Foweraker, Joe, and Ann L. Craig, eds. 1990. *Popular Movements and Political Change in Mex-*

ico. Boulder: Lynne Rienner.

Foweraker, Joe, and Todd Landman. 1997. *Citizenship Rights and Social Movements: A Comparative and Statistical Analysis*. Oxford: Oxford University Press.

Fox, Jonathan. 1992. "Democratic Rural Development: Leadership Accountability in Regional Peasant Organizations." *Development and Change* 23 (2): 1-36.

———. 1994. "The Difficult Transition from Clientelism to Citizenship: Lessons from Mexico." *World Politics* 46:151-184.

———. 1996. "How Does Civil Society Thicken? The Political Construction of Social Capital in Rural Mexico." *World Development* 24 (6): 1089-1103.

———. 2000a. "Assessing Binational Civil Society Coalitions: Lessons from the Mexico-US Experience." Paper presented at annual meeting of the Latin American Studies Association. October, Miami, Fl.

———. 2000b. "The World Bank Inspection Panel: Lessons for the First Five Years." *Global Governance* 6 (3): 279-318.

Fox, Jonathan, and L. David Brown, eds. 1998. *The Struggle for Accountability: The World Bank, NGOs, and Grassroots Movements*. Cambridge: MIT Press.

Francisco Segura, Jesús J. 1999. "Tres momentos en la expansión de la capital de Oaxaca." *Cuadernos del Sur* 5 (14): 55-80.

Frank, Andre Gunder. 1978. *World Accumulation and Underdevelopment*. New York: Monthly Review Press.

———. 1980. *Crisis in the World Economy*. New York: Holmes and Meier.

Franzosi, Roberto. 1996. "A Sociologist Meets History. Critical Reflections upon Practice." *Journal of Historical Sociology* 9 (3): 354-391.

———. 1998. "Narrative Analysis--or Why (and How) Sociologists Should Be Interested in Narrative." *Annual Review of Sociology* 24: 517-554.

———. 2004. *From Words to Numbers: Narrative, Data, and Social Science*. Cambridge and New York: Cambridge University Press.

Freeman, Carla. 2001. "Is Local:Global as Feminine:Masculine? Rethinking the Gender of Globalization." *Signs* 26(4): 1007-1037.

Fourcade-Gourinchas, Marion and Sarah L. Babb. 2002. "The Rebirth of the Liberal Creed: Paths to Neoliberalism in Four Countries." *American Journal of Sociology* 108 (3): 533-579.

Fukuyama, Francis. 1989. "The End of History?" *The National Interest* 16: 3-18.

Fung, Archon, Dara O'Rourke and Charles Sabel. 2001. *Can We Put an End to Sweatshops?* Boston: Beacon Press.

Gabriel, Christina, and Laura MacDonald. 1994. "NAFTA, Women and Organising in Canada and Mexico: Forging a 'Feminist Internationality.'" *Millennium Journal of International Studies* 23 (3): 535-562.

Gallego, Marisa. 2004. "Introducción." Pp. 7-13 in *Luchar Siempre: Las Marchas de la Resistencia, 1981-2003*, I. Vázquez, U. Gorini, M. Gallego, G. Nielsen, E. Epstein, and C. Rodriguez, eds. Buenos Aires: Ediciones Madres de Plaza de Mayo.

Galván, Mario. 2001. National Commission for Democracy in Mexico, Sacramento, CA. E-mail interview, received August 23.

Gamson, William A. 1992. *Talking Politics*. Cambridge and New York: Cambridge University Press.

Gamson, William A., and David S. Meyer. 1996. "Framing Political Opportunity." Pp. 275-290 in *Comparative Perspectives on Social Movements: Political Opportunities, Mobilizing Structures, and Cultural Framings*, Doug McAdam, John D. McCarthy, and Mayer N. Zald ,eds. Cambridge: Cambridge University Press.

Gamson, William A., Bruce Fireman, and Steven Rytina. 1982. *Encounters with Unjust Authority*. Chicago, IL: Dorsey Press.

Garcia Márquez, Gabriel, and Roberto Pombo. 2001. "Habla Marcos." *Revista Cambio*, March 25.

García-Gorena, Velma. 2001. "Mothers as Leaders: The Madres Veracruzanas and the Mexican Antinuclear Movement." In *Women on Power: Leadership Redefined*, S. J. M. Freedman, S.

C. Bourque, and C. M. Shelton, eds.. Boston: Northeastern University Press.

Garretón, Manuel Antonio. 1989. "Popular Mobilization and the Military Regime in Chile: The Complexities of the Invisible Transition." Pp. 259-277 in *Power and Popular Protest: Latin American Social Movements*, Susan Eckstein, ed. Berkeley: University of California Press.

George, Susan. 1988. *A Fate Worse Than Debt*. New York: Grove Press.

Gertler, Meric S. 1997. "Between the Global and the Local: The Spatial Limits to Productive Capital." Pp. 45-63 in *Spaces of Globalization: Reasserting the Power of the Local*, Kevin Cox, ed. New York: Guilford Press.

Giarracca, Norma, et al. 2001. *La protesta social en la Argentina: Transformaciones económicas y crisis social en el interior del país*. Buenos Aires: Alianza Editorial.

Giarracca, Norma, and Karina Bidaseca. 2001. "Introducción." Pp. 19-39 in *La protesta social en la Argentina: Transformaciones económicas y crisis social en el interior del país*, N. Giarracca, ed. Buenos Aires: Alianza Editorial.

Gilley, Bruce. 2001. "Sweating It Out." *Far Eastern Economic Review*. Available online at http://www.feer.com/010510/p.o4innov.html.

Giugni, Marco, Doug McAdam, and Charles Tilly, eds. 1999. *How Social Movements Matter*. Minneapolis: University of Minnesota Press.

Gleijeses, Piero. 1991. *Shattered Hope: The Guatemalan Revolution and the United States, 1944-1954*. Princeton, NJ: Princeton University Press.

Goldstone, Jack. 2004. "More Social Movements or Fewer? Beyond Political Opportunity Structures to Relational Fields." *Theory and Society* 33: 333-365.

_____. 2003. "Introduction: Bridging Institutionalized and Noninstitutionalized Politics." Pp.1–24 in *States, Parties, and Social Movements*, edited by Jack Goldstone. Cambridge: Cambridge University Press.

Goldstone, Jack, and Charles Tilly. 2001. "Threat (and Opportunity): Popular Action and State Response in the Dynamic of Contentious Action." Pp. 179-194 in *Silence and Voice in the Study of Contentious Politics*, R. Aminzade, J. Goldstone, D. McAdam, E. Perry, W. Sewell, S. Tarrow, and C. Tilly, eds. Cambridge: Cambridge University Press.

Gómez Calcaño, Luis, and Margarita López Maya. 1990. *El Tejido de Penélope. La Reforma del Estado en Venezuela (1984-1988)*. Caracas: CENDES-APUCV-IPP.

González de la Rocha, M. 2000. "Private Adjustments: Household Responses to the Erosion of Work." UNDP Paper Series.

González, Luis Armando, and Luis Alvarenga. 2002. "La Huelga en el Sector Salud: Consideraciones Políticas." *Estudios Centroamericanos* 57 (649-650): 1140-1143.

Goodwin, Jeff. 2001. *No Other Way Out: States and Revolutionary Movements, 1945-1991*. New York: Cambridge University Press.

Goodwin, Jeff, and James M. Jasper. 1999. "Caught in a Winding, Snarling Vine: The Structural Bias of Political Process Theory." *Sociological Forum* 14 (1): 27-55.

———. Eds. 2004. *Rethinking Social Movements: Structure, Meaning, and Emotion*. Boulder: Rowman & Littlefield.

Goodwin, Jeff, James Jasper, and Francesca Polletta, eds. 2001. *Passionate Politics. Emotions and Social Movements*. Chicago: Chicago University Press.

Gould, Roger. 1995. *Insurgent Identities: Class, Community, and Protest in Paris from 1848 to the Commune*. Chicago: University of Chicago Press.

Granovetter, Mark S. 1973. "The Strength of Weak Ties." *American Journal of Sociology* 78 (6): 1360-1380.

Graziano Da Silva, José. 1982. *A Modernização Dolorosa: Estrutura Agrária, Fronteira Agrícola e Trabalhadores Rurais no Brasil*. Rio de Janeiro: Zahar Editores.

Green, Duncan. 2003. *Silent Revolution: The Rise and Crisis of Market Economics in Latin America*, 2nd ed. London: Latin American Bureau.

Greenhouse, Steven. 1997. "Accord to Combat Sweatshop Labor Faces Obstacles." *New York Times*, April 13.

Guidry, John A., and Mark Q. Sawyer. 2003. "Contentious Pluralism: The Public Sphere and Democracy." *Perspective on Politics* 1: 273-289.

Guidry, John A., Michael D. Kennedy, and Mayer N. Zald. 2000. "Globalizations and Social

Movements." Pp. 1-32 in *Globalizations and Social Movements: Culture, Power, and the Transnational Public Sphere*. John A. Guidry, Michael D. Kennedy, and Mayer N. Zald, eds. Ann Arbor: University of Michigan Press.

Gurr, Ted. 1970. *Why Men Rebel*. Princeton, NJ: Princeton University Press.

Gutmann, Matthew C. 2002. *The Romance of Democracy: Compliant Defiance in Contemporary Mexico*. Berkeley: University of California Press.

Haber, Paul. 1994. "Political Change in Durango: The Role of National Solidarity." In *Transforming State-Society Relations in Mexico: The National Solidarity Strategy*, W.A. Cornelius, A. L. Craig, and J. Fox, eds. San Diego, CA: Center for U.S.-Mexico Studies.

Haggard, Stephan. 1985. "The Politics of Adjustment: Lessons from the IMF's Extended Fund Facility." *International Organization* 39 (3): 505-534.

Halberstam, David. 1998. *The Children*. New York: Ballantine.

Hamel, Pierre, Henri Lustiger-Thaler, Jan Nederveen Pieterse, and Sasha Roseneil. 2001. "Introduction: The Shifting Frames of Collective Action." Pp 1-18 in *Globalization and Social Movements*, Pierre Hamel, Henri Lustiger-Thaler, Jan Nederveen Pieterse, and Sasha Roseneil, eds. New York: Palgrave.

Hanson, Susan, and Geraldine Pratt. 1995. *Gender, Work, and Space*. New York: Routledge.

Harnecker, Marta. 2003. "El Salvador: Un partido al servicio de los movimientos sociales." *Rebelión* (October 10).

Harris, Richard L., and Seid, Melinda J. 2000. "Critical Perspectives on Globalization and Neoliberalism in the Developing Countries." *Journal of Developing Societies* 16 (1): 1-26.

Harvey, David. 1990. *The Condition of Postmodernity: An Inquiry into the Origins of Cultural Change*. Cambridge: Blackwell.

Harvey, Neil. 1998a. *The Chiapas Rebellion: The Struggle for Land and Democracy*. Durham: Duke University Press.

———. 1998b. "The Zapatistas, Radical Democratic Citizenship, and Women's Struggles." *Social Politics* 5 (2): 158-187.

Havemann, Paul. 2000. "Enmeshed in the Web? Indigenous Peoples' Rights in the Network Society." Pp. 18-32 in *Global Social Movements*, Robin Cohen and Shirin M. Rai, eds. London: The Athlone Press.

Heller, Peter S. 1988. "The Implications of Fund-Supported Adjustment Programs for Poverty." Washington, DC: IMF (Occasional Paper # 58).

Hellman, Judith Adler. 1992. "The Study of New Social Movements in Latin America and the Question of Autonomy." Pp. 52-61 in *The Making of Social Movements in Latin America*, A. Escobar and S. Alvarez, eds. Boulder, CO: Westview Press.

———. 1994. "Mexican Popular Movements, Clientelism, and the Process of Democratization." *Latin American Perspectives* 21 (2): 124-142.

———. 1997. "Structural Adjustment in Mexico and the Dog That Didn't Bark." *CERLAC Working Paper Series*. Toronto: Centre for Research on Latin America and the Caribbean.

Henisz, Witold J., Bennet A. Zelner, and Mauro Guillén. 2005. "The Worldwide Diffusion of Market-Oriented Infrastructure Reform." *American Sociological Review* 70 (6): 871-897.

Hernández, Horténsia. 1996. SIOAC presentation at Maclovio Rojas community meeting. Tijuana, Baja California, Mexico. October.

Hernández, Viviana M. Abreu. 2002. "The Mothers of the Plaza de Mayo: A Peace Movement." *Peace & Change* 23:385-411.

Hillman, Richard. 1994. *Democracy for the Privileged. Crisis and Transition in Venezuela*. Boulder, CO: Lynne Reiner.

Holloway, John. 1998. "Dignity's Revolt." Pp. 159-198 in *Zapatista! Reinventing Revolution in Mexico*, John Holloway and Eloína Peláez, eds. London: Pluto Press.

Holloway, John, and Eloína Peláez. 1998. "Introduction: Reinventing Revolution." Pp. 1-18 in *Zapatista! Reinventing Revolution in Mexico,* John Holloway and Eloína Peláez, eds. London: Pluto Press.

Holston, James. 1991. "The Misrule of Law: Land and Usurpation in Brazil." *Comparative Studies in Society and History* 33 (4): 695-725.

Holzner, Claudio A. 2002. "Poverty of Democracy: Political Opportunities and Political Participation of the Poor in Mexico." Ph.D. diss., University of Michigan.

Houtzager, Peter P. 1997. "Caught Between State and Church: Popular Movements in the Brazilian Countryside, 1964-1989." Ph.D. diss., University of California, Berkeley.

Houtzager, Peter P., and Markus J. Kurtz. 2000. "The Institutional Roots of Popular Mobilization: State Transformation and Rural Politics in Brazil and Chile, 1960-1995." *Comparative Studies in Society and History* 422: 394-424.

Human Rights Watch, Women's Rights Project. 1996. *Mexico. No Guarantees: Sex Discrimination in Mexico's Maquiladora Sector*. New York: Human Rights Watch.

Hunt, Scott A., Robert D. Benford, and David A. Snow. 1994. "Identity Fields: Framing Processes and the Social Construction of Movement Identities." Pp. 185-208 in *New Social Movements: From Ideology to Identity*, Enrique Laraña, Hank Johnston, and Joseph R. Gusfield, eds. Philadelphia, PA: Temple University Press.

Indymedia-Chiapas. 2001. San Cristóbal de las Casas, Chiapas, Mexico. E-mail interview, November 1.

INEGI. 1996. "Cuaderno Estadístico Municipal: Oaxaca de Juárez." Aguascalientes: INEGI.

Iñigo Carrera, Nicolas. 1999. "Fisonomía de las Huelgas Generales de la Década de 1990." *PIMSA 1999*: 155-73.

Iñiguez, A., and A. Sanchez. 1996. "El conurbano bonaerense y la provincia de Buenos Aires: Condensación de la tragedia nacional de la desocupación y la subocupación." *Cuadernos del IBAP* 7: 1-32.

Instituto Brasileiro de Geografia e Estatísticas (IBGE). 1990. *Censos Econômicos-1985*, two volumes. Rio de Janeiro: Brazilian Institute for Geography and Statistics.

International Labor Organization (ILO). 2003. "Employment and Social Policy in Respect of Export Porcessing Zones." Report of ILO Governing Body (March). Geneva: ILO.

Jasper, James M. 1997. *The Art of Moral Protest: Culture, Biography, and Creativity in Social Movements*. Chicago and London: University of Chicago Press.

Jenkins, J. Craig. 1995. "Social Movements, Political Representation and the State: An Agenda and Comparative Framework." Pp. 14-34 in *The Politics of Social Protest: Comparative Perspectives on States and Social Movements*, J. Craig Jenkins and Bert Klandermans, eds. Minneapolis: University of Minnesota Press.

Jenkins, J. Craig, and Bert Klandermans. 1995. "The Politics of Social Protest." Pp. 1-13 in *The Politics of Social Protest: Comparative Perspectives on States and Social Movements*, J. Craig Jenkins and Bert Klanderman, eds. Minneapolis: University of Minnesota Press.

Jenkins, J. Craig., and Charles Perrow. 1977. "Insurgency of the Powerless: Farm Worker Movements (1946-1972)." *American Sociological Review* 42: 249-268.

Jenkins, J. Craig, and Kurt Schock. 1992. "Global Structures and Political Processes in the Study of Domestic Political Conflict." *Annual Review of Sociology* 18: 161-185.

Jenkins, J. Craig, and William Form. 2005. "Social Movements and Social Change." Pp. 331-349 in *The Handbook of Political Sociology: States, Civil Societies, and Globalization*, T. Janoski, R. Alford, A. Hicks, and M. Schwartz, eds. New York: Cambridge University Press.

Jennings, M. Kent, and Ellen Ann Andersen. 2003. "The Importance of Social and Political Context: The Case of AIDS Activism." *Political Behavior* 25: 177-199.

Johnston, Hank. 2002. "Verification and Proof in Frame and Discourse Analysis." Pp. 62-91 in *Methods of Social Movement Research*, Bert Klandermans and Suzanne Staggenborg, eds. Minneapolis: University of Minnesota Press.

———. 2005. "Talking the Walk: Speech Acts and Resistance in Authoritarian Regimes." Pp. 108-137 in *Repression and Mobilization*, Christian Davenport, Hank Johnston, and Carol Mueller, eds. Minneapolis: University of Minnesota Press.

Johnston, Hank, and Józef Figa. 1988. "The Church and Political Opposition: Comparative Perspectives on Mobilization against Authoritarian Regimes." *Journal for the Scientific Study of Religion* 12 (1): 32-47.

Johnston, Hank, and Bert Klandermans, eds. 1995. *Social Movements and Culture*. Minneapolis: University of Minnesota Press.

Johnston, Hank, and Aili Aarelaid-Tart. 2000. "Generations, Microcohorts, and Long-Term Mobilization: The Estonian National Movement, 1940-1991." *Sociological Perspective* 43:

671-698.

Jonas, Susanna. 2000. *Of Centaurs and Doves: Guatemala's Peace Process*. Boulder, CO: Westview Press.

Jonas, Susanne. 1991. *The Battle for Guatemala: Rebels, Death Squads, and U.S. Power*. Boulder, CO: Westview Press.

Kalman, R.E. 1980. "A System-Theoretic Critique of Dynamic Economic Models," *International Journal of Policy Analysis and Information Systems* 4 (1): 3-22.

Kamel, Rachel, and Anya Hoffman, eds. 1999. *The Maquiladora Reader: Cross-Border Organizing Since NAFTA*. Philadelphia, PA: American Friends Service Committee.

Keck, Margaret E. 1992. *The Workers' Party and Democratization in Brazil*. New Haven, CT: Yale University Press.

Keck, Margaret, and Kathryn Sikkink. 1998a. *Activists Beyond Borders*. Ithaca, NY: Cornell University Press.

———. 1998b. "Transnational Advocacy Networks in the Movement Society." Pp. 217-238 in *The Social Movement Society: Contentious Politics for a New Century*, David S. Meyer and Sidney Tarrow, eds. Lanham, MD: Rowman & Littlefield.

———. 1999. "Transnational Advocacy Networks in International and Regional Politics." *International Social Science Journal* 51 (1): 89-101.

———. 2000. "Historical Precursors to Modern Transnational Social Movements and Networks." Pp. 35-53 in *Globalizations and Social Movements: Culture, Power, and the Transnational Public Sphere*. John A. Guidry, Michael D. Kennedy, and Mayer N. Zald, eds. Ann Arbor: University of Michigan Press.

Kellner, Douglas. 2002. "Theorizing Globalization." *Sociological Theory* 20 (3): 285-305.

Kendall, M. G. 1976. *Time Series*, 2nd ed. London: Charles Griffin.

Kentor, Jeffrey. 2001. "The Long Term Effects of Globalization on Population Growth, Inequality, and Economic Development." *Social Problems* 48(4): 435-456.

Kepne, Alison. 2000. "For Two Students, Spring Break Trips Offer a Glimpse into Clothing Factories." *The Digital Collegian*, April 13.

Khagram, Riker, and Kathryn Sikkink. 2002. *Restructuring World Politics: Transnational Social Movements, Network and Norms*. Minneapolis: University of Minnesota Press.

Khan, Mohsin S., and Malcolm D. Knight. 1985. "Fund-Supported Adjustment Programs and Economic Growth." Washington, DC: IMF.

Kidd, Dusty. 2001. "Kukdong-Mexmode Update from Nike." Available online at http://www.nikebiz. org. November 30.

Kielbowicz, Richard B., and Clifford Scherer. 1986. "The Role of the Press in the Dynamics of Social Movements." *Research in Social Movements, Conflicts and Change* 9: 71-96.

Klachko, Paula. 1999. "Cutral Co y Plaza Huincul. El Primer Corte de Ruta." *PIMSA 1999*: 121-154.

Klandermans, Bert. 1997. *The Social Psychology of Protest*. Oxford: Blackwell.

———. 2004. "The Demand and Supply of Participation: Social Psychological Correlates of Participation in Social Movements." Pp. 360-379 in *The Blackwell Companion to Social Movements*, D. Snow, S. Soule and H. Kriesi, eds. Malden, MA: Blackwell.

Kline, Harvey F. 1995. *Colombia: Democracy Under Assault*, 2nd ed. Boulder, CO: Westview Press.

Kohan, Aníbal. 2002. *A las Calles! Una Historia de los Movimientos Piqueteros y Caceroleros de los '90 al 2002*. Buenos Aires: Ediciones Colihue.

Koopmans, Ruud. 2004. "Political. Opportunity. Structure. Some Splitting to Balance the Lumping." Pp. 61-73 in *Rethinking Social Movements*, Jeff Goodwin and James Jasper, eds. Boulder, CO: Rowman & Littlefield.

Koopmans, Ruud, and Paul Statham. 1999. "Political Claims Analysis: Integrating Protest Event and Political Discourse Approaches." *Mobilization* 4 (1): 40-51.

Köpke, Ronald. 2000. "Las experiencias del equipo de monitoreo independiente de Honduras." Pp. 100-119 in *Códigos de Conducta y Monitoreo en la Industria de Confección: Experiences Internacionales y Regionales*, Ronald Köpke, Norma Molina, and Carolina Quinteros, eds. San Salvador, El Salvador: Fundación Böll.

Korner, P., G. Maass, T. Siebold, and R. Tetzlaff. 1986. *The IMF and the Debt Crisis*. London: Zed Books.

Korten, David. 2001. *When Corporations Rule the World*. Bloomfield, IN: Kumarian Press.

Korzeniewicz, Roberto Patricio, and William C. Smith. 2000. "Poverty, Inequality, and Growth in Latin America: Searching for the High Road to Globalization." *Latin American Research Review* 35 (3): 7-54.

———. 2004. "Redes Regionales y Movimientos Sociales Transnacionales en Patrones Emergentes de Colaboración y Conflicto en las Américas." *América Latina Hoy* 36: 101-

Kriesberg, Louis. 1997. "Social Movements and Global Transformation." Pp. 3-18 in *Transnational Social Movements and Global Politics: Solidarity Beyond the State*, Jackie Smith, Charles Chatfield, and Ron Pagnucco, eds. Syracuse: Syracuse University Press.

Kriesi, Hanspeter. 1995. "The Political Opportunity Structure of New Social Movements: Its Impact on their Mobilization." Pp. 167-198 in *The Politics of Social Protest: Comparative Perspectives on States and Social Movements*, J. Craig Jenkins and Bert Klandermans, eds. Minneapolis: University of Minnesota Press.

———. 2004. "Political Context and Opportunity." Pp. 67-90 in *The Blackwell Companion to Social Movements*, David Snow, Sarah Soule, and Hanspeter Kriesi, eds. Malden, MA: Blackwell.

Kriesi, Hanspeter, Ruud Koopmans, Jan Willem Duyvendak, and Marco G. Giugni. 1995. *New Social Movements in Western Europe: A Comparative Analysis*. Minneapolis: University of Minnesota Press.

Kurzman, Charles. 1996. "Structural Opportunity and Perceived Opportunity in Social Movement Theory: The Iranian Revolution of 1979." *American Sociological Review* 61 (1): 153-170.

La Botz, Dan. 1998. "Mexico's Labor Year in Review." *Mexican Labor News and Analysis* 3 (1): 3-16.

———. 2001. "Debate over Maquiladoras Takes New Turn: The China Question." *Mexican Labor News and Analysis* 6 (10): 1.

———. 2005. "Social Statistics." *Mexican Labor News and Analysis* 10 (6): 15.

Laclau, Ernesto, and Chantal Mouffe. 1985. *Hegemony and Socialist Strategy*. London: Verso.

LaFeber, Walter. 1993. *Inevitable Revolutions: The United States in Central America*, 2nd edition. New York: W.W. Norton and Co.

Lamas, Marta, Alicia Martínez, María Luisa Tarrés, and Esperanza Tuñon. 1995. "Building Bridges: The Growth of Popular Feminism in Mexico." Pp. 324-347 in *The Challenge of Local Feminisms: Women's Movements in Global Perspective*, Amrita Basu, ed. Boulder, CO: Westview Press.

Larner, Wendy. 2000. "Neo-liberalism: Policy, ideology, and governmentality." *Studies in Political Economy* 2 (63): 5-25.

Las Madres de Plaza de Mayo. 2002. "La resistencia tuvo hijos." *Periodico Mensual de la Asociación Madres de Plaza de Mayo*, March.

Laufer, Ruben, and Claudio Spiguel. 1999. "Las 'Puebladas' Argentinas a partir del 'Santiagueñazo' De 1993. Tradición Histórica y Nuevas Formas de Lucha." Pp. 15-44 in *Lucha Popular, Democracia, Neoliberalismo: Protesta Popular en América Latina en los Años del Ajuste*, Margarita Lopez Maya, ed. Caracas: Nueva Sociedad.

Lawson, Joseph Chappell H. 2002. *Building the Fourth Estate: Democratization and the Rise of a Free Press in Mexico*. Berkeley: University of California Press.

Le Bot, Yvon. 1997. *El sueño zapatista*. Barcelona: Plaza y Janés.

Lee, Ching Kwan. 2000. "The 'Revenge of History': Collective Memories and Labor Protests in North-Eastern China." *Ethnography* 1 (2): 217-37.

Lefebvre, Henrí. 1991 [1974]. *The Production of Space*. Cambridge, MA: Basil Blackwell.

Lehmann, David. 1990. *Democracy and Development in Latin America: Economics, Politics and Religion in the Post-War Period*. Philadelphia: Temple University Press.

Levine, Daniel H. 1992. *Popular Voices in Latin American Catholicism*. Princeton: Princeton University Press.

———. 2006. "Civil Society and Political Decay in Venezuela." In *Civil Society and Democracy in Latin America*, R. Feinberg, C. Waisman, and L. Zamosc, eds. New York: Palgrave Macmillan.

Levine, Daniel H., and Catalina Romero. 2002. "Urban Citizen Movements and Disempowerment in Peru and Venezuela." Paper presented at "The Crises of Democratic Representation in the Andes," Kellogg Institute, University of Notre Dame.

Levy, Daniel, and Kathleen Bruhn, with Emilio Zebadúa. 2001. *Mexico: The Struggle for Democratic Development*. Berkeley: University of California Press.

Lewis, Tammy L. 2000. "Transnational Conservation Movement Organizations: Shaping the Protected Area Systems of Less Developed Countries." *Mobilization: An International Journal* 5: 105-123.

Lewis, Tom. 2004. "Bolivia: The Gas War." *International Socialist Review* 36: 48-52.

Lins, Carlos. 1996. *Programa de Ação para o Desenvolvimento da Zona da Mata do Nordeste*. Recife, PE: Superintendent for the Development of the Northeast.

Linz, Juan J., and Alfred Stepan. 1996. *Problems of Democratic Transition and Consolidation*. Baltimore, MD: Johns Hopkins University Press.

Lipset, Seymor Martin. 1981 (1960). *Political Man: The Social Bases of Politics*. Baltimore, MD: Johns Hopkins University Press.

Lodola, Germán. 2002. "Social Protests under Industrial Reorganization Process. Argentina in the Nineties." Manuscript, Department of Political Science, University of Pittsburgh.

López Barcenas, Francisco. 1998. "Constitución y Derechos Indígenas en Oaxaca." *Cuadernos Agrarios* 8 (16): 128-146.

López Maya, Margarita. 1999. *Lucha Popular, Democracia, Neoliberalismo: Protesta Popular en América Latina en los Años de Ajuste*. Caracas: Editorial Nueva Sociedad.

———. 2003a. "The Venezuelan *Caracazo* of 1989: Popular Protest and Institutional Weakness," *Journal of Latin American Studies* 35: 117-138.

———. 2003b. "Movilización, institucionalidad y legitimidad." *Revista Venezolana de Economía y Ciencias Sociales* 9: 211-228.

Lorde, Audre. 1984. "Age, Race, Class, and Sex: Women Redefining Experience." Pp. 114-123 in *Sister Outsider: Essays and Speeches by Audre Lorde*. Trumansburg, NY: Crossing Press.

Lozano, Claudio. 2001. "Contexto económico y político en la protesta social de la Argentina contemporánea." *Revista del Observatorio Social de América Latina* 5: 1-12.

Lummis, Douglas. 1996. *Radical Democracy*. Ithaca, NY: Cornell University Press.

Lustig, Nora. 1992. *Mexico, the Remaking of an Economy*. Washington, DC: Brookings Institution.

Macdonald, Barbara, with Cynthia Rich. 1983. *Look Me in the Eye: Old Women, Aging, and Ageism*. San Francisco: Spinsters, Ink.

MacEwan, Arthur. 1990. *Debt and Disorder*. New York: Monthly Review Press.

"Madres de Plaza de Mayo tomaron la Catedral Metropolitana." 2002. *La Nación*, June 5.

Maguire, Diarmuid. 1995. "Opposition Movements and Opposition Parties: Equal Partners or Dependent Relations in the Struggle for Power and Reform?" Pp. 199-228 in *The Politics of Social Protest: Comparative Perspectives on States and Social Movements*, J. Craig Jenkins and Bert Klandermans, eds. Minneapolis: University of Minnesota Press.

Mainwaring, Scott. 1986. *The Catholic Church and Politics in Brazil, 1916-1985*. Stanford, CA: Stanford University Press.

Mainwaring, Scott, and Eduardo Viola. 1984. "New Social Movements, Political Culture and Democracy: Brazil and Argentina in the 1980s." *Telos* 61: 17-51.

Malamud, Diana. 2002. "Una voz en el horror." *Página 12*, April 30.

Maney, Gregory M. 2001a. "Transnational Structures and Protest: Linking Theories and Assessing Evidence." *Mobilization* 6 (1): 83-100.

———. 2001b. "Rival Transnational Networks and Indigenous Rights: The San Blas Kuna in Panama and the Yanomani in Brazil." *Research in Social Movements, Conflicts and Change* 23: 103-144.

Manley, Michael. 1987. *Up the Down Escalator: Development and the International Economy: A Jamaican Case Study*. Washington, DC: Howard University Press.

Mann, Michael. 2000. "Has Globalization Ended the Rise of the Nation-State?" Pp. 136-147 in *The Global Transformations Reader: An Introduction to the Globalization Debate*, David Held and Anthony McGrew, eds. Cambridge: Polity Press.

Mannheim, Karl. 1952. "The Problem of Generations." Pp. 276-320 in *Essays on the Sociology of Knowledge*, P. Kecskemeti, ed. London: Routledge and Kegan Paul.

Mansbridge, Jane, and Aldon Morris, eds. 2001. *Oppositional Consciousness. The Subjective Roots of Protest*. Chicago: University of Chicago Press.

Maquila Solidarity Network. 2001. "Nike Concedes Victory: Sportswear Giant Promises to Place Orders with Unionized Factory." December 12.

Marchand, Marianne, and Anne Sisson Runyan, eds. 2000. *Gender and Global Restructuring: Sightings, Sites, and Resistances*. New York: Routledge.

Marks, Gary, and Doug McAdam. 1999. "On the Relationship of Political Opportunities to the Form of Collective Action: The Case of the European Union." In *Social Movements in a Globalizing World*, Donatella della Porta, Hanspeter Kriesi, and Dieter Rucht, eds. London: Macmillan.

Marshall, Monty G., and Keith Jaggers. 2002. *Polity IV Project*. College Park, MD: Integrated Network for International Development and Conflict Management.

Martin, David. 2000. Interview in Denver, CO, October 24.

Massey, Doreen. 1984. *Spatial Division of Labour: Social Structures and the Geography of Production*. London: Macmillan.

———. 1994. *Space, Place, and Gender*. Cambridge: Polity Press.

Maybury-Lewis, Biorn. 1994. *The Politics of the Possible: The Brazilian Rural Workers' Trade Union Movement, 1964-1985*. Philadelphia, PA: Temple University Press.

McAdam, Doug. [1982] 1999. *Political Process and the Development of Black Insurgency, 1930-1970*. Chicago: University of Chicago Press.

———. 1986. "Recruitment to High-Risk Activism: The Case of Freedom Summer." *American Journal of Sociology* 92: 64-90.

———. 1988. *Freedom Summer*. New York: Oxford University Press.

———. 1994. "Culture and Social Movements." Pp. 36-57 in *New Social Movements: From Ideology to Identity*, Enrique Laraña, Hank Johnston, and Joseph Gusfield, eds. Philadelphia, PA: Temple University Press.

———. 1996a. "Conceptual Origins, Current Problems, Future Directions." Pp. 23-40 in *Comparative Perspectives on Social Movements: Political Opportunities, Mobilizing Structures, and Cultural Framings*, Doug McAdam, John D. McCarthy, and Mayer N. Zald, eds. Cambridge: Cambridge University Press.

———. 1996b. "The Framing Function of Movement Tactics: Strategic Dramaturgy in the American Civil Rights Movement," Pp. 338-355 in *Comparative Perspectives on Social Movements: Political Opportunities, Mobilizing Structures, and Cultural Framings*, Doug McAdam, John D. McCarthy, and Mayer N. Zald, eds. Cambridge: Cambridge University Press.

———. 1998. "On the International Origins of Domestic Political Opportunities." Pp. 251-267 in *Social Movements and Political Institutions in the United States*, Anne Costain and Andrew McFarland, eds. Boulder, CO: Rowman & Littlefield.

McAdam, Doug, John D. McCarthy, and Mayer N. Zald, eds. 1996. *Comparative Perspectives on Social Movements: Political Opportunities, Mobilizing Structures, and Cultural Framings*. Cambridge, England: Cambridge University Press.

McAdam, Doug, Sidney G. Tarrow, and Charles Tilly. 2001. *Dynamics of Contention*. New York: Cambridge University Press.

———. 1996. "To Map Contentious Politics." *Mobilization* 1 (1): 17-34.

McCarthy, John D. 1996. "Constraints and Opportunities in Adopting, Adapting, and Inventing." Pp. 141-151 in *Comparative Perspectives on Social Movements: Political Opportunities, Mobilizing Structures, and Cultural Framings*. Doug McAdam, John D. McCarthy, and Mayer N. Zald, eds. Cambridge: Cambridge University Press.

———. 1997. "The Globalization of Social Movement Theory." Pp. 243-259 in *Transnational Social Movements and Global Politics: Solidarity beyond the State*, Jackie Smith, Charles

Chatfield, and Ron Pagnucco, eds. Syracuse, NY: Syracuse University Press.

McCarthy, John D., Clark McPhail, and Jackie Smith. 1996. "Images of Protest: Dimensions of Selection Bias in Media Coverage of Washington Demonstrations, 1982 and 1991." *American Sociological Review* 61: 478-499.

McCarthy, John D., Clark McPhail, Jackie Smith, and Luis J. Crishock. 1998. "Electronic and Print Media Representations of Washington, D.C. Demonstrations, 1982 and 1991: A Demography of Description Bias." In *Acts of Dissent: New Developments in the Study of Protest*, Dieter Rucht, Ruud Koopmans, and Friedhelm Neidhardt, eds. Berlin: Edition Sigma.

McCarthy, John D., and Mayer N. Zald. 1973. *The Trend of Social Movements in America: Professionalization and Resource Mobilization.* Morristown, NJ: General Learning Press.

———. 1977. "Resource Mobilization and Social Movements: A Partial Theory." *American Journal of Sociology* 82 (6): 1212-1241.

McMichael, Philip. 2000. *Development and Social Change.* Thousand Oaks, CA: Pine Forge Press.

Medeiros, Leonilde S. d. 1989. *História dos Movimentos Sociais no Campo.* Rio de Janeiro: FASE.

Melucci, Alberto. 1996. *Challenging Codes: Collective Action in the Information Age.* Cambridge: Cambridge University Press.

Mendez, Jennifer Bickham. 2002. "Creating Alternatives from a Gender Perspective: Central American Women's Transnational Organizing for Maquila Workers' Rights." Pp. 121-141 in *Women's Activism and Globalization: Linking Local Struggles and Transnational Politics,* Nancy A. Naples and Manisha Desai, eds. New York: Routledge Press.

———. 2005. *From the Revolution to the Maquiladoras: Gender, Labor, and Globalization in Nicaragua.* Durham, NC: Duke University Press.

Meyer, David S. 2004. "Tending the Vineyard: Cultivating Political Process Research." Pp. 47-59 in *Rethinking Social Movements,* Jeff Goodwin and James Jasper, eds. Boulder, CO: Rowman & Littlefield.

Meyer, David S., and Debra C. Minkoff. 2004. "Conceptualizing Political Opportunity." *Social Forces* 82 (4): 1457-1492.

Meza, Humberto. 1997. "Trabajadores apoyan Zona Franca Industrial." *La Tribuna,* November 25.

Meza, Patricia. 2003. "Alianza Ciudadana Exige Libertad de Capturados en Troncal del Norte." *Co-Latino,* April 14, p. 5.

MHSSN (Maquiladora Health and Safety Support Network). 2001. 5 (4). December 9.

Michels, Robert. 1962. *Political Parties. A Sociological Study of the Oligarchical Tendencies of Modern Democracy.* New York: Collier Books.

Migdal, Joel S. 1975. *Peasants, Politics, and Revolution: Pressures Toward Political and Social Change in the Third World.* Princeton, NJ: Princeton University Press.

Miller, Byron A. 1992. "Collective Action and Rational Choice: Place, Community, and the Limits to Individual Self-Interest." *Economic Geography* 68 (1): 22-42.

———. 2000. *Geography and Social Movements: Comparing Antinuclear Activism in the Boston Area.* Minneapolis, MN: University of Minnesota Press.

Ministerio Extraordinário da Política Fundiária (MEPF). 1998. *Programa Integrado de Reforma Na Zona da Mata Nordestina.* Recife, PE: MEPF.

Miyagiwa, K. 1993. "On the Impossibility of Immiserizing Growth." *International Economic Journal* 7 (2): 1-13.

Moaddel, Mansoor. 1994. "Political Conflict in the World Economy: A Cross-National Analysis of Modernization and World-System Theories." *American Sociological Review* 59 (2): 276-303.

Molina, Norma, and Aída Carolina Quinteros. 2000. "El monitoreo independiente en El Salvador." Pp. 82-99 in *Códigos de Conducta y Monitoreo en la Industria de Confección: Experiences Internacionales y Regionales,* Ronald Köpke, Norma Molina, and Carolina Quinteros, eds. San Salvador, El Salvador: Fundación Böll.

Molotch, Harvey. 1979. "Media and Movements." Pp. 71-93 in *The Dynamics of Social Movements,* Mayer N. Zald and John D. McCarthy, eds. Cambridge, MA: Winthrop.

Molyneux, Maxine. 1985. "Mobilization Without Emancipation? Women's Interests, the State, and Revolution in Nicaragua." *Feminist Studies* 11: 227-254.

———. 1998. "Analysing Women's Movements." *Development and Change* 29: 219-245.

Monsiváis, Carlos, and Hermann Bellinghausen. 2001. "Marcos a Fox: Queremos garantías; no nos tragamos eso de que todo cambió," *La Jornada*, January 8.

Montgomery, Tommie Sue. 1997. "El Salvador's Extraordinary Elections." *LASA Forum* 28 (1): 4-8.

Morris, Aldon D., and Carol McClurg Mueller, eds. 1992. *Frontiers in Social Movement Theory*. New Haven, CT: Yale University Press.

Morris, Aldon. 1984. *The Origins of the Civil Rights Movement: Black Communities Organizing for Change*. New York: Free Press.

Mouffe, Chantal. 1993. *The Return of the Political*. London: Verso.

Movimiento de Mujeres Trabajadoras y Desempleadeas, "María Elena Cuadra" (MEC). 1999. "Diagnóstico sobre las condiciones socio laborales de las Empresas de las Zonas Francas." Managua: Movimiento de Mujeres Trabajadoras y Desempleadas, "María Elena Cuadra."

MPMLF, (Madres de Plaza de Mayo Línea Fundadora). 2003. "Historia breve," retrieved April 4, 2003, from www.madreslineafundadora.org.ar

———. 2005. "Nuestro 28° Aniversario: Más ancianas, sí, pero más animosas," retrieved June 1, 2005, from http://www.madresfundadoras.org.ar/opinion.shtml?AA_SL_Session= cedalcc9 e159bdb8c46a9fea2a79c1de&x=37184

Müller, Gerard. 1985. *A Dinâmica da Agricultura Paulista*. São Paulo: Foundation for the State System of Data Analysis.

Murillo, Maria Victoria. 2001. *Labor Unions, Partisan Coalitions, and Market Reforms in Latin America*. Cambridge: Cambridge University Press.

Nahmad Sittón, Salomón, ed. 1994. *Fuentes Etnológicas Para el Estudio de los Pueblos Ayuuk (Mixes) del Estado de Oaxaca*. Oaxaca: CIESAS-Oaxaca, Instituto Oaxaqueño de las Culturas.

Naím, Moisés, and Ramón Piñango. 1984. *El caso Venezuela: una ilusión de armonía*. Caracas: Ediciones IESA.

Naím, Moisés. 2000. "The FP Interview: Lori's War." *Foreign Policy* (Spring): 29-55.

Naples, Nancy A. 2002. "The Challenges and Possibilities of Transnational Feminist Praxis." Pp. 267-281 in *Women's Activism and Globalization: Linking Local Struggles and Transnational Politics,* Nancy A. Naples and Manisha Desai, eds. New York: Routledge.

Naples, Nancy A. and Manisha Desai, eds. 2002. *Women's Activism and Globalization: Linking Local Struggles and Transnational Politics*. New York: Routledge.

Nash, June. 1992. "Interpreting Social Movements: Bolivian Resistance to Economic Conditions Imposed by the International Monetary Fund." *American Ethnologist* 19 (2): 275-293.

Nash, June, and Helen I. Safa. 1986. *Women and Change in Latin America*. South Hadley, MA: Bergin and Garvey.

Navarro, Marysa. 1989. "The Personal Is Political: Las Madres de Plaza de Mayo." Pp. 241-258 in *Power and Popular Protest: Latin American Social Movements*, Susan Eckstein, ed. Berkeley: University of California Press.

Navarro, Zander. 2000. "Breaking New Ground: Brazil's MST." *NACLA Report on the Americas* 33 (5): 36-39.

Needleman, Ruth. 1998. "Women Workers: Strategies for Inclusion and Rebuilding." Pp. 151-70 in *A New Labor Movement for a New Century*, Gregory Mantsios, ed. New York: Monthly Review Press.

Nef, Jorge, and Robles, Wilder. 2000. "Globalization, Neoliberalism, and the State of Underdevelopment in the New Periphery." *Journal of Developing Societies* 16 (1): 27-48.

Nepstad, Sharon Erickson. 1997. "The Process of Cognitive Liberation: Cultural Synapses, Links, and Frame Contradictions in the US-Central American Peace Movement." *Sociological Inquiry* 67 (4): 470-487.

———. 2001. "Creating Transnational Solidarity: The Use of Narrative in the U.S.-Central America Peace Movement." *Mobilization: An International Journal* 6: 21-36.

Noakes, John A. and Hank Johnston. 2005. "Frames of Protest: A Road Map to a Perspective."

Pp. 1-29 in *Frames of Protest: Social Movements and the Framing Perspective*, Hank Johnston and John A. Noakes, eds. Lanham, MD: Rowman and Littlefield.

Noonan, Rita K. 1995. "Women Against the State: Political Opportunities and Collective Action Frames in Chile's Transition to Democracy." *Sociological Forum* 10 (1): 81-111.

Oberschall, Anthony. 1973. *Social Conflict and Social Movements*. Englewood Cliffs, NJ: Prentice-Hall.

———. 1993. *Social Movements: Ideologies, Interests and Identities*. New Brunswick, NJ: Transaction.

———. 1996. "Opportunities and Framing in the Eastern European Revolts of 1989." Pp. 93-121 in *Comparative Perspectives on Social Movements: Political Opportunities, Mobilizing Structures, and Cultural Framings*, Doug McAdam, John D. McCarthy, and Mayer N. Zald, eds. New York: Cambridge University Press.

O'Brien, Robert, Anne Goetz, Jan Scholte, and Marc Williams. 2000. *Contesting Global Governance: Multilateral Economic Institutions and Global Social Movements*. New York: Cambridge University Press.

O'Donnell, Guillermo A., and Philippe C. Schmitter. 1986. *Transitions from Authoritarian Rule*. Baltimore, MD: Johns Hopkins University Press.

Olesen, Thomas. 2005a. *International Zapatismo: The Construction of Solidarity in the Age of Globalization*. London: Zed Books.

———. 2005b. "World Politics and Social Movements: The Janus Face of the Global Democratic Structure." *Global Society* 19 (2): 109-129.

Oliver, Pamela E., and Daniel J. Myers. 1999. "How Events Enter the Public Sphere: Conflict, Location, and Sponsorship in Local Newspaper Coverage of Public Events." *American Journal of Sociology* 105 (1): 38-87.

Olson, Mancur. 1971. *The Logic of Collective Action: Public Goods and the Theory of Groups*. Cambridge, MA: Harvard University Press.

Onimode, Bade, ed. 1989. *The IMF, The World Bank, and the African Debt*. London: Zed Press.

Organización Internacional de Trabajo. 1996. *La Situación Sociolaboral en las Zonas Francas y Maquiladoras de Centroamérica y República Dominicana*. San José, Costa Rica: Organización Internacional de Trabajo.

Orme, William, ed. 1997. *A Culture of Collusion: An Inside Look at the Mexican Press*. Miami, FL: North-South Center Press.

Ortner, Sherry B. 1995. "Resistance and the Problem of Ethnographic Refusal." *Comparative Studies of Society and History* 37 (1): 173-193.

Oviedo, Luis. 2001. *Una Historia del Movimiento Piquetero*. Buenos Aires: Ediciones Rumbos.

Oxhorn, Phillip D. 1991. "The Popular Sector Response to an Authoritarian Regime: Shantytown Organizations Since the Military Coup." *Latin American Perspectives* 18 (1): 66-91.

———. 1994. "Understanding Political Change after Authoritarian Rule: The Popular Sectors and Chile's New Democratic Regime." *Journal of Latin American Studies* 26 (3): 737-759.

———. 1995. *Organizing Civil Society*. University Park: Pennsylvania State University Press.

———. 1996. "Surviving the Return to 'Normalcy': Social Movements, Democratic Consolidation and Economic Restructuring." *International Review of Sociology* 6 (1): 117-134.

Oxhorn, Philip, and Graciela Ducatenzeiler. 1998. "Economic Reform and Democratization in Latin America." Pp. 3-19 in *What Kind of Democracy? What Kind of Market?: Latin America in the Age of Neoliberalism*, Phillip Oxhorn and Graciela Ducatenzeiler, eds. University Park, PA: The Pennsylvania State University Press.

Pacenza, Matt. 1996. "A People Dammed: The Chixoy Dam, Guatemalan Massacres and the World Bank." *Multinational Monitor*, July/August: 8-12.

Pagnucco, Ron. 1997. "The Transnational Strategies of the Service for Peace and Justice in Latin America." Pp. 123-138 in *Transnational Social Movements and Global Politics: Solidarity Beyond the State*, Jackie Smith, Charles Chatfield, and Ron Pagnucco, eds. Syracuse, NY: Syracuse University Press.

Paige, Jeffery M. 1975. *Agrarian Revolution: Social Movements and Export Agriculture in the Underdeveloped World*. New York: Free Press.

Paige, Jeffrey. 1997. *Coffee and Power: Revolution and the Rise of Democracy in Central Amer-*

ica. Cambridge, MA: Harvard University Press.

Palencia Prado, Tania. 1996. *Peace in the Making: Civil Groups in Guatemala*. London: Catholic Institute for International Relations.

Paredes Díaz, Jennyfer. 2005. "Diputados aprueban de urgencia nacional el TLC." *Prensa Libre*, March 11, p. 2.

Passy, Florence. 1999. "Supranational Political Opportunities as a Channel of Globalization of Political Conflicts: The Case of the Rights of Indigenous Peoples." In *Social Movements in a Globalizing World*, Donatella della Porta, Hanspeter Kriesi, and Dieter Rucht, eds. London: Macmillan.

Pastor, Manuel. 1987a. "The Effects of IMF Programs in the Third World: Debate and Evidence from Latin America." *World Development* 15 (2): 249-262.

———. 1987b. *The International Monetary Fund and Latin America: Economic Stabilization and Class Conflict*. Boulder, CO: Westview Press.

———. 1989. "Latin America, the Debt Crisis, and the International Monetary Fund." *Latin American Perspectives* 16 (1): 79-110.

Pateman, Carol. 1970. *Participation and Democracy*. Cambridge, UK: Cambridge University Press.

Paulilo, Maria. 1996. *Terra a Vista. . . e ao Longe*. Florianopolis, SC: Editora da Universidade Federal de Santa Catarina.

Paulson, Justin. 2001. E-mail interview, October 1.

Payne, Charles M. 1995. *I've Got the Light of Freedom: The Organizing Tradition and the Mississippi Freedom Struggle*. Berkeley: University of California Press.

Peña, Devon G. 1997. *The Terror of the Machine. Technology, Work, Gender, and Ecology on the U.S.-Mexico Border*. Austin, TX: Center for Mexican American Studies, University of Texas, Austin.

Peoples' Global Action. 2000. Available online at www.nadir.org/nadir/initiativ/agp/infopool /pgabulletin5en_history.htm.

Pereira, Anthony W. 1997. *The End of the Peasantry: The Rural Labor Movement in Northeast Brazil, 1961-1988*. Pittsburgh, PA: University of Pittsburgh Press.

Perelli, Carina. 1994. "Memoria de Sangre: Fear, Hope, and Disenchantment in Argentina." In *Remapping Memory: The Politics of TimeSpace*, J. Boyarin, ed. Minneapolis: University of Minnesota Press.

Petras, James. 1997. "Latin America: The Resurgence of the Left." *New Left Review* 223: 17-47.

Petras, James, and Henry Veltmeyer. 2002. "The Peasantry and the State in Latin America: A Troubled Past, an Uncertain Future." *Journal of Peasant Studies* 29 (3-4): 41-82.

Petrich, Blanche. 2001. "Monos blancos, fruto del desempleo en Europa." *La Jornada*, March 14.

Petrini, Evel. 2003. Personal interview conducted on June 6, Buenos Aires.

Pieterse, Jan Nederveen. 2001. "Globalization and Collective Action." Pp. 21-40 in *Globalization and Social Movements*, Pierre Hamel, Henri Lustiger-Thaley, Jan Nederveen Pieterse, and Sasha Roseneil, eds. New York: Palgrave.

Piven, Frances Fox, and Richard A. Cloward. 1979. *Poor People's Movements: Why They Succeed, How They Fail*. New York: Vintage Books.

———. 1993. *Regulating the Poor*, 2nd ed. New York: Vintage.

Polanyi, Karl. 1944. *The Great Transformation*. Boston: Beacon Press.

Poletto, Ivo. 1997. "O Movimento dos Trabalhadores Rurais Sem Terra e a Luta Pela Terra." *Cadernos de Estudos Sociologicos* 97: 14-28.

Politeia. 1989. Special issue on the *Caracazo*.

Pollack, Aaron. 1999. "A New 'Internationalism' in the Making: Encounters, Networks, Alliances." *Transnational Associations* 4: 205-217.

Polletta, Francesca. 1998a. "Contending Stories: Narrative in Social Movements." *Qualitative Sociology* 21 (4): 419-46.

———. 1998b. "'It Was Like a Fever'. . . Narrative and Identity in Social Protest." *Social Problems* 45 (2): 137-159.

Portes, Alejandro, and Kelly Hoffman. 2003. "Latin American Class Structures: Their Composition and Change During the Neoliberal Era." *Latin American Research Review* 38 (1): 41-82.

Provea. 1989 to 2002. *Situación de los derechos humanos (Annual Reports).* Caracas: Provea.

Putnam, Robert D. 1993. *Making Democracy Work.* Princeton: Princeton University Press.

Ragin, Charles C., and York Bradshaw. 1992. "International Economic Dependence and Human Misery, 1938-1980: A Global Perspective." *Sociological Perspectives* 35 (2): 217-247.

Ramírez Sáiz, Juan Manuel. 1986. *El Movimiento Urbano Popular en México.* Mexico City: Siglo XXI Editores.

———. 1989. "Emergencia y politización de la Sociedad Civil: (los Movimientos Sociales en México, 1968-1983.)" In *Movimientos sociales 2,* Jamie Tamayo, ed. Guadalajara: Centro de Investigaciones sobre los Movimientos Sociales.

———. 1992. "Entre el corporativismo social y la lógica electoral. El Estado y el movimiento Urbano Popular." In *El Nuevo Estado Mexicano: Estado, Actores y Movimientos Sociales.* Mexico City: Nueva Imágen.

Ramos, Sandra López. 1996. *Zona Franca: Rostros de Mujer.* Managua, Nicaragua: Movimiento de Mujeres Trabajadoras y Desempleadas "María Elena Cuadra."

Randall, Margaret. 1994. *Sandino's daughters revisited: Feminism in Nicaragua.* New Brunswick: Rutgers University Press.

Renzi, María Rosa. 1996. "Las zonas francas en Nicaragua." *El Observador Económico* 52: 34-44.

Renzi, María Rosa, and Sonia Agurto. 1993. *¿Qué hace la mujer nicaragüense ante la crisis económica?* Managua, Nicaragua: FIDEG.

Rey, Juan Carlos. 1989. *El futuro de la democracia en Venezuela.* Caracas: Universidad Central de Venezuela.

Ribeiro, Gustavo Lins. 1998. "Cybercultural Politics: Political Activism at a Distance in a Transnational World." Pp. 325-352 in *Cultures of Politics, Politics of Cultures,* Sonia Alvarez, Evelina Dagnino, and Arturo Escobar, eds. Boulder, CO: Westview Press.

Risse, Thomas, and Kathryn Sikkink. 1999. "The Socialization of International Human Rights Norms into Domestic Practices: Introduction." Pp. 1-38 in *The Power of Human Rights: International Norms and Domestic Change.* New York: Cambridge University Press.

Robinson, William A. 1992. "The São Paulo Forum: Is There a New Latin American Left?" *Monthly Review* 44 (7):1-13.

———. 2003. *Transnational Conflicts: Central America, Social Change, and Globalization.* London: Verso.

———. 2004. "Global Crisis and Latin America." *Bulletin of Latin American Research* 23 (2): 135-153.

Robles, Wilder. 2001. "The Landless Rural Workers Movement: MST in Brazil." *Journal of Peasant Studies* 282: 146-161.

Roddick, Jackie. 1988. *The Dance of the Millions: Latin America and the Debt Crisis.* London: Latin American Bureau.

Rodriguez Rouanet, Francisco. 1986. *Rabinal.* Guatemala City: Subcentro Regional de Artesenías y Artes Populares.

Rodrik, David. 2000. "Has Globalization Gone Too Far? Pp. 323-327 in *The Global Transformations Reader: An Introduction to the Globalization Debate,* David Held and Anthony McGrew, eds. Cambridge: Polity Press.

Rofman, Alejandro. 2000. "Destrucción de las Economias Provinciales." *Le Monde Diplomatique,* August: 6-7.

Roniger, Luis. 1990. *Hierarchy and Trust in Modern Mexico and Brazil.* New York: Praeger.

Rosa, Kumudhini. 1994. "The Conditions and Organizational Activities of Women in Free Trade Zones: Malaysia, Philippines and Sri Lanka, 1970-1990." In *Dignity and Daily Bread: New Forms of Economic Organizing among Poor Women in the Third World and First,* Sheila Rowbotham and Swasti Mitter, eds. New York: Routledge.

Rosenstone, Steven J., and John Mark Hansen. 1993. *Mobilization, Participation, and Democracy in America.* New York: Macmillan.

Rosenthal, Anton. 2000. "Spectacle, Fear and Protest: A Guide to the History of Urban Public

Space in Latin America." *Social Science History* 24: 33-73.

Ross, John. 2001. E-mail interview, received September 1.

Rothman, Daniel, and Pamela E. Oliver. 1999. "From Local to Global: The Anti-Dam Movement in Southern Brazil, 1979-1992." *Mobilization* 4: 41-57.

Rowbotham, S. and S. Mitter, eds. 1994. *Dignity and Daily Bread: New Forms of Organizing among Poor Women in the Third World and the First*. London: Routledge.

Rubin, Jeffrey W. 1997. *Decentering the Regime: Ethnicity, Radicalism, and Democracy in Juchitán, Mexico*. Durham, NC: Duke University Press.

Rubins, Roxana, and Horacio Cao. 2000. "Las Satrapías de Siempre." *Le Monde Diplomatique* August: 8-9.

Rucht, Dieter. 1999. "The Transnationalization of Social Movements: Trends, Causes, Problems." Pp. 206-222 in *Social Movements in a Globalizing World*, Donatella Della Porta, Hanspeter Kriesi, Dieter Rucht, eds. New York: St. Martin's Press.

Ruddick, Sara. 1994. "Notes Toward a Feminist Maternal Peace Politics." Pp. 621-628 in *Living with Contradictions*, A. M. Jaggar, ed. Boulder, CO: Westview.

Rude, George. 1964. *The Crowd in History*. New Yor: John Wiley and Sons.

Russell, Grahame. 1995. *The Dedication of the Río Negro Monument: A First Hand Account*. Washington, DC: Campaign for Peace and Life.

———. 1999. "Human Rights: Solution to, or Problem of Globalization?" Available online at http:// www. rightsaction.org.

———. 2000a. "Chixoy Reparations Campaign Communiqué Number One." Available online at http:// www. rightsaction.org .

———. 2000b. "Chixoy Reparations Campaign Communiqué Number Four." Available online at http:// www.rightsaction.org .

———. 2000c. "Chixoy Reparations Campaign Communiqué Number Seven." Available online at http://www.rightsaction.org.

Sachs, Aaron. 1996. "Upholding Human Rights and Environmental Justice." *The Humanist* 56: 5-7.

Sader, Emir, and Ken Silverstein. 1991. *Without Fear of Being Happy: Lula, the Workers Party, and Brazil*. London: Verso.

Safa, Helen I. 1990. "Women and Industrialization in the Caribbean." Pp. 72-97 in *Women, Employment, and the Family in the International Division of Labor*, Sharon Stichter and Jean L. Parpart, eds. Philadelphia, PA: Temple University Press.

———. 1998. "Free Markets and the Marriage Market: Structural Adjustment, Gender Relations, and Working Conditions among Dominican Women Workers." *Environment and Planning* 31 (2): 291-304.

Sage, George H. 1999. "Justice Do It! The Nike Transnational Advocacy Network: Organization, Collective Actions, and Outcomes." *Sociology of Sport Journal* 16 (3): 206-235.

Salazar Villava, Claudia M. 2002. "Procesos de Democratización en América Latina: La Participación de las Organizaciones Civiles." *Acta Sociológica* 36: 155-185.

Sampedro, Victor. 1997. "The Media Politics of Social Protest." *Mobilization* 2 (2): 185-205.

Sandoval, Salvador. 2001. "The Crisis of the Brazilian Labor Movement and the Emergence of Alternative Forms of Working-Class Contention in the 1990s." *Revista Psicología Política* 1 (1): 173-195.

Sarmiento, Sergio. 1997. "Trial by Fire: The Chiapas Revolt, the Colosio Assassination and the Mexican Press in 1994." In *A Culture of Collusion: An Inside Look at the Mexican Press*, William A. Orme, Jr., ed. Miami: North-South Center Press, University of Miami.

Savoia, Claudio. 2002. "Como el primer día." *Viva: La Revista de Clarín*, April 28, pp. 18-25.

Schirmer, Jennifer. 1993. "The Seeking of Truth and the Gendering of Consciousness: The Co-Madres of El Salvador and the CONANIQUA Widows of Guatemala." Pp. 30-64 in *Viva: Women and Popular Protest in Latin America*, S. A. Radcliffe and S. Westwood, eds. London: Routledge.

———. 1994. "The Claiming of Space and Body Politic within National-Security States: The Plaza de Mayo Madres and the Greenham Common Women." In *Remapping Memory: The Politics of TimeSpace*, J. Boyarin, ed. Minneapolis: University of Minnesota Press.

Schlesinger, Stephen, and Stephen Kinzer. 1983. *Bitter Fruit: The Untold Story of the American Coup in Guatemala.* Garden City: Anchor Press.

Schmink, Marianne, and Charles H. Wood, eds. 1984. *Frontier Expansion in Amazonia.* Gainesville, FL: University of Florida Press.

Schneider, Cathy Lisa. 1995. *Shantytown Protest in Pinochet's Chile.* Philadelphia: Temple University Press.

Schock, Kurt. 2005. *Unarmed Insurrections: People Power Movements in Nondemocracies.* Minneapolis: University of Minnesota Press.

Schrader, Jordan. 2002. "Sweatshop Worker Credits University of Michigan for Better Working Conditions." *Michigan Daily*, Dec. 4.

Schuld, Leslie. 2003. "El Salvador: Who Will Have the Hospitals?" *NACLA Report on the Americas* 36 (4): 42-45.

Schulz, Marcus. 1998. "Collective Action Across Borders: Opportunity Structures, Network Capacities, and Communicative Praxis in the Age of Advanced Globalization." *Sociological Perspectives* 41 (3): 587-616.

Schuster, Federico. 1999. *La Protesta Social en la Argentina Democrática: Balance y Perspectivas de una Forma de Acción Política.* Buenos Aires, unpublished manuscript.

———. 2002. *La Trama de la Crisis. Modos y Formas de Protesta Social a partir de los Acontecimientos de Diciembre de 2001.* Buenos Aires: Instituto Gino Germani, UBA.

Schwade, Elisete. 1992. *A Luta Não Faz Parte da Vida. . . É a Vida: O Projeto Político-Religioso de um Assentamento no Oeste Catarinense.* Florianopolis, SC: Universidade Federal de Santa Catarina.

Scott, James C. 1972. "Patron-Client Politics and Political Change in Southeast Asia." *American Political Science Review* 66 (1): 91-113.

Scott, James. 1977. *The Moral Economy of the Peasant: Rebellion and Subsistence in Southeast Asia.* New Haven: Yale University Press.

Scribano, Adrian. 1999. "Argentina 'Cortada': Cortes de Ruta y Visibilidad Social en el Contexto del Ajuste." Pp. 45-72 in *Lucha Popular, Democracia, Neoliberalismo: Protesta Popular en America Latina en los Años del Ajuste*, Margarita Lopez Maya, ed. Caracas: Nueva Sociedad.

Scribano, Adrián, and Federico Schuster. 2001. "Protesta Social en la Argentina de 2001: Entre la normalidad y la ruptura," *OSAL* Septiembre: 17-22.

Seidman, Gay. 1994. *Manufacturing Militance: Workers' Movements in Brazil and South Africa, 1970-1985.* Berkeley: University of California Press.

———. 2000. "Adjusting the Lens: What Do Globalization, Transnationalization, and the Anti-Apartheid Movement Mean for Social Movement Theory?" Pp. 339-357 in *Globalization and Social Movements,* John Guidry, Michael Kennedy, and Mayer Zald, eds. Ann Arbor: University of Michigan Press.

Sewell, William H., Jr. 2001. "Space in Contentious Politics." Pp. 51-89 in *Silence and Voice in the Study of Contentious Politics*, R. Aminzade, J. Goldstone, D. McAdam, E. Perry, W. Sewell, S. Tarrow, and C. Tilly, eds. New York: Cambridge University Press.

Shapiro, Gilbert, and John Markoff. 1998. *Revolutionary Demands: A Content Analysis of the Cahiers De Doléances of 1789.* Stanford: Stanford University Press.

Shayne, Julie. 2004. *The Revolution Question: Feminisms in El Salvador, Chile, and Cuba.* New Brunswick, NJ: Rutgers University Press.

Shefner, Jon. 1999. "Sponsors and the Urban Poor: Resources or Restrictions?" *Social Problems* 46 (3): 376-397.

———. 2001. "Coalitions and Clientelism in Mexico." *Theory & Society* 30: 593-628.

———. 2004. "Globalization and Democracy in Mexico." *Soundings*, Volume 87, No. 1-2.

———. 2006. "Do You Think Democracy Is a Magical Thing?: From Basic Needs to Democratization in Informal Politics." In *Out of the Shadows,* Patricia Fernandez-Kelly and Jon Shefner, eds. University Park: Pennsylvania State University Press.

Shemtov, Ronit. 1999. "Taking Ownership of Environmental Problems: How Local NIMBY Groups Expand Their Goals." *Mobilization* 4: 91-106.

Sheridan, Mary Beth. 1999. "Girl, 14, May Be the Key to Solving Some Juárez Murders." *San*

Antonio Express-News, May 21. p. A4.

Shrivastava, Rashmi. 1996. "Don't Give a Dam! Woman Leads Tribals against Indian Dam." *Women & Enrivonments* 39-40: 8-11.

Sigaud, Lygia. 1977. "A Idealização do Passado numa Area de Plantation." *Contraponto* 22: 115-126.

———. 1979. *Os Clandestinos e os Direitos: Estudo Sobre Trabalhadores da Cana-De-Açúcar de Pernambuco*. São Paulo: Livraria Duas Cidades.

Sikkink, Kathryn, and Jackie Smith. 2002. "Infrastructures for Change: Transnational Organizations, 1952-1993." Pp. 24-43 in *Restructuring World Politics: Transnational Social Movements, Networks and Norms*, Sanjeev Khagram, Kathryn Sikkink, and James Riker, eds. Minneapolis: University of Minnesota Press.

Skidmore, Thomas E. 1999. *Brazil: Five Centuries of Change*. Oxford: Oxford University Press.

Sklair, Leslie. 1989. *Assembling for Development. The Maquila Industry in Mexico and the United States*. Boston, MA: Unwin Hyman.

———. 1995. "Social Movements and Global Capitalism." *Sociology* 29 (3): 495-512.

———. 1998. *Social Movements and Global Captialism: The Cultures of Globalization*. Durham, NC: Duke University Press.

Sklar, Leonard, and Patrick McCully. 1994. *Damming the Rivers: The World Bank's Lending for Large Dams*. Berkeley: International Rivers Network.

Skocpol, Theda. 1979. *States and Social Revolutions: A Comparative Analysis of France, Russia, and China*. New York: Cambridge University Press.

Slater, Candace. 2002. *Entangled Edens: Visions of the Amazon*. Berkeley, CA: University of California Press.

Slater, David, ed. 1985. *New Social Movements and the State in Latin America*. Amsterdam: CEDLA.

Slevin, James. 2000. *The Internet and Society*. Cambridge: Polity Press.

Smith, Christian. 1996. *Resisting Reagan: The U.S. Central American Peace Movement*. Chicago: University of Chicago Press.

Smith, Hilda L. 2001. "'Age': A Problematic Concept for Women." *Journal of Women's History* 12: 77-86.

Smith, Jackie. 1997. "Characeristics of the Modern Transnational Social Movement Sector." Pp. 42-58 in *Transnational Social Movements and World Politics*, Jackie Smith, Charles Chatfield, and Ronald Pagnucco, eds. Syracuse, NY: Syracuse University Press.

———. 1998. "Global Civil Society? Transnational Social Movement Organizations and Social Capital." *American Behavioral Scientist* 42 (1): 93-107.

———. 2001a. "Behind the Anti-Globalization Label," *Dissent* (Fall): 14-18.

———. 2001b. "Globalizing Resistance: The Battle of Seattle and the Future of Social Movements." *Mobilization: An International Journal* 6 (1): 1-19.

———. 2002. "Bridging Global Divides? Strategic Framing and Solidarity in Transnational Social Movement Organizations," *International Sociology* 17 (4): 505-528.

Smith, Jackie, and Hank Johnston. 2002. "Globalization and Resistance: An Introduction." Pp. 1-10 in *Globalization and Resistance: Transnational Dimensions of Social Movements*, Jackie Smith and Hank Johnston, eds., Lanham, MD: Rowman and Littlefield.

Smith, Jackie, and Joe Bandy. 2005. "Introduction: Cooperation and Conflict in Transnational Protest," pp. 1-17 in *Coalitions across Borders: Transnational Protest and the Neoliberal Order*, Joe Bandy and Jackie Smith, eds. Lanham, MD: Rowman and Littlefield.

Smith, Jackie, Ron Pagnucco and Charles Chatfield. 1997. "Social Movements and World Politics: A Theoretical Framework." Pp. 59-77 in *Transnational Social Movements and Global Politics: Solidarity Beyond the State*, Jackie Smith, Charles Chatfield, and Ron Pagnucco, eds. Syracuse, NY: Syracuse University Press.

Smith, Neil. 1984. *Uneven Development: Nature, Capital and the Production of Space*. New York: Basil Blackwell.

Smith, William C. and Carlos H. Acuña. 1994. "Future Politico-Economic Scenarios for Latin America." Pp. 1-28 in *Democracy, Markets, and Structural Reform in Latin America*, W. Smith, C. Acuña, and E. A. Gamarra, eds. Coral Gables, FL: University of Miami, North-

South Center.

Smith, William C., and Roberto Patricio Korzeniewicz. 1997. "Latin America and the Second Great Transformation." Pp. 1-20 in *Politics, Social Change, and Economic Restructuring in Latin America*, W.C. Smith and R.P. Korzeniewicz, eds. Coral Gables, FL: University of Miami North-South Center.

Smulovitz, Catalina, and Enrique Peruzzonti. 2000. "Societal Accountability in Latin America." *Journal of Democracy* 11 (4): 147-158.

Snow, David A. 2004. "Framing Processes, Ideology, and Discursive Fields." Pp. 380-412 in *The Blackwell Companion to Social Movements*, edited by David A. Snow, Sarah A. Soule, and Hanspeter Kriesi, eds. Malden, MA: Blackwell Publishing.

Snow, David, and Robert D. Benford. 1988. "Ideology, Frame Resonance, and Participant Mobilization." Pp. 133-155 in *From Structure to Action: Comparing Social Movement Research across Cultures*, Bert Klandermans and Sidney Tarrow eds. Greenwich, CT: JAI Press.

———. 1992. "Master Frames and Cycles of Protest." Pp. 133-155 in *Frontiers in Social Movement Theory*, Aldon D. Morris and Carol McCluerg Mueller, eds. New Haven, CT: Yale University Press.

Snow, David A., Daniel M. Cress, Liam Downey, and Andrew W. Jones. 1998. "Disrupting the 'Quotidian': Reconceptualizing the Relationship between Breakdown and the Emergence of Collective Action." *Mobilization* 3 (1): 1-22.

Snow, David A., E. Burke Rochford, Steven K. Worden, and Robert D. Benford. 1986. "Frame Alignment Processes, Micromobilization, and Movement Participation." *American Sociological Review* 51 (4): 464-481.

Snow, David, Sarah Soule, and Hanspeter Kriesi. 2004. "Mapping the Terrain." Pp. 3-16 in *The Blackwell Companion to Social Movements*, D. Snow, S. Soule, and H. Kriesi, eds. Oxford: Blackwell.

Soja, Edward W., and Barbara Hooper. 1993. "The Spaces that Difference Makes." Pp. 183-205 in *Place and the Politics of Identity*, Michael Keith and Steve Pile, eds. London: Routledge.

Spar, Debora, and David Yoffe. 1999. "Multinational Enterprises and the Prospects for Justice." *Journal of International Affairs* 52 (2): 557-581.

Stallybrass, Peter, and Allon White. 1986. *The Politics and Poetics of Transgression*. Ithaca, NY: Cornell University Press.

Stamp, Elizabeth. 1982. "Oxfam and Development." Pp. 84-104 in *Pressure Groups in the Global System: The Transnational Relations of Issue-Oriented Non-Governmental Organizations*, Peter Willetts, ed. New York: St. Martin's Press.

Stearns, Linda Brewster, and Paul D. Almeida. 2004. "The Formation of State Actor-Social Movement Coalitions and Favorable Policy Outcomes." *Social Problems* 51: 478-504.

Stedile, João Pedro, and Bernardo M. Fernandes. 1999. *Brava Gente: A Trajetória do MST e a Luta Pela Terra No Brasil*. São Paulo: Editora Fundação Perseu Abramo.

Stedile, João Pedro, ed. 1997. "O MST e a Questão Agrária: Entrevista com João Pedro Stedile." *Estudos Avançados* 11 (31): 69-98.

Steinberg, Marc. 1999. *Fighting Words. Working-Class Formation, Collective Action, and Discourse in Early Nineteenth-Century England*. Ithaca, NY: Cornell University Press.

———. 1998. "The Riding of the Black Lad and Other Working-Class Ritualistic Actions: Toward a Spatialized and Gendered Analysis of Nineteenth-Century Repertoires. *In Challenging Authority. The Historical Study of Contentious Politics*. Eds. Michael Hanagan, Leslie Page Moch, and Wayne te Brake. Minneapolis: University of Minnesota Press.

Stephen, Lynn. 1991. *Zapotec Women*. Austin: University of Texas Press.

Stiglitz, Joseph E. 2002. *Globalization and Its Discontents*. New York: W.W. Norton.

Stinchcombe, Arthur. 1965. "Social Structure and Organizations." Pp. 142-193 in *Handbook of Organizations*, J. March, ed. New York: Rand McNally.

Stoddard, Ellwyn R. 1987. *Maquila: Assembly Plants in Northern Mexico*. El Paso: University of Texas Press.

Stokes, Susan C. 1995. *Cultures in Conflict: Social Movements and the State in Peru*. Berkeley: University of California Press.

Stonich, Susan C., and Conner Bailey. 2000. "Resisting the Blue Revolution: Contending Coalitions Surrounding Industrial Shrimp Farming." *Human Organization* 59 (1): 23-36.

Storper, Michael. 1997. *The Regional World: Territorial Development in a Global Economy.* New York: Guilford Press.

Strange, Susan. 2000. "The Declining Authority of States." Pp. 148-155 in *The Global Transformations Reader: An Introduction to the Globalization Debate*, David Held and Anthony McGrew, eds. Cambridge: Polity Press.

Sutton, Barbara. 2004. *Body Politics and Women's Consciousness in Argentina.* Ph.D. diss., University of Oregon.

Swidler, Ann. 1986. "Culture in Action: Symbols and Strategies." *American Sociological Review* 51 (2): 273-286.

Swyngedouw, Erik. 1997. "Neither Global nor Local: 'Glocalization' and the Politics of Scale." Pp. 137-66 in *Spaces of Globalization: Reasserting the Power of the Local*, Kevin Cox, ed. New York: Guilford.

Tamayo Flores-Alatorre, Sergio. 1999. *Los Veinte Octubres Mexicanos: la Transición a la Modernización y la Democracia, 1968-1988.* México, DF: Universidad Autónoma Metropolitana-Azcapotzalco.

Tarrow, Sidney G. 1989. *Democracy and Disorder: Politics and Protest in Italy, 1965-1975.* Oxford: Oxford University Press.

———. 1992. "Mentalities, Political Cultures, and Collective Action Frames: Constructing Meanings through Action." Pp. 174-202 in *Frontiers in Social Movement Theory*, Aldon D. Morris and Carol McClurg Mueller, eds. New Haven, CT: Yale University Press.

———. 1995. "The Europeanization of Conflicts: Reflections from a Social Movement Perspective." *Western European Politics* 18 (2): 223-51.

———. 1998. *Power in Movement: Social Movements and Contentious Politics.* Cambridge: Cambridge University Press.

———. 2001. "Transnational Politics: Contention and Institutions in International Politics." *Annual Review of Political Science* 4: 1-20.

———. 2002. "From Lumping to Splitting: Specifying Globalization and Resistance." Pp. 229-249 in *Globalization and Resistance: Transnational Dimensions of Social Movements*, Jackie Smith and Hank Johnston, eds. Lanham, MD: Rowman & Littlefield.

———. 2005a. "The Dualities of Transnational Contention: 'Two Activist Solitures' or a New World Altogether?" *Mobilization* 10: 53-72

———. 2005b. *The New Transnational Activism.* New York: Cambridge University Press.

Tasso, Alberto. 1999a. *Juárez. Epica y ocaso de una pasión provinciana.* Santiago del Estero, unpublished manuscript.

———. 1999b. *Sistema Patronal, Dominación y Poder en el Noroeste Argentino.* Santiago del Estero, unpublished manuscript.

———. 1997. "¿Cómo somos y por qué?" *Quipu de Cultura* 8: 5-6.

Taylor, Diana. 2002. "'You Are Here': The DNA of Performance." *The Drama Review* 46: 149-169.

Tenti, Emilio. 2000. "Exclusión Social y Acción Colectiva en la Argentina de Hoy." *Punto De Vista* 67: 22-28.

Testa, Vilson M., Raul d. Nadal, Luiz C. Mior, Ivan T. Baldissera, and Nelson Cortina, with John Wilkinson. 1996. *O Desenvolvimento Sustentavel do Oeste Catarinense.* Florianopolis, SC: EPAGRI.

Thayer, Millie. 2000. "Traveling Feminisms: From Embodied Women to Gendered Citizenship." Pp. 203-233 *Global Ethnography: Forces, Connections and Imaginations in a Postmodern World*, Michael Burawoy, ed. Berkeley: University of California Press.

Theil, H. 1958. *Economic Forecasts and Policy.* North Holland: Amsterdam.

Thompson, E.P. 1971. "The Moral Economy of the English Crowd in the Eighteenth Century." *Past and Present* 50: 76-136.

———. 1993. *Customs in Common.* New York: The New Press.

Thornton, Sally Webb. 2000. "Grief Transformed: The Mothers of the Plaza de Mayo." *Omega* 41:279-289.

Tiano, Susan. 1994. *Patriarchy on the Line: Labor, Gender, and Ideology in the Mexican Ma-*

quila Industry. Philadelphia, PA: Temple University Press.

Tilly, Charles. 1978. *From Mobilization to Revolution*. New York: Addison Wesley.

———. 1995. *Popular Contention in Great Britain, 1758-1834*. Cambridge, MA: Harvard University Press.

———. 1997. *Roads from Past to Future*. Lanham, MA: Rowman & Littlefield.

———. 2003a. *Contention and Democracy in Europe, 1650-2000*. New York: Cambridge University Press.

———. 2003b. *Stories, Identities, and Political Change*. Lanham, MA: Rowman & Littlefield.

———. 2004. *Social Movements, 1768-2004*. Boulder, CO: Paradigm.

Tocqueville, Alexis de. 1961. *Democracy in America*. 2 vols. New York: Schocken Books.

Tong, Mary. 1998. "Two Cases of Cross-Border Organizing." Presentation. Social Movements Across Borders conference. Los Angeles: Social and Political Responses to Globalization in Latin America Project (LAREGLO) and Latin American Studies Program, California State University. Los Angeles. April 15.

Trevizo, Dolores. 2006. "Between Zapata and Che: A Comparison of Social Movement Success and Failure in Mexico." *Social Science History* 30(2): 197-229.

Tuirán, Alejandro. 2000. "El Voto de los Pobres: Rezago Social y Elecciones." *Reforma*, Sunday, June 25.

Twin Plant News. 1999. "Indicators." www.twin-plant-news.com

U.S. Department of Labor-National Administrative Organization (USDOL/NAO) 2001. Submission No. 9701. www2.dol.gov/dol/ilab/public/programs/nao/status.htm#iia6.

Umaña, Lorena. 2003. "La ruptura de la política y nuevas nociones de la participación en San Salvador." *Estudios Centroamericanos* 58: 905-911.

United Nations Development Program (UNDP). 1999. *World Survey on the Role of Women in Development: Globalization, Gender and Work*. New York: United Nations.

———. 2000. *Human Development Report 2000*. New York: Oxford University Press.

Van Cott, Donna Lee. 2005. *From Movements to Parties in Latin America: The Evolution of Ethnic Politics*. Cambridge: Cambridge University Press.

Van Dyke, Nella. 2003. "Crossing Movement Boundaries: Factors that Facilitate Coalition Protest by American College Students, 1930-1990." *Social Problems* 50 (2): 226-250.

Vargas, Humberto, and Eduardo Córdova. 2004. "Bolivia: Un país de re-configuraciones por una cultura de pactos políticos y de conflictos." Pp. 85-102 in *Movimientos Sociales y Conflicto en América Latina*, J. Seoane, ed. Buenos Aires: CLACSO.

Vázquez, Inés. 2004. "Palabra de resistencia." Pp. 195-214 in *Luchar Siempre: Las Marchas de la Resistencia, 1981-2003*, I. Vázquez, U. Gorini, M. Gallego, G. Nielsen, E. Epstein, and C. Rodriguez, eds. Buenos Aires: Ediciones Madres de Plaza de Mayo.

Vázquez, Inés, Ulises Gorini, Marisa Gallego, Gerardo Nielsen, Elisa Epstein, and Carlos Rodriguez. 2004. *Luchar Siempre: Las Marchas de Resistencia 1981-2003*. Buenos Aires: Ediciones Madres de Plaza de Mayo.

Vélez-Ibañez, Carlos G. 1983. *Rituals of Marginality: Politics, Process and Culture Change in Urban Central Mexico, 1969-1974*. Berkeley: University of California Press.

Veltmeyer, Henry. 1997. "New Social Movements in Latin America: The Dynamics of Class and Identity." *Journal of Peasant Studies* 251: 139-169.

Veltmeyer, Henry, and James Petras. 2000. *The Dynamics of Social Change in Latin America*. New York: St. Martin's Press.

Veltmeyer, Henry, James Petras, and Steve Vieux. 1997. *Neoliberalism and Class Conflict in Latin America: A Comparative Perspective on the Political Economy of Structural Adjustment*. New York: St. Martin's Press.

Verba, Sidney, Kay Lehman Schlozman, and Henry E. Brady. 1995. *Voice and Equality: Civic Voluntarism in American Politics*. Cambridge, MA: Harvard University Press.

Verité. 2001. "Comprehensive Factory Evaluation Report on Kukdong International Mexico, S.A. De C.V. Atlxico, Puebla Mexico." Available online at http://www.verite.org

Villalón, Roberta. 2002. "Piquetes, Cacerolazos y Asambleas Vecinales: Social Protests in Argentina, 1993-2002." Master's thesis, University of Texas at Austin.

Viotti da Costa, Emilia. 2000. *The Brazilian Empire: Myths and Histories*. Chapel Hill, NC:

University of North Carolina Press.

Wallerstein, Immanuel. 1974. *The Modern World-System: Capitalist Agriculture and the Origins of the European World-Economy in the Sixteenth Century.* New York: Academic Press.

———. 1980. *The Modern World-System II: Mercantilism and the Consolidation of the European World-Economy, 1600-1750.* New York: Academic Press.

———. 1989. *The Modern World-System III: The Second Era of the Great Expansion of the Capitalist World-Economy, 1730-1840s.* New York: Academic Press.

Walsh, Catherine E. 2001. "The Ecuadorian Political Irruption: Uprisings, Coups, Rebellions, and Democracy." *Nepantla: Views from the South* 2 (1): 173-204.

Walton, John. 1989. "Debt, Protest, and the State in Latin America." Pp. 299-328 in *Power and Popular Protest: Latin American Social Movements*, Susan Eckstein, ed. Berkeley, CA: University of California Press.

———. 1992. "Making the Theoretical Case." Pp. 121-138 in *What is a Case?*, Charles Ragin and Howard Becker, eds. Cambridge: Cambridge University Press.

———. 1998. "Urban Conflict and Social Movements in Poor Countries: Theory and Evidence of Collective Action." *International Journal of Urban and Regional Research* 22 (3): 460-481.

Walton, John, and Charles Ragin. 1990. "Global and National Sources of Political Protest: Third World Responses to the Debt Crisis." *American Sociological Review* 55: 876-890.

Walton, John, and David Seddon. 1994. "Food Riots Past and Present." Pp. 23-54 in *Free Markets and Food Riots: The Politics of Global Adjustment*, J. Walton and D. Seddon, eds. Oxford: Blackwell.

Walton, John, and Jonathan Shefner. 1994. "Latin America: Popular Protest and the State." Pp. 97-134 in *Free Markets and Food Riots: The Politics of Global Adjustment*, J. Walton and D. Seddon, eds. Oxford: Blackwell.

Wasserman, Stanley, and Katherine Faust. 1994. *Social Network Analysis: Method and Applications.* Cambridge, England: Cambridge University Press.

Whalen, Jack, and Richard Flacks. 1989. *Beyond the Barricades.* Philadelphia: Temple University Press.

Wickham-Crowley, Timothy. 2001. "Winners, Losers, and Also-Rans: Toward a Comparative Sociology of Latin American Guerrilla Movements." Pp. 132-181 in *Power and Popular Protest: Latin American Social Movements*, Susan Eckstein, ed. Berkeley: University of California Press.

Willetts, Peter. 1982. "Pressure Groups as Transnational Actors." Pp. 1-27 in *Pressure Groups in the Global System: The Transnational Relations of Issue-Oriented Non-Governmental Organizations*, Peter Willetts, ed. New York: St. Martin's Press.

———. 1982. "The Impact of Promotional Pressure Groups on Global Politics." Pp. 179-200 in *Pressure Groups in the Global System: The Transnational Relations of Issue-Oriented Non-Governmental Organizations*, Peter Willetts, ed. New York: St. Martin's Press.

Williams, Heather L. 1996. *Planting Trouble: The Barzón Debtors' Movement in Mexico.* La Jolla, CA: Center for U.S.-Mexican Studies.

———. 2001. *Social Movements and Economic Transition: Markets and Distributive Conflict in Mexico.* Cambridge: Cambridge University Press.

Wiltfang, Gregory L., and Doug McAdam. 1991. "The Costs and Risks of Social Activism: A Study of Sanctuary Movement Activism." *Social Forces* 69: 987-1010.

Winston, Morton. 2002. "NGO Strategies for Promoting Corporate Social Responsibility." *Ethics and International Affairs* 16 (1): 71-88.

Witness for Peace Guatemala Team. 1996. *A People Dammed: The Impact of the World Bank Chixoy Hydroelectric Project in Guatemala.* Washington, DC: Witness for Peace.

Wolford, Wendy. Forthcoming a. "Of Land and Labour: Agrarian Reform on the Sugarcane Plantations of Northeast Brazil," in *Latin American Perspectives*.

———. Forthcoming b. "Producing Community: The MST and Land Reform Settlements in Brazil," in *Journal of Agrarian Change*.

Wolfson, Mark. 2001. *The Fight Against Big Tobacco: The Movement, the State, and the Public's Health.* New York: Aldine de Gruyter.

Wood, Elisabeth Jean. 2000. *Forging Democracy from Below: Insurgent Transitions in South*

Africa and El Salvador. Cambridge: Cambridge University Press.

Wood, Robert E. 1986. *From Marshall Plan to Debt Crisis*. Berkeley: University of California Press.

Woortmann, Ellen F. 1995. *Hedeiros, Parentes e Compadres: Colonos do Sul e Sitiantes do Nordeste*. São Paulo: Hucitec.

World Bank. 2000. "Nicaragua at a Glance." www.worldbank.org/data/countrydata.

———. 2001. *World Development Indicators 2001 CD-ROM*. Washington, DC: World Bank.

World Social Forum. 2001. "World Social Forum Charter of Principles," Available online at *www.forumsocialmundial.org.br/main.php?id_menu=4&cd_language=2*.

WRC (Worker's Rights Consortium). 2002. Available online at http://www.workersrights.org.

Wright, Angus, and Wendy Wolford. 2003. *To Inherit the Earth: The Landless Movement and the Struggle for a New Brazil*. Oakland, CA: Food First Books.

Ya Basta. 2001. "The Age of Clandestinity." Available online at www.contrast.org/borders/tampere/materials/age-of-clandestinity.html.

Yashar, Deborah. 2005. *Contesting Citizenship in Latin America: The Rise of Indigenous Movements and the Postliberal Challenge*. Cambridge: Cambridge University Press.

Zamosc, Leon. 2004. "The Indian Movement in Ecuador: from Politics of Influence to Politics of Power." Pp. 131-157 in *The Struggle for Indigenous Rights in Latin America*, N. Postero and L. Zamosc, eds. Brighton: Sussex Academic Press.

Zuo, Jiping, and Robert D. Benford. 1995. "Mobilization Processes and the 1989 Chinese Democracy Movement." *Sociological Quarterly* 36 (1): 131-156.

INDEX

ABOUT THE CONTRIBUTORS

Paul Almeida is assistant professor of sociology at Texas A&M University. His research focuses on the dynamics of social movement mobilization in lesser-developed countries. His articles on social movements have appeared in the *American Journal of Sociology, Latin American Perspectives, Mobilization, Realidad* (El Salvador), *Research in Political Sociology, Research in Social Movements, Conflicts and Change,* and *Social Problems.* He is currently completing a book manuscript on waves of popular unrest in El Salvador between 1925 and 2005.

Javier Auyero is associate professsor of sociology at SUNY-Stony Brook. He is the author of *Poor People's Politics, Contentious Lives,* and *Routine Politics and Explosive Collective Violence.* Javier is the current editor of the journal *Qualitative Sociology.*

Joe Bandy is associate professor of sociology at Bowdoin College where he teaches courses in sociology, environmental studies, and Latin American studies. His research has investigated the many ways that social movement organizations have responded to the economic changes associated with globalization, especially the formation of transnational coalitions among environmental justice and labor movements in the United States and Mexico. His latest research focuses on the transnational dimensions of corporate social responsibility and human rights. His most recent publications include *Coalitions Across Borders: Transnational Protest and the Neo-Liberal Order* (coedited with Jackie Smith, 2004), "Paradoxes of a Transnational Civil Society in a Neoliberal World: The Coalition for Justice in the Maquiladoras" in *Social Problems* (2004), and "So What Is to Be Done?: Maquila

267

Justice Movements, Transnational Solidarity, and Dynamics of Resistance" in *The Social Costs of Maquiladora Development* (edited by Kathryn Kopinak, 2004).

Cory Blad is assistant professor of sociology at Southern Illinois University Edwardsville. His research examines the intersection of global political economy and local culture with respect to state and national relationships. He is currently writing several research reports examining the role of social policy in the development of Canadian and Québécois national projects and state institutions.

Elizabeth Borland is assistant professor of sociology at the College of New Jersey. Her recent publications have focused on women in Argentina, particularly women's collective action in the democratic period. Her interests include social movements, coalitions, decision making in organizations, gender, and intergenerational dynamics.

Victoria Carty is assistant professor of sociology at Chapman University. Her areas of interest include social movements, globalization, and Latin America. Specifically, her work has centered on the labor movement, the international peace movement, and the role that the Internet has played in facilitating contemporary social change. Recent publications include "Protest, Cyberactivism, and New Social Movements: The Reemergence of the Peace Movement Post 9/11" in *Social Movement Studies* and "Labor Struggles, New Social Movements, and America's Favorite Pastime: New York Workers Take on New Era" in *Sociological Perspectives*. She is currently doing work on the labor struggle in the banana farm industry in Panama.

Claudio A. Holzner is assistant professor of political science at the University of Utah. He has been awarded postdoctoral fellowships and grants by the Center for U.S.-Mexican Studies at the University of California, San Diego, the Tanner Humanities Institute at the University of Utah, and the National Science Foundation. He has done extensive fieldwork in both Mexico and Italy since 1995. He has published articles and monographs on political participation and on immigration, including articles in *Mobilization*, *Latin American Politics and Society* (forthcoming), and *Italian Politics and Society*. His current research explores the effects of economic and political reforms on the political participation of citizens in Mexico.

Hank Johnston is editor of *Mobilization: An International Quarterly* and associate professor of sociology at San Diego State University. He is author of *Tales of Nationalism: Catalonia, 1939-1979*, as well as many research articles and chapters about social movement theory and about protest and resistance in repressive states. Also he has coedited several collections of social movement research: *Social Movements and Culture*, *New Social Movements*, *Globalization and Resistance*, *Frames of Protest*, and *Repression and Mobilization*. Currently he is researching protest repertoires in newly industrializing states. In 2003, Professor Johnston received the Exceptional Service Award by the American Sociological Association Section on Collective Behavior and Social Movements.

Luis Lander is professor of economic and social sciences at the Central University of Venezuela. He is the author of more than forty academic articles in Venezuelan and international journals. His most recent articles include: "Referendo revocatorio y elecciones regionales en Venezuela: geografía electoral de la polarización" (with

Margarita López Maya); "Petróleo y democracia en Venezuela: del fortalecimiento del Estado, a la subversión soterrado y la insurrección abierta"; "La insurrección de los gerentes: Pdvsa y el gobierno de Chávez"; "Gobierno de Chávez: nuevos rumbos en la política petrolera venezolana." Professor Lander is currently director of the journal, *Revista Venezolana de Economia y Ciencias Sociales.*

Margarita López Maya is senior professor at the Center of Development Studies of the Central University of Venezuela. She has dedicated twenty-five years to research on the political and social history of twentieth-century Venezuela. Her present fields of research are popular protest and political and social actors in contemporary Venezuela. Her recent publications, such as "The Venezuelan Caracazo of 1989: Popular Protest and Institutional Weakness" in *Journal of Latin American Studies* (2003), and her book *Del Viernes Negro al Referendo Revocatorio* (2005) deal with the recent critical political events of her country. Professor López-Maya has also functioned as the director-editor of *Revista Venezolana de Economía y Ciencias Sociales.*

Jennifer Bickham Mendez is associate professor of sociology at the College of William and Mary. Her book, *From the Revolution to the Maquiladoras: Gender, Labor and Globalization in Nicaragua* (2005) presents an ethnographic case study of a Nicaraguan working women's organization in order to demonstrate how globalization affects grassroots advocacy for social justice, particularly as it relates to the situation of women maquila workers. She has published articles in various journals including *Social Problems, Organization, Mobilization,* and *Identities.* Her current work focuses on Latino/a transnational migration in Williamsburg, VA, and explores migrants' exclusion and incorporation in this new immigration receiving site.

Thomas Olesen is lecturer at the department of political science at the University of Aarhus and at the Danish School of Journalism. His research interests are social movements and globalization. He has recently published a book-length study of the transnational network supporting the Zapatistas in Mexico: *International Zapatismo: The Construction of Solidarity in the Age of Globalization* (2005).

George Pasdirtz is a consultant at the University of Wisconsin–Madison. His previous publications have been in the area of statistical methodology, computer simulation, health policy analysis, and quantitative history. He is currently developing time series models for the U.S. economy within the world system and is using the models to forecast world system development.

Jon Shefner is associate professor of sociology and director of the Global Studies Interdisciplinary Program at the University of Tennessee-Knoxville. He is coeditor, with Patricia Fernandez-Kelly, of *Out of the Shadows: Political Action and the Informal Economy in Latin America* (2006). In addition to working on the impact of IMF stabilization policies on national politics, his research focuses on the political economy of development and social movements. His book addressing the impact of globalization and democratization on Mexico's urban poor will soon be published by Pennsylvania State University Press.

Julie Stewart is an assistant professor in the department of sociology at the University of Utah. Her dissertation explored the role of transnational activism in shaping the post-war trajectories of two Guatemalan villages. Her research interests include transnational social movements, international non-governmental organizations, community development, and globalization.

Takeshi Wada is assistant professor of sociology at the University of Missouri, Columbia. His publications include "Civil Society in Mexico: Popular Protest amid Economic and Political Liberalization" in *International Journal of Sociology and Social Policy* (2005) and "Event Analysis of *Claim* Making in Mexico: How Are Social Protests Transformed into Political Protests?" in *Mobilization* (2004). His research explores the impact of globalization and democratization on the ways civil society actors make claims upon the authorities. He is currently developing a global database of political events using computer-automated coding technology to carry out a cross-national study of popular protests.

Wendy Wolford is assistant professor of geography at the University of North Carolina at Chapel Hill. Her work has focused on social mobilization in rural Brazil, with a coauthored book, *To Inherit the Earth* (2003) on the Rural Landless Workers' Movement in South and Northeast Brazil. She has published several articles in journals such as *Environment and Planning, Mobilization: An International Quarterly,* and the *Journal of Agrarian Change.* Her research interests include social movements, the political economy of development, and political ecology. Recent awards include a fellowship at the Yale Program in Agrarian Studies and a three-year grant from the National Science Foundation to study institutional aspects of land distribution in Brazil.